# NATO's European Allies

# NATO's European Allies
## Military Capability and Political Will

Edited by

### Janne Haaland Matlary
*Professor of International Politics, Department of Political Science, University of Oslo, Norway*

and

### Magnus Petersson
*Professor of Modern History, Norwegian Institute for Defence Studies, Norway*

Selection, introduction and editorial matter © Janne Haaland Matlary and Magnus Petersson 2013
Individual chapters © Respective authors 2013

All rights reserved. No reproduction, copy or transmission of this publication may be made without written permission.

No portion of this publication may be reproduced, copied or transmitted save with written permission or in accordance with the provisions of the Copyright, Designs and Patents Act 1988, or under the terms of any licence permitting limited copying issued by the Copyright Licensing Agency, Saffron House, 6–10 Kirby Street, London EC1N 8TS.

Any person who does any unauthorized act in relation to this publication may be liable to criminal prosecution and civil claims for damages.

The authors have asserted their rights to be identified as the authors of this work in accordance with the Copyright, Designs and Patents Act 1988.

First published 2013 by
PALGRAVE MACMILLAN

Palgrave Macmillan in the UK is an imprint of Macmillan Publishers Limited, registered in England, company number 785998, of Houndmills, Basingstoke, Hampshire RG21 6XS.

Palgrave Macmillan in the US is a division of St Martin's Press LLC, 175 Fifth Avenue, New York, NY 10010.

Palgrave Macmillan is the global academic imprint of the above companies and has companies and representatives throughout the world.

Palgrave® and Macmillan® are registered trademarks in the United States, the United Kingdom, Europe and other countries.

ISBN 978–1–137–03499–1

This book is printed on paper suitable for recycling and made from fully managed and sustained forest sources. Logging, pulping and manufacturing processes are expected to conform to the environmental regulations of the country of origin.

A catalogue record for this book is available from the British Library.

A catalog record for this book is available from the Library of Congress.

Transferred to Digital Printing in 2013

# Contents

| | |
|---|---|
| List of Tables | vii |
| Acknowledgements | viii |
| Notes on Contributors | ix |

1 Introduction: Will Europe Lead in NATO?    1
  J. H. Matlary and M. Petersson

## Part I  Determinants of the Use of Force

2 From Mars to Venus? European Use of Force from a
  Historical Perspective    25
  M. Petersson

3 A Farewell to Arms: Europe's Meritocracy and the
  Demilitarization of Europe    37
  C. Coker

4 Towards an Affordable European Defence and Security
  Policy? The Case for Extensive European Force Integration    57
  S. Diesen

5 Strategy, Risk and Threat Perceptions in NATO    71
  Ø. Østerud and A. Toje

## Part II  Application: Case Studies

6 No More Free-Riding: The Political Economy of Military
  Power and the Transatlantic Relationship    97
  S. Kay

7 Between Theory and Practice: Britain and the Use of Force    121
  P. Porter

8 France: The State with Strategic Vision    141
  Y. Boyer

9 The Reluctant Ally? Germany, NATO and the Use of Force    161
  B. Schreer

| | | |
|---|---|---|
| 10 | Willing and Able? Spanish Statecraft as Brokerage<br>*D. Coletta and D. García* | 178 |
| 11 | Poland's Participation in NATO Operations<br>*M. Pietras* | 205 |
| 12 | Hungary in NATO: The Case of a Half Empty Glass<br>*T. Magyarics* | 232 |
| 13 | Punching above Its Weight: Denmark's Legitimate Peripheral Participation in NATO's Wars<br>*M. V. Rasmussen* | 262 |
| 14 | Norway: Militarily Able but Politically Divided<br>*J. H. Matlary* | 279 |
| *Index* | | 301 |

# List of Tables

11.1 Attitude of the Poles towards the presence of Polish troops in Afghanistan (%)    211

# Acknowledgements

First of all, we would like to thank the research programme 'NATO in a Changing World' at the Norwegian Institute of Defence Studies (IFS) of the Norwegian Defence University College, and the Department of Political Science, University of Oslo, for generous support for the making of this book. The programme, financed by the Norwegian MOD, supports research on various aspects of NATO and is interdisciplinary.

Furthermore, we are grateful to colleagues for comments on various drafts of our chapters, especially Associate Professor Paal S. Hilde and Lieutenant Colonel Dr Harald Høyback, and to the chapter authors for being precise and prompt in delivering their contributions.

Finally, we would like to thank Christina Brian, Julia Willan and Harriet Barker at Palgrave Macmillan for encouraging and supporting the book project from the beginning to the end.

*Janne Haaland Matlary and Magnus Petersson*
*Oslo and Boston, July 2012*

# Contributors

**Yves Boyer** is Professor at the École Polytechnique, France, where he teaches International Security Affairs, and is Deputy Director of the Paris-based Fondation pour la Recherche Stratégique (FRS).

**Christopher Coker** is Professor of International Relations at the London School of Economics and Political Science, UK. He is a regular lecturer at the Royal College of Defence Studies (London), the NATO Defence College (Rome), the Centre for International Security (Geneva) and the National Institute for Defence Studies (Tokyo).

**Damon Coletta** is Professor of Political Science at the United States Air Force Academy, USA. His research interests include transatlantic relations, international crisis management and civil–military relations. He is the author of *Trusted Guardian: Information Sharing and the Future of the Atlantic Alliance* (2008), and co-editor of the eighth edition of *American Defense Policy*.

**Sverre Diesen** is a former Chief of Defence of Norway. He is a graduate of the Norwegian Military Academy (1979), Norwegian Army Staff College I and II (1986–1988); and Staff College Camberley, UK (1990). He also holds a master of science degree in Civil Engineering from the Norwegian University of Science and Technology, Norway (1976).

**David García** is Professor of International Relations, Department of International Studies, at the Complutense University of Madrid, Spain. His areas of interest are US foreign policy, transatlantic relations and security in Asia-Pacific.

**Sean Kay** is Professor of Politics and Government, Chair of International Studies, Ohio Weslean University, and Associate, Mershon Center for International Security Studies at the Ohio State University, USA. He specializes in international politics, international security, globalization, international organizations and US foreign and defence policy.

**Tamás Magyarics** is Hungarian Ambassador to Ireland. He is currently on leave from Eötvös Loránd University, Budapest, where he is an associate professor, and the Hungarian Institute of International Affairs, Hungary, where he was Director and Senior Research Fellow. His major fields of interest are transatlantic relations, US foreign affairs and international security.

Øyvind Østerud is Professor at the Department of Political Science at the University of Oslo, Norway, and Adjunct Professor at the Norwegian Defence University College. He received his PhD from the London School of Economics and Political Science, UK. He was Head of Department during 1993–1996 and 2007–2012, and President of the Norwegian Academy of Science and Letters during 2008–2011. His latest books include *Denationalisation of Defence* (2007) and *Hva er krig* [*What is War*] (2009).

Marek Pietraś is Professor of International Relations at the Maria Curie-Skłodowska University in Lublin, Poland. He is the author of 135 publications on contemporary international relations, with a particular focus on non-traditional security threats and the impact on international security of systemic factors including globalization processes.

Patrick Porter is Reader in Strategic Studies at the University of Reading, UK. He is also a Fellow of the UK Chief of the Defence Staff's Strategic Forum, and a contributing editor to *Infinity*, a new online strategy journal. His areas of interest include strategic studies, geopolitics, war and orientalism and US grand strategy in the Asia-Pacific.

Mikkel Vedby Rasmussen is Professor of Political Science at the University of Copenhagen, Denmark, where he is the Director of the Centre for Military Studies. Previously, he worked at the Danish Institute for Military Studies and the Danish Institute for International Affairs. He is a regular lecturer at the Royal Danish Defence College, Denmark, and the NATO Defence College, Italy.

Benjamin Schreer is Deputy Head of the Strategic and Defence Studies Centre (SDSC) and Senior Lecturer at the Australian National University, Australia. Previous positions included Deputy Director of the Aspen Institute, Germany, and Deputy Head of the research unit 'European and Atlantic Security' at the Stiftung Wissenschaft und Politik (SWP) in Berlin.

Asle Toje is Lecturer at the Political Science Department, University of Oslo, Norway. He is also Research Director at the Norwegian Nobel

Institute in Oslo. He holds a PhD in international relations from Pembroke College, Cambridge, UK. He has authored several books, including *America, the EU and Strategic Culture: Renegotiating the Transatlantic Bargain* (2008) and *The European Union as a Small Power: After the Post Cold War* (2010).

# 1
# Introduction: Will Europe Lead in NATO?

*J. H. Matlary and M. Petersson*

## The purpose and the relevance of the book

In a speech at the National Defence University in Washington, DC, in February 2010, former US Defence Secretary Robert Gates talked about the 'demilitarization of Europe' (Gates, 2010). When he gave his last major speech at NATO's ministerial meeting in Brussels in June 2011, he argued that NATO had become a 'two-tiered' alliance,

> between members who specialize in 'soft' humanitarian, development, peacekeeping, and talking tasks, and those conducting the 'hard' combat missions, between those willing and able to pay the price and bear the burdens of alliance commitments, and those who enjoy the benefits of NATO membership – be they security guarantees or headquarters billets – but don't want to share the risks and the costs.
>
> (Gates, 2011)

At a closed-door meeting with NATO Defence Ministers, Gates also named two states – Germany and Poland – that could contribute to the Libya operation but did not, and three states – the Netherlands, Spain and Turkey – that could do more (Spiegel, 2011). As a commentator put it later: 'the real danger comes from within – from European reluctance to pay for its own defence and from growing US indifference towards what Washington sees as feckless allies' (Stevens, 2011).

The US criticism has continued since then, and the gist of the criticism is the same: Allies do not carry their share of the burden, neither in terms of defence spending – which stands 75/25 in American's favour today – nor in terms of military contributions to operations.

How valid is this criticism? Which of NATO's European allies are 'able' militarily and 'willing' politically to undertake 'sharp operations' and to actually use force for the purpose of policy? Robert Kagan has argued that Americans are 'from Mars' and Europeans are 'from Venus' (Kagan, 2002, 2003), and that the attitude to the use of military force differs between the United States and Europe. How accurate is that picture?

The question of burden sharing has always been important in NATO – it has resulted in a 'crisis literature' on NATO (Thies, 2009) – but it has an acute relevance today because the United States will cut its defence budget over a ten-year period and is no longer automatically willing to lead military operations. The Libya mission 'Unified Protector' is a case in point. The United States did not want to lead, but was forced to 'lead from behind' because allies lacked some of the necessary capacities: 'shortages in allied intelligence-gathering, aircraft, aerial refuelling tankers and precision-guidance kits for bombs proved that the US remained the backbone of NATO-offensives' (Shanker and Schmitt, 2011, see also Hallams and Schreer, 2012). Thus, even if Europeans are politically willing, as in this case, they may not be militarily able.

In this book, we provide the first in-depth analysis of the relationship between these factors – political willingness and military ability to use force – asking whether Europe in this new situation of economic austerity and postmodern political values can play a key role in regional and global security and defence. Hitherto Europeans have been called upon to rise to the occasion of matching the United States with minor contributions, ranging from 'showing the flag' to militarily important contributions. But when the US signals that its lead role no longer is automatic, what about the European allies? Can they and will they undertake sharp operations on their own, assuming leading roles?

This issue is of key importance for policy as well as for scholarship on NATO. European defence today is marked by sharp cuts in budgets and a lack of integration of materiel. This happens while many national defence systems are not yet modernized or transformed towards expeditionary forces. Further, we need to ascertain whether it is true that Europe is a civilian power that refrains from using the military tool for coercion, deterrence or war-fighting in general (Sheehan, 2007).

Put differently, how important are domestic factors in security policy? There is ample research on the importance of geopolitics for the defence and security policy of the state if we look to realism in its various forms. Indeed, the main reason for military defence and for military alliances lies in the self-help fact of international anarchy. Especially for great powers, geopolitics and power-balancing matter as explanations for their willingness to maintain and use their armed forces (Nye, 2009). For smaller states, however, there is little they alone can do about their geopolitical position or about changes in threats. They are too small to matter in their domestic defence and security policies, hence their dependence on allies, especially the hegemonic power of the United States. This is often referred to as the 'alliance dilemma' in NATO (Snyder, 1984). For instance, Ringsmose has shown that Denmark, a small NATO member, is influenced by US pressure rather than by geopolitical changes in its security and defence policy (Ringsmose, 2010).

This is logical – small states depend on the hegemonic power for their security and are therefore prone to being influenced by its demands and wishes. Geopolitical threats and risks are second-order concerns, but matter as the 'prime movers' for being an alliance member. Thus, we can expect that European NATO members will be influenced by US pressure and expectations more than by geopolitical changes such as the current development of a multi-polar system (Strachan, 2009). Thus, what happens in US security and defence policy is of prime importance in Europe: On the one hand, less US engagement in NATO may lead to 'relaxation' due to less pressures in European states. On the other hand, the same phenomenon may lead to more European engagement because one can no longer 'pass the buck' to the United States. The worst outcome would be the former, but it may be the most likely, as we shall discuss below.

If we assume that alliance dependence explains most European NATO members' security and defence policy, the question becomes how true this will be in the time ahead. Whereas political elites seem to want to prioritize alliance dependence, Krebs finds that only an elite consensus across parties allows for this: European NATO states defy public unpopularity regarding International Security Assistance Force (ISAF) and continue to send troops, but this may be because there is (still) agreement across parties on this. Conversely, if this consensus is broken and parties take advantage of public opinion in order to get elected, alliance dependence no longer commands the importance it has had throughout the Cold War and beyond (Kreps, 2010).

The role of domestic politics in security and defence was secondary to alliance dependence during the Cold War. This was because the threat was clear, something which led to unity among political factions. Security and defence policy dynamics was different from domestic politics. However, when threats are less clear and look more like risks, the national interest is also unclear, and security and defence policy moves down the ladder of political priorities (Williams, 2008).

This has clearly happened in most European states after the Cold War. The academic study of such processes – policy-making in security and defence under diffuse threats and uncertain national outcomes – is still relatively scant (Matlary, 2009). As we know, even under the very clear risk of nuclear war during the Cuban missile crisis the policy response in Washington depended on the actors and organizations behind the policy (Allison, 1971).

Security and defence studies have traditionally either been in the realist 'camp', emphasizing geopolitics, or in the liberal 'camp', looking at alliance dependence, general foreign standing in NATO, the UN, etc., on the part of states as explanatory variables. After 1990, however, especially in Europe, the relevance of domestic factors as *explananda* seems to rise. In studies of Germany we find that political culture and ideology matter much (Matlary, 2009; Noetzel and Schreer, 2009). We can also expect that domestic factors will trump alliance dependence should this factor become less relevant, given US reticence to lead like before in NATO. Domestic factors therefore suggest themselves to become increasingly more important in explaining NATO policy in Europe.

## Burden-sharing in NATO

In their classic study of security as a public good, Olson and Zeckhauser showed that the economic theory of public goods applies to defence spending in an asymmetric alliance such as NATO (Olson and Zeckhauser, 1966). This point is underlined by Jason Davidson in his recent analysis of transatlantic burden-sharing: 'The scholarly literature on alliance burden-sharing...suggests that America's allies contribute rarely or never to US-led uses of force' (Davidson, 2011, p. 4).

Yet free riding is not normal in NATO, and most European allies contribute to operations where the United States is in the lead. The main explanation for this in the scholarship is the so-called 'alliance dilemma' in NATO (Snyder, 1984). In a study based on more than 50 elite interviews in France, the United Kingdom, and Italy, Davidson argues that national interest rather than alliance loyalty explains many contributions by these states in recent years (Davidson, 2011). He tries to weigh the following variables: national security interests, prestige, alliance loyalty, national public opinion, and human rights/values. He concludes that 'alliance value is significantly less important than threat and prestige: strong evidence supported threat and prestige in twice as many cases as alliance value (Davidson, 2011, p. 175). Yet he also agrees that 'interests and prestige overlap with alliance value' in most cases: states that want to be close to the United States want this in order to be important in world politics and/or to have US protection in security terms. Thus, if Norway places most weight on geopolitics and Denmark on prestige, they will both support the United States. However these foreign policy or external variables are weighed, what they have in common is that they are 'external' to the state. But in which ways do domestic variables matter in the decision to contribute?

In the Cold War, external factors clearly mattered most as the threat was existential. Europe really needed a US security guarantee. After the Cold War there is no clear-cut external variable – as seen above, the foreign policy reasons for NATO contributions are weighed differently. As the threat is no longer common and existential, there is also much greater scope for domestic variables. External factors no longer automatically trump domestic ones.

The study of the role of domestic variables is rather scant. The study of national strategic cultures is rarely done comparatively. One recent example of a comparative study is Kirchner and Sperlings' book *National Security Cultures* (Kirchner and Sperling, 2010). In the book, their aim is to study the impact of domestic cultures on various security policy issues, one of them being compellence, which we term coercive diplomacy in this book. The other factors studied in that volume do not involve military force.

With the exception of the few studies on national strategic cultures in Europe there is little systematic scholarly work on how domestic factors influence the political and military ability of NATO's European allies. The few studies of public opinion concur that it plays little role unless it is used by the political opposition in election campaigns. Davidson finds that public opinion is only relevant as an explanatory factor when it is coupled with opposition parties that may capitalize on this in (re)election efforts (Davidson, 2011, p. 176).

This concurs with Kreps' conclusion, which points out that ISAF contributions are not stopped by unfavourable publics. She finds that an elite consensus across parties allows for this: European NATO states defy public unpopularity regarding ISAF and continue to send troops, but this may be because there is agreement across parties on this. Conversely, if this consensus is broken and parties take advantage of public opinion in order to get elected, alliance dependence no longer commands the importance it has had throughout the Cold War and beyond (Kreps, 2010). But we can nonetheless assume that the role of domestic politics in Europe will increase in the time ahead, given budget cuts, austerity in general, and a generally negative view about the 'success' of ISAF.

Moreover, the great difference among European NATO allies in terms of risk-willing and relevant contributions needs explanation. ISAF illustrates how some states opt for caveats and play little role in dangerous operations, whereas others carry much more of the common burden. All NATO allies contributed to ISAF, but very few to the war-fighting in the dangerous south. NATO's European allies, therefore, seem to fall into at least two groups today. This classification is based on the degree of risk-willing, relevant military contribution to operations like ISAF. Yet there are also divisions among states regarding strategy for NATO – the most common division is between the so-called 'globalists' and 'traditionalists' (Noetzel and Schreer, 2009).

We can discern groups of states also in other international organizations, that is in the EU, where the inner core in security policy is made up of the contributing states to any one mission, but led by France and Britain (Matlary, 2009). Multi-tier NATO is a consequence of the lack of a common strategic vision. Noetzel and Schreer describe the 'traditionalists' as reversal-oriented, comprising Central European countries, favouring an alliance still focused on Article 5, based on the perception of a resurgent Russian threat. After all, the functioning of collective defence was their primary reason for joining the alliance (Noetzel and Schreer, 2009, p. 216). But even for the 'traditionalists' contributions to international operations are needed if the motive is Article 5 guarantee.

Burden-sharing in NATO today is very difficult for governments. Allies expect just burden-sharing in terms of carrying risk, whereas domestic publics are in 'deep peace' and not sympathetic to national casualities or political causes in far-away lands. What can a government do about this dilemma? It has to 'deliver' on two arenas, at home and internationally, where the demands are conflicting. They have to make painful choices. This is why the modern burden-sharing 'equation' is so difficult for states: they must take risk and suffer losses of their own soldiers in wars that are not in their own national interest in a traditional sense.

The 'alliance dilemma' formulated by Snyder in 1984 is today characterized by 'fear of abandonment rather than of entrapment'. Whereas there was a direct dependence between the United States and European allies in the Cold War, allies could be quite certain that they would not be abandoned. But as bipolarity has given way to more of a multipolar system today, and the threat has become diffuse and variously interpreted, 'abandonment outweighs entrapment fears' (Snyder, 1984, p. 484). As stated, Ringsmose has studied the behaviour of Denmark, one of the key contributors in coalition warfare, both in Iraq and Afghanistan, and found that the key determinant was Danish interest in closeness to Washington. Denmark has no geopolitical security calculus to consider, surrounded as it is by NATO states. The Danish abandonment of submarines testifies to this. Yet Denmark strongly supports US policy, to the point of being one of the most loyal supporters and contributors to US-led coalitions. Ringsmose argues that for Norway, the geopolitical relationship with Russia determines coalition contributions, whereas the main point for Denmark is general foreign and security policy (Ringsmose, 2010).

Thus, the perception of the importance of alliance dependence may not be related to national security concerns, contrary to realist theory. The Norwegian and Danish cases are paralleled in the Central-European cases, which like Norway seek US proximity because of geopolitics ('traditionalists'); and in the British and Dutch cases, which are global partners with the United States although they do not have national geopolitical security concerns ('globalists'). These two groups of states in NATO both seek closeness to the United States, albeit for different reasons.

In sum, both 'globalists' and 'traditionalists' among European NATO states need the US security guarantee if the alliance is to be real and deterring. Germany needs the United States as much as Denmark, and we should therefore expect both these states to contribute where the United States asks. But as noted, contributions differ very much within NATO Europe. It must be the case that some states are both willing and able, some are probably willing but unable, some the other way round, and some both unwilling and unable, at least relatively speaking.

## Outline of the book

As stated, in this book we analyse European 'political willingness and military ability' to use force within a NATO context, both in terms of coercion as well as in actual deployments. The book consists of two distinctive parts. In Part I (Chapters 2–5) which is thematic, important generic factors – history, culture, economy and military structure, and threat and risk perceptions – are discussed. This part forms the analytical basis for the country studies in Part II (Chapters 6–14). The point of departure in this part is the analysis of US strategic thinking and its implications for NATO. Then we examine four major states (the United Kingdom, France, Germany and Spain), two Central European states (Poland and Hungary), as well as two small states (Denmark and Norway).

Through this analysis we are able to detect and empirically show which political dynamics are at work in these states with regard to the political will and military ability to use force for the purpose of policy. The background factors that affect the military ability and political will to use force for political purposes are many. Yet we have to choose a relatively small but important number of them. Clearly 'politics' and 'ideology' must be important, as socialist parties generally are more sceptical about military force than liberal-conservative parties. The type of government of a given state must play a role, but this variable alone cannot explain the willingness and ability to use force (Herring, 2007).

'Military or Strategic Culture' is another factor. For instance, Italy, and Spain have in many ways an almost pacifistic culture, as does indeed Germany, but none of these states have had by long-time socialist governments. The state's 'historical experience' thus matters, and plays a role in forming cultures – both political and military ones. It can be argued that the United Kingdom, France, the Netherlands, Poland and Denmark have different political and military cultures from those of Germany, Italy and Spain. The concept of culture is, however, notoriously difficult as an analytical concept, being used both as an explanatory variable and as a social practice (Lock, 2010). There are examples of ideology trumping and changing culture, as in the case of Denmark, which through political leadership changed its political and military culture from low political willingness and low military ability to high political willingness and high military ability to use force for the purpose of policy after the Cold War (Saxi, 2010).

However, even when there is a will there may not be a way: in security and defence, the 'nuts and bolts' matter more than in other policy areas. Without military capacity, there is no effect or contribution. Factors such as 'military structure' and 'economic strength' are therefore important. How a state chooses to organize its armed forces has a great influence on how operational and expeditionary it will be, something which can be analysed in terms of deployable and sustainable forces, money for investment rather than wages and so on. Modern armed forces are capital-intensive, not manpower-intensive. The size of defence budgets is quite important to any analysis of military ability, but military ability also depends on how the money is spent (Farell and Terriff, 2010).

'Threat perceptions', finally, have always been one of the most central background factors for the build-up and use of military force as well as for alliance cohesion. Charles Kupchan argues that alliance members cooperate more when threat increases and vice versa: 'allies check rising threats by seeking to cooperate more closely with each other' (Kupchan, 1988, p. 324).

The 'operationalization' of 'political will' and 'military ability' is not easy. All states in NATO have defence structures (apart from Iceland) and they are all contributing to various NATO missions, be it in Kosovo, Afghanistan or Libya. They all qualify as 'willing and able' by a wide definition of these terms. This is also the diplomatic way of putting things: all are on board. However, the question that the ISAF mission has high-lighted lies in unequal burden-sharing in terms of 'risk and treasure'

If Europe has to assume more responsibility for its own security in the future, given a new multipolarity and a weaker United States, and concomitantly play a global role, it will have to engage in coercive diplomacy, too. The 'use of military force' that we define as interesting in this study is, therefore, not primarily related to low-risk peace-keeping operations, but to high-risk complex, sharp operations where ISAF is a good example. These are the types of operations that are hard to commit to both politically and militarily but which can be assumed to occur also beyond ISAF in a blend of counter-insurgency and easier forms of 'wars among the people', be they induced by humanitarian catastrophes or terrorism.

Further, the 'use of military force' is related to coercive diplomacy which we assume will be increasingly necessary in the time ahead in Europe. Multipolarity means that powerful non-NATO states will probably use coercion, and Europe must be prepared to put pressure as well as use incentives in diplomacy beyond its borders. Although coercion very often fails, it is normally the precursor to the actual use of force and is of course preferable to the latter (Byman and Waxman, 2002). In many cases, there is no 'carrot-only' alternative, as Europe learnt in Bosnia and Kosovo.

## The chapters

In Chapter 2, Magnus Petersson discusses European use of force from a historical perspective. He argues that in the pre-modern and modern ages – when use of force for political purposes was the rule and not an exception – it is more or less irrelevant to the present situation. He also argues that it is wrong to suggest that European states have not used force for political purposes after the Second World War. In particular France and the United Kingdom, but also other European NATO states, have actually used force for political purposes and have had both the military ability and political will to do so. However, he argues, the motives for the use of force have changed from securing the power and integrity of the state towards securing the values of the Western community. Furthermore, the threshold for using force inside Europe has been much higher than the threshold for using force outside Europe. The use of force, finally, has been exercised integrated and collectively rather than individually. There is a clear difference between France and the United Kingdom, both 'willing and able' both to coerce, use force and to lead, and the rest of European NATO.

In Chapter 3, Christopher Coker analyses political culture and the 'demilitarization' of Europe, and the 'growing apart' between Europe and the United States both intellectually and psychologically. He argues that Europe's demilitarization is pre-eminently a 'cultural' phenomenon: 'The political class cannot see the point of war, and has not, for a long time, had to think about it seriously, with the US always leading from the front.' Coker argues that Europe's demilitarization began with the collapse of the Soviet Union, when the 'Eurocrats' started to build 'a structure that was transnational, passionless and above all, safe'. It is a problem, he argues, to believe that it is possible to be a civilian power in a mutlipolar world: 'As Asia re-arms, and China flexes its muscles, they may use hard power (or at least the threat of it) to change the rules of engagement that the Europeans tend to take for granted.' In Coker's chapter, political culture has strong explanatory power as a background factor for military ability and political will to use force: 'Europe has developed a distinctive political culture that looks at war very differently from the United States.'

In Chapter 4, Sverre Diesen looks into economy and organization as drivers for the use of force, or – as he expresses it – the 'fundamental mechanisms behind the ever increasing cost and consequent dwindling capabilities of modern defence forces, known as the problem of critical mass'. The 'bottom line', Diesen argues, 'is that European countries in the face of the economic realities of sustaining today's force structures cannot afford the price of today's policies'. Soon they must therefore 'decide on some kind of defence integration strategy'. If not, they will lose military ability to use force for political purposes – in particular global military reach – and 'the political influence and status depending on that'. And NATO's smaller powers will, according to Diesen, even lose 'basic capabilities' (such as tanks, submarines or fighters) because of the problem of critical mass, which will make them dependent on others even when it comes to national crisis management. For Diesen, economy and organization are powerful drivers for the use of force. It is the defence budgets that are 'driving security policy' and not the other way around.

In Chapter 5, Asle Toje and Øyvind Østerud discuss NATO's transformation after the Cold War and the variation in threat perceptions between the members causing internal disagreements: 'In terms of military force, NATO retained some of its basic features from the former period. The disparities in capabilities (US hegemony) prevail, while there are new disparities in threat perceptions and willingness to take risks.' The authors argue that NATO has struggled to find a new meaning after the Cold War and that it has not succeeded. The United States wants NATO to be a 'global police force', the European members want American security guarantees, while European defence budgets have fallen by about 2 per cent yearly since the 1990s: 'The experience of Afghanistan has been that decision makers in Washington task whether it really is in its interests to cover defence costs for countries that only partially support US geopolitical objectives.' The authors paint a dark picture of NATO's future with unclear US leadership, European infighting, and fragmentation: 'NATO was a collective alliance – one for all, all for one. What NATO is today, is less clear.'

In Part II of the book, the country studies provide detailed analyses of different NATO members' military ability and political will to use force for political purposes. We compare a range of different NATO members: Four large states (France, the United Kingdom, Germany and Spain), two Central European states that are relatively new members (Poland, Hungary), as well as two small states (Denmark, Norway).

As the point of departure, in Chapter 6, Sean Kay starts off with a description of the US' current view of NATO, Europe and the use of force. Kay argues that United States will not for much longer tolerate 'status quo' in the transatlantic relationship. To rebalance, the European NATO members have to be able and willing to take real responsibility for crises in Europe, for example sustain a Balkans-style peace support operation and a Libya-style war simultaneously: 'there is a deepening assumption in the United States that America's allies must pick up the leadership in their area'. Kay concludes that it will not be possible for the United States to implement its new defence strategy (that is deep cuts in the defence budget 'and' more focus on Asia) without such a rebalancing. In addition, he argues that such a rebalancing would 'serve to advance the broadest of common interests and create a more sustainable and viable sharing of responsibility across the Atlantic'.

In Chapter 7, Patrick Porter discusses British attitudes to the use of force. He demonstrates that the political will is there, but also that there is – and has been for long – a 'mismatch' between ambition and investment, between theory and practice, and between strategy and identity. The Libyan war, he argues, 'demonstrates that there is an enduring tendency to see force as a potentially effective means of shaping the external environment' and that use of force is symbol of British 'stateness'; it 'reflects and reinforces Britain's identity as a serious power at the top table'. According to Porter, the will to use force has survived 'disappointing experiences in recent wars', lack of public support and cuts in the defence budget. The implications of the mismatch between resources and goals could be more focus on alliances, coalitions and defence integration with allies. It could also be a British revision of its ambitions to remain a 'global player' with the power projection capabilities to support it. Thus, Britain is willing and able, has shown willingness despite popular opposition in some cases, but needs military integration in order to keep its ability. The French and the British have a major bilateral cooperation in this regard.

In Chapter 8, Yves Boyer analyses the French government's military ability and the political will to use force. He argues that the organization of security and defence policy in France has been quite efficient, thanks to the strong role of the President, who is constitutional head of the armed forces, gives guidance on the overall strategy and military organization, controls their execution through the military staff, and directs their implementation through the chairing of the High Council on Defence. So, although France is also suffering from the financial and economic crisis, it can still keep up a 'traditional ambitious' policy, that is, 'working for preserving a certain degree of autonomy, acting as a fair player in NATO to wait for the favourable moment to speed up a genuine European defence policy while developing ad hoc bilateral cooperation with the American ally'. The French are willing and able to use force, and cooperate with the British bilaterally and in NATO, as well as with the United States. French strategic thinking seems to continue along the same lines under Socialist President Hollande, something which indicate that political ideology and public opinion are of limited importance in France with regard to the use of force.

In Chapter 9, Benjamin Schreer discusses Germany and the use of force since the end of the Cold War. Schreer argues that 'Germany has come quite a long way... when it comes to the political will to use military force as an NATO ally'; the political willingness has grown and the transformation of the *Bundeswehr* into a more expeditionary force has created military ability. However, the German government at the same time 'grew more self-confident in terms of taking decisions about the use of force from a purely national interest perspective', which was demonstrated in connection with the Iraq War in 2003 and NATO's Libya Campaign in 2011. Schreer thinks that it will continue that way, that Germany 'most likely' will remain a 'selective NATO ally' in out-of-area operations, and not be able to play a 'leadership role' within the alliance. The Germans seems no longer to be motivated primarily by alliance dependence and do not want to lead in a military operation. They can therefore be placed in the category rather unwilling, despite being able.

In Chapter 10, Damon Coletta and David Garcia investigate Spain's military ability and political will to use force. They argue that Spain has been seen as a both unable and unwilling NATO member, but that these views to some extent have been unfair: 'Appreciating Spain's potential for effective statecraft and accepting Spain for twenty-first century diplomacy in a broker's role requires a shift in perspective from the typical Anglo-American lens.' A new view undertaken both by outside observers and by the Spanish public 'could prepare the way for reinvigoration of Spanish statecraft', they argue. The most important factor seems to be the unwillingness to engage because of public opinion. Democratic communication and public outreach from Spain's statesmen is what is needed, according to the authors: 'Brilliant statecraft goes for naught if citizens can neither see a state worth defending nor feel the emotional tug of republican virtue.' In Spain there is no great willingness to use force, both a rather pacifistic culture and political ideology matter. Under Aznar alliance dependence was evident as a cause for contributions to the Iraq war; but with the Socialist government of Zapatero which was propelled into office after the Madrid terror attacks, there was an immediate withdrawal from this operation.

In Chapter 11, Marek Pietraś discusses Polish attitudes to the use of force. He demonstrates that Poland has been a willing and able NATO partner though limited by financial shortcomings. The goal of Poland's participation in NATO's operations has been 'to enhance its international position and attain the status of a US strategic partner'. However, public opinion has developed a growing scepticism against Polish out-of-area engagement, which has made Poland hesitate towards such operations, as in the Libyan case. The Polish government is also concerned that such operations could undermine NATO's collective defence. Poland is both willing and able, and is motivated primarily by alliance dependence for geopolitical reasons. Yet its disappointment over the status of the US-Polish relationship allows public opinion to matter more than before. In terms of military capability, Poland is better off than many other states.

In Chapter 12, Tamás Magyarics analyses the Hungarian military ability and political will to use force. As the other smaller European NATO allies, he argues, Hungary is 'less and less capable of thinking globally as far as military matters concerned'. Hungary has not lacked the political will to be a reliable ally within the alliance – the track record of the Hungarian governments in the past 20 years has shown that – but the military capabilities have not been in place. Necessary and expensive defence reforms have been very difficult to carry through, especially in times of difficult economic circumstances when resources are badly needed elsewhere. That resulted in a situation where 'Budapest repeatedly promised more than it has been able to deliver'. According to Magyarics, the situation has now changed and become more realistic: 'Hungary will not be punching below its weight in NATO in the future.' Here the picture is clear: Political willingness but lacking military capability, whereas alliance dependence is the main motivator, for geopolitical reasons.

In Chapter 13, Mikkel Vedby Rasmussen discusses Danish political will and military ability to use force. Since the end of the Cold War Denmark has shown that it is one of NATO's most loyal members, and that it does not hesitate to use force for political purposes. It has also built up military capability, and taken many painful decisions, to be able and ready to use force: 'With the experience from Afghanistan and Libya the Danish armed forces had acquired the skills of expeditionary warfare' Rasmussen argues. The Danish status as 'journeyman' was also confirmed by the appointment of the former Prime Minister Anders Fogh Rasmussen to NATO's Secretary General. The problem is, according to the author, not quality but quantity, because Denmark is a small country, and the solution of the problem is more cooperation with other allies and partners: 'If Denmark wants to maintain its status as a 'journeyman' in NATO, the Danish government will have to continue to develop its ability to network the Danish armed forces with partners.' Danish political will is crystal clear, and alliance dependence explains it. The underlying motive is probably rather general foreign policy prestige rather than geopolitics. Denmark needs military integration with others in order to sustain the desired level of contributions.

In Chapter 14, Janne Haaland Matlary analyses the Norwegian government's military ability and political will. She shows how Norway has been an eager and consistent contributor to international operations, starting with UN operations. Norway goes where NATO goes, and has the military ability to do so for the most part. Norwegian defence capabilities have been restructured towards expeditionary warfare since about 2000, but Norway retains a national focus as the primary one, situated as it is next to Russia. Regarding political ability, the left-Socialist party (Sosialistisk Venstreparti, SV) is shown to have influenced the contributions to ISAF in the period when this party retained much influence, but this was a relatively brief interlude. In conclusion, Norway seeks closeness to the United States for the most part, based on the geopolitical strategy that NATO must deter Russia, but sometimes domestic politics takes precedence or at least modifies traditional security and defence policy. There is a will for the most part, and a way, but also Norway needs 'smart defense' integration in order to sustain its contributions to international operations in the longer run.

## Will European NATO states carry more burden?

The country chapters bring out the importance of national strategic culture and history. In the United Kingdom, Porter argues, four 'themes' well connected to history have 'shaped' Britain's use of force today: 'the tension between continental and global commitments; the Anglo-American relationship; the retreat from empire; and one of the most difficult contexts for relating theory to practice, nuclear weapons'. And Spain's 'brokering role' for twenty-first century diplomacy rests, according to Coletta and Garcia, on 'the skill with which Spain across multiple centuries negotiated the twisting and at times violent course of great power competition'. With regard to Poland, Pietraś points out that a 'vitally significant factor for Poland's participation in NATO peacekeeping operations' has been the prior experience of participation in many of the most important UN peacekeeping missions since 1953. These experiences became, according to Pietraś, a kind of 'value added' to the Polich NATO operations conducted from 1996 and onwards.

Political ideology seems to have been a prominent driver in Germany and Norway. According to Schreer, Germany is not unwilling and unable to play a major military role within a changing NATO – and has also done so after the end of the Cold War in the Balkans, and in Afghanistan – but it has also for a long time developed 'a strategic culture of military restraint', which has a great impact on German attitudes to the use of force. In Norway, domestic politics (rather than political culture) has influenced the government's will to use force for political purposes. 'Norway has, on the whole, been militarily able', Matlary argues, but the political realities have from time to time reduced the political will.

Economy and organization appear to have been important drivers for the use of force in France and Hungary. As already mentioned, the key role of the French President in policy making and implementation is an organizational factor that has great implications, but – as Boyer underscores – the extent of the likely reduction of the French defence budget could jeopardize the coherence of the French military model. Lack of relevant military capabilities has been Budapest's biggest problem when it comes to Hungarian use of force, according to Magyarics. This, in turn, has been the effect of the scarcity of resources (i.e. economy), and – as already has been touched upon – inability to reform the defence forces (i.e. organization).

For Denmark organization and political culture have also been of crucial importance for the government's active and engaged NATO policy; it seems to be consensus in Danish politics that the ability to deploy troops shall be maintained and the Danish Armed Forces are in great shape for NATO missions. But a prerequisite for the changed Danish attitude to the use of force after the end of the Cold War seems – like in no other country – to have been changed 'threat perceptions'. The Danish Armed Forces have, as Rasmussen argues, transformed 'from a force dedicated to fighting a war of necessity in the defence of the national territory to a force that fights wars of choice'.

Taken together the findings indicate that it is quite important to, in depth, understand what affects military ability and political will to use force for political purposes in every single case. There is no single European attitude to the use of force. This, in turn, has implications for the burden-sharing within NATO.

Kay concludes that Europeans simply have to assume responsibility for their own security in a real way now. Yet they are not rising to this occasion, judging from the European country chapters. In the two major military powers in Europe, France and the United Kingdom, there is (still) the ability to project and use force globally, but only France appears to have a global strategy for military power. Yet France has only recently returned to the military structure of NATO and is as such a 'newcomer' – or perhaps 'latecomer' in the alliance. The United Kingdom, the major actor alongside the United States with its 'special relationship', undergoes changes in the political willingness to use force: while it is a prerogative (FPP – foreign policy prerogative) of the prime minister, it does not seem to be based on a clear strategy. Afghanistan has meant major mobilization of public opinion against the use of force, and it seems likely that the latter will influence the decisions on this in the future. Thus, France may be the most 'insulated' with regard to decision to use force, public opinion having little impact. The United Kingdom is more prone to being influenced by the latter, yet retains the FPP as well.

In other states in this study, we see that Germany is very influenced by its historical experience as well as its public opinion, adverse to the use of force. Here Christopher Coker's point that the attitude to the use of force is cultural is surely correct. In Poland the recent reticence to the use of force is rather political than cultural: the desire to have a special relationship with the United States was frustrated, we learn. In Spain, domestic public opinion matters, as well as cultural antipathy to using force. In Hungary the government has followed the United States, but also has genuine national interests in the Balkans. In Denmark and Norway, we see evidence of political and ideological factors playing a key role: both states have variation in their contributions over time – Denmark has moved from being a 'laggard' in NATO to being the most responsive to US expectations, while Norway has maintained closeness to the United States as a major strategy since 1945, but in the 2005–2009 Socialist government with left-wing SV in the coalition we have seen how domestic factors trumped this policy line.

Regarding political willingness to use force, we therefore can conclude that political ideology matters directly for NATO contributions and for the relationship to the United States, that is, for burden-sharing. But we also see that states with military cultures that are strategic in nature, thus actively using force, are less influenced by political factors. The United Kingdom and France use force in a habitual manner regardless of ideology: there is no discernible difference between Sarkozy and Hollande, or between Brown and Cameron. Moreover, Germany continues to be averse to the use of military force even when a conservative chancellor is governing – there seems to be little difference between Schröder and Merkel with regard to the aversion to the military instrument.

It is no surprise that military ability is closely correlated with political will, in fact, it is a function of political will. In these chapters we learn that the major 'smart defence' project in Europe is the British–French collaboration which has lasted more than a decade. The major military actors in Europe politically are also the major trail-blazers for military modernization and integration. Germany, on the other hand, does not go for much expeditionary force, but continues to keep a large mobilization army. Denmark and Norway are both active in getting to the best levels in terms of modernization, seeking to be interoperable with the United Kingdom and United States. One interesting feature of the German case is the relaxation regarding the United States and NATO pressures to contribute. Germany seems to say that 'we have different priorities', the use of force is not one of them.

The country chapters show that most governments look to the United States when deciding to contribute to international operations. Alliance loyalty or dependence is the major reason why contributions come. This finding is consistent with the literature discussed above, but it also raises a very important question: What will happen to military contributions once the United States is no longer in the lead of an operation? If Libya is the first example of things to come, it will be up to European states and not the United States to both initiate, lead and take full responsibility for operations in the vicinity of the region. As Kay's chapter brings out, the United States is serious about its new strategic priority in Asia and also about the need for Europe not only to carry much more burden but also to lead operations.

Given this, what do the chapters tell us about such political willingness? The Libya operation was both initiated and led by France, in close cooperation with the United Kingdom. As we have seen, these are the two major military cultures in Europe which both have the FPP and militaries with a global reach. If European allies will continue to conduct international operations, it will probably have to be under French and/or British leadership.

In France the FPP obtains without any important restrictions in terms of political ideology or public opinion. As Boyer underlines, there is no major change in strategy brought by the ideological change of Hollande versus Sarkozy. The French institutional system is so designed that long-term (30 years!) strategic planning is possible, and the system is on purpose insulated from political change in the short term. France is clearly the state where the 'score' on political ability or willingness to use force is the highest.

The United Kingdom is similar in terms of FPP, but in the United Kingdom public opinion seems to have become important as a function of the Iraq and Afghanistan wars. Iraq was agreed to by Tony Blair without much consultation, as necessary given the importance of the 'special relationship', but it turned out to be a controversial decision as the situation in the field worsened. The Afghan operation has brought home many fallen, and British public opinion has become engaged in a new manner. The Libya operation was agreed to by Prime Minister Cameron against the strategic advice of advisors, military as well as civilians. This decision was not the result of long-term strategic thinking.

Thus, the two leading military states of Europe are both equipped with the FPP, making their leaders able to decide themselves on the use of force. However, the United Kingdom seems less clear about strategy today than before, whereas France shows continuity because of its institutional 'lock-in'.

These states are of course able to deploy globally and to sustain such deployments over time. However, also they experience budget cuts, and have started very important bilateral cooperation as far back as in 1998. These states initiated the EU's development of battle groups and defence policy with the St. Malo declaration in 1998, and are today more focused on national-level and NATO-level cooperation (Matlary, 2009). The British–French military equipment deal is significant for two reasons: Firstly, it shows that even the biggest states of Europe have to find partners if they are to maintain their status in the future; secondly, it shows that the time is ripe or even overdue for such deals. This arrangement was started more than a decade ago, but to date, few if any other states – which need partners even more – have moved into such encompassing deals with others.

Germany, the third large power of Europe, made a furore over Libya by abstaining from the UN Security Council. Schreer makes the point that this decision can be read as an expression of national interest: Germany is wary of international operations and finds that economic interests are much more important than military interests. Germany simply does not want to be a great power in the world in traditional coercive diplomacy, he argues. Perhaps Schreer is right in pointing out that German assertiveness today means to opt for another type of great power status, that is based on economic power and soft power diplomacy. If this is the case, Germany will continue this strategic line in NATO – not follow the United States, not deploy in international operations as a main rule, in short, be a 'selective ally', as he puts it.

The implications of this are that the leading states of NATO regarding the use of force will be France and the United Kingdom to an even greater extent in the future than today. The future model of NATO operations in and around Europe looks like it will centre on British–French leadership around which coalitions will be built. This is a model that is already in place – coalitions have been common in NATO for a long time, starting with Kosovo. The new element is that the United States will no longer lead such operations where its own interests are not involved.

But even if the United States is not in the lead, it will matter greatly to the United States whether European NATO carries more of the burden, even in operations where the United States is not involved. If NATO is to deter, it has to be able both to coerce and to fight. This is the essential point. An alliance that is unable to act is no deterrent. Therefore, there will be expectations that all members of NATO contribute, as an alliance with 'dead weight' is not only burdened by free riders but this also has a detrimental effect on the deterring ability of the alliance. This means that the importance of alliance dependence will not go away.

The fundamental need for Europe to keep NATO alive implies that the United States keep a keen interest in Article 5. The United States demands that Europe carry more of the burden and that Europe undertake to lead operations from now on. This demand can be seen as a *sine qua non* for NATO to continue as the deterrent and security guarantee that it is today. If Europeans do more, the United States will also do its part. This 'new deal' in NATO will have to function if the United States is to continue taking interest in the alliance. Therefore European allies must continue not only to contribute but also to accept responsibility for operations.

One may object that there will not be a need for new international operations after ISAF and Libya. This objection presupposes that NATO plans for which operations it will undertake. It does not. 'Events, my dear boy, events', is reputed to have been Harold Macmillan's response when asked what determines international politics. Events determine where NATO goes – no one ever planned to be in sharp operations in Bosnia, Kosovo, Afghanistan or Libya.

## Bibliography

Allison, G. T. (1971) *Essence of Decision: Explaining the Cuban Missile Crisis* (Boston: Little, Brown).
Byman, D. and Waxman, M. (2002) *The Dynamics of Coercion: American Foreign Policy and the Limits of Military Might* (Cambridge: Cambridge University Press).
Davidson, J. W. (2011) *America's Allies and War: Kosovo, Afghanistan, and Iraq* (Basingstoke: Palgrave Macmillan).
Farell, T. and Terriff, T. (2010) 'Military Transformation in NATO: A Framework for Analysis', in Terriff, T., Osinga, F. and Farell, T. (eds) *A Transformation Gap? American Innovations and European Military Change* (Stanford: Stanford University Press), pp. 1–13.
Gates, R. (2010) 'NATO Strategic Concept Seminar (Future of NATO)', http://www.defense.gov (homepage), date accessed 23 May 2012.
Gates, R. (2011) 'The Security and Defense Agenda (Future of NATO)', http://www.defense.gov (homepage), date accessed 18 September 2011.

Hallams, E. and Schreer, B. (2012) 'Towards a "post-American" Alliance? NATO Burden-sharing after Libya', *International Affairs*, Vol. 88, No. 2, pp. 313–327.
Herring, E. (2007) 'Introduction: The Scope of the Military Security Agenda', in Collis, A. (ed.) *Contemporary Security Studies* (Oxford: Oxford University Press), pp. 129–145.
Kagan, R. (2002) 'Power and Weakness', *Policy Review*, Vol. June & July, No. 113, pp. 3–28.
Kagan, R. (2003) *Of Paradise and Power: America and Europe in the New World Order* (New York: Alfred A. Knopf).
Kirchner, E. J. and Sperling, J (2010) *National Security Cultures: Patterns of Global Governance* (London: Routledge).
Kreps, S. (2010) 'Elite Consensus as a Determinant of Alliance Cohesion: Why Public Opinion Hardly Matters for NATO-led Operations in Afghanistan', *Foreign Policy Analysis*, Vol. 6, No. 3, pp. 191–215.
Kupchan, C. (1988) 'NATO and the Persian Gulf: Examining Intra-alliance Behaviour', *International Organization*, Vol. 42, No. 2, pp. 317–346.
Lock, E. (2010) 'Refining Strategic Culture: Return of the Second Generation', *Review of International Studies*, Vol. 36, No. 3, pp. 685–708.
Matlary, J. H. (2009) *European Union Security Dynamics in the New National Interest* (Basingstoke: Palgrave Macmillan).
Noetzel, T. and Schreer, B. (2009) 'NATO's Vietnam? Afghanistan and the Future of the Atlantic Alliance', *Contemporary Security Policy*, Vol. 30, No. 3, pp. 529–547.
Nye, J. S. (2009) *Understanding International Conflicts: An Introduction to Theory and History* (New York: Pearson Longman).
Olson, M. and Zeckhauser, R. (1966) *An Economic Theory of Alliances* (Santa Monica, CA: RAND).
Ringsmose, J. (2010) 'NATO Burden-Sharing Redux: Continuity and Change after the Cold War', *Contemporary Security Policy*, Vol. 31, No. 2, pp. 319–338.
Saxi, H. L. (2010) 'Defending Small States: Norwegian and Danish Defense Policies in the Post-Cold War Era', *Defense and Security Analysis*, Vol. 26, No. 4, pp. 415–430.
Shanker, T. and Schmitt, E. (2011) 'Seeing Limits to "New" Kind of War in Libya', *The New York Times*, 21 October.
Sheehan, J. J. (2007) *The Monopoly of Violence: Why Europeans Hate Going to War* (London: Faber and Faber).
Snyder, G. (1984) 'The Security Dilemma in Alliance Politics', *World Politics*, Vol. 36, No. 4, pp. 461–495.
Spiegel, P. (2011), 'Gates Criticises Five Allies Over Libya', *Financial Times*, 8 June.
Stevens, P. (2011) 'NATO's Long Drift towards Irrelevance', *Financial Times*, 23 September.
Strachan, H. (2009) 'The Strategic Gap in British Defence Policy', *Survival*, Vol. 51, No. 4, pp. 49–70.
Thies, W. J. (2009) *Why NATO Endures* (Cambridge: Cambridge University Press).
Williams, M. J. (2008) *NATO, Security and Risk Management: From Kosovo to Kandahar* (London: Routledge).

# Part I
# Determinants of the Use of Force

# 2
# From Mars to Venus? European Use of Force from a Historical Perspective

*M. Petersson*

## Introduction

On several occasions, US former Secretary of Defence, Robert Gates, criticized European NATO allies for not sharing a reasonable part of the military burden within the alliance. In his final policy speech on NATO's future in Brussels, 20 June 2011, his message was quite clear. The ISAF mission in Afghanistan had exposed 'significant shortcomings in NATO – in military capabilities, and in political will'. The Libya operation showed similar shortcomings that had the potential to 'jeopardize the alliance's ability to conduct an integrated, effective and sustained air-sea campaign' (Gates, 2011).

The (European) NATO members had to find out new approaches 'to boosting combat capabilities' to avoid 'collective military irrelevance', he continued, and to avoid that future US political leaders 'may not consider the return on America's investment in NATO worth the cost' (Gates, 2011). Gates' successor, Leon Panetta, has expressed similar views, and his predecessor, Donald Rumsfeld, famously talked about 'old Europe', a group of countries built around the Franco-German relationship unwilling to follow the US lead before the Second Gulf War (Sedivy and Zaborowski, 2005; Hallams and Schreer, 2012).

Since the formation of NATO in 1949, this kind of criticism has not been unusual from the US side (Hallams and Schreer, 2012). During the 1950s, for example, when the Soviet Union had large conventional forces threatening Western Europe, the United States tried to persuade the European allies to build up more forces to defend the continent, without much success: 'many Alliance members', Doris M. Condit writes, 'felt that the Soviet threat was abating, and they disliked American pressures for additional and possibly unnecessary military expenses' (Condit, 1988, pp. 383–84). And, as Wallace J. Thies has pointed out, there is a 'vast literature filled with claims that NATO is in disarray, is about to fall apart, or even has ceased to exist in all but name':

> If we take these claims seriously, relations between the United States and its European allies fell to the lowest point since the Second World War in 1980, 1981, 1983, and 1987. Predictions that the Alliance was on the verge of collapse or that it had already ceased to exist in all but name found their way into print in 1981, 1982, 1983, 1986, 1987, 1988, 1989, and 1990.
>
> (Thies, 2009, pp. 12–14)

It is, however, fair to argue that the US criticism has increased after the end of the Cold War, and especially after 9/11. The US population seems to be more and more negative towards Europe in general and NATO in particular (Bateman, 2010), something which is also underscored by Sean Kay in Chapter 6.

Furthermore, in the scholarly debate attention has been paid to the growing 'rift' in the transatlantic relation. Robert Kagan, probably the most influential analyst on the topic, has argued that Americans are from Mars and Europeans are from Venus (Kagan, 2002; Kagan, 2003), and he has been followed by several others.

Against that background, it seems that the attitude to the use of force for political purposes differs between the United States and Europe. How true is that picture?

The aim of this chapter is to analyse European attitudes to the use of force from a historical perspective, to discuss those attitudes in a present context and to present some reflections on the issue for the future.

In the first part of the chapter, I will briefly describe which role the use of force for political purposes has played in European history, especially in the democratic, post-modern age (i.e. after the Second World War). I will argue that motives for the use of force have shifted from securing the power and integrity of the state towards securing the values of the Western community ('the why'); that the threshold for using force inside Europe has been much higher than the threshold for using force outside Europe ('the where'); and that the use of force has been exercised integrated and collectively rather than individually ('the how').

In the second part of the chapter, I will discuss the post-modern European attitudes to the use of force in a present context and try to identify what consequences these attitudes could have for the military ability and political will to use force today and in the future. Especially important here is to elaborate upon how important history is as a background factor for today's and tomorrow's use of force for political purposes.

## European use of force from a historical perspective

Before going into the issue of European use of force in a historical perspective it is reasonable to present Kagan's and other scholars' main arguments about Europe's changing role in world politics after the Second World War.

Kagan argues that the Europeans' 'more peaceful strategic culture' is 'quite new' and that it differs from the strategic culture 'that dominated Europe for hundreds of years and at least until World War I': 'The European governments – and peoples – who enthusiastically launched themselves into that continental war believed in *machtpolitik*.' In short, Americans and Europeans have shifted roles, according to Kagan: when the United States was weak it practiced 'the strategies of weakness', when the Europeans were strong 'they believed in strength and martial glory', and now when the United States is strong 'it behaves like powerful nations' (Kagan, 2003, pp. 5–6).

Other scholars, such as James J. Sheehan, also argue that '[t]he ability and willingness to make war' has changed in Europe after the end of the Second World War, but do so from a rather different perspective: 'the obsolescence of war is not a global phenomenon but a European one ... the disappearance of war after 1945 created both a dramatically new international system within Europe and a new kind of European state'. According to Sheehan, 'the long peace' during the late nineteenth and early twentieth century represents 'the historical roots of the civilian policies and institutions that would eventually dominate European public life':

> Violence declined in importance and it was concealed from view by something else – that is, by the state's need to encourage economic growth, provide social welfare, and guarantee personal security for its citizens.
>
> (Sheehan, 2007, pp. xvi–xviii and xx)

Sheehan argues that the combination of economic strength and military weakness is not 'illogical'. Rather it represents a different – 'civilian' – identity, culture or state: 'As a result, the European Union may become a superstate – a super *civilian* state – but not a superpower', he declares (Sheehan, 2007, pp. 221, 224, emphasis added by Sheehan).

Yet other scholars, such as Adrian Hyde-Price, take a position in between Kagan and Sheehan. Hyde-Price is reluctant to generalize about a European strategic culture, but he argues that the 'recasting' of strategic culture that took place after the Second World War in Europe contains 'certain themes that are broadly shared':

> The first is a view of war as destructive and uncontrollable and consequently something to be avoided at almost any cost. The second is the belief that a primary role – if not *the* primary role – of armed forces is deterrence and collective territorial defence.
> (Hyde-Price, 2005, p. 140)

There are several other examples of scholarly literature dealing with the issue of Europe's diminishing military role on the world scene and reluctant attitude to the use of force for political purposes after the Second World War (Cooper, 1996; Dalgaard-Nielsen, 2004). However, it can be argued that this picture of the European states is debatable.

First of all it is problematic to compare the pre-modern age and the modern age with the post-modern age, which Kagan and others do to a large extent. Second, it is not obvious to argue that European attitudes to the use of military force have changed dramatically during the post-modern age, as many scholars do. In the following sections, I will develop those two arguments further.

## Courts, cabinets and commons

The use of military force for political purposes in Europe during the pre-modern (before the nineteenth century) and modern (during the late eighteenth, the nineteenth and early twentieth centuries) age was a frequent phenomenon. However, for several reasons it is not unproblematic to compare European use of force after the Second World War with those periods.

First of all, it can be argued that the decisions to wage war during the pre-modern and modern ages were normally not much, or not at all, influenced by the people and their representatives – especially not during the pre-modern age. Monarchies were hereditary and the monarch's loyalty was directed to the family rather than the state (and the people). As Jeremy Black expresses it:

> Rulers were conscious of their position as part of a family, and of their responsibility to it. This encouraged a stress not only on dynastic and personal honor, but also on the specific rights that were held to be the family's inheritance.
> (Black, 2002, p. 10)

During the nineteenth century, 'the modern age', the influence of the Parliaments became greater, at least in some countries, and the waging of war became more directly connected to the state (and the people – or perhaps more correctly those who were allowed to vote) than to the family. But it was still mainly the heads of state and their cabinets that made the decisions to wage war, not the people and their representatives (Anderson, 2007).

Second, the reasons for waging war during this period were often religious and/or family related, especially in the pre-modern period. Even after 1648 religion played a great role in creating tensions within and between states, according to several scholars. During the nineteenth and early twentieth centuries, however, nationalism became more important as a conflict driver (Black, 2002; Howard, 1976).

To sum up, war fighting was, as Michael Howard argues, a matter for 'priests' and 'princes' during the pre-modern age, for 'peoples' and 'nations' during the modern age and for 'idealists' and 'ideologues' during the post-modern age (Howard, 2001). Therefore, it is not unproblematic to compare European use of force for political purposes during the post-modern age with the use of force during the modern and pre-modern age.

## European use of force during the post-modern age

Kagan's description of European use of force after the Second World War has been criticized for being too 'German centric'. As, for example, Anja Dalgaard-Nielsen puts it:

> He overlooks that European countries like France and the United Kingdom have a tradition of projecting power and have no qualms about using it as a perfectly normal instrument for pursuing the national interest in extra-European parts of the world.
> (Dalgaard-Nielsen, 2004, p. 74)

30  *Determinants of the Use of Force*

Sheehan makes this point as well, that is, that the bipolar world order 'made it possible for Europeans to live at peace with one another, but it did not bring peace to the rest of the humanity'. Sheehan's conclusion, however, is that European states 'lost not only the ability but also the will to retain their empires; they no longer assumed that they could and should dominate the globe':

> ...by the 1960s, *grandeur* was no longer an important goal for European states. What mattered...was material well-being, social stability, economic growth. This is what European electorates demanded of their governments, and that is what governments struggled to provide.
>
> (Sheehan, 2007, pp. 166–71)

Sheehan's and Kagan's arguments – in simplified form – that Europeans do not use military force for political purposes after the Second World War, can, however, be scrutinized further, both from a quantitative and a qualitative perspective.

First of all, almost independently of how one reckons, both France and the United Kingdom have – individually – used major military force for political purposes more often than the United States after the Second World War – in Malaya, in Indochina, in Madagascar, in Tunisia, in Cyprus, in Algeria and in Uganda, to mention but some cases. The decolonization after the Second World War was violent, and France and the United Kingdom used military force, sometimes massive force, for political purposes quite often. Sometimes – as the Suez operation in 1956 shows – they worked together, and in that specific case direct against the will of the United States (Bernard, 2009).

Second, the use of force has not always been connected – at least not directly connected – to the decolonization process. The British use of force for political purposes in Greece towards the end of and directly after the Second World War, in Jordan in 1958, and in the Falklands in 1982 are examples of that. In Greece the UK government wanted to hinder communist expansion, in Jordan to defend the Jordanian regime and in the Falklands – perhaps the most spectacular British operation after the Second World War – to throw out the Argentinean invaders (Iatrides and Rizopoulos, 2000; Groove, 2002; Yitzhak, 2004).

Third, the European NATO members have used military force for political purposes side by side with the United States in all major US-led operations since the end of the Cold War. In the Gulf War in 1991 the United Kingdom contributed with more than 45,000 troops, France with almost 15,000 and Italy with over 1,000 – just to mention the three largest contributors. In Afghanistan (ISAF, September 2011) the United Kingdom contributed with almost 10,000 troops, Germany with almost 5,000, Italy and France with almost 4,000 and several other European NATO members (such as Poland, Romania and Spain) with more than 1,000. Even in Iraq in 2003, the United Kingdom contributed with 46,000 troops during the invasion phase, and several other European NATO members deployed large amounts of troops thereafter. In Libya in 2011, finally, France and the United Kingdom alone flew one-third of the overall sorties, attacking 40 per cent of the targets (Chin, 2011; Panetta, 2012; Devore, 2012).

### Post-modern European use of force – why, when and how?

As the very brief analysis above indicates, the arguments of Kagan, Sheehan and other scholars need modification. The European NATO members have neither lacked military ability nor political will to use force for political purposes after the end of the Second World War. It is, however, true that their relative military ability to do so has declined compared to earlier periods, and that NATO – because of that – lacks a sustainable burden-sharing model (Hallams and Schreer, 2012).

On the other hand, many of the European NATO members' defence forces have undergone a fundamental transformation, from a 'threat-based' to a 'capabilities-based' model as the basis for defence planning, which has made their forces more mobile, more ready and more interoperable with US forces (on transformation, see, for example, Neal, 2006).

Anyway, it is reasonable to argue that the political will to use force has changed character slowly from a state-centric to a people-centric approach, especially after the end of the Cold War. Both the Kosovo operation in 1999 and the Libya operation in 2011 illustrate that. 'The Kosovo crisis was a watershed event in the reformulation of a doctrine of intervention', Michael W. Doyle argues: 'When the UN did not protect the Kosovars, NATO did' (Bellamy and Williams, 2011; Doyle, 2011, p. 79).

Furthermore, European states have seldom used force inside Europe after the Second World War. The British operations in Greece (1944–1947) and the engagement in former Yugoslavia after the end of the Cold War are exceptions to that rule, but both during the Cold War and after the Cold War the use of force has been concentrated outside Europe, especially in Africa and Asia. During the Cold War, France fought major wars in Indochina and Algeria, and the United

Kingdom primarily in the Middle East. After the Cold War coalitions of NATO members and non-NATO members have been using force for political purposes in Africa, Asia and the Middle East.

Lastly, it is fair to argue that the use of force by European states after the Second World War, and especially after the Cold War, has been multinational and undertaken collectively rather than individually. The operations in Kuwait, the former Yugoslavia, Afghanistan, Iraq and Libya are all examples.

To sum up, there seems to be a slow change in 'why' European states use force, 'where' European states use force and 'how' European states use force after the Second World War. Taken together, this seems to indicate that the European NATO members' military ability and political will to use force for political purposes still exists, but that the ends, means and strategies are slowly changing. However, one should also remember that there are important differences between the European NATO allies when it comes to why, where and how force should be used. As Timo Noetzel and Benjamin Schreer have shown, NATO consists of three tiers of members – a 'reformist' tier, a 'status quo' tier and a 'neo-traditionalist' tier – that have different opinions regarding central issues, such as threat perception, collective defence and enlargement (Noetzel and Schreer, 2009).[1]

## History, military ability and political will

How important is history as a background factor for the European NATO members' military ability and political will to use force for political purposes today and tomorrow? Philosophically speaking, the answer to that question depends on epistemological standpoints regarding the scope and character of history as an academic discipline. Can generalizations be drawn from history? Can predictions be made on the basis of history?

E. H. Carr – British historian, journalist and international relations theorist – argues that the picture of history dealing with 'the unique and particular, and science with the general and the universal' is wrong. 'The historian', he continues, 'is not really interested in the unique, but what is general in the unique' (Carr, 1961, pp. 62–63).

According to Carr those who reject generalization are those who deny that something can be learned from history, but the historian is bound to generalize and thus provide 'general guides for future action which, though not specific predictions, are both valid and useful'. Specific events cannot be predicted because they are unique and because 'the element of accident enters to it':

To learn about the present in the light of the past means also to learn about the past in the light of the present. The function of history is to promote a profounder understanding of both past and present through the interrelation between them.

(Carr, 1961, pp. 68–69)

John Lewis Gaddis takes a similar position when he argues that history cannot help us 'predict' the future (as replicable sciences can), but it can – for sure – 'prepare' us for it and it provides us with methods for 'coping' with it (Gaddis, 1997, p. 84). Michael Howard, lastly, formulates it in the following way:

... the past is a foreign country; there is little we can say about it until we have learned its language and understood its assumptions; *and in deriving conclusions about the processes which occurred in it and applying them to our own day we must be very careful indeed.*

(Howard, 1991, p. 13, my emphasis)

So, in that perspective, how much does history influence the European NATO members' military ability and political will to use force for the purpose of policy? Probably a lot, but that does not mean that we know exactly how. The air war in Libya is a good example of that. Who would have guessed that such an operation would take place at all, that 'the Europeans' would lead it and that the United States would play a supportive role?

However, given that the Europeans' actually engaged in the conflict, it is not – for historical reasons – surprising that France and the United Kingdom took the lead. They had during and after the Cold War demonstrated that they had the military ability and political will to use force for political purposes a number of times. It is neither surprising that Germany – of historical reasons – did not support the operation and did not take part in it. This created tensions within the alliance, but it is understandable from a historical point of view.

As Pascal Vennesson et al. (2009, pp. 638–639) argue:

Because of its traumatic past and the international context Germans have been skeptical about the use of military force and the deployment of Bundeswehr abroad.... Military force is not perceived as an efficient or exclusive instrument of security policy, it has to be embedded in a comprehensive security approach, and the notion that it can only be a very last resort is prevalent.

## Concluding remarks

The aim of this chapter has been to analyse European attitudes to the use of force from a historical perspective, to discuss those attitudes in a present context and to present some reflections on the issue for the future.

I have argued that the use of force in European history – that is, until the end of the Second World War – is not quite relevant for the situation today. If we want to understand the present situation we must concentrate on the democratic, post-modern age (i.e. after the Second World War). I have also argued that European states – in particular France and the United Kingdom, but also others – actually have used force for political purposes after the end of the Second World War, and that they have both the military ability and political will to do so.

However, it seems that the motives for the use of force have shifted from securing the power and integrity of the state towards securing the values of the Western community ('the why'); that the threshold for using force inside Europe has been much higher than the threshold for using force outside Europe ('the where'); and that the use of force has been exercised integrated and collectively rather than individually ('the how').

Finally, I discussed how important history is as a background factor for the European NATO members' military ability and political will to use force for political purposes today and tomorrow, and here I agree with several of my history colleagues that we cannot make predictions of future behaviour of the European NATO states by looking at history, but we can understand their action better by looking at history and we can handle the present and the future better by knowing our history. 'Nobody can abolish the past', Sir Michael Powike argues (Quoted in Howard, 1991, p. 19). History – like culture, economy and threat perceptions – influences the present military ability and political will to use force for sure, but we still do not know exactly how.

## Notes

1. Timo Noetzel and Benjamin Schreer: 'NATO's Vietnam? Afghanistan and the Future of the Atlantic Alliance', *Contemporary Security Policy*, Vol. 30, No. 3, pp. 529–547.

## Bibliography

Anderson, S. (2007) 'Metternich, Bismarck, and the Myth of the "Long Peace," 1815–1914', *Peace and Change*, Vol. 32, No. 3, pp. 301–328.

Bateman, R. L. (2010) 'The Death of NATO', *US Naval Institute Proceedings*, Vol. 136, No. 12, pp. 48–55.

Bellamy, A. J. and Williams, P. D. (2011) 'The New Politics of Protection? Côte d'Ivoire, Libya and the Responsibility to Protect', *International Affairs*, Vol. 87, No. 4, pp. 825–850.

Bernard, J-Y. (2009) 'Disregarding the Atlantic "Special Relationship": The Eden Cabinet in the Lead-Up to the Invasion of the Suez Canal Zone', *Canadian Journal of History*, Vol. XLIV, Spring–Summer, pp. 39–61.

Black, J. (2002) *European International Relations 1648–1815* (Basingstoke: Palgrave).

Carr, E. H. (1961) *What is History?* (London: Macmillan).

Chin, W. (2011) 'British Defence Policy and the War in Iraq 2003–2009', *Defence & Security Analysis*, Vol. 27, No. 1, pp. 65–76.

Condit, D. M. (1988) *The Test of War, 1950–1953* (Washington, DC: Historical Office, Office of the Secretary of Defence).

Cooper, R. (1996) *The Post-modern State and the World Order* (London: Demos).

Dalgaard-Nielsen, A. (2004) 'Looking to Europe: American Perceptions of the Old World', *Cooperation and Conflict*, Vol. 39, No. 1, pp. 69–76.

Devore, M. C. (2012) 'Armed Forces, States, and Threats: Institutions and the British and French Responses to the 1991 Gulf War', *Comparative Strategy*, Vol. 31, No. 1, pp. 56–83.

Doyle, M. W. (2011) 'International Ethics and the Responsibility to Protect', *International Studies Review*, No. 13, Vol. 1, pp. 72–84.

Gaddis, J. L. (1997) 'History, Theory, and Common Ground', *International Security*, Vol. 22, No. 1, pp. 75–85.

Gates, R. (2011) 'The Security and Defense Agenda (Future of NATO)', http://www.defense.gov (homepage), date accessed 18 September 2011.

Groove, E. (2002) 'The Falklands War and British Defence Policy', *Defense and Security Analysis*, Vol. 18, No. 4, pp. 307–317.

Hallams, E. and Schreer, B. (2012) 'Towards a "Post-American" Alliance? NATO Burden-sharing after Libya', *International Affairs*, Vol. 88, No. 2, pp. 313–327.

Howard, M. (1976) *War in European History* (Oxford: Oxford University Press).

Howard, M. (1991) *The Lessons of History* (Oxford: Clarendon Press).

Howard, M. (2001) *The Invention of Peace and the Reinvention of War* (London: Profile Books).

Hyde-Price, A. (2005) 'European Security, Strategic Culture, and the Use of Force', in K. Longhurst and M. Zaborowski (eds) *Old Europe, New Europe and the Transatlantic Agenda* (London: Routledge), pp. 137–157.

Iatrides, J. O. and Rizopoulos, N. X. (2000) 'The International Dimension of the Greek Civil War', *World Policy Journal*, Vol. 17, No. 1, pp. 87–103.

Kagan, R. (2002) 'Power and Weakness', *Policy Review*, Vol. 113, June & July, pp. 3–28.

Kagan, R. (2003) *Of Paradise and Power: America and Europe in the New World Order* (New York: Alfred A. Knopf).

Neal, D. J. (2006) 'Do We Really Understand What is Meant by Transformational Change for Defence?', *Defence Studies*, Vol. 6, No. 1, pp. 73–96.

Noetzel, T. and Schreer, B. (2009) 'Does a Multi-tier NATO Matter? The Atlantic Alliance and the Process of Strategic Change', *International Affairs*, Vol. 85, No. 2, pp. 211–226.

Panetta, L. E. (2012) *Remarks by Secretary Panetta at Carnegie Europe, Brussels, Belgium* (Washington, DC: US Department of Defence).

Ronen, Y. (2004) 'The Formation and Development of the Jordanian Air Force: 1948–1967', *Middle Eastern Studies*, Vol. 40, No. 5, pp. 158–174.
Sedivy, J. and Zaborowski, M. (2005) 'Old Europe, New Europe and Transatlantic Relations', in K. Longhurst and M. Zaborowski (eds) *Old Europe, New Europe and the Transatlantic Agenda* (London: Routledge), pp. 1–27.
Sheehan, J. J. (2007) *The Monopoly of Violence: Why Europeans Hate Going to War* (London: Faber and Faber).
Thies, W. J. (2009) *Why NATO Endures* (Cambridge: Cambridge University Press).
Vennesson, P., Breuer, F., de Franco, C. and Schroeder, U. (2009) 'Is There a European Way of War? Role Conceptions, Organizational Frames, and the Utility of Force', *Armed Forces & Society*, Vol. 35, No. 4, pp. 628–645.
Yitzhak, R. (2004) 'The Formation and Development of the Jordanian Air Force: 1948–1967', *Middle Eastern Studies*, Vol. 40, No. 5, pp. 158–174.

# 3
# A Farewell to Arms: Europe's Meritocracy and the Demilitarization of Europe

*C. Coker*

## Introduction

> 'The name of the song is called *War*.' 'Oh, that's the name of the song, is it,' Alice said, trying to look interested.
>
> 'No, you don't understand,' the Knight said, looking a little vexed. 'This is what the name is *called*. The name really is *Peacekeeping*'.
>
> 'Then, I ought to have said,' 'that's what the *song* is called', Alice corrected herself.
>
> 'No, you oughtn't; that is quite another thing. The *song* is called a Peace Policy (*Friedenspolitik*). That is only what it's called you know'.
>
> 'Well, what *is* the song, then?' said Alice, by this time completely bewildered.
>
> 'I was coming to that,' the Knight said. 'The song really is *Peace* and the tune is my own invention'.
>
> (Freely adapted from Lewis Carroll, *Alice Through the Looking Glass*)

In 1959, the famous scientist C.P. Snow stirred up a hornet's nest of controversy when he warned that Western society was split into two hostile cultures facing each other across a gulf of mutual incomprehension.

> For constantly I felt I was moving among two groups – comparable in intelligence, identical in race, not grossly different in social origin, earning about the same incomes, who had almost ceased to communicate at all, who in intellectual, moral and psychological climate, had so little in common... that one might have crossed an ocean.
>
> (Snow, 1959, p. 5)

It is a passage which could well stand as a commentary for the current state of the Western Alliance. Two political cultures, Europe and the United States, with similar intellectual accomplishments, not grossly disparate in income, do indeed face each other across the Atlantic. Intellectually as well as psychologically they have been growing apart. The distance between their respective political elites is particularly alarming. It was magnified by differences over the War on Terror; it has been thrown into even greater relief by differences over the management of the economic crisis which has engulfed the West since 2008.

Snow was not talking about the Western Alliance, of course. He was describing the gap in incomprehension between two different elites: one scientific, the other literary. He himself straddled both. He was both an eminent scientist and a famous novelist. And he was aware, or perhaps should have been, that the division he drew, even at the time, was a gross caricature. There is no single scientific culture. The scientific community has split into cells, or different fields, equally inaccessible to each other. It has never been easy to take a uniform view of science, which is why one still speaks of the 'sciences'. But if Snow's Jeremiad no longer describes the real split between the sciences and humanities, it can be employed to illustrate a growing divide between two political cultures in the 'imagined community' we still call 'the West'.

In his valedictory speech in Brussels, Robert Gates, the outgoing US Defence Secretary, warned of a 'dim if not dismal future for the transatlantic alliance' (Gates, 2011). He was moved to speak by his increasing disquiet over the deficiencies exposed by the Libyan campaign on which the United States and at least some European powers had been able to agree. Philip Guedalla, a British writer in the 1920s, once remarked pithily that you could judge the success of a British expedition abroad by the extent of the soldiers' tan. If they had failed to acquire one, the mission had clearly not been a success. If it looked as though they had been out in the sun for too long, it was clear that something had gone wrong with the mission. A five and a half month war to topple a fourth-rate dictator was not a very striking success. Indeed the Libyan operation expressed deeper problems with Western interventionism, or what David Cameron liked to call at the time, 'muscular liberalism'. The United States may well have only 'facilitated' success, but it played a disproportionate role in air-to-air refuelling, the suppression of Libyan radar and the use of Unmanned Aerial Vehicles (UAVs) for reconnaissance, three essential 'enablers' of modern warfare. Only nine members of NATO were willing to take casualties or inflict them. Only two were willing to commit attack helicopters. And some of the big European powers, such as Germany and Poland, chose to sit the war out, aligning themselves with the BRICs (Brazil, Russia, India and China), who had not been able to bring themselves to vote for or against the expedition. Writing of the general campaign, *Newsweek*'s national security correspondent, John Barry, was unequivocal in his judgement that 'Libya has probably consigned notions of a "European defence identity" to the scrapheap of history' (Barry, 2011).

It might even be claimed that without the need to make NATO itself still 'relevant' in American eyes, it is doubtful whether the Europeans would be doing very much fighting at all. It was in bid to heal the wounds left by the Iraq war (2003) that the Europeans committed themselves to fighting in Afghanistan, the Danes in Helmand besides the British; the Dutch in Oruzgan. Norwegian Special Forces prioritized the NATO deployment, though they often found themselves protecting the Germans in Kunduz who were in no condition to protect themselves. By 2010, 500 European soldiers had lost their lives in Afghanistan, and the European contribution at the time was still the largest. Even so, Afghanistan and Libya notwithstanding, we may be witnessing the swansong of European military power and the progressive demilitarization of the continent. And Gates identified the cause a year before his Brussels speech. In early 2010 he first voiced his concerns over what he identified as a culture of 'demilitarization' in Europe, a situation 'where large swathes of the general public and political class are averse to military force and the risks that go with it' (Gates, 2010). It is the role played by 'political culture' that is the theme of this chapter.

## Discourses on war

The demilitarization of Europe has been going on for some time. It is rarely, if ever, officially acknowledged. Instead defence budgets continue to be cut, and armed forces downsized with only a few exceptions (Sweden/Poland). The process has been accompanied by the near collapse of a Common Security and Defence Policy (CDSP). Only one new initiative in crisis management has been undertaken since 2008.

The creation of a new European Union (EU) foreign policy chief and a European diplomatic service is particularly telling in this regard; the language used is of 'peacekeeping', 'stabilization' and even 'mediation', but the word 'defence' is notably absent (Witney, 2011, p. 2). What has emerged is a discourse described by Jurgen Habermas as 'cosmopolitan law enforcement'.

Discourse is an ill-defined term which has many uses in the social sciences, and almost as many meanings. The widely held view, however, is that it is a set of ideas, beliefs and practices that provide ways of representing knowledge. A discourse enables the presentation of certain forms of knowledge while precluding the construction of others.

The American military historian John Lynn uses the term to refer to cultural conceptions of war that tend to structure off sections of its essence, its purpose and the problems it presents. A discourse helps to make sense of the world 'out there' and thus to reduce it to manageable proportions. It makes it more open to reason, although the decisions we take on the basis of what we perceive to be reality are not necessarily rational at all.

Lynn is a historian, not a political scientist, and he is no social constructivist. Indeed, he is very critical of the rise of fashionable social science approaches to military history: '"Deconstruction" means one thing to our "cutting edge colleagues" [military historians] just need something like carpet bombing'. Irony apart, Lynn's discourses are cultural lenses through which particular groups in the military at different times choose to perceive reality. Different groups will contend with each other, but only one discourse will prevail at any given time. As he acknowledges:

> ...culture has no single discourse on war. Rather, a number of distinct discourses encompass the values, expectations, etc, of varied groups which harbour potentially very different and at time opposing interests and points of view.
>
> (Lynn, 2003, p. 365)

Different social groups may well structure different discourses specific to themselves. It follows that there are discourses of power – or empowerment – and that it is generally true to say that the dominant group in society will produce the prevailing discourse. The Italian philosopher Pareto called ideologies 'elite derivations', and the same term might be usefully applied as well to the dominant discourse on war.

In distinguishing between what he terms the 'discourse' and the 'reality' of war, Lynn adds:

> The fundamental assertion of cultural history is that human communities impose cultural constructions upon reality, that they make the 'actual' fit the 'conceptual'. Cultural historians sometimes insist that reality is simply what is perceived and thus culturally constructed. Such an attitude in war is fatal, in the literal sense of the word. But avoiding foolish intellectual excess, this principal applies to the cultural history of war within limits set by the objective facts of armed conflict.
>
> (2003, p. 365)

This concept of the reality of war is comparable with another definition of reality offered by John Vasquez: 'The word "reality" refers to the resistance of the world to conform to every imaginable conception humans create' (Vasquez, 1995, p. 225). As Steven Lukes notes on a related point:

> All cultures... are, apart from everything else that they are, a setting within which their members individually and collectively, engage in the cognitive enterprise of reasoning and face the common human predicament of getting the world right, of understanding, predicting and controlling their environment.
>
> (Lukes, 2003, p. 59)

This is true of all forms of cultural conception and it has particularly important implications for war. Historically, there exists a 'feedback loop' between the discourse and the reality of war. Military culture, as a conceptual medium, may be deeply embedded in society, yet as a cognitive enterprise engaged in understanding and controlling the military environment, it always encounters the resistance imposed by reality that is independent of its own cultural construction. Reality, in Vasquez' sense of the word, confronts every society with a particularly harsh truth: success or failure in battle owes a lot to its 'cognitive enterprise', its dialogue with the real world. A military discourse is difficult to sustain in the face of persistent failure in the field. Indeed, it may even prove to be severely dysfunctional if it does not reflect reality as it is, rather than as one would like it to be. It is my contention that Europe's political class has allowed Europe's hard power portfolio to diminish because it has an imperfect understanding of the 'real world'.

One explanation for this is the striking fact that while the EU has a political culture it has no 'European' strategic culture. The EU has no intention of becoming a military power, writes James Sheehan.

> Because the EU does not claim Carl Schmitt's 'monstrous capacity', the power of life and death, it does not need citizens who are prepared to kill and die. It needs only consumers and producers who recognize that the community serves their interests and advances their individual well-being. And as consumers and producers, most Europeans have usually been rather satisfied with the Union's accomplishments.
>
> (Sheehan, 2007, p. 220).

And this was always going to be the problem with pursuing European Security and Defence Policy (ESDP) even after the European citizenry ceased to be satisfied with the EU's economic performance. Some commentators have also expressed deep scepticism about whether there is sufficient political will to realize ambitious statements such as the Cologne Declaration (1999) with its call for 'autonomous action' or the Declaration on Strengthening Capabilities (December 2008) and its declared wish to remedy the Union's capability shortfalls. All attest to an extraordinary degree of wishful thinking.

In the absence of a political union the Europeans are struggling to save the Euro; in the absence of a single strategic culture they have to make the best they can in coalitions of the willing of a plurality of 'national' discourses on war. This in turn gives rise to strategic incoherence, as it did in the Balkans in the 1990s and in Afghanistan in the past ten years.

Take Europe's strongest military power, the United Kingdom. 'If there was a single overriding lesson of the Iraq War', wrote Wesley Clark, NATO's former Supreme Allied Commander Europe (SACEUR), 'it would be that American military power, especially when buttressed by Britain's, is virtually unchallengeable today'. It was a comforting thought when the United Kingdom went to war with America in 2003. For out of all the European armies, including the French, the war fighting ethos has been central to Britain's national discourse. *The British Defence Doctrine* promotes a 'war fighting ethos, as distinct from a purely professional one [which] is absolutely fundamental to all those in the British Armed Forces' (King, 2011, p. 274). It also stresses that they have a legal right to apply lethal force and potentially unlimited liability to lay down their lives in performance of their duty. Notwithstanding the proportion of their career engaged in duties other than war fighting, the doctrine goes on to say that it is essential that all servicemen and women develop and retain 'the physical and moral fortitude to fight'. In short, Britain's armed forces, when recruiting, training and promoting their personnel on the basis of performance in the field, stress over and over again the importance of combat.

But the recent British military record has been disappointing. The operation to seize and then secure Basra (2003–2007) was a defeat which, according to one British colonel, permanently diminished its reputation in the eyes of its American allies (Ledwidge, 2011, p. 38). Afghanistan was going to be a good war, which made up – in American eyes – for the defeat in Iraq. It did not. All it confirmed was that the British are not as good at war as they think they are. The British have been in Helmand longer than the Soviets. Their declared objective in 2006 was to provide security in the province's 14 districts. Today, a force three times the size of the initial deployment clings onto three districts, and even this deployment is apparently difficult. British interest in Helmand, writes Frank Ledwidge, has been not only a blundering catastrophe but a violent tragedy (Ledwidge, 2011, p. 84). The same, perhaps, could be said of all the Afghan wars in which the British have fought – the present campaign is their fourth.

Was this a failure of culture? Difficulties abounded. British forces in both Iraq and Afghanistan were under-funded and under-equipped. But the real failure, adds Ledwidge, lies with the Generals, who were ill-trained and inadequately educated in strategy, and unable to stand up to the politicians. The military elite simply under-performed. They were asked to do too much with too little. Ledwidge suggests that the British Army will find it difficult to survive the next 'strategic shock', especially if it is closer to home.

The German military was even worse shaped because of their own discourse on war. During the Cold War, the *Bundeswehr* provided the Corps to the central front in Europe and was widely regarded at the time as being one of the best NATO formations. German officers are still among the best trained in Europe, and their staff skills are still highly regarded. Yet the army has met with a string of failures in the field. Especially problematic was the deployment of the German-Dutch Multinational Brigade in Afghanistan in 2003–2004, when different national caveats had operational complications (with the Dutch being sent on dangerous patrols whilst the German remained safely in their armed vehicles). As one Dutch officer complained, 'we don't have a problem with the Afghans; we have a problem with the Germans' (King, 2011, p. 256).

And one of the problems can be traced directly to the military discourse that prevails in Germany still. It is called *Innere Führung* (usually rendered in English as 'civic education') and it is designed to remind soldiers that they are citizens first. It was specifically intended in the 1950s to ground the new *Bundeswehr* on the idea that ethics in war relies on inner moral conviction (after the fatal *Wehrmacht* oath of loyalty to Hitler in 1938 blunted any independent resort to conscience). It was, if you like, the price of re-arming Germany, and during the Cold War when the army was not used, it was seen to legitimize military service, and it made sense for a largely conscript army. But as Anthony King writes, today it offers little direction to German soldiers. It is an individual principle, not a collective resource. He quotes a German officer he interviewed in 2006 who claimed it had become a dangerous dogma which severely compromised operational effectiveness.

He was echoing a widespread feeling that leadership was lacking after the dismal performances during the riots in Kosovo, especially in Prizren two years earlier, which almost led to the dismissal of the German KFOR Commander, General Kammerhoff (King, 2011, p. 193). During the riots, a *Bundeswehr* sergeant was tasked with protecting a Serbian monastery near Prizren. Confronted by a large crowd, he ordered his platoon to escort the monks from the monastery to safety, but he also allowed the Albanians to burn the UNESCO World Heritage site to the ground. The sergeant's decision was perfectly compatible with the concept of *Innere Führung*. He fulfilled his duty of protecting the monks without escalating the level of violence. Yet clearly, the protection of the monastery from criminal destruction was minimally implied in the orders he had been given. The incident demonstrated the way in which senior German officers can conveniently redefine their mission in order to justify the lowest level of engagement. More critically, adds King, this process of redefinition absolves commanders of the responsibility to act. Other European officers have noted the unwillingness of the *Bundeswehr* to take command responsibility in a number of settings. Indeed, even on exercises, they note that the German armed officers will typically exaggerate the time it takes for their command to perform a function in order to ensure that they can never be embarrassed by failure.

But in recent years, even the competence of the smaller nations, once noted for their commitment in the field, has been reassessed, not always to their advantage. The Dutch army, whilst acting credibly in Afghanistan, arguably has not fully recovered from its low status in society following the fall of Srebrenica in 1995. The massacre caught the Dutch public by surprise and provoked an eruption of public anger.

Both the press and members of Parliament began to ask embarrassing questions about the 'passivity' or even 'cowardliness' of the Dutch UN soldiers. On 4 August 1995, the headline of the weekly newspaper, *HP/De Tijd*, declared that Dutch soldiers were 'too sweet and innocent for war' (Sion, 2006, p. 457).

The events at Srebrenica turned out to have been one of the most important landmarks in a fraying relationship between the military and society, which has diminished the status of the military even further. In their desire to overcompensate, some Dutch soldiers deliberately played up their self-image as 'warriors' capable of going round for round with the combat soldiers of the American or British armed forces. One Dutch artilleryman interviewed by Liora Sion claimed:

> This is a job for real men... A real man is someone who is sturdy, who doesn't get scared quickly, and is ready for action... if a clerk will try to do our work, then he'll be done for in a week. You must be a person who likes living outdoors and doing stuff.
>
> (2006, p. 460)

This image of army life as a masculine adventure recalls the phenomenon of 'weekend warriors': men who join workshops, retreats and seminars in the United States and Canada to experience 'the warrior within', at a time when many men are also experiencing widespread confusion over the meaning of manhood.

## Cosmopolitan discourse

Sheehan is right to argue that there is no European strategic culture. In other words, when Europe's armed forces deploy either in association with each other or independently (France and the Ivory Coast, the United Kingdom and Sierra Leone) they apply different discourses of war. But when they are deployed by governments, there is a distinctive 'way of warfare' – a European style, given to it by the meritocratic political class that runs Europe, and which is increasingly replacing democratically elected leaders in countries like Greece and Italy with technocrats of its own ilk. Europe has developed a distinctive political culture that looks at war very differently from the United States.

The EU has become what Sheehan recognizes as the first post-Schmittian state, one that has no clearly defined enemies. It is committed to the proposition that interdependence decreases the need or even rationality of power politics. Instead, it pursues a cosmopolitan vision, and 'cosmopolitan states', writes Ulrich Beck, differ significantly from 'surveillance states' like the United States which keep the world under scrutiny all the time (quite literally through satellites, UAV flights, etc.). Cosmopolitan states 'do not only fight against terrorism, but also against the causes of terrorism in the world. Out of the solutions of global problems which appear insoluble at the level of the individual state, they regain and renew the power of the 'political' to shape and convince' (Beck, 2001).

The word 'political' is important here. Robert Cooper too sees the EU as a 'post-modern system' which is more transnational than supranational, a community that considers the resort to war to be a failure. Europe lives in a post-modern system that instead of applying the balance of power embraces 'the rejection of force' and promotes 'self-enforcement behaviour'. 'In the post-modern world, *raison d'état*, the amorality of Machiavelli's theory of statecraft...has been replaced by moral consciousness in international affairs' (Cooper, 2002).

Whether or not such a system is ultimately sustainable in what Lynn would call the 'real world', especially as European power seems to be going gently downwards, is a matter I will raise at the end of this chapter. But it is worth asking why the political elite of Europe thinks in the way that it does. To do this let me invoke the school of 'sociological institutionalism' which is rapidly gaining ground in international relations theory. Those who espouse it are strongly of the opinion that organizational practices (or institutions) mould the preferences, identities and interests of actors in the social world. The institutions of the EU, for example, are bound over time to produce specific 'outcomes' or policy behaviour.

> Institutions influence behaviour by providing the scripts, categories and models that are indispensable for action. Not least because without them the world and the behaviour of others cannot be interpreted...It follows that institutions do not simply affect strategic calculations of individuals, as rational choice institutionalists contend, but also mould them as basic preferences.
> (Hall and Taylor, 1996, p. 15)

What distinguishes this school is the claim that organizations often adopt practices (or opt for particular policies) not only because they advance the instrumentally rational, the means/end efficiency of the organization concerned but also because they enhance its social prestige. In other words, the fact that the EU pursues inter-government bargaining and consensus politics can be explained, at least in part, by the extent to which its members expect this of each other.

In conceptualizing security in such terms, the Europeans act in the light of their own understanding of how the world works, which, in turn, is rooted in their own experience at home: the recognition that their own freedom of action is severely prescribed. A trans-national community is only as strong as the trans-national states that make up its individual members. And the trans-national state is one that has to come to terms with certain realities.

1. The institutional and organizational context of national decision-making is increasingly internationalized. For the members of the EU political life has become 'inter-mestic' (the international and domestic and now inextricably interlinked).
2. National autonomy is compounded in some cases radically. Sovereignty is now divided. Politics increasingly involves a partnership between the public, private and voluntary sectors. The social contract between state and citizen has given way to individual contracts with interest groups or ethnic minorities. Trans-national states seek to empower themselves by sharing power, not surrendering it. Only in this way, they believe, can nation-states secure themselves against the risks, real and imagined, in the outside world.
3. In the end, this is all framed by a unique twenty-first-century ideology – what John Fonte calls 'trans-national progressivism'. It is an ideology that, as an American writer, he finds deeply alienating because it challenges the traditional American idea of self-determination and common citizenship. For a trans-national progressivist state is one in which ethnic claims take precedence over those of the individual citizen and the social contract; where the state follows a 'democratic impulse' to de-link itself from the nation in order to promote greater multi-culturalism; where post-national citizenship makes imperative the dismantling of national myths and narratives (Fonte, 2002, p. 207).

As Fonte acknowledges, many of these cultural preferences are also the favoured choice of many Americans. The United States and Europe, after all, do inhabit a common Western world, and norms are not exclusive to either. Hence the debate on the multi-cultural 'assault' on American values by writers who share Fonte's stance, most of them conservatives such as Francis Fukuyama and John o'Sullivan, the former editor of the *National Review*. But whilst they would all concede that this represents an ideological struggle within the West, Fonte himself is firmly of the belief that the EU alone embodies trans-national progressivism at the 'state' level and cites this as a major source of conflict with the United States, especially after 9/11, when liberal-democratic supporters of the liberal state rallied to the flag and committed themselves to a new war: the War on Terror.

How does this translate into war? If the Americans still see war in Clausewitzian terms, as a 'continuation of politics by other means', the Europeans tend to see it differently, as the promotion of international law. As the West Point military lawyer, Michael Nelson puts it, the Europeans seem to prefer 'lawfare' to warfare. They prefer to pursue traditional strategic objectives by employing legal manoeuvres, and when the use of force becomes unavoidable, to constrain it severely with legal norms. America's criteria for 'just wars' are essentially ethical in nature and their application is not subject to verification by international courts of law, but remains a matter for domestic debate. The Europeans prefer to pursue what Habermas calls 'cosmopolitan law enforcement' (Habermas, 2006, p. 101). It is a process that can be dated back in origin to Kant's vision of a normative taming of political power through the law. In opposition to America's 'moralisation' of war, the Europeans prefer its 'juridification'. War takes the form of policing operations and those accused of war crimes, like ordinary criminals, enjoy the safeguards of due process accorded to defendants in domestic criminal proceedings. Accordingly, Europeans try to target their enemies as carefully as they do criminals who obstruct justice at home. Only this can explain why a German Foreign Minister could describe the Kosovo War (1999) as a *Friedenspolitik*, or peace policy.

What the Americans complain about most is that the Europeans talk the language of 'ultimate causes' but practice the art of minimum risk. Whatever explanation we volunteer for this normative gap between the United States and Europe, it is pretty clear that the United States itself is not on the road to becoming a cosmopolitan power any time soon.

Ultimately, however, the Americans still do war in their own fashion, and the American elite (both Democrats and Republicans) suspects that the European transnational state lacks the cultural ruthlessness which the exercise of power demands. Is international security best underwritten by transnational progressivism, or what Cooper calls, 'the old-fashioned double standards' of an earlier era? Is it best secured by force? Is international law best underwritten by the norms of global government and the inter-state networks and institutions of our multi-lateral world? If a transnational state may be better placed to promote 'sustainable development', climate change reform and even fight humanitarian wars (Libya) in the hard world of inter-state conflict, is military power still not the best currency?

Taking Fonte's argument one stage further, I would contend that the problem Europe faces is that its transnational elite derives neither status nor value from war.

## Status

Honour still holds a central place in international politics. The desire to be esteemed by others is a basic human drive, and as such a component of human nature. Similarly the desire to be acknowledged for one's sense of self is equally important and fundamental to the human condition. The point is that honour involves power. To be dishonoured is to be disempowered; to be humiliated is to forfeit respect in the eyes of others, including one's friends.

The word 'state' actually derives from the Latin 'status' (in its sense of standing or position). Status is important, as Hobbes realized, in helping the members of a community to construct their identities. He writes about it in terms of respect or value, and he writes as one would expect in the language of early market capitalism. A man's pride is treated as a commodity; regular dealing in the social market establishes his price. 'The value or worth of a man is of all things his price, that's to say so much as he would be given for the use of his power; ... for to let a man (as most men do) rate themselves at the highest value they can; yet their true value is no more than it is esteemed by others' (Macpherson, 1962, p. 37). The language is still familiar and pre-supposes a marketplace in which competitiveness thrives. The language of society and politics, even more than it was in Hobbes' day, is infused with market terms. We talk of 'moral capital' and 'social capital'. One British general during the Kosovo War insisted that the British army could only be asked to undertake what 'the market will allow' (Moskos, 2000, p. 95).

In our world standing has been instrumentalized. It can mean different things: 'honour', 'work', 'price' or 'estimate'. Like individuals, nations are still concerned with worth because value is intimately linked to authority. If we take honour to mean 'fame' or 'renown', then it may indeed appear somewhat old fashioned. But if we understand it to mean 'deference', 'just due' or 'prestige', then it is still an important factor in international opinion, and extremely important in dissuading others from attacking you. States may no longer fight to win status, but they do to retain it; for with it goes something else which is central to power:

honour. In our world, honour means credibility (the word introduced into common parlance during the Cold War). Credibility requires one to occasionally inflict pain on others. Honour, in that sense, is a social bond, and winning it back is a social obligation. And in much of the world the defence of honour is not only confined to the present but is also shared with the ancestors with whom it is important to keep faith. Cultures of honour, which we now tend to engage in war in places like Afghanistan, spring up because they amplify human emotions like pride, anger and revenge and because they reinforce solidarity, the clanship links or gang membership from which their members derive safety. They are often a perfectly sensible response to external challenges. Honour represents a kind of social reality. It exists because everyone agrees it exists, and it must be defended on a hair-trigger response because it is dangerous not to. To be seen to be as risk-averse as the Europeans is to invite dishonour, which, as Hobbes warns, can be dangerous. And the United States is still in the business of defending its honour, if necessary by the use of force.

Military honour codes of the military are important, too, for the way honour is taught within the military is usually indicative of the extent to which a society values it or not. Take the example of Canada. When their government committed itself to fighting in Afghanistan in 2003 most Canadians believed that their country only engaged in peacekeeping. To the political class, as well as the public, writes Douglas Bland, it would have been surprising to have learned that a country does not earn a reputation for its peacekeeping ability by having a military for whom peacekeeping represents the high end of the capability spectrum. You can only keep the peace if you can make war. In Bland's own words, 'the success of Canada's early peacekeeping efforts flowed form the fact that the Canadian Forces had well-equipped units trained to fight wars which could be rapidly deployed without the assistance of other nations' (Bland, 1999, p. 19). Writing in 1999 about Canada's missions in the former Yugoslavia, Bland identified a fundamental disconnect between perceptions of the 'Canadian way of warfare and its reality'. The problem has become more marked since. 'There may be two ways of warfare in this nation', he wrote, 'a domestic, politically supported way and a military way and they often compete with each other. Clearly, no rational national policy can be built and sustained on such an unstable foundation' (Bland, 1999, p. 21).

But in a democratic society no military stands outside the social mainstream for long and in the case of Canada we can see a gradual convergence over time of civil and military norms. A controversial study conducted by the Canadian Army in 1997, based on interviews with 800 officers involved in overseas operations during the 1990s, concluded that military forces had begun to internalize the expectations of ordinary Canadians. The traditional warrior ethos just would not wash with public opinion anymore. Perhaps, it concluded, the very idea of a hero had changed. And here, sport was indicative. It noted changing attitudes to the game of ice hockey, one of the most violent of all male contact sports. Instead of the individual heroism of a former age, it noted the team spirit of the present; against the old ethos, it observed a more balletic *pas de deux*, or grace under pressure. Perhaps, the Canadians want a different kind of hero who wants to make a difference.

A single example will suffice to illustrate the point. Captain Nicola Goddard, an Artillery Forward Observation Officer, was killed in an ambush in Afghanistan on 17 May 2006. She was trained to direct artillery fire and call in air strikes, as she had done on several occasions in the past. But her ultimate mission, to cite her own words from a letter to her parents, was to be 'part of something so much bigger than myself':

> We are where we are now with the choices that we have available to us. It seems to me that we have such a burden of responsibility to make the world a better place for those who were born into far worse circumstances. It's more than donating money to charity – it's taking action and trying to make things better.
>
> (Goddard, 2006)

For sacrifice to define heroism, it must be down to something meaningful, otherwise it is mere suicide. Meaning, to be understood and shared widely and therefore form a basis for social actions, cannot be defined merely on purely idiosyncratic grounds, but must accord with the expectations of society. And Canadian society has changed enormously in recent years.

In that respect, Canada is much more like Europe than the United States. If there is a West to be salvaged, some writers suppose, it is because of the values it represents. But what are those values? Scepticism, competition, restraint, tolerance, fairness or, for lack of a better label, being Canadian. Canadians have all the virtues. They do not spend more money than they have; they are reasonable multiculturalists, Anglo-centric Francophiles and stalwart peacekeepers. They may be the best chance to defeat any rivals, from religious fundamentalists to those who espouse the Beijing Consensus. But whenever one thinks of Canada, one is drawn to the wry remark of the South African poet Breyten Breytenbach: 'The problem with Canada is that it's all accent, and no master text'. In the end, it is not America; it has no message of manifest destiny or exceptionalism. I suspect that in the early twenty-first century some nations will still subscribe to a master text, China being one.

## Value

As for 'value', the difference between the political elites of Europe and America is even more striking. Europe attaches no spiritual value to war because its founding myth is different from America's. America is sustained by two historical memories: the War of Independence in 1776 and the American Civil War. In the first, the citizens' right to bear arms reflects the fact that Americans have a right to fight for freedom. The Civil War reaffirmed the values of the American Revolution and can be seen as a consecration of national values. What is especially interesting about the United States is that both founding myths have allowed it to marry two visions of Western life which had been in conflict in Europe in the past 30 years – the celebration of the West for its democratic vision and the condemnation of the West for militarism and imperialism of the past. Instead of seeing these as irreconcilable, the Americans tend to see them as inseparable. Without democratic accountability, they would not be the military power they are today, and without military power the world would not have been made safer for democracy. For the Europeans, democratic power offers a more attractive alternative to military power. As Habermas insists, the juridification of war marks a larger project: the normatizing of international relations.

Europe also has a military foundation myth but one that resonates very differently in the collective imagination, or the *conscience historique*. For the French and Germans it is the battle of Verdun in which hundreds of thousands of soldiers died in an area little larger than the combined acreage of the London parks. In Abel Gance's iconic film, *J'Accuse*, Europe is seen preparing for the next war. '*Morts de Verdun, levez-vous!*' (Arise, dead of Verdun) cries a deranged veteran at the heart of the film, and the dead do just that, emerging from their mass graves to reproach the living. Caught on the screen, as in life, an army of ghosts in rotting uniform with close-ups of disfigured faces (*les gueules cassées* (broken mugs in the language of the time)) reproach the living for producing a second disaster. It is in Verdun's shadow that European integration was born (Sontag, 2003, p. 26). As early as the 1930s French veterans returning to the battlefield to commemorate the Fallen began to celebrate the battle not so much as a French victory, or even a German defeat, as a European catastrophe.

In the United States it is very different. With nearly 2 million men in arms, every large American city has a large, well-staffed military base. Every major community has reservists, many on active duty in the War on Terrorism. *Hurricane Katrina* (2005) found 35 per cent of the Louisiana National Guard in Iraq, hence the bonds that link elected leaders with the Head of State or the Commander in Chief. George Bush understood this very well which is why the Europeans were caught out by his re-election in 2004.

The ethic of value has been translated to the soldier level, too. Many of the most combat-intense soldiers in the American military come from Kansas, the south-west, the Bible belt. At this stage in American political life, the Scottish-Irish constituency (some 30 million strong) has an influence well beyond its size. Back in 1896, Theodore Roosevelt wrote a book, *Winning the West*, in which he claimed that they had played the largest role in taming the frontier, and pushing back the Indians. And they are today essential to the American frontier experience in another respect: the frontiers on which American soldiers find themselves fighting. James Webb (a former US Under-Secretary of the Navy) thinks so, and he wrote a book some years ago on this largely forgotten ethnic group. Anatol Lieven in a recent book on American nationalism wrote that the values of the American South still permeate the US political consciousness in ways that most West Coast liberals and East Coast intellectuals do not even suspect. Paranoia (what Hofstader called the US 'cultural style') and honour translated in foreign policy terms into a preoccupation with credibility and a willingness to defend it with force are both highly ingrained in American military thinking.

And there is something else that allows Americans to attach value to war which is unique to themselves. It is a specifically American norm: the connection between violence and religion. Let me take one example when the US Marines retook the city of Fallujah in November 2004. A US military chaplain told a detachment before going into battle that they were fighting a 'just cause' and that they were 'tools of God's mercy'. No European military padre is likely to invoke God and has probably not done so since the Korean War.

One of the things that most puzzled De Tocqueville on his visit was the extent to which religion was at the heart of America, just at the moment that it was receding from the imagination of Europeans. For Americans, religion strengthened democracy, choice and freedom, rather than undermined it. In separating state from religion (which the Europeans did not), they established religious entrepreneurism. Jefferson saw scepticism as good for religion because it would promote competition; Madison saw it as good for the state because, in his own words, religion could be free 'to promote public morality' (unencumbered by state patronage). What the Americans created was the world's first free market in religious beliefs in which different cults and faith-based communities were constantly able to renew themselves, as they are doing today.

Indeed, politics and religion, rather than separated as in most European countries, are intimately bound up with a normative framework of American power. The American religion is what Robert Bellah calls 'a public theology'. Religion has been at the centre of every major political crisis in American life, from abolitionism to the campaign for civil rights in the 1960s. The evangelical impulse has been at the heart of the American political debate and is at the heart of war today.

No Western nation is as violent or religious as America. Only a minority of Americans do not believe in God, and the majority (when interviewed) believe that God loves them on an individual basis. Americans worship a customized God, of course. It was Spinoza, the great Dutch-Jewish philosopher of ethics, who famously remarked that it was essential for all of us to love God, even if we suspect that He does not love us in return. I do not know of a more un-American statement. Of two chosen people, many Jews have probably always suspected that God did not love them much; the Americans, from the moment the United States was founded, turned Calvinism into a religion of hope, not despair, on the curious understanding that the Elect (the saved) were Americans, not Europeans.

## Conclusion

The demilitarization of Europe is pre-eminently a cultural phenomenon. The calculation about threats and future risks is interesting enough, but the organizing currents are cultural. The political class cannot see the point of war, and has not, for a long time, had to think about it seriously, with the United States always leading from the front. Now that the United States has resorted to default mode and merely 'facilitates' Europe's own efforts, it is time to ponder the point we have reached.

Europe's demilitarization began well before the onset of the present financial crisis with its deficits, debt sustainability and defaults, all of which will be invoked to cut back on defence even further in the years ahead. The end of the Soviet threat removed the existential threat; peace and prosperity were assumed to be the natural order in a unipolar American world. The Eurocrats chose to build an economic and legal superstructure without a linguistic, cultural or civic base; they chose to build a structure that was transnational, passionless and above all safe. The problem is that there is little moral solidarity underpinning the European Project. If the Germans are not prepared to bleed for Greece economically, why should they ask their soldiers to bleed for the EU? When economic sacrifices are necessary, solidarity haemorrhages away quickly. The real blame lies not with weak political leadership at home but with a technocratic mindset which imagined it was possible to engineer a new society oblivious to history, language, culture, values and place.

And the same will probably be found to be true of the belief that it is possible to be a civilian power in a mutlipolar world. The talk in Washington, as well as Beijing and Delhi, is of Europe's strategic irrelevance. Much of this is due to its own economic profligacy and the failure of national governments to make a national interest case for the EU itself. But part of the explanation lies with its obsession with soft power to the exclusion of everything else. As Asia re-arms and China flexes its muscles, they may use hard power (or at least the threat of it) to change the rules of engagement that the Europeans tend to take for granted. They may even apply it for their own 'reset' button with the West.

## Bibliography

Barry, J. (2011) *Lessons of Libya for Future Western Military Forays* (Washington, DC: The European Institute).
Beck, U. (2001) 'The Cosmopolitan State: Towards a Realistic Utopia', *Eurozine*, 5 December 2001.
Bland, D. (1999) 'War in the Balkans, Canadian-style', *International Review of Policy Options*, October 1999, pp. 18–21.
Cooper, R. (2002) 'The New Liberal Imperialism', *The Observer*, 7 April 2002.
Fonte, J. (2002) 'Liberal Democracy vs. Transnational Progressivism: The Ideological War within the West', *Orbis*, Vol. 46, No. 3, pp. 449–467.
Gates, R (2010) 'NATO's Strategic Concept Seminar (Future of NATO)', http://www.defense.gov (homepage), date accessed 26 May 2012.
Gates, R. (2011) 'The Security and Defense Agenda (Future of NATO)', http://www.defense.gov (homepage), date accessed 26 May 2012.
Goddard, T. (2006) 'Eulogy for Captain Nichola Kathleen Sarah Goddard 1980–2006', in OnCampus Weekly, 2 June, http://www.ucalgary.ca (homepage), date accessed 26 May 2012.
Habermas, J. (2006) *The Divided West* (Cambridge: Polity).

Hall, P. and Taylor, R. (1996) 'Political Science in the Three Institutionalisms', Max Plank Institute Discussion Paper, 96/6.
King, A. (2011) *The Transformation of Europe's Armed Forces: From the Rhine to Afghanistan* (Cambridge: Cambridge University Press).
Ledwidge, F. (2011) *Losing Small Wars* (Newhaven: Yale University Press).
Lukes, S. (2003) *Liberals and Cannibals: The Implications of Diversity* (London: Verso).
Lynn, J. (2003) *Battle: A History of Combat and Culture* (Boulder, CO: Westview Press).
Macpherson, C. B. (1962) *The Political Theory of Possessive Individualism* (Oxford: Clarendon Press).
Moskos, C. C. (ed.) (2000) *The Post-Modern Military: Armed Forces after the Cold War* (Oxford: Oxford University Press).
Sheehan, J. (2007) *The Monopoly of Violence: Why Europeans Hate Going to War* (London: Faber & Faber).
Sion, L. (2006) '"Too Sweet and Innocent For War?": Dutch Peacekeepers and the Use of Violence', *Armed Forces and Society*, Vol. 32, No. 3, pp. 454–474.
Snow, C. P. (1959) *The Two Cultures* (London: Routledge and Kegan Paul).
Sontag, S. (2003) *Regarding the Pain of Others* (London: Hamish Hamilton).
Vasquez, J. A (1995) 'The Post-Positivist Debate: Reconstructing Scientific Enquiry – An International Relations Theory after Enlightenment's Fall', in K. Booth and S. Smith (eds) *International Relations Theory Today* (Cambridge: Polity).
Witney, N. (2011) *How to Stop the Demilitarisation of Europe* (London: European Council on Foreign Relations).

# 4
# Towards an Affordable European Defence and Security Policy? The Case for Extensive European Force Integration

*S. Diesen*

## Introduction – the state of European defence

The will and ability of NATO's European members to act consistently and decisively in any future crisis threatening the security interests of the Alliance are increasingly in question. This is hardly surprising after more than a decade of conflicts – from Kosovo and Afghanistan to Libya – where reservations, caveats and straightforward refusals to become involved have been the rule rather than the exception for many of the allies. So far, this has mainly been a token of political indecision or reluctance, rather than a lack of actual military capability. However, looking to the future, the question is whether the constraints on Alliance coherence and joint action are going to be as much a matter of limited military means as of limited political determination – of ability as much as willingness. This may well be the case, unless appropriate strategies for dealing with diminishing European force structures and vanishing capabilities are developed over the next five to ten years.

What sort of defence and security posture will be possible within the limits imposed by defence budgets and the rising cost of the military tool-box itself? In other words, the perception that limits to NATO's power are set by what can be agreed politically will be challenged by a realization that they are set as much by what forces can be made available, deployed and sustained in the field, particularly by the European allies. Security policy, in short, is about to be overtaken by economy as the primary consideration in this respect. Furthermore, this is not just a threat to NATO's ability to act in distant theatres of operation. It applies just as much to its ability to deal effectively with a crisis on the European continent itself.

This chapter will explore the implications of such a development and what NATO must do to remain a credible alliance with a viable military capability – in or out of area. The Section 'Technology-Driven Cost Increase and the Emerging Problem of Critical Mass' explains the fundamental mechanisms behind the ever-increasing cost and consequent dwindling capabilities of modern defence forces, known as the problem of critical mass. In the Section 'Smart Defence – Three Strategies for European Defence Integration', three different strategies for dealing with this problem are examined, constituting three different approaches to European defence integration – or 'smart defence' to use the more commonly employed phraseology. The Section 'NATO, EU or Both – the Perceived Importance of Formal Alliances' explores the challenges to defence cooperation and integration posed by the affiliation of European countries to different security organizations, and the applicability of the three different strategies in that regard. Finally, in Section 'Conclusion – towards a More Rational European Defence Structure', the chapter concludes with an assessment of the way ahead and the probability – as well as the ultimate necessity – of serious European defence integration, if Europe is to retain the military capability required to be a global political actor.

## Technology-driven cost increase and the emerging problem of critical mass

The most crucial challenge for today's European defence planners is the spiralling cost of modern military equipment and the consequent unaffordability of the complete range of capabilities that make up a modern defence force. The integration of ever more and improved technology into weapon systems and platforms as well as in sensors, C4I systems and precision-guided munitions means that the performance of these systems is improving in leaps and bounds compared to the systems they replace – but at an ever-increasing price. This is a cost increase in real terms, that is, it comes on top of ordinary inflation and runs to something like 3–5 per cent per year as an average across the spectrum of conventional military capabilities. In practical terms, this means that the cost of re-equipping a nation's armed forces doubles in fixed prices every 20 years or so. Or, to put it that way, every 20 years nations have to double the purchasing power of their defence budgets, if they wish to modernize their force structure as well as maintain it in terms of its size (Diesen, 2011).

Although this development is something all defence ministers and chiefs of staff will testify to, it is often questioned by economic experts outside the military community, since it goes against the experience of most other sectors of industrial production. Things tend to become cheaper as technology develops, rather than more expensive. And since the digital components used to enhance the performance of today's weapons and military equipment are much the same as those used in consumer electronics, you would expect the same development there. However, although many of the *components* are the same, it is the integration of components into military *systems* – built to operate and survive in a completely different environment from TV sets and mobile phones, and produced in much smaller numbers – that keeps driving costs upwards.

After the end of the Cold War, therefore, practically no country[1] – large or small – has been able to afford an annual growth in defence procurement of 3–5 per cent per year in real terms. This invariably has meant that platforms and capabilities have been acquired in smaller numbers, and that, consequently, the forces of almost all countries have been shrinking significantly. This applies to the great powers as well as to small- and medium-sized states. At the end of the Cold War, the Royal Navy had 50 frigates and destroyers, whereas the British Army had 900 main battle tanks. Today, the target numbers in the Strategic Defence and Security Review are 19 and 200, respectively (HM Government, 2010).

Among the small states, the Norwegian navy has gone from 36 to 6 fast patrol boats (FPBs) over the same period, whereas the air force will go from 87 fast jets (F-5 Freedom Fighter, F-16 Fighting Falcon) in 1990 to 48 (F-35 Lightning II) by 2020. An interesting implication of this is that today it is the affordability of the equipment rather than the force ceilings allowed under the arms reduction treaties negotiated during the 1990s which limits the size of European defence forces. It is also fair to presume that as long as the major players in the defence market – the great powers – regard the operational and strategic advantage of having state-of-the-art military technology and systems as greater than the disadvantage of having a smaller force, this trend will continue.

Particularly for the small- to medium-sized countries, however, this development has brought the size of their forces, in terms of the number they can field of the more sophisticated and expensive systems, down to or near the level of 'critical mass' – the least number of such systems which is economically and operationally sustainable. Economically because the unit cost of marginal systems becomes extremely high, since the logistic support organization cannot be scaled down at the same rate as the systems themselves. The actual number of any given system in the force structure doesn't make much of a difference to the cost of supporting it; it is having it in the inventory in the first place which accounts for much of the necessary expense going into workshops, tools, spares, expertise, simulators and training facilities and so on. The implication of this is that it is the *width* of the force structure – the number of different systems and platforms – that matters, rather than its *depth* – that is, the number of units of each platform or system.

Operationally, a similar logic applies, since the number of platforms or systems of a given type cannot be scaled down to zero while retaining a sufficiently large professional environment to sustain the required competencies. For example, a navy operating conventional submarines will need a certain number of vessels to generate the number of officers and specialists required for submarine operation purposes in the operational headquarters, in the logistic support system and in the training organization (Innset, 2010). Exactly what this minimum or critical number of systems is will vary from one capability to another, and it depends on a number of factors – some generic and some specific to the force structure in question. Even if it is the smaller countries that have been hit the hardest by the critical mass effect, the writing is on the wall even for major European powers like France, Britain or Germany – albeit in a slightly different way or on a different scale. Whereas small- and medium-sized countries can already feel the strain of sustaining basic capabilities and systems like main battle tanks, submarines and fighter aircraft, the major powers experience the same effect when it comes to aircraft carriers or submarine-based nuclear retaliation capability.

The recent French–British agreement about building and operating aircraft carriers jointly is a case in point – scarcely an imaginable scenario even as late as ten years ago. But the underlying mechanisms are exactly the same as for the smaller countries: The number of systems or units of each capability, and hence its operational value, becomes too small to justify the initial cost of acquiring and supporting it, while the ability to sustain the necessary professional competencies becomes marginal (Diesen, 2011). This also explains why the European allies put together only manage to generate a fraction of the military might of the United States, despite spending considerably more money than this fraction would suggest. The Europeans use a multitude of different guns, tanks, vehicles and other equipment, instead of focusing their efforts on one type of each platform or system. And because they all pay the logistic 'entrance fee' for each of the different capabilities in their inventories separately, the number of units of each system will obviously be much smaller than in the United States, where the same fee is only paid once for each capability or type of platform.

Although the critical mass effect is felt by all European countries to some degree or at some level, it is first and foremost a threat against the smaller nations, calling for a new approach to defence cooperation or integration. Otherwise, these countries will find themselves with potentially dangerous capability gaps opening up when important systems simply disappear as they become unsustainable. Arguably, this isn't equally unacceptable to all countries, since security requirements are not in any way the same for all nations on the European continent. Denmark is an interesting example, situated as an extension of German territory jutting out into the North Sea and sheltered on all sides by allied or friendly countries. Any hostile power attempting to use force against Denmark would have to violate the territorial integrity of one or several other countries to gain access to Danish territory, waters or air space. Consequently, the Danes have dealt with the critical mass problem by disbanding their submarine force. Furthermore, the ground-based air defence capability is gone, as well as most of the army's heavy artillery. Instead, the Danish armed forces have deliberately been tailored as a small, expeditionary force designed to support NATO operations anywhere with specific capabilities, closely linked to US and UK forces (Saxi, 2010). However, as geopolitical realities as well as security policy ambitions vary, a number of even the smaller European countries are not yet prepared to go down that road.

## Smart defence – three strategies for European defence integration

Broadly speaking, this has brought into existence three different models for coping with the problem of increasingly unaffordable national capabilities. These models may be termed *role specialization, pooling and sharing,* and *joint force generation* (see, for example, Borchert and Eggenberger, 2007). Role specialization, as the name suggests, means that a group of countries within the Alliance decides to divide their overall defence and security tasks between them. Each country will retain basic military capabilities and competencies, whereas responsibility for fielding some of the more expensive systems in the capability spectrum will be shared between them on a complementary basis, depending on economic factors as well as historical and other circumstances.

For example, three nations situated along the same seaboard might decide that only one of them will retain maritime patrol aircraft to provide joint situational awareness, one will keep a submarine force and one large surface combatants like frigates or destroyers – whereas all of them would still keep some kind of fast patrol boat for maintaining a presence and a capability in the littoral. Carried to extremes, this approach would mean that one country would have an army, another a navy, with a third partner looking after the air force. However, since this means depending entirely on your partners, even for peacetime security purposes like air policing, patrolling territorial waters or maintaining a military presence on your own territory, this kind of advanced role specialization has so far not been seriously considered anywhere. And even in its less radical form, the crucial weakness of this strategy is that it presupposes joint action by all, should one partner request it. Since each country is giving up specific capabilities, and since an adversary wishing to confront any of the partner countries militarily would obviously be in a position to adapt his strategy to the gaps in its capability spectrum, this creates a significant vulnerability. The ability of each government to handle political crisis management at the national level is, to a greater or lesser degree, impeded.

During the Cold War, when the reason for being of all NATO forces was the threat of a Soviet invasion, this was perhaps a minor consideration. But today, with a number of different scenarios where nations may wish to have some kind of independent national capability, at least initially, to deal with a local or regional security situation, this is a real challenge. Governments cannot take for granted that all allies and partners are willing immediately to come to their aid in a crisis, nor may they in fact want to. The inherent weakness of role specialization, therefore, is that it takes for granted joint political and military action from the earliest stages of a crisis or a conflict. This is the sort of political straitjacket for which today's European politicians have displayed a notable distaste, even when serious common interests are at stake.

*Pooling and sharing* is a more structured approach to the same problem, in many ways taking the full consequence of allied interdependence and creating a truly allied force or capability. Current and successful examples of this are NATO's fleet of Airborne Warning and Control System (AWACS) aircraft operating from Geilenkirchen in Germany, and the Heavy Airlift Wing flying C-17 cargo planes out of Papa in Hungary. Under this arrangement, nations will provide a proportional share of the cost of manning and operating the capability, which is under permanent command of NATO (NATO, 2011).

With the Heavy Airlift Wing, the share paid by each nation will also entitle it to a certain number of flight hours to cover its national requirements, for example, logistic flights to and from Afghanistan. Although a rational and economic way of giving access to important capabilities for the alliance as such, this approach is even more dependent on joint action – or at least on political acceptance across the Alliance of granting release of the capability for use. This is not just an implication of the fact that they are genuine NATO assets, under command of SACEUR. It is also an implication of the fact that nations disagreeing strongly with a mission could withdraw their own nationals from the normally multinational crews, thereby creating manning shortfalls. However, this is not an objection to the general principle of pooling and sharing at a lower level. For all practical purposes, Belgium and the Netherlands today have a joint navy based on this principle. The as-yet theoretical case of air policing and defence of the former Yugoslav republics may serve as another useful example. These six or seven (depending on whether one recognizes Kosovo or not) republics in the western Balkans are, albeit to a different degree, too small and have too limited economic resources to sustain national air forces with modern, multi-role fighter aircraft, at least in meaningful numbers.

In addition to the economic problem, there is also the fact that they are small countries geographically, with an air space significantly limiting operations with fast jets. One way around this would be for all or at least some of them to pool resources and create a joint fighter force within a joint air space. Such a scheme would benefit from the fact that they share a common geography as well as a common language and history. Geographical proximity implies common geopolitical and strategic interests within the wider European area, whereas their shared language and history – despite ethnic and religious differences – would facilitate cooperation in both cultural and practical terms. The fact that they are not all full members of NATO need not be an insuperable obstacle, and we will return to this in a moment. However, given the scars left by the civil wars of the 1990s, this is probably not a practical proposition today. Suffice it to say that it is a useful example of the sort of circumstances where, other factors permitting, a pooling and sharing concept could be expected to work reasonably well, not least bearing in mind that such an arrangement is a *sine qua non* in the longer term for the countries in question having a modern fighter force at all.

The last concept of multinational defence integration so far is the *joint force generation* approach, which is the basis for the Nordic Defence Coooperation (NORDEFCO) cooperation scheme between the five Nordic countries: Denmark,[2] Finland, Iceland,[3] Norway and Sweden. The essence of this is that each nation will retain its entire spectrum of capabilities, the necessary economy of scale being achieved by having a common logistic and training organization supporting the forces. The first prerequisite to make this work is that the countries in question procure the same equipment for their forces, at least when it comes to major items such as main battle tanks, artillery, helicopters and so on, thereby achieving a certain commonality of systems. This will enable them to have a joint basis for force generation, such as maintenance facilities, training infrastructure, specialist courses for technical as well as operational personnel and so on. Each country will need to retain front-line supply and maintenance capacity, the integration principle applying to higher echelon, stationary logistic and training facilities. Although such an arrangement will also create a degree of mutual interdependence, this will be in the field of logistics and support, as opposed to the more immediate kind of operational dependence created by the role specialization approach (Saxi, 2011).

Comparing these two strategies, we see that whereas role specialization presupposes joint action in a crisis, joint force generation will facilitate it without making it a prerequisite – at least in the shorter term. Precisely in its ability to preserve a complete spectrum of capabilities for national crisis management in a short warning scenario lies the comparative advantage of joint force generation. Something like this approach was demonstrated in the 1970s, when four European countries (Belgium, Denmark, the Netherlands and Norway) were looking for a replacement for their ageing fleets of F-104 and F-5 fighters. When they all settled for Lockheed-Martin's F-16, a comprehensive logistics and maintenance package known as European Participating Air Forces (EPAF) was negotiated. This programme has been a huge success in terms of its effect on major maintenance, upgrading and support of the F-16. But essentially it came about as an opportunistic rather than a preconceived scheme, as the four countries found themselves in the market for an important weapon system at roughly the same time and decided to do something about it.

For this approach to take full effect, a more deliberate strategy of defence procurement is required, the participating nations coordinating their investments in at least a 5–10 year time perspective. Precisely in the requirement for commonality of systems lies the downside of the approach, since this is a major constraint on each nation's freedom to pursue an independent procurement policy – not just in terms of *what* they buy but also in terms of *when* they buy it. Joint force generation, in short, requires very carefully coordinated if not unified long-term defence planning. This is not an easy thing to achieve, particularly because it also has industrial implications in an area where national prestige as well as genuine security concerns and the political requirement to sustain thousands of jobs have traditionally created very strong protectionist policies in most countries.

Consequently, all three strategies for dealing with the critical mass problem of European defence forces have their strengths and weaknesses. For governments assessing these strategies, therefore, there will be pros and cons to all of them, in many cases forcing upon them what must be perceived as choosing between pestilence and cholera. This leads us to yet another prerequisite common to all three approaches. For any of them to work, there must be a certain amount of political and military symmetry between the participating countries, in order to create the same sense of urgency in the respective capitals. The squeeze of the critical mass problem, and the consequent need to do something, must be experienced as equally strong by all governments, in order to create approximately the same degree of motivation to tackle the political inconveniences and share the political downsides in an equitable fashion. Furthermore, the will to sacrifice the short-term national interest does not only depend on symmetry but also on the size of the countries and their forces in absolute terms. The smaller the country the more acute the problem, and consequently the stronger the will to compromise. Militarily, the force structures must be of comparable size and type for the right conditions to exist in practical terms, particularly for the joint force generation approach. These are conditions which will only be met by countries of roughly the same size, preferably also located in approximately the same part of Europe to cut down on the consumption of both time and treasure associated with movement of forces and equipment between them – be it for operational or logistic and training purposes.

## NATO, EU or both – the perceived importance of formal alliances

The most important stumbling block in the path of defence integration between at least some European countries has been perceived to be their different affiliation with international alliances and organizations, mainly NATO and the EU (Hoffmann, 2009). This applies particularly to some of the smaller countries, for whom some kind of defence integration is all the more important precisely because they are small. Of the Nordic countries, Sweden and Finland belong to the EU but are not members of NATO, Norway and Iceland are the other way around, whereas Denmark is a member of both organizations – but has reservations against EU's common security and defence policy, the European Security and Defence Policy (ESDP). In the Balkans, there is a similar situation with the different countries being either members or non-members of the EU, or members or partners of NATO. This begs the question of whether defence cooperation and integration, with its inherent interdependencies of one kind or another, is acceptable across the boundaries of alliances and permanent security structures, in particular between members and non-members of NATO. The answer to that is yes – first of all because NATO is changing, second because there is a notable lack of viable alternatives.

Since the end of the Cold War, the number of NATO member countries has almost doubled. This in itself means that the strategic perspectives and priorities across the alliance have diversified significantly. On top of that the common and existential threat to all of them, in the shape and form of the Soviet Union, has disappeared, leaving the alliance with a new and different rationale. Out of area, the alliance has taken on responsibility for conflicts like Afghanistan or Libya. On the continent of Europe, its role is one of building stability and security cooperation, while maintaining a deterrent against the use of force from an outside power – not for permanent territorial expansion, but more likely as part of a strategy of coercive diplomacy in support of more limited political objectives. The most important implication of this is that NATO is no longer purely a military alliance for a specific purpose – that of deterring a Soviet attack on Europe – but is instead developing into *a political organization with a military capability* (Ringsmose and Rynning, 2011).

The subtle difference between the two is that joint action by all member states in the event of a crisis – even a crisis in Europe – cannot be taken for granted to the same extent, let alone a crisis occurring out of area. If a crisis has a distinctly local character and concerns less than the national survival of the country or countries involved, considerations of national interest and domestic policy implications must be expected to strongly influence decisions in capitals as to if and how the alliance should get involved. Should Norway have to confront Russia in a crisis developing in the high north over Spitsbergen, it is probably fair to say that there will be little enthusiasm among the Central and South European countries to go out on a limb over an issue like that. Similarly, one can find causes and scenarios involving the countries at the opposite end of the continent which would hardly excite the North European members sufficiently to go to war over them.

Conversely, if a modern conflict in Europe can be expected to be local, the common geopolitical and strategic interest will probably be strong between countries situated in the affected region, irrespective of their formal defence and security affiliations. A community of genuine strategic interest will be at least as strong an incentive to joint political and military action as membership in the same security organization. Consequently, claiming that defence cooperation partners outside NATO can never be trusted, whereas fellow NATO members always and unreservedly can, is probably a simplification of today's realities (Edström, Matlary and Petersson, 2011).

Furthermore, refusing to cooperate with countries outside one's own security organization may well be a strategy going nowhere when it comes to solving the actual problem of critical mass and disappearing capabilities. This is because the closest political and military allies of a small country are not necessarily in the same situation in terms of the risk of losing important capabilities unless drastic measures are taken. As previously mentioned, the necessary motivation and will to accept the political downsides of such measures require a degree of political and military symmetry which is not correlated with alliance membership or geographical proximity. However, there is a difference between the three outlined approaches to defence integration in terms of how suitable they are in this regard. Role specialization as well as pooling and sharing are no doubt more vulnerable strategies when there are weaker security obligations and guarantees – be they formal or real – between the partners. This is because they are based on the presumption of immediate reinforcement in a crisis of a threatened partner with the capabilities he is lacking, and for which he has chosen to rely on his partners.

In other words, the weaker the obligation to support a threatened partner the greater the comparative disadvantage of this approach. The joint force generation strategy, on the other hand, will leave all participating countries with at least a limited national capacity across the spectrum of capabilities, but with logistic and training support facilities spread out between the partners. Hesitation or reluctance of the partners to become involved will, therefore, only hurt the logistic ability to support a military effort beyond a certain time limit. If we assume that an armed conflict in Europe today will be of limited duration, and that systems and weapon platforms undergoing heavy repair or upgrading in workshops and factories therefore may not be reassembled in time to be employed anyway, the question of in what country these workshops are located must necessarily be of limited consequence.

## Conclusion – towards a more rational European defence structure

The above line of argument seems to suggest that the joint force generation approach is objectively the preferable solution, minimizing security risk for a maximum gain in terms of economy of scale. Despite this, there is more focus in NATO today on the two other approaches – 'role specialization and pooling and sharing' – when it comes to the much-debated issue of 'smart defence'. This is perhaps to be expected in an alliance, where there will be a natural reluctance to admit that the commitment to the treaty and the solidarity between its members are not as strong and unconditional as during the Cold War.

Furthermore, the negative industrial consequences of the force generation strategy and its commonality of systems requirement are very distasteful political implications in peace. This is all the more so in the face of an economic crisis in Europe of unprecedented scope and gravity. With unemployment already in double figures in most European countries, streamlining defence procurement with its implicit rationalization of defence industries, laying off tens of thousands of workers, is not a vote-winning policy; nor is the attempt to sustain complete national inventories and support organizations by steadily increasing defence budgets in an attempt to keep up with both investment and operating cost increases. The slightly disturbing implication of this, therefore, is that from a political point of view a strategy of cutting defence expenditure by disbanding certain marginal capabilities, simply presupposing that friends and allies will come to your assistance in a crisis, will be vastly preferable to minimizing the strategic risk at the expense of jobs in your own defence industry. In the first alternative, the downside is hypothetical and long term – in the second it becomes a tangible fact here and now.

Add to this the protected if not privileged position of the defence industry in many countries, and the instinctive aversion of the great powers to sacrifice national prestige and freedom of action in these matters, we see that the way ahead for sensible and economically rational defence policies in Europe is a bumpy one indeed. There are few prime ministers around like Margaret Thatcher, who on the eve of the First Gulf War in 1990 threatened to buy German Leopard IIs as the main battle tank for the British Army should the newly developed British Challenger fail to perform.[4]

Consequently, given its many economic and political complications, there is no cause for great optimism when it comes to the prospect of imminent and comprehensive European defence cooperation. On the contrary, there is every reason to believe that things will get worse before they get better. But the bottom line – in more senses than one – is that European countries in the face of the economic realities of sustaining today's force structures cannot afford the price of today's policies. Within a matter of few years, they must decide on some kind of defence integration strategy. Failing to do so will be a decision in itself, with serious implications for all, whether we are great powers or small countries. For major powers like Britain and France, it is a question of maintaining a global military reach and the political influence and status depending on that, as well as a leading role beside the Americans in NATO. For small countries, where carriers or nuclear retaliation capability have never been an ambition, the critical mass challenge is rapidly threatening basic capabilities like tanks, submarines or fighters – and thereby minimal military requirements for national crisis management.

Unless something quite unexpected happens – which can never be ruled out, but which is scarcely a sound assumption for defence planning purposes – these underlying trends will continue. Time has come, therefore, to accept that the days are over when security policy was driving defence budgets. Today, defence budgets are driving security policy, thereby imposing new and hitherto unknown solutions to security problems. We cannot, in short, have a more ambitious defence and security policy than the one we can afford at the price European electorates are willing to pay. To quote the former Chairman of NATO's Military Committee, General Klaus Naumann, and former Supreme Allied Commander Europe, General Joe Ralston: 'European defense integration is not an interesting option – it is an imperative' (CSIS, 2004).

## Notes

1. China is a notable exception, her defence budgets growing with an annual average of 15 per cent over the period 2000–2010. Approximately 30 per cent of Chinese defence budgets are spent on equipment (GlobalSecurity, 2012).
2. Denmark's participation has so far been limited, since that country, as previously explained, has largely accepted the loss of several of its former capabilities

3. Iceland's participation is purely political, since it has no military forces of its own.
4. Quoted by Major General R Swinburne of the UK MOD to the students at the Army Command and Staff College in Camberley at a briefing during the build-up to Op GRANBY, the deployment of British forces to the Gulf in September 1990. Authors own notes.

## Bibliography

Borchert, H. and Eggenberger, R. (2007) 'European Security and Defence Policy, Role Specialization and Pooling of Resources: The EU's Need for Action and What It Means for Switzerland', *Contemporary Security Policy*, Vol. 24, No. 3, pp. 1–25.
CSIS (2004) 'Joint Declaration on European Defense Integration', 19 August 2004, http://csis.org (homepage), date accessed 26 May 2012.
Diesen, S. (2011) *Fornyelse eller forvitring? Forsvaret mot 2020* (Oslo: Cappelen Damm).
Edström, H., Matlary, J. H. and Petersson, M. (2011) 'Utility for NATO – Utility of NATO?', in H. Edström, J. H. Matlary and M. Petersson (eds) *NATO: The Power of Partnerships* (Basingstoke: Palgrave Macmillan), pp. 1–17.
GlobalSecurity (2012) http://www.globalsecurity.org (homepage), date accessed 26 May 2012.
HM Government (2010) *Securing Britain in an Age of Uncertainty: The Strategic Defence and Security Review* (London: HM Government).
Hoffmann, S. (2009) 'Overlapping Institutions in the Realm of International Security: The Case of NATO and ESDP', *Perspectives on Politics*, Vol. 7, No. 1, pp. 45–52.
Innset, B. (2010) *Integrasjon med grenser eller grenseløs integrasjon: En analyse av nordisk forsvarssamarbeid* (Oslo: Den norske Atlanterhavskomite).
NATO (2011) 'Strategic Airlift Capability. A Key Capability for the Alliance', 7 December 2011, http://www.nato.int (homepage), date accessed 2 June 2012.
Ringsmose, J. and Rynning, S. (2011) 'Introduction. Taking Stock of NATO's New Strategic Concept', in J. Ringsmose and S. Rynning (eds) *NATO's New Strategic Concept: A Comprehensive Assessment*, DIIS Report 2011:02 (Copenhagen: DIIS).
Saxi, H. L. (2010) *Norwegian and Danish Defence Policy. A Comparative Study of the Post-Cold War Era* (Oslo: The Norwegian Institute for Defence Studies).
Saxi, H. L. (2011) *Nordic Defence Cooperation after the Cold War* (Oslo: The Norwegian Institute for Defence Studies).

# 5
# Strategy, Risk and Threat Perceptions in NATO

Ø. Østerud and A. Toje

## Introduction

When NATO's Heads of State and Governments assembled in Chicago in May 2012 for the alliance's 25th summit they did so in a sombre mood. NATO is, arguably, facing the gravest challenge since its creation. A lack of shared purpose translating into weak support for alliance ventures. The unspoken tension was between the American desire to use the alliance's role as a political and military support framework for its global geopolitics and the European allies who would like to focus on American security guarantees in Europe and less on what they are to be expected to deliver in return. The pending failure of NATO's mission in Afghanistan has increased European scepticism towards out-of-area interventions. American policy makers added to NATO's sclerosis by, in 2012, unilaterally reducing the American troop levels stationed in Europe to record lows, adding to concerns regarding the viability of collective defence in an alliance with only one primary security producer. Although the 2010 Strategic Concept stressed that NATO would do both Article 5 defence and out-of-area operations, in reality the members are preparing to do neither (NATO, 2010).

Studies of NATO strategy have tended to concentrate on deterrence and defence functions of the alliance, notably on how changing understandings of the military balance of power (Senghaas, 1972; Kaldor, 1981; Schwartz, 1983). Far less attention has been directed towards NATO's role as a forum of political consultation and cooperation and, by extension, the role that it played with regard to the military ability and political will to use for political purpose. NATO was always cast as an alliance of like-minded states united by shared norms and values. The defence of territory was from the outset fused with ideological and economic ideals. It is on this basis that the allies have executed a coherent grand strategy, giving guidance to security policy, defence strategy and military posture on a national and supranational level (AHA, 1974; Heller and Gillingham; 1992; Wenger, 2006). This is by no means a novel observation, but one that deserves restating, not least because it is an essential factor in the ways in which NATO has evolved as a catalyst for agreed understandings regarding the use of force and why this is, as will be argued here, no longer the case.

The outline of this chapter is straightforward. The text is structured into three sections, beginning with the nature and function of NATO strategy from 1949 and up to 1991. The second section deals with three core transatlantic tensions that arose with the demise of the Soviet Union over questions of burden-sharing – referring to the persistent and rapidly growing gap across the Atlantic in terms of defence capabilities; the question of power-sharing – pertaining to the role of the United States as alliance leader; and finally, the question of threat assessment – what would be NATO's mission in the post-Cold War world. The final section assesses the operations of NATO in Afghanistan and Libya, with an emphasis on the effects these missions have had on the alliance. In the Concluding Remarks section some thoughts are offered on the *status quo* and challenges facing the NATO in the years to come.

## A Cold War creature

Since 1949, NATO has provided the West's foreign policy gravitas, informing the full range of foreign policy for its members. Membership in NATO was a decision that took a great many other decisions with it. Joining the Western Alliance influenced who to trade with, how sovereignty was defined and on what arenas to seek prestige objectives. As the sole transatlantic institutional link NATO played a vital part throughout the Cold War in maintaining strategic cohesion and Western unity. The efforts at unity, first captured in the Vandenberg Resolution (1948), the Brussels Treaty (1948) and the North Atlantic Treaty (1949), were later joined by a plethora of parallel dialogues ranging from intergovernmental contacts to scholarly forums and a web of interlocking institutions.

NATO of 2012 is a different organization from what it was at its creation. The western alliance was a reflection of the Cold War, delineating the boundaries between East and West in Europe and beyond. It was designed to stabilize the continent, contain Soviet expansion, and defend Western Europe and North America collectively against threat embodied in the Warsaw Pact. NATO was a military, political and ideological framework for transatlantic cooperation, while at the same time also being an instrument for American influence in Europe. This approach has been a source both of NATO's strength and resilience, but it was also a source of tension that has granted the alliance few periods of inner peace over the past six decades. The alliance's *raison d'être* was to make the allies capable of resisting, and if possible avoiding, war with the Soviet bloc. How this single threat would be best met was the crux of all the main intra-alliance debates during the Cold War.

The credibility of NATO as a defence pact was from the onset based on American pre-eminence. On a military level, Western Europe was an American protectorate, captured in Geir Lundestad's label 'Empire' by invitation (Lundestad, 2003). Throughout the Cold War the United States was a European power (as opposed to a power in Europe) by virtue of a substantial troop presence fluctuating between 150,000 and 400,000 personnel. Article 5 of the Treaty stated that an attack on any member state was an attack on all, understood to imply a collective obligation to mobilize and counterattack. American bases and military personnel in Europe were seen as a guarantee of the American commitment to Europe. The strategic posture of NATO during the Cold War was unstable in two key respects. One, it was uncertain whether the overarching nuclear 'balance of terror' would deter conflict also at lower levels. Did the prospect of escalation into a full-scale war deter also minor armed clashes, or could incidents develop and multiply because the nuclear balance of power made escalation less likely? Two, the idea of extended deterrence meant that the American nuclear umbrella effectively covered the allied countries. Was US assistance credible if such assistance implied a direct nuclear threat against the American homeland?

As early as the 1950s, the Atlantic alliance was seen as a 'troubled partnership'. Richard L. Kugler singles out four key developments that NATO underwent during its first decade: the creation of an integrated military structure, the establishment of a lasting US military presence in Central Europe, the acceptance of American strategic leadership and the agreement on the rearmament of West Germany (Kugler, 1990). The year 1954 was arguably the most important year in NATO's existence. That year saw the inclusion of the Federal Republic of Germany (FRG) into the transatlantic alliance (Fursdon, 1980, p. 9; Bozo, 2001, pp. 10–23). The US military planners had already in 1948 arrived at a conclusion that Western Europe could not be defended without substantial German contributions (Harder, 2000). In 1950 Pentagon plans for a highly developed NATO force posture including a large US force presence in Europe were contingent on German rearmament. The debate on German rearmament in the early 1950s ended in the landmark Paris agreement of October 1954, which bestowed sovereignty on Western Germany and allowed for the creation of an army of such size that it could feasibly defend itself (Kanarowski, 1982).

This happened only after less feasible plans, such as a Soviet-sponsored initiative to reunite Germany and the Pleven Plan for an autonomous European Defence Community, had foundered (Fursdon, 1980). The Paris agreement allowed for the western victory powers and West Germany to pool their forces in the effort to protecting the exposed central flank in a posture that would endure more or less unchanged for three decades (Park, 1990). The problem was, of course, that Europe was at the height of post-war reconstruction and there was generally little desire to divert scarce funds from public works towards the sort of near-wartime levels of defence spending envisioned by American military planners. In practice, the German contribution was taken as a green light to scale back armies in other European countries. As a result, the European allies would not shoulder their portion of the defence burden of the West: the American resources committed to Europe became far more substantial than was initially envisaged, handing down what Stanley Sloan calls 'a legacy with which NATO struggled until the end of the Cold War' (Sloan, 2003, p. 3).

The inherent ambiguities of nuclear deterrence were reflected in the official Strategic Concepts of NATO. The first fundamental debate on the tenets of NATO strategy was sparked by the Soviet Union gaining and rapidly expanding a nuclear arsenal combined with residual tensions over the Korean War, as well as the Hungarian uprising and Suez crisis of 1956. The issue of the debate was whether 'New Look' was having more far-reaching strategic implications than supposed. The NATO military planners were in a dilemma with regard to the integration of nuclear weapons due to the shift in US policy. In 1953 the Ridgeway Report concluded that nuclear weapons necessitated larger conventional forces because the casualty rates were expected to be higher (Winand, 1993; Schwartz, 1983; Deporte, 1986). But as such contributions were not politically feasible. NATO in 1957 agreed to the MC 14/2, which envisaged the immediate use of the alliance's nuclear weapons in response to a major attack, the strategy that came to be known as 'massive retaliation'. This scenario for mutual assured destruction, known by its acronym MAD, was deterrence pure and simple.

From the 1960s, European uneasiness over American dominance in defining NATO strategy was voiced, most explicitly by the French. The mechanics of nuclear deterrence raised concerns: would, as the French asked themselves, the United States be willing to risk New York and Washington in order to defend Paris? The French answer to this question was, on balance, not affirmative. The strategic rationale of an independent French nuclear force – the *Force de Frappe* – was to make European deterrence more credible and to give France a seat at the table at a time when the dealings between the two power blocs were increasingly determined by the Russo-American bilateralism. The price was a discord in NATO strategy and command that extended well into the post-Cold War era. During the Cold War, NATO was a collective defence pact for the member states, confined to the boundaries of this area. The organization was not, accordingly, geared towards projecting force out of area. Separate defence leagues and bilateral agreements were in operation in other parts of the world. NATO's role was not that of extraterritorial police force, or indeed a support framework for American geopolitics. When the United States sent troops to Vietnam in 1965, they did so alone.

Disagreement over NATO's political role built up through the Berlin and Cuban missile crises and erupted in January 1963, when Charles de Gaulle announced his veto to Britain's admission to the Common Market, rejected hosting US Polaris missiles and signed a bilateral treaty of friendship with Konrad Adenauer. As the French President explained to the German Chancellor, 'America only envisages an alliance on the condition that it commands it' (De Gaulle, 1987, p. 267, authors' translation). The machinations of the mid-1960s revolved around such important questions as the management and application of nuclear power and the perception of the Soviet threat. One response lay in the assembling of additional political NATO structures that would add multilateralism to the emerging US-Soviet détente and accommodate the needs of an economically revived, and politically more assertive, Europe. Since a complete reliance on nuclear deterrence was risky brinkmanship or, alternatively, not credible due to the prospect of catastrophic retaliation, internal debates paved the way for a new strategic concept. In 1967, the strategy was rephrased as *flexible response*, adapting the means of reply to the level and character of the threats and aggressive advances at hand.

The doctrine of flexible response had two origins: one in the United States and one in Europe. The result was that the strategies first advocated by the Kennedy administration in 1962 and the MC 14/3 were different. The American debate reflected a shifting tactical emphasis away from counter-city targeting to counter force and counter value as well as renewed emphasis on conventional defence. The idea presented was one of controlled nuclear escalation as opposed to the practice of permanent targeted soviet cities, while it did not imply American unwillingness to make first use of nuclear weapons. There was considerable resistance in Europe where the policy shift was met with concerns that the United States was weakening its alliance commitment (Stromseth, 1988, pp. 151–174).

The doctrinal shift was only accepted in Europe after the new version of the MC 14/3 spelled out how escalation would work in practice. Flexible response predicated less severe response to minor episodes which would have political price, but it reduced the risk of lower-level conflicts spiralling out of control. In European NATO capitals there was a shared sense that the reduced tensions should be met with renewed dialogue with the aim of reducing threats further. The new balance between NATO's military and its political functions was articulated in the 1967 *Harmel Report on the Future Tasks of the Alliance*, the first effort to develop a strategy for NATO in a political sense. The Report has been referred to as the "Magna Carta" of NATO, and somewhat correctly so in that the document defines an 'ultimate political purpose' of the alliance (Brockpähler, 1990). The Report made it clear that NATO would pursue a policy of détente, with the explicit aim of de-escalating East–West rivalry.

There are four statements in the Harmel Report that needs highlighting in the context of this chapter. While reaffirming the alliance's primary tasks as being to deter and defend, paragraph 8 of the Report affirms NATO's determination to resolve the underlying political issues such as the division of Germany. Paragraph 5 of the Report carries a vision of détente, meaning a balance of force that would help create a climate of stability, security and confidence. The dual approach of credible collective defence combined with cohabitation with the Eastern bloc was to carry NATO into the post-Cold War world. But the Report also had forward-looking elements. Paragraph 9 of the Harmel Report states that 'the ultimate political purpose of the alliance is to achieve a just and lasting peaceful order in Europe accompanied by appropriate security guarantees'. This goal remains unchanged to this date. Finally, paragraph 15 of the document outlines the global role of NATO: 'The North Atlantic Treaty Area cannot be treated in isolation from the rest of the world. Crisis and conflicts arising outside the area may impair its security either directly or by affecting the global balance' (NATO, 1967). This phrase was to receive new relevance as the threat that NATO has been created to avert subsided with the abolition of the Warsaw Treaty Organization in 1991.

## Consensus lost

The immediate implication of the end of the Cold War – the fall of the Berlin wall and the dissolution of the Soviet Union – was that NATO found itself without the threat it had been created to deter. As one of the alliance's leading thinkers, Jamie Shea, noted:

> In the post-Cold War era security has become muffled. Although the classic threat has disappeared, new security threats and challenges have proliferated and allies do not necessarily have the same perceptions as to what they are. The threats are today latent and whether or not to address them is voluntary as opposed to the imperatives of the Cold War threats exemplified by Soviet tanks on the inner-German border.

Since 1991, NATO strategy has been revised several times. The organization has been transformed radically, and the level of internal disagreement has increased, since the overall *rationale* of NATO remains contested.

The alliance was faced with the challenge of transforming its *raison d'être*; first, by deciding how to relate to the former adversaries in the Soviet bloc, and second, by redefining its Strategic Concept and changing its mode of operation. Resolving these questions were made harder by NATOs Cold War legacy: first, despite half a century of debate, NATO had proved incapable of generating anything resembling an equal transatlantic burden-sharing. This gap grew into a chasm as European states reaped the peace dividend, reducing defence spending. This trend was compounded by a steadily growing gap in technology and military capabilities across the Atlantic that hampered inter-operability. Second, much of the same situation was reflected in the case of power-sharing within the alliance, where the United States had grown accustomed to holding a position of primacy akin to that held by the USSR in the Warsaw Treaty Organisation. Finally, the collapse of the USSR, the great unifier, left NATO without a common enemy to justify its policies and without an agreed purpose underpinning its future.

A RAND Corporation study published in the mid-1990s is widely regarded as having had a vital impact on the shaping of American NATO policies. The study recommended transforming NATO from a collective defence alliance into a communal security grouping based on common democratic values (Asmus and Nurick, 1996, p. 142 – see also Asmus et al., 1993). For this reason Eastern enlargement came to be considered by many as the solution to NATO's self-preservation challenge. Some, including former US National Security Adviser Zbigniew Brzezinski, hoped that the act of enlargement would bring a new momentum to the alliance (Brzezinski, 2001). The question of enlargement would soak up NATO's political and administrative resources for much of the 1990s. Enlargement proceeded in two stages. From 1999 NATO comprised the Czech Republic, Hungary and Poland, and from 2004 also Bulgaria, Estonia, Latvia, Lithuania, Rumania, Slovakia and Slovenia. On the one hand, the gradual enclosure of Russia was partially softened by an agreement of diplomatic consultations, although Russia reacted negatively to the enlargement as well as to NATO's deployment of a proposed missile shield in former Warsaw Pact countries. On the other hand, enlargement meant, 'not least' because the frontline defences were not extended into the new frontline members, that NATO became less coherent as a collective defence pact.

The 1991 Strategic Concept was formally revised in 1999 to reflect the new security situation in Europe amidst the final chapter of the Balkan wars. The document went through a great many drafting processes and ended up as a sprawling blend of ideological affirmations and listings of potential threats. Where the Strategic Concept had less to offer was on the topic of NATO's purpose. The absence of any agreed clear and present threat undercut the strategic aspects of the strategy. The limited added value of the document and the excruciating nature of the drafting process led several of the people involved in the drafting process to question whether the exercise had been worth the effort.[1]

In 1999 NATO stressed the importance of cooperation with former adversaries, to improve the security of all of Europe. NATO forces could be scaled down while mobility and adaptability to new circumstances were to be increased. This was a response to the American notion that NATO would have to go 'out of area or out of business' (Patrick, 2009). This meant that the new *quid pro quo* for US security guarantees would be for the NATO members to provide military support for American global politics. NATO's structure of planning and command was adapted according to the new idea of rapid deployment in a variety of crisis scenarios. Based on experience with handling the Yugoslav civil war of the mid-1990s, the strategic revision was brought a long step further. Consequently, the new Strategic Concept suggested that NATO's traditional role of collective territorial defence, stemming from the member states' commitment under Article 5, though still necessary, was no longer sufficient to underpin the alliance (NATO, 1999). The deployment of forces out of area was explicitly endorsed. NATO was redefined as an instrument for crisis management both within and beyond the collective defence area.

During the first decade of the new century, NATO faced the challenge of becoming over-burdened. The major tasks were not clear, and the tendency was that a wide array of challenges, potential or otherwise, were elevated to the level of threat. In the revised Strategic Concept of 2010, the tripartite function of collective defence, crisis management and cooperative security was addressed (NATO, 2010). NATO hoped to better its relations with Russia while at the same time building an anti-missile defence system that would undercut Russian deterrence. The alliance also declared its intention to expand into fighting terrorism, organised crime and piracy. Civil–military relations in conflict areas became part of the expanded NATO doctrine. The threat perception became wider, but also less focused and more controversial. With regard to the military ability and political will to use for political purpose, the compromise reached was that NATO should be both about collective defence and out-of-area activities. The problem not addressed was that the Afghan operation had shown that the two types of tasks require vastly different capabilities, institutional frameworks and training. As had been the case so many times in the past, political impasse translated into decreased defence spending. Both the United States and its European allies sharply reduced military spending (Hallams and Schreer, 2012, p. 315).

## Repurposing NATO

### Bosnia and Kosovo: Attempts at crisis management

A major operational turning point for NATO occurred in Bosnia-Herzegovina towards the mid-1990s. Neither the UN Security Council nor the European Union (EU) was able to concentrate on a joint course of action in the Balkans crisis. As this was a European crisis, NATO was the likely military instrument, provided that the 1991 Strategic Concept's phrase 'appropriate crisis management measures... including those in the military field' was understood to include operations beyond the north Atlantic area. (NATO, 1991, Art 32). After the UN mandate was given, the SFOR (Stabilization force) in Bosnia, followed by KFOR in Kosovo, drove NATO into a more active crisis management role. These operations demonstrated that the political and military capacity of NATO depended on American leadership, but also that NATO was unprepared for these types of operations. The NATO members had difficulties in deploying, then in sustaining forces once in the field as well as in interacting effectively with other NATO forces (NATO, 1997).

The NATO operation in Kosovo in 1999, with air strikes towards Belgrade, again highlighted the unevenness of the alliance. During the Kosovo air campaign the Americans would shoulder most of the burden of the military operations. American warplanes flew 80 per cent of the 10,484 strike missions, supplied 90 per cent of the command, control and communications facilities and launched over 90 per cent of the 'smart' weapons (Drozdiak, 1999). KFOR was the immediate backdrop to the new strategic concept in which out-of-area operations were codified. NATO, in the Balkan crisis, followed from the revised threat perceptions after the Cold War – regional instability, the risk of wider repercussions in neighbouring states and refugee flows across borders. Jihadists from Arab countries also played a role in the Yugoslav conflicts, a prelude to the challenges that would later be faced by NATO in Afghanistan.

The Kosovo War also gave birth to a new Eurocentric security framework – what came to be known as the EU's Common Security and Defence Policy (CSDP). The initiative sprung from a bilateral initiative launched at the French port of Saint Malo where France and Britain agreed to breathe new life into the old vision of a joint European force. Although the two countries differed in strategic outlooks they were equally appalled that Europe again had proved manifestly unable to prevent a relatively small crisis on its own doorstep from spiralling out of control. The Saint Malo statement charted a middle path between the French position – 'The European Union needs to be in a position to play its full role on the international stage' with a 'capacity for autonomous action, backed up by credible military force' – and the British view: 'while acting in conformity with our respective obligations in NATO, we are contributing to the vitality of a modernised Atlantic alliance which is the foundation of the collective defence of its members' (Joint Declaration on European Defence).

This agreement did little to resolve the inter-institutional tensions that ensued. The uneasiness in the EU–NATO interaction is well known. Despite overlapping members and missions there is surprisingly little substantial cooperation between the Europe's two primary security institutions. The formal framework for dialogue, the Political and Security Committee (PSC)–North Atlantic Council (NAC) meetings, has not become the forum envisioned in the 2003 Berlin-Plus agreement. When NATO and EU ambassadors meet, they are only authorised to discuss select capability initiatives and 'joint EU–NATO operations' – both of which there have been preciously few. Other important issues, such as anti-terror cooperation, Iraq, Afghanistan and Sudan are simply not on the agenda. It is no secret that this state of affairs may to no small degree be attributed to the impasse between EU member Cyprus and NATO member Turkey. The intricacies of the dispute are too complex to revisit in detail, but the outcome of the impasse has been that NATO and the EU for the first decade of the 2000s were an either–or configuration, with little formal or indeed informal cooperation (for more on the Turkey–Cyprus issues, see Duke, 2008).

### Afghanistan: In together, out separately

The Afghanistan operation has – even more explicit than SFOR/KFOR – made the tensions and varieties of concerns within NATO evident. The US intervention started as a direct response to the terrorist attacks that took place on 11 September 2001, directed against terrorist safe havens provided for by the Taliban regime. NATO theatrically invoked the collective defence Article 5 for the first time in the history of the alliance the day after the attacks and reluctantly recognized the Afghan intervention in late 2001 to be an Article 5 operation. What is notable is that the member states did not interpret Article 5, as had been agreed during the Cold War, as a promise of immediate military assistance but rather as an invitation to consultations about troop contributions. The European member states were for the most part adamant that Article 5 did not entail any automatic military support in Afghanistan, or indeed the Iraq conflict two years later. Despite the best of intentions, it is hard to escape the conclusion that this intermezzo weakened NATO's claim to be a traditional alliance.

In Afghanistan, the strategy was at first a limited military deployment in support of the Northern Alliance in the civil war against the Taliban regime. The limited aim of regime change met with success at an early stage, but the wider aim of stabilising the country, containing terrorism and hunting down Al-Qaida fighters turned out to drag the intervention forces into a quagmire. The allied ISAF operation was transformed into a formal NATO responsibility from August 2003. The transfer was accompanied by a proliferation of objectives, from strengthening human rights to democratizing Afghanistan, promoting gender equality, economic development and so on, and it gave the foreign intervention a hint of the surreal, as the revolt spread, the narcotics production grew and corruption permeated what was widely seen as a marionette government (Suhrke, 2011). The shared operational responsibility did not make the operation more efficient, but it was seen to make it more legitimate, particularly with domestic European audiences. As eventually all NATO members dispatched forces to the country, there were inter-alliance disputes over nearly every aspect of the military operations. And so it was that an alliance that had only a handful of troops in Afghanistan at the time of Kabul's fall in 2001 counted upwards 130,000 troops ten years later. This was, as Astrid Suhrke points out in her authoritative work on the conflict, more soldiers than the Soviet Union had in Afghanistan at any point during its brutal war of the 1980s (Suhrke, 2011, p. 262).

The escalation is inextricably linked to the kaleidoscopically shifting objectives of the operation, not least because the ever-growing ambitions have – in tandem with the lack of goal achievement – been cited as the reason for the escalation in a self-reinforcing circular argument. The ISAF operation can be said to fall into five distinct narrative phases. The period from 2001 to 2003 can be summarized under the heading 'war on terror'. NATO was in Afghanistan to eliminate terrorists and their supporters. This led in 2003 to the 'Marshall Plan Hindu Kush' phase where the major combat operations were assumed to be over and focus was on getting the economic and social wheels turning. The years 2006–2009 noted that 'the first bomb, then build' of civil–military cooperation was in accordance with NATO's 'shape, clear, hold, build' doctrine. The period 2009–2010 was marked by 'We are President Karzai's soldiers' where the United States sent 30,000 new troops while 'Afghan ownership' was a central theme. This has in 2011 led into 'not Switzerland' – where the focus is on lowering expectations that Western powers had built up under the Marshall planning phase. In 2011 President Obama announced that the bulk of US troops would be out of Afghanistan by the end of 2014. Most experts agree that NATO will most likely leave Afghanistan with little to show for its considerable efforts.

In Afghanistan NATO took on an operation that absorbed much of its political and military resources throughout the first decade of the 2000s. The difficulties involved in reforming NATO, while at the same time carrying out a large out-of-area operation, are illustrated in the fate of the NATO Response Force (NRF). The initiative was launched at the 2002 Prague NATO Summit and declared operational four years later at the summit in Riga. The NRF was branded as a dynamo for the continued relevance of NATO and a catalyst for the transformation of the alliance – a reformed instrument of collective action. The 24,000 strong task force was to be drawn from the best capabilities available among the NATO members. The NRF was intended to give the alliance an immediate capacity for defence that had been lost with the abandonment of the Cold War contingency plans (NATO, 2002). The NRF did not deliver on its initial promise (Winkler, 2007). In 2012, Defense Secretary Leon Panetta pledged to contribute a US-based Army brigade to the NRF, in an attempt to reassure European allies after a round of cuts in American troops that brought the number to a record low of little more than 30,000. This meant that the inter-allied joint exercises will be less frequent than in the past, leaving renewed concerns over NATO inter-operability.

## Libya: NATO as a coalition of the willing

While NATO was planning for what promises to be a tumultuous retreat from Afghanistan, the member states were taken by surprise by the Arab Spring. The upheavals in Tunisia, Egypt and in the Middle East did not call for Western intervention, but the unrest that rose towards a civil war in eastern Libya led to a bombing campaign by NATO countries. Gadhafi's forces threatened to crush the ragtag revolutionaries in their stronghold in Benghazi. The Transitional National Council tried to coordinate the rebellion and seek foreign support. As the regular army rolled back the rebels by mid-March 2011, the UN Security Council passed a resolution that authorized outside measures to protect civilians and impose a no-fly zone in the Libyan air space (IISS, 2011, pp. 67–72). The air attacks that started on 19 March effectively stopped the regime's forces on the road to Benghazi, and imposition of the no-fly zone started shortly afterwards. NATO forces from several countries took part in ground attacks against the Libyan army, while some Arab countries flew supporting missions and assisted in overseeing the no-fly zone. The rebellion against Gadhafi's regime would most likely have failed without NATO support. As operations evolved the NATO allies stretched the UN mandate's no-fly zone to include attacks on the infrastructure of Gadhafi's regime and – if media reports are to be believed – put irregular forces on the ground to assist the inexperienced rebels.

France took the lead in forming a consensus for intervention. After briefly considering an EU mission and being rebuffed by German opposition, the case was put before the NATO council. What came to pass in these debates remain murky. Newspaper reports indicated that France and Britain were the chief proponents pro while Germany and Turkey led those opposed to the mission (Dempsey and Myers, 2012). The United States, reluctant to take ownership of the mission, as they had done in Kosovo, took the back seat in the deliberations. The result, by some accounts, was the most hostile debate in the alliance's history. As one NATO official who was present put it, 'accusations were made from both camps that will not be easily forgotten'.[2] With little time to spare as the revolutionaries were in imminent danger of being overrun, NATO arrived at an arrangement that may have fateful consequences for the future of the alliance: the bulk of the allies abstained, leaving only six members to carry out the mission on behalf of the alliance.

The international operation in Libya was, it should be noted, atypical for Western military interventions after the end of the Cold War. The Libyan campaign started on European initiative, specifically from France and the United Kingdom. The main argument was that the regime's reoccupation of Benghazi would result in a massacre of civilians, and that the international community had endorsed the principle of a 'responsibility to protect' in other crisis areas. This moved the UN resolution, even if China and Russia abstained. The United States initially supported the French–British initiative with some reluctance, but saw an advantage in an operation led by European powers with US military support. Increasingly, the United States took the lead from behind, as one commentator succinctly phrased it:

> Discreet US military assistance with France and Britain doing the trumpeting was sensible. Discreet does not mean desultory. The United States took out Libya's air defence system. It provided more than 70 per cent of the surveillance, intelligence and reconnaissance capabilities. It flew 70 per cent of refuelling missions. What it did not do was wade into Libya with the army it had in the vanguard of a motley coalition of the willing.
>
> (Cohen, 2011)

It was not only the French–British initiative that was noteworthy. NATO was more than usually fragmented over the Libyan campaign. Turkey was vocally opposed to the mission, and Germany took no stand, neither did Poland. In fact, less than half of the alliance members participated, and strike missions were undertaken by less than a third of the member states. US officials complained about the unwillingness of NATO members, but also about their inadequate military capabilities, a result of persistent cuts in defence spending (Gates, 2011). The Libyan mission, further, raised questions about the command structure of NATO in action. A joint French–British command was unacceptable to other NATO members and does not seem to have tempted the British either. The United States was from the beginning eager to avoid the forefront. The chosen option – a joint NATO command – was not noteworthy as such, but it was questionable since several member states did little to hide their opposition to the operation. In this respect, the Libyan mission seems to have heralded the end of the collectively engaging alliance.

Another notable feature of the NATO campaign in Libya was the mission creep during the air raids. What started out as an operation to protect civilians soon became an operation for regime change and ousting Gadhafi from power. By mid-2011, this was an explicit objective in US, French and British interpretations of the UN mandate. At the same time, the initial pretexts for intervention – a regime committing 'genocide', Gadhafi's forces 'killing the Libyan people' – turned out to be gross exaggerations. The number of civilian casualties was not staggering, even if a reoccupation of Benghazi might have become nasty. For the rebels in the civil war, and probably also for the intervention forces, getting rid of Gadhafi was a primary objective (Roberts, 2011). President Sarkozy may have had exterior motives, being criticized for passivity during the upheavals in Tunisia and eager to show French initiative and strength on the doorstep to the hexagon. The unconventional role of the philosopher and activist Bernhard-Henri Lévy has also been singled out as a factor; he was travelling to Benghazi and bringing representatives from the Transitional National Council to Paris at an early stage.[3] The episode points to a key topic: the tribulations of France in NATO.

### France in NATO: quest for a new transatlantic bargain

The end of the Cold War transformed the security situation in Western Europe. The European NATO countries were no longer fused by having a mutual enemy and a joint protector. Soon, centrifugal forces were tugging at the alliance as Germany focused its geopolitical interest eastwards, forging close ties with Russia. Britain continued to look west, to America for cooperation, and France was vacillating on whether to pull back from its Cold War sphere of interest in Mediterranean and North Africa, in order to seek more gainful relations and fears that such a move would remove the last semblance of great power status. Among the other NATO members the ambition was defensive, to prolong the traditional Atlantic alliance and the inexpensive security guarantees that came with it. In geopolitical terms, the fringes of Europe gravitated towards the United States as a major security guarantor, while the central continental powers – France and Germany – developed a more independent stance in the core of the EU.

France was seen as a reluctant ally during the Cold War. When President Charles de Gaulle and France withdrew from NATO's military command in 1966, this was the culmination of a series of specific grudges and one overall uncertainty. The US hegemonic leadership of NATO ran counter to French interests. The Suez crisis in 1956 and lack of American support for France's claims in Algeria were but examples of a broader struggle: America's geopolitical leadership of the West. France objected to this by developing its own deterrent, the *Force de Frappe*, accordingly. French attempts at establishing itself as an independent 'third force' was met with limited success during the Cold War. After the Cold War, France lost no time on taking charge of those who believed that security tight and asymmetrical transatlantic alliance was surplus to Europe's strategic requirements. There were Franco-American clashes over NATO enlargement policies, Middle East policies and the post-2001 'war on terror'.

The many French attempts at rapprochement were not met by Washington in a spirit of equality, so strongly desired in France. This basic lesson was repeated by Presidents Pompidou and Nixon, Giscard and Carter, and more recently, François Mitterrand and George Bush the Elder, and Jacques Chirac in his relations with Bill Clinton and George Bush the Younger. It is in this context that the French desire for European autonomy should be understood. But France was isolated in NATO on this position. In what many saw as a surprise move President Sarkozy effectuated a turnaround in French policies. What made French leaders reassess their position were three worrying trends. One, 'demand' factors outstripped 'supply' in European security. However, after a decade of the CSDP the initiative had yet to translate into a credible collective presence, which, due to the rapid decline of France and Britain, meant that Europe would have no seat at the high table in a multipolar system. Two, there was a shift in the American position. Under President George W. Bush, American scepticism towards EU military cooperation shifted from grudging acceptance to vocal support, raising the spectre of an American pull-out from Europe (Rees, 2011). Three, NATO's sustainability was in doubt. The operations in the Balkans, Afghanistan and Libya had done little to disprove the image of a politically fractured and militarily un-interoperable alliance (Toje, 2010).

In bringing about the French rapprochement President Sarkozy has been criticized in France for being overly pro American, but pro-American inclinations are hardly necessary to account for the French reorientation in 2008. By rejoining NATO's integrated military structure, France not only gained greater leeway for a French leadership in the alliance, as the French leadership in bringing about NATO air strikes in Libya indicate. The French shift was also seen, by decreasing American concerns on European 'ganging up', as increasing the scope for 'G-6' military cooperation within the EU – between Britain, France, Germany, Italy, Poland and Spain; attempts at independent military planning capability within the EU; and preserving a common EU arms market. What President Sarkozy was attempting was to build a genuine European power presence, but chose to do so in the spirit of the Saint Malo compromise, that is, within a broader transatlantic framework. NATO is perceived from Paris as less vital and therefore easier to accept.

In attempting to bring about a new transatlantic security architecture with a more equal EU presence, the French sought to avoid the sort of mistakes that had marred past attempts at Franco-American *rapprochement* (Bozo, 2008). A seasoned diplomat, Levitte sought to build confidence by strengthening Sarkozy's Atlanticist credentials: he offered 700 additional French troops to the NATO mission in Afghanistan and proposed French reintegration into NATO's military structure.[4] Importantly, the French made these offers without asking for the sort of high-profile *quid pro quo* that had scuttled previous attempts at reintegration (Menon, 2000). Instead, France sought to persuade the Americans that EU defence would be the more likely venue to bring about the sort of force generation that NATO initiatives had failed to deliver (Wikileaks, 2011). This perspective found a sympathetic hearing in Washington. The position was put in plain terms by Victoria Nuland, the American ambassador to NATO, in a speech in Paris given in early 2008: 'I am here today in Paris to say that we agree with France'; she continued, 'Europe needs, the United States needs, NATO needs, the democratic world needs – a stronger, more capable European capacity' (Nuland, 2008). The American shift in *Europapolitik* was enduring and has been continued under the Obama administration, concerned that the current arrangements was slowly depleting NATO's military ability and political will to use for political purpose (Biden, 2009).

Sarkozy described his ambition as encompassing 'an independent European Defence and an Atlantic organization in which we play a full role' (Sarkozy, 2007). Three policy questions were singled out: interinstitutional cooperation, capability initiatives and intra-institutional reform. The Defence Minister, Hervé Morin, surprised his colleagues by stressing that these processes would be carried out in concert with the Americans (Lequesne, 2008). The strategy was based on 'untangling'. The overarching aims of revised transatlantic power and burden-sharing appear to have been compartmentalized into three main policy processes: unblocking EU–NATO cooperation; effective bolstering of European military capabilities; and making the CSDP into an actual fighting force. The idea was that rather than seeking another 'grand bargain', such as the 1998 Franco-British Saint Malo Declaration, the French would pursue a series of separate policy initiatives that it was hoped – given time – would fuse, synergise and bring about a new transatlantic security bargain. All three of these efforts were contingent on gaining British, German and American acceptance of and support for an autonomous European CSDP.

When added together, French initiatives undertaken during their 2008 presidency of the EU were less than successful. The promised revamped transatlantic security framework with one North American and one EU pillar bridged by NATO did not come to pass. One lesson learnt is that the United States carries less sway in Europe than is sometimes assumed. Although Paris managed to win wholehearted support in Washington for their defence agenda, this failed to result in similar support in London and, more notably, in Berlin. Painstaking negotiations failed during the French presidency to translate general objectives into detailed compromises. Throughout this process a recurrent challenge has been to strike a balance between the desirable and the possible. Sarkozy discovered that the scope for initiative in military matters was less than he had originally envisioned.

## Concluding remarks

NATO formally survived after the end of the Cold War because it was redesigned and redefined. The enlargement into Eastern Europe was meant to stabilize substantial parts of the former Warsaw Pact, without provoking Russia. The reassurance of Russia was sought by formalized cooperation short of NATO membership. This balance has proved difficult to maintain in practice and NATO-Russo relations remain uneasy. In military operations, the development of NATO since the 1990s is 'mission creep' in the most literal sense. The engagement in Bosnia-Herzegovina – where NATO, in contrast to the United Nations and the EU, was led by a hegemonic superpower – opened up for a new doctrine and operations 'out of area'. NATO members even agreed to military operations against Serbia without a UN mandate and without a threat to the member area itself.

The Afghanistan campaign from late 2001 was formally defined as an Article 5 operation in the war against terror after 9/11, but gradually internal disagreements evolved. The ISAF force became a test case for the coherence and relevance of the alliance, with differentiated participation in various parts of the operation and different views on the objectives and modalities of the mission. In the Libya bombardments these fissures became manifest with open German and Turkish objections, and with the United States following behind a French–British initiative.

On the one hand, NATO was more relevant to the new challenges and conflict situations, but on the other hand – and accordingly – less monolithic. The alliance had become more of a diplomatic field in a complex and opaque international environment. Fragile states has been a focal point for interventionism after the Cold War. NATO projected force into this new anarchic environment, while collective defence and security as defined in the Cold War era receded into the background.

France left the integrated military structures in 1966, only to return in 2010. One reason why the reintegration failed to spark much interest was that France rejoined a different alliance than the one it had left. NATO is set to leave Afghanistan with little to show for its efforts. The underwhelming response to the Libyan intervention is an indicator that this may well be the last of the post-Cold War liberal interventions, at least for some time. One might say that the alliance has fallen into the trap of trying to please everyone; it ends up pleasing no-one. The 2010 strategic concept underlines this point by simply agreeing to focus on Article 5 operations (the penchant of the European allies) and out-of-area operations, the code word for supporting American geopolitical goals on a global stage. Developments outlined in this chapter give cause to question the viability of this compromise.

'The transatlantic alliance is dead.' The remark came after Western powers' annual security conference in Munich during spring 2012. Judy Dempsey, one of Europe's leading defence correspondents, said, put in plain words, what has long been whispered in the corridors of power.[5] NATO has struggled to find a new meaning after the Soviet Union, often jokingly referred to as 'the great uniter'. Somewhat simplified, the United States wanted NATO to take on the role of global police force, at America's request. European countries have generally been more concerned with American security guarantees to its allies in Europe. Since 1999, NATO has undertaken a number of overseas missions, mostly in defence of the UN Charter. In contrast to the rhetorical support for these operations, the European allies demonstrated their lack of enthusiasm for the new activism by cutting the defence budgets. NATO ex-UD defence spending as percentage of GDP fell from 2.05 in 1999 to 1.65 in 2008 (IISS, 2010, p. 110). The simple logic seems to be that those who do not own the equipment cannot be expected to send it to Afghanistan or Libya.

The European defence budgets have fallen by about 2 per cent year on year since the 1990s, while they grew in most other parts of the world, notably Asia (IISS, 2011, Chapter 5). France, Britain, Germany and Italy are still to be found among the ten countries in the world who spend the most on defence, but the funds are only to a limited extent translated into expeditionary intervention capabilities. The result is a dramatic drop in defence capacity. Countries that once mobilized hundreds of thousands now have difficulty to put a few hundred men in the field. Former US Secretary of Defense, Robert Gates, addressed this in a speech to the European allies. He condemned European defence cuts, saying that America is tired of taking more than their share of the burden on behalf of those who 'evade the risks and costs' (Financial Times, 2011). The experience of Afghanistan has made the decision-makers in Washington to ask themselves whether it really is an interest to cover defence costs for countries that only partially support US geopolitical objectives.

The objective of NATO was – according to the alliance's first Secretary-General, Lord Ismay – to keep 'the Americans in, Russians out and the Germans down'.[6] The crux of NATO's geopolitical challenge is to be found in this trio. For many allies, NATO's feeble response to the Russian settlement in South Ossetia was disturbing – will the allies look the other way if a member state finds itself in the same situation? Part of the reason for NATO's response was that Germany shields Russia in NATO. Germany is not held down, on the contrary: perhaps the most important result of the current financial crisis is that 'where goes Germany, so goes Europe'. And the United States is no longer 'in'. In its new strategy, announced in January, the United States reduced its troop presence in Europe from what already was the lowest numbers since the creation of NATO. This is noteworthy because NATO, anno 2012, has the capacity for collective defence, if the United States would choose to sit on the fence as many member states chose to do during the Libyan war. American defence expenditure fell from around 6 per cent of GNP in 1989 to 3 per cent in 2000 (Hallams and Schreer, 2012, p. 315). In the coming years the country will likely lose at least some of the technological edge that enabled them to defeat the opponents almost without loss. It will inevitably raise the threshold for intervention. NATO response force, the alliance's 'fire brigade', is in reality an American brigade, stationed in the United States. Superpower geopolitical refocusing means that the helper – and thus help – is further away than in the past.

In terms of military force, NATO has only to a limited degree transformed away from territorial defence capabilities towards out-of-area deployable forces. While it has been customary to blame this state of affairs on European misspending and non-military considerations, there may be cause to look closer. David Blagden and Anand Menon (forthcoming) have found that that the more vulnerable European states are to the threat of territorial aggression – that is, their perceived vulnerability to a military threat from a potentially hostile Russia – the less likely they are to generate out-of-area deployable capability at the expense of territorial defence capabilities. This argument dovetails with US accusations of 'free-riding' – a lack of shared threat perception will necessarily lead to different strategic priorities.

It would seem that a mutually reinforcing dynamic is in play: shifting US geopolitical objectives leads to reduced interest in Europe which impacts European defence priorities, leading to reduced ability and willingness to join NATO to further US geopolitical objectives, leading to further reduced US interest in NATO. This opens a pregnant question: will NATO continue to be a military alliance or is it destined to become a political-military forum and a reservoir for ad hoc 'coalitions of the willing'? We may be seeing a shift from the Article 5 spirit of solidarity towards the more discretionary logic of Article 4 of the North Atlantic Treaty (Daalder and Goldgeier, 2006, pp. 105–114).

Over Libya the alliance fragmented under pressure. This is important to note, because the very purpose of NATO has been to generate the military ability and political will to use for political purpose. This is arguably no longer the case. There is genuine cause for concern. The one factor that has allowed NATO to survive a persistent crisis, the one factor that the alliance cannot do without – American support – is diminished. Whether the creeping American disengagement will amount to forced equality with the EU picking up the slack or whether Europe will fragment – with different countries drawn to different poles in the emerging multipolar world order – remains to be seen. What remains certain is that NATO is no longer the alliance that it used to be.

## Notes

1. Interview NATO HQ, 22 May 2011.
2. Interview with a political adviser to NATO Secretary-General's Policy Planning Unit, 12 September 2011.
3. Lévy's role was extensively covered and discussed in the French press in Spring 2011.
4. It was suggested to the authors that respective French and American spheres of interest in Africa were also discussed during this initial process.
5. Judy Dempsey speaking at the Leangkollen-seminaret of the Norweghian Atlantic Commitee, 7 February 2012.
6. As is so often the case with well-worn quotations, one has (so longing we can find) not been able to find some original source on when and where the precise words were actually first uttered.

# Bibliography

AHA (1974) 'After Twenty-Five Years: NATO as a Research Field', *AHA Newsletter*, Vol. 12 (November 1974), pp. 3–9.

Asmus, R. D. and Nurick, R. C. (1996) *NATO Enlargement and the Baltic States* (Santa Monica, CA: RAND Corporation).

Asmus, R., Kugler, R. and Larrabee, S. (1993) 'Building a New NATO', *Foreign Affairs*, Vol. 72, No. 4, pp. 28–40.

Biden, J. R. (2009) 'Remarks by Vice President Biden at the 45th Munich Conference on Security Policy', 7 February 2009, www.whitehouse.gov (homepage), date accessed 26 May 2012.

Blagden, D. W. and Menon, A. (forthcoming) 'The Secure, the Wary, and the Scared: Explaining Variation in European Military Postures'.

Bozo, F. (2001) *Two Strategies for Europe: de Gaulle, the United States and the Atlantic Alliance* (Lanham: Rowman & Littlefield).

Bozo, F. (2008) *Alliance atlantique: La fin de l'exception française? Document de Travail* (Paris: Fondation pour l'Innovation Politique).

Brzezinski, Z. (2001) 'Enlargement and the Way Ahead', *Financial Times*, 11 June 2001.

Brockpähler, J. (1990) 'The Harmel Philosophy: NATO's Creative Strategy for Peace', *NATO Review*, Vol. 38, No. 6, pp. 17–21.

Cohen, R. (2011) 'Leading from Behind', *International Herald Tribune*, 1 November 2011.

Daalder, I. H. and Goldgeier, J. (2006) 'Global NATO', *Foreign Affairs*, Vol. 85, No. 5, pp. 105–114.

De Gaulle, C. (1987) *Lettres, notes et carnets. Janvier 1964–juin 1966* (Paris: Plon).

Dempsey, J. and Myers, S. L. (2012) 'NATO Showing Strain Over Approach to Libya', *The New York Times*, 14 April 2012.

Deporte, A. W. (1986) *Europe Between the Superpowers: The Enduring Balance*, 2nd ed. (New Haven: Yale University Press).

Drozdiak, W. (1999) 'War Showed US-Allied Inequality', *Washington Post*, 28 June 1999.

Duke, S. (2008) 'The Future of EU-NATO Relations: a Case of Mutual Irrelevance through Competition?', *Journal of European Integration*, Vol. 30, No. 1, pp. 27–43.

*Financial Times* (2011) 'Beginning of the End for NATO?', 10 May 2011.

Fursdon, E. (1980) *The European Defence Community: A History* (London: Macmillan).

Gates, R. (2011) 'The Security and Defense Agenda (Future of NATO)', http://www.defense.gov (homepage), date accessed 26 May 2012.

Hallams, E. and Schreer, B. (2012) 'Towards a "post-American" Alliance? NATO Burden-sharing after Libya', *International Affairs*, Vol. 88, No. 2, pp. 313–327.

Harder H-J. (ed.) (2000) *Von Truman bis Harmel. Die Bundesrepublik Deutschland im Spannungsfeld von NATO und europäischer Integration* (München: R. Oldenbourg).

Heller, F. H. and Gillingham, J. (1992) 'After Forty Years: Reflections on NATO as a Research Field', in F. H. Heller and J. Gillingham (eds) *NATO: The Founding of the Atlantic Alliance and the Integration of Europe* (Basingstoke: Macmillan), pp. 11–27.

IISS (2010) *The Military Balance: 2010* (London: Routledge).
IISS (2011) *The Military Balance: 2011* (London: Routledge).
IISS (2012) *Strategic Survey 2011: The Annual Review of World Affairs* (London: IISS).
Joint Declaration on European Defence (3–4 December 1998) Saint Malo: The Heads of State and Government of France and the United Kingdon.
Kaldor, M. (1981) *The Baroque Arsenal* (New York: Hill and Wang Publishers).
Kanarowski, S. M. (1982) *The German Army and NATO Strategy*. National security affairs monograph series, 82-2 (Fort Lesley J. McNair, Washington, DC: National Defense University Press).
Kugler, R. L. (1990) *Laying the Foundations: The Evolution of NATO in the 1950s* (Santa Monica: RAND).
Lequesne, C. (2008) *La France dans la nouvelle Europe: Assumer le changement d'échelle* (Paris: Presses de Sciences Po).
Lundestad, G. (2003) *The United States and Western Europe – from Empire by Invitation to Transatlantic Drift* (Oxford: Oxford University Press).
Menon, A. (2000) *France, NATO, and the Limits of Independence, 1981–97: The Politics of Ambivalence* (Basingstoke: Macmillan).
NATO (1967) 'The Future Tasks of the Alliance ("The Harmel Report")', *Key Policy Documents*, Brussels, 13–14 December 1967, https://www.nato.int (homepage), date accessed 10 January 2012.
NATO (1991) *The Alliance's New Strategic Concept* (NATO: Brussels).
NATO (1997) *Lessons Learned in Peacekeeping Operations* (NATO: Brussels).
NATO (1999) *The Alliance's Strategic Concept* (NATO: Brussels).
NATO (2002) 'Prague Summit Declaration', http://www.nato.int (homepage), date accessed 26 May 2012.
NATO (2010) *Active Engagement, Modern Defence* (NATO: Brussels).
Nuland, V. (2008) 'American NATO Ambassador Victoria Nuland's Speech to the Press Club and AmCham Paris, France, 22 February 2008', http://www.america.gov (homepage), date accessed 26 May 2012.
Park, W. H. (1990) 'Defense, Deterrence, and the Central Front: Around the Nuclear Threshold', in L. S. Kaplan, S. V. Papacosma, M. R. Rubin and R. V. Young (eds) *NATO after Forty Years* (Wilimington, Del.: Scholarly Resources Inc., 1990), pp. 222–228.
Patrick, S. (2009) 'Out of Area, Out of Business?' *The National Interest*, 25 March 2009, http://nationalinterest.org (homepage), date accessed 12 April, 2012.
Rees, G. W. (2011) *The US-EU Security Relationship: The Tensions between a European and a Global Agenda* (Basingstoke, Basingstoke, Hampshire: Palgrave Macmillan).
Roberts, H. (2011) 'Who Said Gadaffi Had to Go?', *London Review of Books*, 17 November 2011, pp. 8–18.
Sarkozy, N. (2007) 'Fifteenth ambassadors' conference, speech by M. Nicolas Sarkozy, President of the Republic', 27 August 2007, http://www.ambafrance-uk-org (homepage), date accessed 8 September 2007.
Schwartz, D. N. (1983) *NATO's Nuclear Dilemmas* (Washington, DC: Brookings Institution).
Senghaas, D. (1972) *Rüstung und Militarismus* (Frankfurt/Main: Suhrkamp).
Sloan, S. R. (2003) *NATO, the European Union and the Atlantic Community* (New York: Rowman & Letterfield).

Stromseth, J. E. (1988) *The Origins of Flexible Response. NATO's Debate over Strategy in the 1960s* (Oxford: Palgrave Macmillan).

Suhrke, A. (2011) *When More Is Less: The International Project in Afghanistan* (London: Hurst).

Toje, A. (2010) *The European Union as a Small Power: After the Post-Cold War* (New York: Palgrave Macmillan).

Wenger, A. (2006) 'The Politics of Military Planning: The Evolution of NATO's Strategy', in V. Mastny, S. G. Holtsmark and A. Wenger (eds), *War Plans and Alliances in the Cold War: Threat Perceptions in the East and West* (London: Routledge), pp. 165–192.

Wikileaks (2011) '07paris3798, a/s fried discusses Nato, Georgia, Kosovo, cfe', http://wikileaks.org/cable/2007/02/07PARIS777.html, date accessed 16 September 2011.

Winand, P. (1993) *Eisenhower, Kennedy and the United States of Europe* (New York: St. Martin's Press).

Winkler, P. (2007) 'Frühes Ende der NATO Response Force?', *Neue Züricher Zeitung*, 13 October 2007.

# Part II
# Application: Case Studies

# 6
# No More Free-Riding: The Political Economy of Military Power and the Transatlantic Relationship

S. Kay

## Introduction

In June 2011, outgoing Secretary of Defence Robert Gates warned that if a more balanced architecture was not achieved within the transatlantic security relationship, NATO (the North Atlantic Treaty Organization) would face a 'dim' and 'dismal' future. Gates sent a strong warning that the American military commitment to Europe should not be taken for granted. Yet the 'burden-sharing' problem is neither new nor solely the fault of the European NATO members. A central problem has been in Washington, where for decades inequity of military contributions was tolerated if it sustained American primacy in Europe. This status quo no longer reflects American national security or economic priorities – and it has a major impact on how Americans are beginning to think about the utility of military intervention.

This chapter examines determinants of military capabilities within NATO as a tool of American power during the Cold War and post-Cold War periods. Brief overviews of the cases of Kosovo, Afghanistan and Libya demonstrate how incentive structures have led to a steep decline in the utility of NATO's existing value as a tool of military intervention for the United States. The chapter concludes with reflection on how NATO might be made stronger via the 'lead from behind' concept, articulated by the United States in the 2011 Libya war, which can be a baseline for a radical realignment in the political economy of transatlantic security.

## Structural conditions and burden-sharing outcomes

Americans today are weary of military interventions. While the recent Afghanistan and Iraq wars have taken their toll, the reality is that America has been in a near constant tempo of military operations of some sort since the end of the Cold War. Starting in 1989 in Panama – then through Iraq, Somalia, Haiti, Bosnia, Iraq no-fly zones and dual containment of Iraq and Iran, Kosovo, Afghanistan, Iraq again, Afghanistan surges, and a war in Libya – this operational tempo has taken a toll both on the American military and on the American public's willingness to sustain military interventions – especially at a time of fiscal crisis. They do not oppose it if missions are clear and success attainable. Crucially, however, Americans also increasingly expect allies that can afford to, not to sit on sidelines and avoid contributing to military interventions. Thus, while there was some outcry against the way the US 'led from behind' in the Libya war, it is now seen as an acceptable model of military intervention. In terms of NATO, nearly 70 years after the Second World War and over 20 years since the end of the Cold War, these pressures are producing a major shift in thinking towards America's role in NATO. Today, a rebalancing is being sought in the transatlantic relationship – as codified in the new American defence guidance published in January 2012 by the US Department of Defense (Department of Defense, 2012).

Public opinion is a good indicator of deepening fissures and frustrations among the American public and across the Atlantic which is creating deepening fissures in the NATO alliance over military intervention. The Pew Global Attitudes survey, for example, reported on transatlantic perspectives on military intervention in late 2011 (Pew Research Center, 2011). The survey shows that 75 per cent of Americans agree that it is 'sometimes necessary to use military force to maintain order in the world' – while European attitudes decline from Britain's 70 per cent, France's 62 per cent, Spain's 62 per cent and Germany's very low 50 per cent. This is significant as these are the largest and most capable military powers in Europe, and if the United States is to find substantive coalition partners in Europe, it would have to come from these states.

The transatlantic alliance is also split over the need for institutional legitimacy for military intervention – generally seen as attained via a United Nations (UN) mandate. Americans are split on this issue with 45 per cent saying it is necessary and 46 per cent arguing it only complicates military operations. In Germany, 76 per cent want the UN mandate and, respectively, in Spain it is 74 per cent, Britain 67 per cent and France 66 per cent. This is an important structural divide because as a rule most Americans also want to know that allies are with them in military interventions – but doing so also means gaining a UN mandate to sell that politically in Europe. Most crucially, Americans today are turning inward in ways that they have not since the Second World War. In the Pew survey, only 39 per cent of Americans agree that the United States should help other countries while 52 per cent say America should handle its own problems and let others manage as best as they can. There is a serious dichotomy in that America wants allies, but not necessarily feeling it needs a mandate to legitimate military intervention. On the other hand, Europeans are not going to spend more on defence and thus find it harder to influence American thinking and military planning. Worse, while Europeans still want American engagement, continued perceptions of European free-riding on American national security spending and capabilities only further exacerbate the growing isolationist trends in America.

Alliances regularly confront 'collective action problems' – the dilemma of who provides for common goals when multiple states are engaged. The central problem being that if there is one large actor who has a broad interest in provision of an outcome, such as security, then smaller countries can reap that benefit without contributing to costs or risk. A particular problem is 'free-riding' which is a public choice dilemma for collective action. During the Cold War, collective defence, as sought in NATO, became a public good – a benefit which once provided is utilized by all recipients whether they contribute to the costs of service provision or not. If one large nation has a greater demand for a public good than others, it will place a higher valuation on its provision. Ultimately, that state provides a disproportionate level of the collective good, as the smaller members of an alliance supply suboptimal outcomes. A small country or countries which view defence costs as a burden could choose not to contribute to military obligations of an alliance, knowing that the larger countries would defend it if threatened (Olson and Zeckhauser, 1966; Olson, 1965).

There were clear concerns about what would become known as the 'burden-sharing problem' in NATO, dating to the institution's founding. In 1947 and 1948, when European officials began sounding out the United States on a transatlantic security architecture, Washington made it clear that Europe should go first, and then America would see how it might assist. Secretary of State George C. Marshall, for example, told his British counterpart in December 1947 that the United States was sympathetic to European overtures for maintaining a post-war alliance, but that the Europeans should first institutionalize their own defence community. Marshall advised that the Europeans should 'come together for their own protection, see what they could do, and then turn to the United States, and see what we could do to make up the difference between what the situation required and what they were able to do by their own efforts' (Bohlen, 1969, pp. 92–93). Other American officials made clear that their preference was a 'European-first' organization – which John Hickerson of the Department of State's Office of European Affairs described as 'a third force which was not merely the extension of US influence but a real European organization strong enough to say "no" both to the Soviet Union and to the United States, if our actions should seem so to require' (FRUS, 1974, p. 11).

The European allies took first steps towards a transatlantic security architecture with the Brussels Treaty of 1948 which bound the United Kingdom, France and the Benelux countries into a political commitment to common defence. Still this grouping lacked the necessary element of economic power and military capabilities US involvement would eventually bring via NATO. As negotiations for the NATO treaty commenced, key moments reinforced the idea that the European allies should be producers, not only consumers, of security along with the United States. For example, the Vandenberg Resolution (approved in June 1948) endorsed creating a regional security architecture involving the United States and Europe but on the basis of 'continuous and effective self-help and mutual aid'. The goal was clear – to strengthen European integration and capacity as the front-line of containing the Soviet threat. Europeans, acting according to self-help, should take lead responsibility, and should not be dependent on American power. Also in June 1948, in secret negotiations over what would become the NATO treaty, the architect of the policy of Soviet containment, George Kennan, argued that the new alliance should be based on a 'dumbbell' concept in which the European allies would assume primary military responsibility.[1]

In this view, the primary role for the United States would be to provide aid while reducing its military presence on the ground. As the treaty moved to completion, Kennan offered a stark and prescient warning about the structure of what would become NATO: 'Instead of the ability to divest ourselves gradually of the basic responsibility for the security of Western Europe we will get a legal perpetuation of that responsibility. In the long-run, such a legalistic structure must crack up on the rocks of reality; for a divided Europe is not permanently viable, and the political will of the US people is not sufficient to enable us to support Western Europe indefinitely as a military appendage' (FRUS, 1974, pp. 283–289). Kennan added that

> We should have clearly in mind that the need for military alliances and rearmament on the part of the western Europeans is primarily a subjective one, arising in their own minds as a result of their failure to understand correctly their own position. Their best and most hopeful course of action, if they are to save themselves from communist pressures, remains the struggle for economic recovery and for internal political stability.
> (FRUS 1974, p. 43)

Kennan's views on building a European capacity supported by, but not dependent on, the United States were rejected because the situation in Europe ultimately required that a substantial American commitment was necessary to get Europe on its feet and to address operational requirements and politically sensitive issues like West German re-armament. Nonetheless, Kennan's warnings did, over time, come true as NATO got locked into a deep structural disequilibrium of burden-sharing. America gained primacy over European security concerns in the North Atlantic Area while Europe benefited by focusing on the strengthening of the west European economic capacity. The goal of burden-sharing was, nonetheless, officially reinforced in Article 3 of the NATO treaty. It read: 'The Parties, separately and jointly, by means of continuous and effective self-help- and mutual aid, will maintain and develop their individual and collective capacity to resist armed attack.' Yet the core of this new 'transatlantic deal' was a tension – between an American desire for primacy and a dual desire to see the European allies simultaneously create more military capabilities and balanced burden-sharing.

In the early and most dangerous moments of the Cold War, NATO succeeded. The alliance deterred Soviet aggression. NATO achieved this at a time when there was an overwhelming Soviet conventional military advantage – with 12 divisions and under 1,000 combat aircraft to defend NATO against 210 Soviet divisions with over 6,000 aircraft. But NATO succeeded as an institutional shell – with no headquarters, no staff or Secretary General, no integrated military command and a residual post-Second World War American occupation, not combat, presence and not forward deployed. Only the political promise of a collective defence consultation in the event of an attack on a member state gave

NATO its real power of purpose. As US Secretary of State Dean Acheson asserted, NATO was conceived as a 'pre-integration organization, aimed to produce general plans for uncoordinated and separate action in the hope that in the event of trouble a plan and forces to meet it would exist and would be adopted by a sort of spontaneous combustion' (Acheson, 1969, p. 329).

By the mid-1950s, however, events ranging from the Soviet acquisition of nuclear weapons, the fall of China to communism, the war in Korea and the consolidation of Soviet troop presence in the Warsaw Pact led the United States and its allies to make the NATO architecture a massive military structure. It was at this point that the lasting burden-sharing imbalances would lock into the NATO alliance capacity for military operations. America held lead responsibility – eventually deploying well over 300,000 troops in Western Europe. During the remaining years of the Cold War the burden-sharing question would bedevil the NATO alliance. The European allies would frequently argue that they would bear the brunt of any actual war on their territory. The Americans wanted the European allies to contribute more to the common defence effort or off-set costs.

Disproportionate cost-sharing for military contributions to NATO is demonstrated by comparing relative defence expenditures as a percentage of Gross National Product (GNP) among major alliance members (Golden, 1983, pp. 24–54; Duke, 1993, pp. 124–150). For example, in 1953 the United States spent 14.7 per cent of its budget on defence while France and Britain spent around 11 per cent, and in the Federal Republic of Germany the spending was less than 5 per cent. By the 1980s, at the height of new Cold War tensions with the Soviet Union – US defence spending rose to 6.5 per cent while European spending remained flat at about 3 per cent. America's global containment role, which took it well beyond Europe, accounted for some of this disparity. However, as one study shows, the United States, with 48 per cent of the aggregated NATO gross domestic product, provided 66 per cent of the NATO defence costs when excluding the costs of the Vietnam War. For balance to have been attained, the United States would have had to spend $1.1 trillion less on defence between 1961 and 1988 (Sullivan Jr and LeCuyer, 1988, pp. 124–150). Meanwhile, the Europeans did make major contributions – especially West Germany, which would have been the primary place of war in an open conflict with the Soviet Union, maintained a large standing army and hosted large numbers of American troops and equipment, including regular exercising on its territory. Europe was also able to make investments in economic aspects of security which signalled an important alternative to the ideology of communism being imposed on Eastern Europe by the Soviet Union. As the Cold War progressed, the United States set out a pattern of complaining about wanting more European capabilities while also frustrating efforts that would have built European capability independent of NATO. Some areas of European contributions and burden-sharing were handled effectively – such as the rearmament of what would become the Federal Republic of Germany in the mid-1950s. As historian Lawrence S. Kaplan writes: 'Not only was it illogical to omit the German component to NATO, it was also unfair... Why should Americans – and Europeans – labor to defend a West that includes Germany without the Germans participating in the common defense?' (Kaplan, 1984, p. 45). France sought to integrate this German role even further into an all-European Army via the plan of Premier Rene Pleven to create a European Defense Community in 1952. Yet France ended up scuttling the plan in part due to American statements that such an action outside NATO might create an 'agonizing reappraisal' of the American commitment to Europe by Secretary of State John Foster Dulles (FRUS, 1983, pp. 711–712). A British alternative of revitalizing the Brussels Pact to create the Western European Union as a nascent European pillar to NATO became the preferred approach to reassuring the American side of both its influence and efforts to advance burden-sharing.

What amounted to mainly political gestures on cost-sharing in NATO were insufficient in the eyes of key American Members of Congress. In 1966, Senator Mike Mansfield began introducing a series of Senate resolutions, asserting that NATO would not be harmed by substantial reductions in US troop levels in Europe. Senator Mansfield hoped to use legislation to incentivize the Europeans to do more on their own behalf and save the American tax payer money. His first resolution stated:

> The commitment by all Members of the North Atlantic Treaty is based upon the full cooperation of all Treaty partners in contributing materials and men on a fair and equitable basis, but such contributions have not been forthcoming from all of the Members: relations between the two parts of Europe are now characterized by an increasing two-way flow of trade, people, and their peaceful exchange; and the present policy of maintaining large contingents of US forces and their dependents on the US continent also contributes further to the fiscal and monetary problems of the US.
>
> (United States Senate, 1967)

These same pressures grew exponentially in the decade following the end of the Cold War while its members sought to adapt NATO to new missions and military engagements such as peace-enforcement and peace-keeping. In the 1990s, various efforts worked through NATO to create organizational structures so that European forces could be separable, but not separate from those in the NATO architecture. Meanwhile, NATO would admit new members but insist that they be 'contributors to' and not 'consumers of' security. Still, America's dual purpose deepened as it wanted more capabilities from its allies, but it also insisted as a 'red-line' that there be no duplication of efforts. Ironically, the United States would stand back while European allies put considerable troops at risk in the early period of the Bosnia crisis in 1993. This reached a point in June 1995 that threatened to break the premise of a post-Cold War role for NATO in European crisis management. A senior French military official described the situation as being: 'If the Europeans are on one side and the Americans on the other, it would be like an earthquake in the Atlantic alliance' (James, 1995). US Secretary of Defense William Perry was blunt: 'Paralyzed into inaction, NATO seemed to be irrelevant in dealing with the Bosnian crisis... it appeared to me that NATO was in the process of unraveling' (Kay, 1998, p. 80).

America eventually led a NATO intervention in Bosnia but only after tens of thousands of people had gone dead or missing and the fabric of the alliance was tested to the limits. NATO was the key institution to helping consolidate peace in Bosnia and to supplying rapidly some 60,000 troops of which one-third were American. The rest were European – thus demonstrating real burden-sharing capacity (facilitated by many months of integrated military command exercises and planning). But the Bosnia experience also reinforced the reality that NATO only really worked when America led – as the previous two years in Bosnia had been a disaster.

## NATO's collective action problem

The end of the Cold War, combined with the need to reorganize operational capacity after the terrorist attacks of September 2001, left NATO with a core dilemma: ever-increasing goals and missions and decreasing will and military capabilities. It made sense to turn to NATO for post-Cold War security operations on the assumption that its institutional attributes would help it to project stability and consolidate core Euro-Atlantic values. NATO became what Kenneth W. Abbott and Duncan Snidal referenced as being a 'community representative' and as 'managers of enforcement' of agreed principles and norms – both in and even outside the European area (Abbott and Snidal, 1998). NATO was presumed to be important at facilitating security provision because of its 'institutional assets', as described by Celeste Wallander. NATO's rules and procedures would 'enable states to cooperate by providing resources such as information on intentions or compliance; by establishing rules for negotiations, decision-making, and implementation; and by creating incentives to conform to international standards necessary for multilateral action' (Wallander, 2000, p. 709). The dilemma for NATO is that while as an institution it could provide these relative benefits for its members, whether it would actually work or not was entirely dependent on the will and capacity of its members. Its members would increasingly ascribe grandiose designs to NATO, even as far as seeking a 'global NATO' without any realistic level of investments in capabilities relative to new missions. These strategic trends undermined NATO's credibility as a reliable means of resolving contemporary security challenges as relative expectations outpaced actual will and capacity.

The conditions under which NATO's institutional assets might be utilized remained unclear and the assumption that NATO allies would invest resources, especially in a benign threat environment, was deeply flawed. These ambitions ignored the basic reality that states act according to their interests and there are limits to how that coincides with delivery of collective goods. Advocates of such institutional adaptation, like Robert O. Keohane, did qualify their assumptions about the willingness of institutional members to actually export principles and norms as a measure of self-help as NATO was now aspiring to do in Europe. He writes: 'Democracies may act to stop starvation or extreme abuses of human rights... but they are unlikely to sacrifice significant welfare for the sake of democracy – especially when people realize how hard it is to create democracy and how ineffective intervention often is in doing so' (Keohane, 2002).

Consequently, the quest for new missions is explained along the lines of rules, procedures and expectations of efficiency in projecting military power via NATO's standing structures, further reformed for new missions. One such expectation was that a European pillar could grow within NATO but not replace it. Another was that Europeans would do more to consolidate their military capacity and increase spending on capabilities to better contribute to new missions of common interest. None of these expected outcomes became reality – in fact the structural inequities of military operational burden-sharing got worse. Interestingly, though the desire for emphasizing NATO as the main vehicle for defence cooperation was assured when France in April 2009 returned to the integrated NATO military command.

Had policy-makers and scholars focused more on the hard cases of the conditions under which NATO's post-Cold War adaptation would matter to security outcomes – rather than on trying to explain why it persisted, a better understanding of what was likely and unlikely to happen could have altered expectations. NATO, instead, experienced an entirely new 'collective action problem' of security provision which exposed severe limits towards meeting these goals. Joseph Lepgold predicted in 1998 (before the major NATO military excursions in Kosovo, Afghanistan and Libya) that: 'Both humanitarian operations and operations designed to affect the political incentives of the actors in a conflict are likely to be seriously undersupplied, which could pose a difficult international problem in view of the need for such operations' (Lepgold, 1998, p. 79). Lepgold used free-riding incentives to explain why NATO allies might endorse operations but have little compelling interest in providing resources and suffering costs for missions not involving their territorial or political integrity. NATO officials and American leaders could call for all the capabilities they wanted to – but the response was not likely to change unless the incentives were changed. So long as the European allies could reap the benefits of American security provision, they would have little reason to change the status quo.

This new, and accelerating, burden-sharing dilemma was starkly and regularly pointed to with alarm by NATO leaders who argued out that Europe collectively spent about two-thirds on defence as the United States, but got only one-third the capability. Indeed, if Europe would do better to coalesce, they could better advance their interests by gaining more influence in global affairs. Still, by 2011 with air power the weapon of choice in NATO, disparity in terms of airlift was considerable – with the US/NATO-Europe ratio in heavy transport aircraft at 285/16, medium transport aircraft at 516/323, tanker aircraft at 538/72, heavy transport helicopters 632/205 and medium-range helicopters at 2090/633. Fighter and fighter ground-attack aircraft holding were woefully out of balance, with the United States having 3,560 and only the British and French showing serious ability with a combined 544 (IISS, 2011, pp. 38–39).

American total naval tonnage was, at the turn of the century, already three times greater than the five biggest European NATO members (the

United Kingdom, France, Germany, Italy and Spain) for nuclear-fuelled ballistic missile-bearing submarines and surface combatants, and four times greater for operational transport and support ships. The United States had 66 nuclear-fuelled submarines, with the top five European NATO allies having 18. The US navy had 12 catapult-launch aircraft carriers and 29 cruisers; the leading five European nations had one cruiser and one catapult-launch aircraft carrier. Measured against America's 400 frigates, the top 5 European NATO members had about 100. American ships are produced as one single type and displace 2,800 tons; the European frigates are of various makes and a third of them displace only 1,300 tons or less. The United States had 7,600 main battle tanks with the five main allies members having 4,800 main battle tanks (with the United States having basically one basic model and the Europeans having six highly different brands) (Yost, 2000/2001, p. 101). Meanwhile, allied armies, while often large, were mainly heavy conscript forces lacking in the professional skills and mobility needed for long-range deployments and sustainability. NATO meetings, studies, summits and paper commitments to increase capabilities followed – but little changed. Operationally, most allies were either unable or unwilling to contribute to high-intensity and high-risk combat operations and, even if they wanted to, were not in a position to act effectively in a coordinated way.

While the expanded nature of missions would require more capabilities – even robust nations like the United Kingdom were, by 2010, engaging in deep cuts in military spending. Germany, to get its defence budget to a common NATO goal of 2 per cent gross national product would require a near doubling of its defence capability. Even before the 2008 global economic crisis, there was a growing divergence in capabilities for military operations. When NATO intervened in Bosnia-Herzegovina in 1995, it sent 60,000 troops. In 2004, when NATO took over the Afghanistan operation its total forces numbered 7,000 and the alliance struggled to get its members to supply more than six helicopters though thousands were available. As another example, in 2004, NATO authorized the deployment of 300 military instructors into Iraq. This was essential to help the United States rebuild the country and to help the Iraqis gain capacity to manage their own security. Meanwhile, a high value interest for Europe, oil and stability in Iraq, could be gained whether they contributed or not, given America's role. Yet, only 16 of the (then) 26 NATO members agreed to participate in this training mission. The Supreme Allied Commander of Europe, General James Jones, called this trend 'disturbing' and said that once NATO decides on a mission it is essential that 'all allies support it.... When nine, 10, of 11 countries in the alliance will not send forces the burden falls on the other 14' (Burgess, 2004).

To many Americans the image of comfortable and wealthy Europeans – enjoying their wine and long summer vacations and reaping the benefits of America's commitment to Iraq while contributing little themselves – left a searing scar on the transatlantic relationship. With America left to provide 90 per cent of the troops, 90 per cent of the costs and left with 90 per cent of the casualties in a place that likely did as much to service European as it did American interests was a bitter pill indeed.

Hallmark NATO programmes, like the heralded 'NATO Response Force' created in 2002, was one way to economize military operations in crises, allowing for about 21,000 troops to move into an urgent crisis. But even if it would be in place, it would take only one member to block deployment – and it would depend on all allies actually contributing the forces they had promised to deliver. Another policy, NATO enlargement required new members to be 'contributors, not just consumers' of security – but once they entered the alliance, leverage to assure this among new members was lost. In Iraq, many of these 'new Europe' allies did contribute, but mainly to bolster their case for NATO admission, not out of a desire to advance a public good outside of their immediate collective defence concerns. These operational dilemmas became acute and were exacerbated exponentially during NATO's three prominent military interventions since 1999 – a war in Kosovo, a counter-insurgency and counter-terrorism campaign in Afghanistan, and in a regime change operation in Libya.

**The Kosovo 'Success'**

The 1999 Kosovo War, though an important tactical success in getting the Serbs to back down from ethnic cleansing in their breakaway ethnic-Albanian province, exposed deep problems in the conduct of combat operations through NATO – in what became known as its 'war by committee' decision-making process. NATO set out to protect a targeted and weak Albanian minority population against Serb forces. However, decision-making rules in NATO only allowed for three days of initial target selection and limited military operations to air power – only flying, however, at above 15,000 feet. These tactical operational constraints put civilians at risk and strategic bombing options which could have shortened the war were politically inhibited. The allies could not agree to threaten a ground option – which limited the utility of airpower.

In an after-action assessment, the commander of AFSOUTH, Admiral James O. Ellis detailed how NATO had negative effects on Joint Task Force activation, staff composition, facilities, command and control, logistics and execution; a lack of coherent campaign planning; a lack of component staffing; and a race to find suitable targets. Admiral Ellis concluded that the institutional environment of NATO affected 'every aspect of planning and execution'. In particular, NATO's institutional attributes caused 'incremental war' instead of decisive operation; excessive collateral damage concerns created sanctuaries and opportunities for the adversary which were successfully exploited; and the difficulty of NATO's conducting out-of-area operations was not anticipated.[2]

Military communications were undermined by the high-tech capabilities of American fighter jets which were not shared by other NATO members. The United States did not share specifics on hundreds of sorties that involved the use of F-117s, B2s and cruise missiles so as to guarantee sole American control over US-only assets (Lambeth, 2001, p. 185). NATO decision-making only allowed for more of the same and the war went on – with final decisions which helped end the war taken by key allies outside NATO. Success had much more to do with Russian diplomacy, economic pressure and a growing willingness by the United States and Britain to insert ground troops. As US National Security Adviser Sandy Berger said on 2 June 1999, victory would be won 'in or outside NATO – a consensus in NATO is valuable, but it can't prevent us from moving' (Erlanger, 1999).

Reflecting on the war, US Defense Secretary, William Cohen, proclaimed: 'If we were to carry out and act unilaterally, we would have a much more robust aggressive and decapitating type of campaign, the difference here, of course, is that we're acting as an alliance' (PBS Frontline). Two years later when European allies offered to go to war alongside the United States in Afghanistan (and thus share the burden) after the 11 September 2001 terrorist attacks, the United States said, effectively: 'Thanks, but no thanks.' Ironically, while now Europe was offering to help, the United States did not want it because it would have allowed European influence over how America might choose to fight and win its war.

### The Afghanistan war

NATO assumed political and command responsibility for the war in Afghanistan in 2005 – and soon was given a mission – counterinsurgency – for which it had no experience. Many NATO allies put operational 'caveats' on what their forces could do. Only a small handful offered combat troops while many allies only allowed for safe engagements in stable areas. NATO inherited a mission suffering from substantial neglect and which had, by 2006, allowed for a substantial Taliban-based insurgency to grow in southern Afghanistan and even into areas in the North that were previously secure. Even after a new approach designed to emphasize counter-insurgency and a surge of 30,000 US troops was adopted in 2009, core assumptions about the new mission were flawed. There was a mistaken belief in Washington that the European allies would do more and that some of their opposition was tied to their views of the administration of George W. Bush. It was actually their perception of their interests that limited European engagement – along with the reality of knowing that America would now do this war with or without European additional contributions. Thus it would be reasonable for Europeans to think, well, then why not save the money and respect our own public opposition to war in Afghanistan and not engage further?

Additionally, the real threat was outside the area of operations - in Pakistan; there was no legitimate partner in Afghan governance, NATO lacked unity of command; caveats remained; insufficient capacity was deployed for training local army and police forces; and NATO lacked adequate 'civilian surge' mechanisms. As American soldiers there often said privately, 'We think of the European role in NATO's ISAF operations as an acronym for: I Saw Americans Fight' (Kay and Khan, 2007). The essential tools of fighting this kind of war (counterinsurgency and counter-terrorism) remained largely in American hands – especially airlift, strategic intelligence, satellite surveillance, unmanned air vehicles, troop carrying helicopters, attack helicopters and experienced special operation forces (Synovitz, 2005). As one exasperated Canadian commander who led expeditionary forces in Afghanistan said in early 2006, Afghanistan was NATO's 'biggest operational and perhaps strategic challenge in years, if not decades' (Norton-Taylor, 2006). Yet, by 2012, the allies were beginning to depart, with even the very mission of why they were there not defined and with few metrics to demonstrate sustainable success.

### Libya

In March 2011, the NATO allies intervened in Libya. Military and paramilitary forces aligned with the brutal government of Muammar Gaddafi were repressing rebels seeking to oust his government.

It appeared that absent external support, the rebels would be crushed at the city of Benghazi (Walt, 2011). Two key NATO allies, Britain and France, pushed for intervention and the United States agreed to go along – but 'leading from behind'. Within days the same political and operational dilemmas that hampered the military cohesion and effectiveness of Kosovo and Afghanistan operations emerged, but even worse. Germany refused to participate – and even walked out of the North Atlantic Council at a key moment of debate. Only a handful of countries agreed to send, but limited airpower and no ground forces were ever to be contemplated. NATO could not agree on the actual mission – humanitarian assistance or regime change. NATO could not agree on a plan for post-conflict peace-building. NATO could not operate without key staging, logistical and intelligence assets that only the United States could provide. Decisive outcomes, consequently, could not be achieved as intended at the outset and there was no 'Plan B' for failure (Marcus, 2011).

The allies lacked available aircraft and capacity in precision-guided weaponry, and sustainability of air operations. Of the countries that provided strike aircraft were Britain and France, with 20 each, and an additional 6 each from Belgium, Canada, Denmark and Norway. All these additional planes were American-made and updated to be compatible with, and dependent on, American operating systems. Even after taking a reduced role in early April 2011, the United States was still flying about 25 per cent of the air activity over Libya – mainly intelligence, jamming and refuelling operations (De Young and Jaffe, 2011). For its part, Britain likely used as much as 20 per cent of its cruise missile capacity in the first weeks of the war (Harding, 2011).

NATO was eventually successful – with Gaddafi killed by his own people (in October 2011) and the relative costs of $1 billion for the United States and no allied lives lost were impressive. On the other hand, Libya's future was entirely unsettled and it was not clear that this was the end of NATO's responsibility for Libya's future, or what it might mean for intervention elsewhere in the region. Key questions unanswered were (1) would NATO, given these exposed capabilities realities, never agree to do something like this again – putting potential areas of greater interest at risk of not being addressed, or (2) would NATO see this as a painless war leading to a sense that it could rush into interventions, only to find out too late it was ill-prepared and ill-equipped? These were not impertinent concerns given both Syria and Iran looming as rising crises in the foreseeable future.

## Saving NATO from itself

It should come as no surprise that the combined military power of NATO was, eventually, able to defeat fragile and weak states run by dictators like Slobodan Milosevic and Moammar Gaddafi. That outcome was always given in terms of raw power capabilities – and that stark reality of how difficult it was to achieve these goals was, at core, a reflection of the deep fraying of the core foundations of the NATO alliance. After 20 years of the post-Cold War adaptation, the European allies either would not or could not fight a war in Libya on their own – culminating the trends already exposed in Kosovo and Afghanistan. By 2011, it became clear that it was time for Washington to rethink how NATO might fit into a rebalanced transatlantic relationship. Conceptually, the value of NATO is clear as the world has many uncertainties and allies with common values and interests are a high commodity. As the new US Secretary of Defense, Leon Panetta said of the Libya war in October 2011:

> With the fall of the Qaddafi regime, our nations saw an example of why NATO matters and why NATO remains indispensable in confronting the security challenges of today.... We need to use this moment to make the case for the need to invest in this alliance, to ensure it remains relevant to the security challenges of the future.
>
> (Erlanger, 2011)

Secretary Panetta also appeared to see this discussion as requiring meaningful outcomes, not mere proclamations. On 5 November 2011, he told the *New York Times* that American strategic planners were reviewing options for cuts in troops deployed in Europe – either to save money or free up resources for Asia. Such an approach would see the United States working with the NATO allies to help them become capable of acting alone.[3] No one would envisage the United States simply walking away abruptly and risk seeing all the gains made in European security over generations lost. This approach towards a realigned NATO, if done at sufficient scale and with good planning, is both the best and most realistic way to make NATO sustainable for the long-haul.

There is no functional reason why European members of NATO cannot be uniquely responsible for security matters in and around the periphery of the Continent. Europe is at peace, and despite its economic crises remains among the wealthiest and most economically integrated region in the world. Within Europe are two nuclear powers and over 2 million people collectively in uniform. Combined, the European allies spend over $150 billion a year on defence, making them collectively the second biggest military spending power in the world. European countries send a significant percentage of the troops allocated to UN peacekeeping operations – with 8.71 per cent of total troops deployed by the UN compared to 3.49 per cent for North America (which includes a high percentage of Canadian forces). Indeed, by 2005, European countries were deploying on average around 70,000 troops in southeast Europe, Afghanistan, central Asia, Iraq and the Persian Gulf and Africa. When British forces in Iraq (at that time) were counted, the number rose to 90,000 sustained troop deployments (Giegerich and Wallace, 2001, p. 6).

Still, there are imbalances even within Europe. The United Kingdom, France, Germany, Italy and Spain account for 80 per cent of all defence spending in Europe. Some allies that spend low amounts are nonetheless among the more active in terms of advancing NATO goals – such as Norway, Denmark and Poland (for example). Yet, even among those more active members, there are major cuts in defence capabilities ongoing. These trends have, however, importantly led towards more integration of defence capacity in Europe. There is little likelihood of 'defence renationalization' in the European context and the extended economic crises have greatly incentivized deeper military integration. Britain and France have developed joint operational concepts as have France and Germany, and Germany and Poland. Not only has Poland called for more European-first defence planning, but they have also called on more leadership by Germany, not less. In a November 2011 speech in Berlin, Polish Foreign Minister Radislaw Sikorski called Germany Europe's 'indispensible nation' and declared that: 'I demand of Germany that, for your sake and for ours, you help [the euro zone] survive and prosper. You know full well that nobody else can do it. I will probably be the first Polish foreign minister in history to say so, but here it is: I fear German power less than I am beginning to fear German inactivity' (*The Economist*, 2011).

In effect, the core European security dilemmas of the past are managed, and increasingly without the United States. An American realignment out of Europe would provide additional incentives to further this integration and if done gradually and in concert with the allies. Crucially, the primary threats to Europe today are economic, not military – and thus not only are these trends happening – they are the right ones relative to the nature of threats. The three major crisis interventions summarized in this chapter each exposed the dysfunctional military trends in NATO.

By 2011, the alliance had become even to its supporters, like Secretary Gates, a serious crisis. Surely these are not good foundations on which to build future capacity for military intervention. While all who care about the transatlantic relationship, this author included, want to see the most capable and relevant NATO possible, decades of experience demonstrate definitively that the existing approach to burden-sharing has failed. So the burden on those who would resist major change in NATO is high, given the proven fact of existing failure to increase the capacity for military operations. This is especially true for an American audience that has grown sceptical of Europeans seen as free-riding; who have their own serious economic woes; and who see Asia as of paramount importance. Worse, NATO as an organization has a seeming incapacity to make the basic adjustments in terms of strategic planning. The 2010 NATO Strategic Concept ignored the global economic crisis and the inevitability that as America focused inward it would have to find dramatic cost savings in its global military force posture. NATO officials did their best, but they cannot affect the core interests and behaviour of the member states unless key incentives were changed.

Consequently, NATO produced a strategically irrelevant strategic plan. This situation became deeply unsustainable in late 2011 when the Eurozone came to near collapse as debt contagion hit Italy and Spain and threatened to engulf the entire currency. A key element of a new agreement on fiscal integration struck by the Eurozone members in December 2011 was that they would enforce a much more rigid requirement of no more than 3 per cent gross national product allocated to budget deficits. The idea that the European allies would increase spending on defence to make up for the structural imbalances in NATO had by 2011 become absurd – bordering on denial. While the Kosovo, Afghanistan and Libya wars exposed deep operational problems within NATO – at least the Kosovo and Libya conflicts can be described as near term tactical 'successes' – the larger costs are strategic, for the alliance.

A new and dramatic change in the burden-sharing structure in NATO is needed to sustain this important transatlantic security relationship by building on three core elements. This shift became apparent in January 2012 when President Obama announced, along with the Secretary of Defense and the Joint Chiefs of Staff, new guidance for defence planning and budgeting. The US Department of Defense announced new strategic guidance for force structure and budgets. Buried in the short public document is a single sentence, originally in italics for emphasis, which moves debates over European security after the Cold War into a new paradigm: '*In keeping with this evolving strategic landscape, our posture in Europe must also evolve'* (US Department of Defense, 2012, p. 3). If President Barack Obama, Secretary of Defense Leon Panetta and the Joint Chiefs of Staff are faithful to their basic assumptions, then it is fair to anticipate dramatic, and highly appropriate, changes in America's role in NATO.

Three key elements of the new strategy make it hard to escape the logic of a major realignment in NATO. First, there is a clear statement that Asia is the priority for American national security planning – and it would not be possible to do this in a serious way without major cuts and changes in America's force posture in Europe. Second, major troop reductions are coming – including shrinking the size of the US Army from 570,000 to possibly as low as 490,000. These cuts have to come from somewhere and Europe is the obvious place to start. Third, the document states that (also with original italics): '*Whenever possible, we will develop innovative, low-cost, and small-footprint approaches to achieve our security objectives,* relying on exercises, rotational presence, and advisory capabilities.' If there is any place in America's global footprint where this approach is most immediately applicable, it is Europe. Some specific shifts within NATO can help to rebalance this essential relationship and sustain a degree of capacity for military intervention among the allies.

First, *limit America's role in NATO to Article V missions*. This means placing the US position in NATO in strategic reserve – hedging against future great power difficulties or shocks to the international system affecting the United States and Europe. Given that the general threat level is very low and warning times long, this means limiting for the foreseeable future American involvement in NATO to missile defence and officer liaison activity for planning. The United States would not just walk away, but rather set a clear goal of working with the allies over a period of time to help them get to a point where they can sustain a Balkans-style peace support operation and a Libya-style war without the United States. Other 'emerging threats' would be handled either with Europe in a lead role within NATO or by the European Union – that is, cyber attack, sanctions regimes, counter-terrorism and peace operations in or around the European area. Second, this approach means *dramatic reductions in American military personnel stationed in Europe*, likely from tens of thousands down to hundreds – mainly manning missile defence operations and in support roles in planning headquarters. This would likely also mean, third, *relocating EUCOM* from Germany to the United States – as there is no command or operational activity done through EUCOM that cannot be done from an American location (modelled, that is, after the fact that wars in Iraq and Afghanistan have been run from Florida and CENTCOM). Remaining major US bases in Europe would be either closed or handed over to Europeans as part of the new operational priorities for European defence. Pre-deployed equipment and integration planning would remain in the event of any Article 5 threat, or any serious non-collective defence operations that in the end required American engagement (for further discussion, see Kay, 2012).

The arguments against this set of recommendations are understandable, but based on assertions, not facts. Some critics of this approach will point out that 'Europe is not ready' to stand on its own – and that means that America must stay and lead. This is a fallacy which proves itself only by a willingness to stay with the status quo – which America has already concluded will lead to a dim and dismal future for NATO. Another argument is that Europe is needed as a vital platform for American logistics and transport flows. Yet, a massive amount of American troop flows into the Persian Gulf have gone through Shannon Airport in Ireland – not a NATO member (Kay, 2011). In other words, bilateral arrangements for air and naval access can address this need in crises. A third argument is that if America is not there as an anchor in Europe, the Europeans will re-nationalize and instinctively return to nationalism and war. This ignores the entire story of progress in Europe since 1945, and in particular ignores the fact that at the most dangerous moment to NATO, the very early years of the Cold War, there was almost nothing there. Irony was present at the founding – when after the signing ceremony for the NATO treaty in Washington DC in 1949, the music played was from the musical Porgy and Bess and the song selection 'Plenty of Nothin'. It was always the core political commitment to each other that made the transatlantic security relationship unique and powerful. Still, some critics will argue that even now America has to be en mass in Europe, because when it was not what ultimately happened was the Hitler regime and the Second World War. However, this again ignores the deep and dramatic historical transformation that has happened in Europe since the Second World War.

Strong evidence shows that Europe is moving well beyond historically derived assumptions about nationalistic competition. For example, in 2010 the British and French leaders announced that they will integrate their military capabilities bilaterally and at a level of depth that was never achieved in NATO. This includes creating a joint expeditionary force, shared use of aircraft carriers and combined efforts on nuclear weapons safety and effectiveness, including unprecedented information sharing on nuclear programs. The deal went into precise detail on sharing programmes on parts, maintenance and training for crews of military transport aircraft – independent of reliance on America's heavy transport aircraft. They also planned cooperation on drone planes and a range of technologies for nuclear submarines and military satellites (Burns, 2010).

The British and French agreement was announced to last for 50 years and is a model for integration growing from within the European elements of NATO. America can play a lead role in fostering that and align with the common interest articulated by British Prime Minister David Cameron. In announcing the agreement with France, Cameron said that the new arrangement would save 'millions of pounds' in part of the larger dynamic of cutting Britain's defence spending. He added: 'It is about defending our national interest. It is about practical, hard-headed cooperation between two sovereign countries.' Cameron went even further and made the key point that this was not at the exclusion of Germany, and that this was something that should be welcomed in Washington because, he said, 'They'd like us to have the biggest bang for our buck that we possibly can' (Burns, 2010).

## Conclusion

The United States needs to make a dramatic, indeed historical, statement that the status quo will no longer be tolerated in the transatlantic relationship. Meanwhile, the European allies also have to recognize that as the American commitment is reallocated, their level of security capacity must economize and become more effective. Neither are mutually exclusive concepts – America can work closely with Europe to achieve this commonly stated objective over a period of time – perhaps three to five years.

There is no doubt, America does have the political will to conduct military interventions – it has been doing so rather steadily since the end of the Cold War. America, however, also has to make major adjustments and there is a deepening assumption in the United States that America's allies must pick up the leadership in their area. In particular, it would not be possible for the United States to implement its 2012 defence strategy unless there are massive rebalancing efforts made in the transatlantic relationship. Major US troop reductions are coming from Europe – but also creative efforts are available to build a bottom-up capacity for a more deeply integrated European lead role. Clearly stating that it is America's goal to get Europe to a place where it can sustain a Balkans-style peace support operation and a Libya-style war simultaneously will help set a clear goal towards effective rebalancing. If successful, this new approach would broaden and deepen the longevity of the strategic American engagement with Europe by creating a more equitable basis for responsibility sharing. Finally, this approach would fulfil one of the primary and most important founding missions and intents of NATO – that it should exist to get Europe on its feet – not as a permanent appendage of American power. The end result will serve to advance the broadest of common interests and create a more sustainable and viable sharing of responsibility across the Atlantic – thus deepening and lengthening the quality of the transatlantic security relationship in NATO.

## Notes

1. The Dutch representative in these negotiations suggested an alternative 'peach' shape with the Brussels Pact serving as the 'hard kernel in the center and a North Atlantic Pact the somewhat less had mass around it' (FRUS, 1974, p. 171).
2. Admiral James O. Ellis, US Navy, 'A View from the Top'. Briefing slides provided to the author.
3. Shanker and Bumiller (2011), and off-the-record discussions with senior US defence planners in summer and fall 2011.

## Bibliography

Abbott, K. W. and Snidal, D. (1998) 'Why States Act through Formal International Organizations', *Journal of Conflict Resolution*, Vol. 42, No. 1, pp. 3–32.

Acheson, D. (1969) *Present at the Creation: My Years in the State Department* (New York: W.W. Norton & Co.).

Bohlen, C. E. (1969) *Transformation of American Foreign Policy* (New York: W.W. Norton & Co.).

Burgess, L. (2004) 'Jones: Failure of Some NATO Nations to Join Iraq Training Effort is "Disturbing" ', *Stars and Stripes*, 24 November 2004.

Burns, J. F. (2010) 'British Military Expands Links to French Allies', *New York Times*, 2 November 2010.

De Young, K. and Jaffe, G. (2011) 'NATO Runs Short on Some Munitions in Libya', *Washington Post*, 15 April 2011.

Duke, S. (1993) *The Burdensharing Debate: A Reassessment* (New York: St. Martin's Press).

*The Economist* (2011) 'Sikorski: German Inaction Scarier than Germans in Action', 29 November 2011.

Erlanger, S. (1999) 'NATO Was Closer to Ground War in Kosovo than is Widely Realized', *New York Times*, 22 November 1999.

Erlanger, S. (2011) 'Panetta Urges Europe to Spend More on NATO or Risk a Hollowed Out Alliance', *New York Times*, 5 October 2011.

FRUS (1974) 'Memorandum of Conversation, by Director of the Office of European Affairs (Hickerson)', *Foreign Relations of the United States, 1948*, Vol. 3, Western Europe (Washington, DC: US Government Printing Office).
FRUS (1983) *Foreign Relations of the United States, 1952–1954*, Vol. 5, Western Europe (Washington, DC: US Government Printing Office).
Giegerich, B. and Wallace, W. (2001) 'Not Such a Soft Power: The External Deployment of European Forces', *Survival*, Vol. 46, No. 2, pp. 163–182.
Golden, J. R. (1983) *The Dynamics of Change in NATO: A Burden-Sharing Perspective* (New York: Praeger, 1983).
Harding, T. (2011) 'Libya: Navy Running Short of Tomahawk Missiles', *The Telegraph*, 23 March 2011.
IISS (2011) *The Military Balance: 2011* (London: Routledge).
James, B. (1995) 'US and Allies Set on Collision Course over Bosnia Policy', *New York Times*, 1 July 1995.
Kaplan, L. S. (1984) *The United States and NATO: The Formative Years* (Lexington, KY: University of Kentucky Press).
Kay, S. (1998) *NATO and the Future of European Security* (New York: Rowman and Littlefield Publishers, Inc.).
Kay, S. (2011) *Celtic Revival? The Rise, Fall, and Renewal of Global Ireland* (Lanham, MD: Rowman and Littlefield, 2011).
Kay, S. (2012) 'A New Kind of NATO', foreignpolicy.com, 11 January 2012.
Kay, S. and Khan, S. (2007) 'NATO and Counter-insurgency: Strategic Liability or Tactical Asset?', *Contemporary Security Policy*, Vol. 28, No. 1, pp. 163–181.
Keohane, R. O. (2002) *Power and Governance in a Partially Globalized World* (New York: Routledge).
Lambeth, B. S. (2001) *NATO's Air War for Kosovo: A Strategic and Operational Assessment* (Santa Monica, CA: RAND Corporation).
Lepgold, J. (1998) 'NATO's Collective Action Problem', *International Security*, Vol. 13, No. 1, pp. 78–106.
Marcus, J. (2011) 'Libya Stalemate Leaves NATO with No Plan B', *BBC News*, 11 May 2011.
Norton-Taylor, R. (2006) 'NATO Will Be in Afghanistan for Years, Says Military Chief', *The Guardian*, 23 February 2006.
Olson, M. (1965) *The Logic of Collective Action: Public Goods and the Theory of Groups* (Cambridge, MA: Harvard University Press).
Olson, M. and Zeckhauser, R. (1966) 'An Economic Theory of Alliances', *The Review of Economics and Statistics*, Vol. 47, No. 3, pp. 266–279.
PBS Frontline: Interviews, William Cohen, War in Europe, www.pbs/org/frontline (homepage), date accessed 28 May 2012.
Pew Research Center (2011) 'The American-West European Values Gap', 17 November 2011, http://www.pewglobal.org (homepage), date accessed 10 January 2012.
Shanker, T. and Bumiller, E. (2011) 'Weighing Pentagon Cuts, Panetta Faces Deep Pressures', *New York Times*, 6 November 2011.
Sullivan Jr, L. and LeCuyer, J. A. (1988) *Comprehensive Security and Western Prosperity* (Washington, DC: The Atlantic Council of the United States).
Synovitz, R. (2005) 'Afghanistan: France Wants to Keep Separate Commands for ISAF and Combat Forces', *Radio Free Europe/Radio Liberty*, 4 October 2005.

United States Senate (1967) 'United States Troops in Europe: Hearings before the Combined Subcommittee of Foreign Relations and Arms Services Committee on the Subject of United States Troops in Europe', 90th Congress, 1st Session, 26 April, 3 May 1967.

US Department of Defense (2012) *Sustaining U.S. Global Leadership: Priorities for 21st Century Defense* (Washington, DC: US Department of Defense).

Wallander, C. (2000) 'Institutional Assets and Adaptability: NATO after the Cold War', *International Organization*, Vol. 54, No. 4, pp. 705–735.

Walt, S. M. (2011) 'Top 5 Reasons We Keep Fighting All These Wars', *Foreign Policy*, 4 April 2011.

Yost, D. S. (2000/2001) 'The NATO Capabilities Gap and the European Union', *Survival*, Vol. 42, No. 4, pp. 97–128.

# 7
# Between Theory and Practice: Britain and the Use of Force

*P. Porter*

## Introduction: Shocking moments

The makers of British strategy faced a hard world. Britain's resources were stretched to the limit. Its armed forces struggled to wage multiple minor wars against guerrillas on far-away continents. Its recent war had featured atrocities against civilians, spurring an outcry from liberal opinion at home and a renewed debate about the purpose of Britain in the world. At home, a society wanting more social welfare made increasing demands on the coffers of the state. Abroad, a power shift was underway. The rise of new giants challenged the status quo, splitting attention and resources between different military capabilities. How should British forces be configured, given the next war could be against guerrillas on the frontiers of empire, or against the conventional forces of nation-states? It had rarely seemed so difficult to balance depleting resources with far-flung commitments. Projecting power at long range had proved to be exhausting and demoralizing. Some prophets argued that military force – even state power itself – was losing its utility, that the future was enlightened dialogue and trade in a more cosmopolitan and tight-knit global village, or that new technologies and costs would make major wars too expensive, too horrific and too futile to be thinkable. These interlocking problems triggered formal enquiries and the attempt to institutionalize strategy in the shape of a formal advisory forum.

For all the differences in context, this story could apply to the Britain of 1902 and of 2011. It points to familiar dynamics in British military and diplomatic history: the cycle of shock and inquest; the mismatch of ambitious far horizons with limited investment; 'guns and butter' budgetary tensions; the surprises and disappointments felt in the gap between theory and practice; the kind of wars Britain prepared for, against the kinds of war it got; and the relationship between strategy and identity – that the use of force was intertwined with deeper questions about the kind of country Britain wants to be.

The differences between both moments also tell us much about the forces shaping and shoving the use of military power today. In 1902, Britain was still a major world power, even if it was also a 'weary Titan' that 'staggers under the too vast orb of its fate' as Secretary of State for the Colonies Joseph Chamberlain told the Imperial conference of that year (Amery, 1956, p. 421). It was a formal empire, and had climbed to Great Power status through financial and maritime supremacy. In 2011, post-imperial Britain still had expeditionary forces abroad, but in the name of building up sovereign, indigenous governments. It was no longer a 'Great Power' in the traditional sense but acted within the constraining parameters of an American grand strategy. America had emerged in the Second World War both as ally and adversary, underwriting Britain's ability to fight but also dismantling its empire. The notion of an autonomous British grand strategy in 2011 was problematic, precisely because since 1945, Britain had become not exactly a province but a constrained client in an American-dominated world order.

In 1902, the shock flowed from the battlespace of the Anglo-Boer war in South Africa (1899–1902), from the unexpected resilience of insurgents, the revelation that a large share of the enlisted men were too unhealthy to operate and the disturbing ease with which British capital and morale were depleted. In 2011, British land forces were also reeling from shocks. They had recently battled against revolts of unexpected intensity in Iraq and Afghanistan, with hopes of a decisive season of war being repeatedly disappointed. General David Richards, then commanding ISAF forces, had claimed that 2006 would be the 'crunch year' for the Afghan Taliban. Four years later, the UK foreign secretary, David Miliband, predicted that 2010 would be a 'decisive year' (Stewart, 2011). Yet resistance was still fierce, and the host government was still seen as illegitimate. The main shock in 2011, though, had flowed from a day of terror in September – not the terrorist attacks in 2001, but the collapse of Lehmann Brothers in 2008 and the wider financial crisis that engulfed the world economy and led directly to the austerity defence review and cuts of 2010. The UK forces had struggled doggedly amidst public disengagement and resource constraints with the difficult jobs of armed state-building in Afghanistan and Iraq. But the graver threat to their future flowed from a crisis incubated in banks. Indeed, their own efforts were tied to the financial threat.

The financial crisis now tempted politicians to regard expensive personnel and weapons systems as luxuries, even while they saw a peripheral war in Central Asia as a compelling priority. Afghanistan, a wildly difficult war in forbidding geopolitical terrain, remained the 'main effort' with resources devoted to it 'ring fenced'. This had more long-term implications (discussed further in Till, 2011, pp. 131–132). The quantity of the cutbacks has qualitatively reshaped the design, allocation and capacity of the armed forces: the army is withdrawing from Germany and has suffered a 40 per cent cut to heavy armour/artillery; major vessels of the surface fleet have been reduced; there will be no carrier aircraft available until 2020; and the Nimrod maritime surveillance aircraft has been retired. At the same time that it cut the armed forces, the government refused to entertain any suggestion of 'strategic shrinkage', waging war on another nation-state in Libya and thereby assigning reduced military forces to ever-more expansive policies.

The priority given to Afghanistan marks a clear and troubling parallel: a dismissal of the prospect of major war between states (Blagden, 2009; Strachan, 2010). Both in the Edwardian period and now, frontier policing not only predominated but captured the imagination of policy-makers. In the contest between 'most likely' and 'worst case' futures, it was probabilistic logic that won out. Accordingly, British forces were reconfigured to have a higher percentage of ground forces (including the Army, Marines and RAF regiment) than the United States, France, Canada and Australia – and without the maritime dominance that the Edwardians had. Britain's Chancellor of the Exchequer expressed the logic that defence forces are assets whose value and 'relevance' depended more on the probability of their use, and less on their reserve value as a means of insurance: 'We are going to have a bunch of kit that makes us extremely well prepared to fight the Russians on the north German plain. That's not a war we are likely to face' (BBC News, 2010). But as the historical record hints, remote contingencies with deadly consequences happen. The penalties for getting this wrong could be severe. As Malcolm Chalmers observes:

> While the probability of direct state-led threats may be lower than that of complex encounters with non-state actors, however, the potential damage done to UK interests by hostile states could be much greater. If nuclear proliferation occurs in the Middle East, or if an intensified great power rivalry accompanies the rise of Asia,

then current preoccupations with terrorism and organised crime will quickly pale in comparison.

(Chalmers, 2011, p. 56)

Both crises triggered formal enquiries. The Committee of Imperial Defence (CID), formed in the wake of the Anglo-Boer war, wrestled with multiple commitments but knew what it was arguing about, because its debates orbited around geopolitical priorities. It discussed India in 50 out of 80 meetings between 1902 and 1905 (Howard, 1972, p. 16, on the CID, see further Prins, 2011, pp. 3–7). India was at the heart of Britain's standing in the world, and along with the balance of power in Europe, there was a sense of territoriality to how Britain defined its interests. By 2011, there was nothing like India or the continental commitment to discipline the ideas around which Britons debated strategy. As the various iterations of the *National Security Strategy* made clear, geography had been supplanted by 'globalism', the turn to absolutes such as democracy, stability or the promotion of 'governance' that lacked geographical limitation. Britain's political class still wanted their country to be 'special', to punch above its weight and be a 'force for good', but these objectives had been disconnected from more precise geopolitics. Whatever the merits of these values, they de-territorialized British interests to the point of incoherence. It had become harder than ever to fix a point beyond which British security interests were implicated. Where strategy is about the limitation of efforts and the ranking of priorities, these were potentially limitless. Where in 1902 grand strategy was fixed to specific, imperial and continental goals, in 2011 it had become about virtually everything, and therefore nothing.

The parallels and the differences between these two moments in time are a good introduction to four themes that have shaped Britain's use of force: the tension between continental and global commitments; the Anglo-American relationship; the retreat from empire; and one of the most difficult contexts for relating theory to practice, nuclear weapons.

## Continental and global commitments

Probably more than any other issue, the tension between continental and imperial and/or global commitments highlights the gap between theory and practice in British strategic history (Baugh, 1987). For centuries, there was a basic, often uncodified geopolitical logic to British grand strategy – to secure Britain by keeping Europe divided and at acceptable cost. Winston Churchill summarized it:

> For four hundred years the foreign policy of England has been to oppose the strongest, most aggressive, most dominating Power on the Continent, and particularly to prevent the Low Countries from falling into the hands of such a Power.... Faced by Philip II of Spain, against Louis XIV under William III and Marlborough, against Napoleon, against William II of Germany, it would have been easy and must have been very tempting to join with the stronger and share the fruits of his conquest. However, we always took the harder course, joined with the less strong Powers, made a combination among them, and thus defeated and frustrated the Continental military tyrant, whoever he was, whatever nation he led. Thus we preserved the liberties of Europe.
> (Churchill, 1961, pp. 186–187)

Ideally, Britain could do so without devoting so much blood and treasure that it could not sustain its other commitments. It would remain an offshore heavyweight, holding together a vastly dispersed empire while maintaining a healthy balance of power on the continent. To do both, it would need to husband and allocate resources carefully. Ideally, it would limit its liability in European wars by using its navy and money to wear down the enemy through a peripheral strategy. Not vulnerable to a snap invasion like continental lands, Britain could exercise greater discretion, or at least in theory, and keep Europeans divided while it kept itself rich and balanced its resources and commitments. To be sure, Britain's empire beyond did not necessarily detract from its capacity to act on the continent: in the eighteenth century, Britain engaged in power struggles with European rivals such as Spain and France in the Atlantic, the Caribbean and north America, and its lucrative command of foreign trade boosted the wealth it could invest in the Royal Navy. But the later weakening of Britain's economic power might along with the prospect of hostile states dominating the continent, from the *Kaiserreich* to the Soviet Union, mean that the question of how and how much to shape the landscape of Europe would never go away.

A peripheral strategy was the ideal way of war advocated by the theorist and polemicist Basil Liddell Hart (Liddell Hart, 1942). Liddell Hart's theory of an 'indirect approach' was an interpretation of history and a prescriptive blueprint for the future. He framed British strategic culture as a legacy of maritime and commercial power avoiding major continental commitments. Liddell Hart's argument proved a misleadingly selective use of history in the narrow context of European wars, to present the First World War as an aberration. Britain's military past was colonial as well as European, and thus its experience of land war more intensive, and its naval power at times insufficient to support an ally's land operations, than Liddell Hart admitted (Howard, 1983; Strachan, 1994).

It was the initial preference of the British cabinets that hoped to outlast Germany in both world wars through a combination of maritime blockade and support for continental allies. However, as Lord Kitchener noted in 1915, while committing the British Army to the Western Front, 'one makes war, not as one would like to, but as one must'. The question of discretion and compulsion is with us still. Coherent strategy is partly about exercising discretion wisely, but at times it must respond to contingency, to the inconvenient, the unforeseen and the unknown. This is true both of grand strategy, the long-haul, 'big picture' logic of relating means to ends, and of military strategy and operational art further down the ladder. As Michael Howard once argued, 'whatever the doctrine the Armed Forces are working on now, they have got it wrong. What matters is their capacity to get it right quickly when the moment arrives' (Cited and discussed in Ledwidge, 2011, p. 266). Britain's preferred posture of balancing European powers without an extensive commitment was less ideal for the continental allies like France in both world wars. To overcome revisionist states in Europe which had formidable land forces, such as the Grand Armee or the Wehrmacht, a lot of hard fighting would have to be done. At times, even to keep allies willingly fighting would require more than a maritime, financial (or later, airborne) commitment.

On first glance, it may seem that the dialectic between global and continental commitments is a thing of the past. After all, Britain's empire is gone; in 1971 it officially withdrew the bulk of its forces from 'east of Suez' and major military bases in Southeast Asia, and it no longer frames its strategy in terms of balancing power in Europe while holding on to India. But the question of relative commitments and the geopolitical ranking regions persists. This is true in terms of the balance of major power projection capabilities across the 'commons' of sea and air to guard choke points, maritime approaches and worldwide traffic, versus the agenda of 'stabilisation', counter-insurgency and state-building, which calls for a predominantly land-based military contribution to improving the political interior of distant countries. Britain is still dependent on the sea lanes as a bread-and-butter matter of survival. Yet the ability of terrorists, for example, to strike from long range underpins the land forces' claims on scarce resources. And a 'Europe'/'World' problem still exists in different form: as the focus of American geopolitics shifts to the Asia-Pacific, possibly in the long term, and as it draws down much of its military protectorate over Europe, the question of European defence will not go away, or Britain's role within it.

## The Anglo-American relationship

Observers of Britain's contemporary use of force often contrast it with continental European and American models. As Timothy Garton Ash argued, Britain stood somewhere in the middle, astutely finding a way between 'cheese eating surrender monkeys' and 'fire eating war junkies'. 'We think you sometimes have to fight to defend your way of life, but that you should fight clever, keeping a cool head, a strong grasp on reality and a sense of proportion' (Ash, 2006). But here, theory is distant from practice. The momentum for the recent coalition war against Colonel Gadaffi's Libya came from London and Paris, not Washington. And the recent stereotype of warlike assertive Americans from Mars being contrasted with less powerful but wiser and more restrained Britons is misleading as a broader picture of the relationship and record of both. The *Human Security Report* of 2005 found that Britain participated in more international conflicts since 1946, followed by France and then the United States (Human Security Centre, 2005, p. 26). This is no indicator of conflict intensity, but it does point to a propensity to use military force as a tool of diplomacy, as a means of preserving colonies, as a weapon of humanitarian intervention and to express British identity as a defender of world order (Freedman, 2006). For a long period after 1945, Britons charged that Americans were not supportively bellicose *enough* when it came to the UK's conflicts – at Suez, in the Falklands, or in Bosnia.

It is hard to understand Britain's use of force, and the shape and posture of its armed forces, without considering one of the most momentous strategic shifts of the twentieth century: the eclipse of British power by America, and Washington's dismantling of the British Empire. Britain's historical capacity to project power was symbiotic with its relative financial and trading clout (Kennedy, 1976, pp. 316ff.).

The Battle of Britain in the summer of 1940 was a critical event in persuading a reluctant United States that Britain could hold on if it got proper support, and that it was worth backing. But in other ways this proved to be a fatal step. As America went from arsenal of democracy, provider and armourer and ocean guardian, to formal belligerent, it proved to be both ally and adversary. With the leverage of Lend–Lease, America exacted strict terms on Britain's export trade, its dollar and gold reserves, indeed the very sinews of its global strength. As it became the senior partner in the relationship and acquired ever more bargaining power, Washington deliberately broke up the Stirling trading bloc created at Ottowa in 1932, and the imperial preference system, and ensured that British industries and traders 'would not recover the markets they had been forced to surrender to their American rivals after 1939.' Its firms moved in on the oil of the Middle East, rubber and tin of Malaya, and the markets of India. At the same time, it willingly underwrote Britain's existence and fought alongside it in the Atlantic, North Africa, the Mediterranean and Europe. America's war aim was not only the defeat of the Axis, but the end of European colonial empires, and to ensure that Europe could no longer be boss continent. The Bretton Woods conference of 1944 confirmed the economic transformation of the world, supplanting the existing, protectionist systems with free trade, the reign of the dollar as the world's reserve currency and the 'Open Door' on America's terms.

These power shifts translated into a strategic imbalance that was keenly felt in joint military planning. Still in 1941–1942, the advantage was temporarily with Britain, which had many more trained troops and a seasoned staff that was skilled at getting its own way. At the ARCADIA conference in Washington (December 1941–January 1942), the better prepared Britons prevailed, getting their desired strategy of avoiding a premature direct assault on Nazi Europe, instead clearing North Africa and opening the Mediterranean in 1942 and 1943 as well as increasing air bombardment. But by late 1943, the balance was shifting and America could impose its will. For example, the Americans made Churchill agree to an invasion of southern France in the aptly named 'Operation Dragoon' in August 1944. The year 1944 was probably the hinge date in the power shift. In the year that the post-war order was planned at the Bretton Woods,

> American power was so great, and British power so depleted, that the United States could and often did force its will upon its erstwhile ally. Indeed, so desperate was the British need for US post-war financial support as to leave London a supplicant.
>
> (Stoler, 2005, pp. 227–228)

To be economically viable even after its empire was gradually liquidated, Britain the world's greatest debtor became dependent on America, the world's greatest creditor. The Second World War became a revered moment in British folk memory despite, or perhaps *because*, it cost Britain its place as an independent Great Power. If surviving and defeating the Axis meant the loss of its empire, this was all the more reason to commemorate the defeat of Hitler, Mussolini and Tojo as the 'finest hour' of a fading colossus.

The coming of the *Pax Americana*, especially through the Second World War, has constrained and complicated Britain's capacity for independent strategy ever since. This was realized sharply in some of Britain's post-war conflicts. During the Suez crisis in November 1956, with British gold and dollar reserves falling, the government turned to International Monetary Fund for emergency loans, but under US pressure, the request was rejected. The 1982 Falklands war again underlined British reliance on American permission and support (in the shape of the Ascension Island base or Sidewinder missiles) in order to operate. Though it has sought to influence and even tutor the new superpower, Britain became a subordinate state of an American grand strategy. In exchange for support and even loyalty when the shooting starts, in exchange for the blood price, British governments hoped to secure unparalleled sway in Washington. Whether this has secured an adequate geopolitical return is another question, and Britain's role as the main coalition partner in Afghanistan and Iraq placed fresh doubts over the transactional aspects of the 'special relationship' (Porter, 2010).

Below the grand strategic level, America is a central reference point around which Britain designs its own forces. Britain plans around US-led coalitions. It builds its forces to be interoperable with America's. Ever since the 1958 US–UK Mutual Defence Agreement, its nuclear deterrent has been dependent on America for design, procurement, infrastructure and satellite guidance. And in terms of enunciating a 'grand strategy', Britain borrows the architecture and style of formal institutionalized strategising from Washington. Traditionally, British strategy (as a logic of how to relate the country's power to its commitments) was not codified or embodied in formal committees or manifestos. So the gulf between theory and practice surfaces in an ironic way. Attempting to articulate a distinctive British world role, the makers of British strategy seek inspiration from American forms and under an American shadow, seeking largely institutional solutions to strategic problems.

## Retreat from empire

Britain's use of force in the post-1945 world has been narrated through one of the most enduring of its imperial myths: that faced with the contraction of its power, the empire graceful retreated. Its campaigns in Kenya, Malaya and Northern Ireland reflected this, as they were marked by restraint, minimal violence and even cultural sensitivity. As night was falling on empire, the constabulary forces at the frontier embodied an enlightened conception about the limits of force and the importance of consent as well as coercion.

This myth was propagated by Britons, such as the 'Sandhurst historians' of the 1980s. It was also propagated by Anglophile American officer-intellectuals such as John Nagl (Nagl, 2005). Especially after America became entangled in Iraq in 2003, Americans turned to the British Empire as a model for their own self-criticism. Major-General Robert Scales, testifying before Congress in 2004, argued that Americans should look to Charles Gordon, T. E. Lawrence and modern Basra as models for inspiration. Britain's success in Basra, he argued, owed much 'to the self-assurance and comfort with foreign culture derived from centuries of practicing the art of soldier diplomacy and liaison' (Scales, 2004a, 2004b). America's acclaimed new Counterinsurgency Field Manual 3–24 was partly a British creation, the result of collaboration with British advisors and incorporating elements of historic British (and French) doctrine. It builds on British theorists and British imperial history.[1] Influential journalist George Packer fuelled the idea that America should take its cues from the benchmark of British history. Packer invoked as a model for America the classic doctrine forged in Malaya that stressed minimum force, enlightened nation-building and the primacy of politics (Packer, 2006). The myth of British Empire, and the belief that it endowed contemporary British statecraft with a profound grasp of exotic peoples, was also an American creation. The state of Basra became the yardstick of criticism and the British legacy became a weapon of American debate. As Thomas Donnelly notes, British military history has 'long been a stick with which American officers are prone to thrash one another' (Donnelly, 2009, p. 4).

In the Anglo-American military dialogue, the seminal moment was UK Brigadier Nigel Aylwin-Foster's scathing article in *Military Review*, charging the US Army with multiple failures in Iraq, including moral righteousness, cultural insensitivity bordering on racism, an addiction to firepower, and inflammatory behaviour that undermined its own cause (Aylwin-Foster, 2005). Americans were not so much Romans as

Spartans, handicapped by their strategic culture of fixing and annihilating the enemy, a narrow ethos of war fighting. Foster's complaints of the US Army's errors in Iraq were not substantively wrong. The American Army between 2003 and 2005 was biased heavily towards major combat operations, and it had marginalized thinking about counter-insurgency after Vietnam. Though he underestimated the extent to which the US military is capable of self-reform. Indeed, US Army Chief of Staff General Peter Schoomaker distributed the article to his generals and Foster was invited to help write the new US counter-insurgency doctrine. Would such a morally righteous Army have been so receptive?

The problem was that Foster's critique was premised upon a falsely nostalgic reading of British imperial history. As his footnotes made clear, he built his case partly on American officer John Nagl's study of counter-insurgency that contrasted British learning and eventual success in Malaya against American failure in Vietnam. In other words, not only was America getting it wrong. It was failing to live up to an historic British standard that established eternal 'lessons' and wisdom about small wars and handling the natives. Foster's article and Nagl's book reflected a feedback loop within Anglo-American dialogue that turned to a mythic version of British imperial history to find answers to the growing crisis in Iraq. The growing appetite within the American forces to reform themselves encouraged a British strand of imperial nostalgia.

The mythologized memory of British small wars is ahistorical (Jackson, 2006; Bennett, 2007; Strachan, 2007, p. 10; Dixon, 2009). In reality, campaigns like Malaya (and Kenya) were far more brutal than their admirers allow. In Malaya, there were detentions without trial, executions, jungle bombing campaigns and forcible resettlement of the population into concentration camps. Divide-and-rule and exemplary punishment marked these campaigns more than 'hearts and minds'. Against the Kikuyu ('Mau-Mau') in Kenya, Britain employed interrogation under torture, hangings, indiscriminate bombings of forest, and white settlers or local proxies applied sadistic violence, dismemberment and killings in custody (Anderson, 2005). Britain's techniques of imperial rule against revolt were both to impose the 'smack of government' itself and to allow or channel brutality through proxies. If these campaigns succeeded, it was not because they were liberal.

Thus the historical debate about Britain's use of force in 'small wars' is not merely driven by empirical disagreements over the historical record. It restages the question of British identity now that its power has been eclipsed by America's. And that very question is also at the heart of debate over Britain's most deadly weapon.

## The bomb

The British government decided in January 1947 to begin a nuclear programme and first successfully tested the bomb in October 1952. There was a clear, visible external motivation for going nuclear, the presence of a superpower with a hostile ideology that might overrun continental Europe and/or develop its own nuclear arsenal. The hardening of the Cold War in this period retired the earlier hopes of Prime Minister Clement Attlee and some of his ministers that nuclear power might come under international control and be shared openly with the Soviet Union. Yet once this novel weapon became part of a global antagonism and competition, the focal point of the Trident programme became the capital city of the Soviet Union. Trident was chosen in 1979 along the lines of the 'Moscow Criterion', a requirement that Britain's nuclear weapons' system be capable of destroying the Soviet Union's capital, despite its anti-missile defences.

Yet the history of the British bomb is tied inextricably not only to questions of hard security in the face of a heavily armed totalitarian Soviet Union but of broader strategic calculations and identity. Britain pursued a nuclear deterrent also in the context of its relationship with the United States. By acquiring its own independent deterrent, as the Defence Secretary Denis Healey argued, Britain would add a centre of decision that would both increase the deterrent effect on Moscow, while also gaining influence over the US nuclear strategy. In practice, this shaped how Britain designed its programme. With both Polaris and its successor Trident, Britain did not produce its delivery systems indigenously but acquired them from America. Here, influence and independence could collide rather than complement one another. Britain compromised its independence in order to influence Washington.

Precisely because British nuclear weapons are tied to broader difficult questions beyond the Soviet threat, the nuclear system survived the end of the Cold War yet receives very little public discussion. The 2010 *Strategic Defence and Security Review* was the most far-reaching defence review in a generation. Yet, remarkably, there was almost no public debate about Britain's nuclear weapons (Norton-Taylor and Hopkins, 2011). In the War on Terror, the cause of disarmament and counterproliferation became central to the justification for war in Iraq and confrontation and sanctions against Iran. The international programme of killing and capturing suspected terrorists is justified partly on the basis of a feared confluence of radical ideology and weapons of mass destruction. Yet the debate about the ultimate violent technology is largely discrete, linked mainly to the fear of rogue states and terrorist networks. A near-silence falls over the issue in other contexts, such as the 2011 war in Libya, where the British debate hardly discussed the international consequences of attacking and overthrowing a regime that had peacefully disarmed its WMD capabilities. Amongst the political class, whether counter-proliferation would benefit from British unilateral disarmament is off the table.

If Britain is to find a conception of the utility and role of force in its national security strategy, what is the basis for having capabilities that its leaders mostly decline to talk about, and which they would hesitate to use? Moreover, why should Britain claim the privilege of possessing nukes? If they are an effective deterrent, this would be a basis for further proliferation, as other states might also desire that insurance. And it is harder for British governments to use the deterrence justification, given their often-declared view of the post-Cold War security environment as too uncertain and too full of irrational actors for passive doctrines such as deterrence to apply. Likewise, if they are a 'Gaullist' symbol of prestige, this could also be a basis for proliferation, as attractive to a regional heavyweight like Tehran as to Britain. With the disappearance of the Soviet Union, the major superpower adversary that was invoked to justify nuclear weapons, the question became murkier. It is now linked not to one overarching contest against a known adversary, but to a difficult set of issues about status and security. This itself might help explain why the political class is reluctant to touch it. It was not ever thus. The nuclear deterrent was debated openly and continuously in British politics decades before. But the Labour Party suffered one of its worst historical defeats in the 1983 election where its platform included a commitment to unilateral disarmament. This precedent did not embolden parliamentarians to doubt the nuclear deterrent publicly. To be sure, Liberal Democrat Nick Clegg openly opposed replacing Trident in the 2010 campaign, but this commitment is likely to be submerged by the weight of the coalition government he subsequently entered.

The evolving views of former Prime Minister Tony Blair offer some clues both about why Britain maintains its nuclear deterrent and why the issue has been steadily marginalized. As a young MP, Blair had been a member of the Campaign for Nuclear Disarmament. Yet it was Blair as premier whose government decided on a 'like for like' replacement of Trident with another submarine launched ballistic missile system. Looking back in his memoirs, he regarded the Trident programme with ambivalence. Ultimately, for him the clinching arguments were prestige, uncertainty, the power of a political taboo:

> We agreed the renewal of the independent nuclear deterrent. You might think I would have been certain of that decision, but I hesitated over it. I could see clearly the force of the commonsense and practical arguments against Trident, yet in the final analysis I thought giving it up too big a downgrading of our status as a nation, and in an uncertain world, too big a risk for our defence. I did not think this was a 'tough on defence' versus 'weak or pacifist' issue at all.
>
> On simple, pragmatic grounds, there was a case either way. The expense is huge, and the utility in a post-cold war world is less in terms of deterrence, and non-existent in terms of military use. Spend the money on more helicopters, aircraft and anti-terror equipment? Not a daft notion.
>
> In the situations in which British forces would be likely to be called upon to fight, it was pretty clear what mattered most. It is true that it is frankly inconceivable we would use our nuclear deterrent alone, without the US – and let us hope a situation in which the US is even threatening use never arises – but it's a big step to put that beyond your capacity as a country.
>
> So, after some genuine consideration and reconsideration, I opted to renew it. But the contrary decision would have not have been stupid. I had a perfectly good and sensible discussion about it with Gordon [Brown], who was similarly torn. In the end, we both agreed, as I said to him: Imagine standing up in the House of Commons and saying I've decided to scrap it. We're not going to say that, are we? In this instance, caution, costly as it was, won the day.
>
> (Blair, 2010, pp. 635–636)

Blair's mixture of views reflects an ongoing theme in its nuclear strategic history, the interplay of questions of identity and security (Croft, 2000, p. 69). Trident had become an institution, indeed part of the status quo itself, and thus was politically dangerous to question. Moreover, like Blair, Trident's defenders often do not rely purely on direct security-based arguments to make their case. Chairman of the Defence Select Committee, James Arbuthnot, argued: 'It's an awful argument to put that it gives us a place on the Security Council of the United Nations but I think it actually is true. When South Africa unilaterally disarmed its nuclear weapons I think it did lose influence' (BBC News, 2009). In theory, Britain was committed to a world of multilateral disarmament and ultimately a nuclear-free world. In practice, it made arguments that recognized the very appeal that nukes might have for other states. There is also a striking paradox: where once the nuclear deterrent was defended in the context of a single, identified adversary, it is now the lack of one and the ambiguity of the contemporary security that is used to justify retaining it. Rather than politically undermining the nuclear deterrent, the replacement of the Cold War with an era of 'uncertainty' leans decision-makers against disarmament. As the former Secretary of Defence Liam Fox explained to the House of Commons; 'We simply do not know how the international environment will change in the next few years, let alone the next 50 years; and as this House concluded in 2007 when it voted on whether the UK should start a programme to renew the deterrent, the time is simply not right to do away with it unilaterally' (Fox, 2011). A conclusive reckoning with the issue of nuclear weapons would require a reckoning with British identity itself. In the absence of confident answers, the question would be postponed.

## The future: A will and a way?

How confident can we be that Britain will continue to have the political will and economic/military capacity to use force globally? Until Operation Unified Protector in Libya in 2011, a war that London spearheaded, it would have been reasonable to predict that the wars in Afghanistan and Iraq, combined with the new age of scarcity and austerity budget cuts, had disenthralled policy-makers and the public against the expeditionary use of force, at least in the medium term. Previous governments believed viscerally that war could work, and the Falklands in 1982, the Gulf War of 1991 and even Serbia in 1999 supported their belief.

But the Libyan war demonstrates that there is an enduring tendency to see force as a potentially effective means of shaping the external environment. In addition, it is attractive as a symbol of 'stateness', as an instrument that reflects and reinforces Britain's identity as a serious power at the top table, and justify its status both as a permanent member of the UN Security Council and as a partner in a transatlantic special relationship. As Michael Clarke argues, retaining military forces and the ability to 'pack a punch' is a bid to remain a global player. The Prime Minister yesterday even used the old phrase of a previous Conservative government that Britain would still 'punch above its weight'. It will do this by recognizing the general alignment of interests it feels with the

United States and aiming to keep its Armed Forces above a threshold that the United States takes seriously (Clark, 2010).

This will to use force has survived disappointing experiences in recent wars, an increasing rate of defence inflation, and a lack of public support for the kind of funding that an expansive use of force would require. If there is a persistent will to use force even amidst straitened circumstances, recent experience suggests some of the possible implications for the future. To shoulder the burdens placed on their shrunken armed forces, spread costs and maintain legitimacy, British governments may continue to turn to alliances and coalitions. The initiative of London and Paris over Libya, and the recent Anglo-French defence cooperation treaties, both point to this dynamic. Secondly, a will to use force may be coupled with a reluctance to risk the liability of troops on the ground en masse. In that respect, British strategy has returned to central dilemmas of the 1990s: a pressure for intervention on the cheap, using hi-tech standoff weapons to apply force while limiting commitment (Biddle, 2011). In terms of public opinion and engagement, while there is a body of sophisticated work that challenges the simplistic notion that Westerners are uniformly 'casualty averse', the political class continues to believe that it is, thus generating a pressure to minimize losses (Gelpi, Feaver and Reifler, 2009). And if the strain of exercising force of any duration is growing, this may encourage continued emphasis on prevention and upstream engagement.

And more deeply, Britain's use of force may reflect the strange mixture of liberalism with the evolution of a 'market state' (Bobbit, 2008, pp. 11–12). In other words, Britain defines its security interests through an expansive liberalism, securing itself by exporting liberal institutions and values and investing its struggles with heightened meaning, seeing them as politically Good, while simultaneously seeking to keep that struggle as private and remote from their citizens. The pressure on defence budgets will be downward, so the burdens will fall mostly on the small fraction of the population who make up the professional armed forces. Thus Britain will likely face a long-term 'gap' between an expansive foreign policy where 'strategic shrinkage' is ruled out, and dwindling resources and limited public appetite for the sacrifices of war. As British power contracts, its commitments widen. The dialectic of ends, ways and means may be ruptured.

Only time can show whether the expansion of 'means' – multilateral burden-sharing, an avoidance of ground commitments or upstream engagement – will be sufficient to close what could be called the 'Lippmann gap' between Britain's resources and its goals. The world around Britain may not cooperate conveniently with the government's preferences. A resumption of great-power rivalries, a resilient enemy that unlike Milosevic or Qaddafi refuses to fold under bombing from afar, or a worsening of the wider financial crisis could all mean that the fragile link of ends, ways and means is snapped, so that 'ends' must be revised as well as means. One major possible strategic shift, the burden shift of the United States as it draws down its presence from Britain's neighbourhood, may make Western Europe, once again, its prime outer defence. The future environment may make it prudent to revisit the question of whether Britain can afford to remain a 'global player' with the power projection capabilities to support it, or whether it will have to rethink its role in the world.

## Conclusion

Over the arc of history, the use of force by Britain has been a story of a continuous shift between theory and practice, doctrine and raw experience. Against preferences and expectations, the continental commitment could become so intensive that it was hard to limit its liability, making it difficult to make war on the continent and still sustain global empire and reach. Likewise, the alignment with the United States to survive and preserve an empire in the face of fascist tyranny had the mixed result of ensuring the endurance of the British state but also the unravelling of empire. The grand bargain of transatlantic solidarity often did not yield the return of influence over Washington, as Britain became more of a satellite than a tutor to the new superpower. After 1945, the story of a graceful post-war retreat from empire through enlightened, restrained soldier-policing flew in the face of practice, the unsentimental harshness of population transfers, concentration camps and coercive violence. And while successive governments have declared themselves supportive of worldwide disarmament in theory, in practice they support maintaining a deterrent for precisely the status and security reasons that they hope will not also motivate other states to go nuclear.

This overall pattern points to the need for humility. That humility would entail a bedrock recognition that we cannot know the future. The shocks of conflict and ironies of strategic history make it wise to accumulate a reserve of surplus power, to develop strategies of 'least regret' (Gray, 2008), to focus on vital interests and the unlikely but deadly ways they could be threatened, instead of the parlour game of betting and acting on future probabilities, and the hubris of routinely using force in world politics while expecting no blowback or unintended consequences. In the spirit of Reinhold Niebuhr, it would be better to recognize the inherently tragic nature of world politics and the limitations on our knowledge and understanding. It would be more prudent to conceive the military not as a surgical tool to be simultaneously shrunken and endlessly used, but as a means of insurance. What kind of country is it insuring? That is the unanswered question at the heart of strategy.

## Note

1. US Army/Marine Corps, FM 3-24 *Counterinsurgency Field Manual* (Chicago, 2006), David H. Petraeus and James F. Amos. The Manual refers to the pantheon of British 'small wars' thinkers, including Charles Calwell, Frank Kitson and T. E. Lawrence, as well as the campaign in Malaya.

## Bibliography

Amery, J. (1956) *The Life of Joseph Chamberlain*, Vol. IV (London: Palgrave Macmillan).
Anderson, D. (2005) *Histories of the Hanged: The Dirty War in Kenya and the End of Empire* (New York: Orion).
Ash, T. G. (2006) 'Between Cheese Eating Surrender Monkeys and Fire-Eating War Junkies', *The Guardian*, 6 July 2006.
Aylwin-Foster, N. R. F. (2005) 'Changing the Army for Counter-insurgency Operations', *Military Review*, Vol. 85, No. 6, pp. 2–15.
Baugh, D. A. (1987) 'British Strategy During the First World War in the Context of Four Centuries: Blue-Water Versus Continental Commitment', in D. M. Masterson (ed.) *Naval History: The Sixth Symposium of the US Naval Academy* (Wilmington: Scholarly Resources), pp. 87–88.
BBC News (2009) 'Generals in Scrap Trident Call', 16 January 2009, http://www.bbc.co.uk (Homepage), date accessed 28 May 2012.
BBC News (2010) 'Defence Budget Chaotic, Says Chancellor George Osborne', 2 October 2010, http://www.bbc.co.uk (Homepage), date accessed 28 May 2012.
Bennett, H. (2007) 'The Other Side of the COIN: Minimum and Exemplary Force in British Army Counterinsurgency in Kenya', *Small Wars and Insurgencies*, Vol. 18, No. 4, pp. 638–664.
Biddle, S. (2011) 'The Libyan Dilemma: The Limits of Air Power', *Washington Post*, 25 March 2011.
Blagden, D. (2009) 'Strategic Thinking for an Age of Austerity', *RUSI Journal*, Vol. 154, No. 6, pp. 60–66.
Blair, T. (2010) *A Journey* (London: Hutchinson).
Bobbit, P. (2008) *Terror and Consent: The Wars for the Twenty-First Century* (London: Penguin)
Chalmers, M. (2011) 'The Lean Years: Defence Consequences of the Fiscal Crisis', in M. Codner and M. Clarke (eds) *A Question of Security: The British Defence Review in an Age of Austerity* (London: RUSI), pp. 33–78.

Churchill, W. S. (1961) *The Gathering Storm* (New York: Bantam).
Clark, M. (2010) 'Defence Review: Can Britain Still Pack a Punch?', *Telegraph*, 20 October 2010.
Croft, S. (2000) 'Britain's Nuclear Weapons Discourse', in Stuart Croft (ed.) *Britain and Defence 1945–2000: A Policy Re-evaluation* (Harlow: Pearson Education Limited), pp. 74–79.
Dixon, P. (2009) 'Hearts and Minds: British Counter-Insurgency from Malaya to Iraq', *Journal of Strategic Studies*, Vol. 32, No. 3, pp. 353–381.
Donnelly, T. (2009) 'The Cousins' Counter-Insurgency Wars', *RUSI Journal*, Vol. 154, No. 3, pp. 4–9.
Freedman, L. (2006) 'The Special Relationship – Then and Now', *Foreign Affairs*, Vol. 85, No. 3, pp. 61–73.
Fox, L. (2011) 'Statement on Nuclear Deterrent', 18 May 2011, Hansard Column 351, http://www.publications.parliament.uk/pa/cm201011/cmhansrd/cm110518/debtext/110518-0001.htm#11051871000003
Gelpi, C., Feaver, P. D. and Reifler, J. (2009) *Paying the Human Costs of War: Casualties in Military Conflicts* (Princeton: Princeton University Press).
Gray, C. (2008) 'Britain's National Security: Compulsion and Discretion', *RUSI Journal*, Vol. 153, No. 6, pp. 12–18.
Howard, M. (1972) *The Continental Commitment: The Dilemma of British Defence Policy in the Era of the Two World Wars* (London: Maurice Temple Smith).
Howard, M. (1983) *The Causes of Wars and Other Essays* (Cambridge, Mass: Harvard university Press).
Human Security Centre (2005) *Human Security Report 2005: War and Peace in the 21st Century* (New York: Oxford University Press).
Jackson, A. (2006) 'British Counter-insurgency in History: A Useful Precedent?', *The British Army Review*, No. 139, pp. 12–22.
Kennedy, P. (1976) *The Rise and Fall of British Naval Mastery* (London: Penguin).
Ledwidge, F. (2011) *Losing Small Wars: British Military Failure in Iraq and Afghanistan* (London: Yale University Press).
Liddell Hart, B. (1942) *The British Way in Warfare* (Harmondsworth, Middlesex: Faber & Faber).
Nagl, J. (2005) *Learning to Eat Soup with a Knife: Counterinsurgency Lessons from Malaya and Vietnam* (Chicago: University of Chicago).
Norton-Taylor, R. and Hopkins, N. (2011) 'UK Weapons Remain Taboo as Iran Faces Increasing Scrutiny', *The Guardian*, 8 November 2011.
Packer, G. (2006) 'The Lesson of Tal Afar: Is It Too Late for the Administration to Correct Its Course in Iraq?', *New Yorker*, 10 April 2006.
Porter, P. (2010) 'Last Charge of the Knights: Iraq, Afghanistan and the Special Relationship', *International Affairs*, Vol. 86, No. 2, pp. 355–375.
Prins, G. (2011) *The British Way of Strategy Making: Vital Lessons for Our Times* (London: RUSI).
Scales, R. (2004a) 'Army Transformation, Implications for the Future', Statement of Major General Robert Scales, House Armed Services Committee, 15 July 2004.
Scales, R. (2004b) 'Culture-Centric Warfare', *US Naval Institute Proceedings*, Vol. 130, No. 10, pp. 32–36.

Stewart, R. (2011) 'What Can Afghanistan and Bosnia Teach Us about Libya?', *Guardian*, 8 October 2011.

Stoler, M. A. (2005) *Allies in War: Britain and America against the Axis Powers 1940–1945* (London: Hodder).

Strachan, H. (1994) 'The British Way in Warfare', in D. G. Chandler (ed.) *The Oxford History of the British Army* (Oxford: Oxford University Press), pp. 399–415.

Strachan, H. (2007) 'British Counter-Insurgency from Malaya to Iraq', *RUSI Journal*, Vol. 152, No. 6, pp. 8–11.

Strachan, H. (2010) 'We Are as Complacent about Major War as the Edwardians', *Telegraph*, 17 September 2010.

Till, G. (2011) 'British Strategy after Afghanistan', in M. Codner and M. Clarke (eds) *A Question of Security: The British Defence Review in an Age of Austerity* (London: RUSI), pp. 131–152.

# 8
# France: The State with Strategic Vision

*Y. Boyer*

Widespread pessimism has grown over the relative decline of Europe. Such climate is primarily due to challenges posed by huge public debts and budgetary deficits and their dreadful repercussions on the status of the *Euro* as well as on the difficulty among *Eurozone* countries to find agreement on how to solve the crisis. The further worsening of the crisis could even move the European Union (EU) to a point of rupture as mentioned by Europeans politicians, 'If we, in our Eurozone do not appear to be capable of pulling together and showing solidarity it could signal the end of the much-praised European model' (Verhofstadt, 2010).

So far, however, the EU is, with the United States, the only grouping of nations able to project its influence worldwide. The EU remains, despite the current crisis, a global economic superpower with the highest GNP on the world scene when combining the various GNP of its members. For a foreseeable future this situation will be preserved allowing the Union to generate financial surpluses used to back its policy of global influence based on diverse forms of 'civilian' power with a central position in various international networks and a significant role in international institutions. Indeed, the EU is the single largest financial contributor to the UN system when, at the end of the last decade, spending 38 per cent of the United Nation's regular budget, a significant amount of UN peacekeeping operations and one-half of all UN member states' contributions to UN funds and programmes. EU member states are also signatories to almost all international treaties currently in force. In the last two decades, the EU has finalized the single market; established a single currency; created a zone without internal frontiers (*Schengen*); launched common defence, foreign and internal security policies; and expanded from 12 to 27 members. These are, indeed, very positive developments in a globalized world where cooperation in trade, social development, environment preservation and so on are the dominant value.

Even in defence matters, Europe does possess know-how and capabilities which also permit fruitful cooperation and interoperability with the United States, the world's leading power in military affairs. With about 20 per cent of the world's military spending the EU is far ahead of China (8–7 per cent), Russia (3 per cent) or India (2 per cent). But precisely for the reason that the influence exerted by the EU is more 'civilian' than 'military', the defence dimension of the EU has never had priority on other aspects of the European construction. Of course, additional reasons (historical, societal, diplomatic, etc.) explain the many difficulties met by the Europeans to further their cooperation in that field and the various ambiguities about the conduct of each of the EU countries in defence affairs.

France shares with her EU's partners, and notably those members of the Eurozone, the appalling effects of the financial and economic crisis. The debts issue, in conjunction with economic stagnation, will affect public spending and notably defence expenditure. However, France's national vague, although persistent, consensus on defence and the prominent status of the executive power *vis-à-vis* the Parliament are key features to contain the extent of the likely reduction of the defence budget and to safeguard the existing coherence of the French military model.

## France's defence organization and cooperation with NATO's countries

Probably one of the key and original characteristics of this model remains that strategic affairs and defence are deeply embedded into the power of the French State. Even the defence industry is closely linked to the State's *nomenklatura*, including privatized firms, whose leaders are by and large selected from *Grandes Écoles* (*École polytechnique* dubbed as *l'X* and *École Nationale d'Administration*, ENA) as are their counterparts in politics and banking systems. In addition, the State remains a key purveyor of investments in hi-tech firms and notably those working in armament development and production. Those many connections serve as a hedge against drastic reduction of the format of those industries. Such realities bear heavily upon collaborative projects in the framework of NATO which are US led and often seen as a potential risk to national and European industries.

In the military domains the French defence organization, whatever its limits, has been purposely organized to be efficient and to maintain the coherence of the French defence posture. The Executive (the *Président de la République*) is constitutionally the head of the armed forces.[1] He gives guidance (subsequently agreed by the Parliament) on the overall strategy and military organization. He carefully controls their execution through his military staff at the Élysée palace and directs their implementation through the chairing of the high council on defence (*Conseil de Défense*). He particularly cares about maintaining autonomy of action in key domains, respecting alliances' commitments (EU, NATO, out-of-areas agreements, such as those with some African countries or Abu Dhabi[2]) and coherence of the French defence posture.

This precise stature gives a wide margin of action to the French Head of State, who can decide on committing French forces without prior acquiescence from the Parliament even if debates are, later, organized where parliamentarians from the National Assembly and the Senate discuss the rationale and the scope of the military operation, sometimes without any vote following the debates. Such debates occur when the issue involves a certain amount of forces and allies. Otherwise in 'small' operations in Africa, the Parliament is seldom consulted. This is, as example, the case for Operation *Épervier* in Chad which is in place since 1986 or Operation *Boali* in the Central African Republic (since 2002) where French forces participate actively to the stability of these countries in the heart of Africa. Operation *Boali* provides a good example of the functioning of the French processes to commit forces in urgency. In 2007 a small detachment of French forces, based in Birao, near the Sudanese border, was attacked and encircled by an important group of rebels. If Birao felt, there was a huge risk of destabilization of Chad and later the Democratic Republic of Congo. The Élysée palace military headquarters was immediately warned of the situation and, after the president's approval, the EMA (*État-Major des Armées*) was ordered to take the appropriate measure in air dropping parachutists flying from Gabon and Djibouti to intervene as a backup force. The French chain of command from the political decision to the actual use of force is probably unique among Western democracies and it continues to give a significant capacity of reactivity to the French president. In his tasks as commander-in-chief, the head of state is supported by diverse structures to implement his decisions. Two are noteworthy.

The first one, already mentioned, is the general staff (EMA) who plans operations, conducts operations through the French national OHQ (operational headquarters), called CPCO (*Centre de Commandement et de*

*Conduite des Opérations*), and looks at the equipment and the training of the forces. The second one is the defence industry directorate (*Direction Générale de l'Armement*, DGA) who oversees the elaboration and the production of defence equipment, in conjunction with the EMA. Both work to preserve the coherence of the French defence architecture. Coherence means that general functions assigned to the military relate to adequate command structure, to proper equipment and adapted training. Five key missions having been identified in the White Paper on defence and internal security of 2008: strategic awareness and anticipation, deterrence, protection, projection, prevention. Each of them requires the ability to execute specific missions: nuclear deterrence at sea necessitates, as example, significant capabilities in anti-submarine warfare (ASW).

Such close collaboration among those key players within the ministry of defence is translated into the yearly programmatic report, PP30 (*Plan Prospectif à 30 ans*), a 30-year forecast plan elaborated by the DGA in cooperation with other organizations from the MoD. Its aim is to provide France with the required means for its defence and security policy with the indispensable level of autonomy while respecting its international commitments. PP30 looks at threats that may be encountered in the future and identifies technologies and equipment answering to them. PP30 is divided into two perspectives. One looks at the next five years' planning and programming that may be revisited according to the level of threats, the defence commitments of France, technological evolution and budgetary constraints. The other, long-term outlook is envisaged mainly around future technological perspectives at 30 years ahead. Such organization, although in some aspects are relatively cumbersome, permits consistency and long-term planning, thus shelving armed forces from hasty cuts that may lead to incoherence in the French military posture. It is also an organization that is by and large relatively isolated from external interference.

On the political chessboard, both the right (UMP, centrist) and the left (Socialist party) are keen to maintain this state of affairs. President François Hollande, alluding to possible reduction of the defence budget,[3] pledged, however, that he will be particularly attentive to maintain the coherence of the 'model', something the British have not been able to achieve in their 2010 Strategic Defence Review (SDR). In the probable decrease of the defence budget, nuclear deterrence will be slightly affected by spending reductions. Hence, cuts will bear upon conventional forces raising the question of the type of military engagement the French want to tackle considering maintaining their capacity to enter first on a theatre of operation as a key requirement to participate efficiently to coalition military operations within the framework of the EU or NATO.

## Conventional forces

Conventional forces have their role and structure defined in large part by three key tasks enunciated in the 2008 White Paper on defence that will be certainly maintained under the leadership of President Hollande: *prevention, protection* and *projection*. For each component (Air, Land and Sea) an adequate command structure for engagement at the operational level exists and each is NATO certified. This certification also includes Special Forces. This certification is important in the sense that it signifies having capabilities to enter first on a theatre of operation. This remains a key requirement in terms of autonomy of decision as well as in the ability to develop cooperation with major allies, such as the United States, Great Britain or Germany. France shares with these countries the participation to the Multinational Interoperability Council (MIC), where complex command structures and new modes of operation are tested in common. MIC

> provides a joint multinational forum for identifying interoperability issues and articulating actions at the strategic and high operational level that, if nationally implemented by MIC members nations, will contribute to more effective coalition operations.... Each of the MIC member nations is considered to be a potential 'lead nation' of a future coalition or multinational operation.
>
> (2012)

France participation to the MIC dates back to the early 2000s (Boyer, 2005). The development of the MIC, although not highly publicized, probably because of the complexity and the technicality of the works being done, also signifies a relative leaving behind of NATO.

Indeed, the slow but steady decrease of defence budget throughout Europe has led most European countries to possess useful and capable but marginal military capabilities. As a result, most of the European countries have lost their ability to fully apprehend modern warfare above the tactical level and failed to develop force structure and equipment corresponding to the higher levels of warfare. This has deep consequences on the prospects of military cooperation and integration of most European nations into the framework of any US-led coalition. To take only one example, this heterogeneity has implication when contemplating force projection. If a 'small' European country is willing to participate in an operation, it can fill a certain quantity of troops and materials but certainly not for a long period of time; accordingly the 'bigger' countries will then be in an obligation to fill the vacuum in sending more troops as a compensation. Hence the necessity to find proper place to discuss new ways of warfare in a highly technical environment brought, notably, by information and communication technologies.

Decrease in European defence budget and its potential implication is becoming a recurring theme for French officials. The French Chief of Staff, Admiral Edouard Guillaud, mentioned, when testifying at the National Assembly, in early January 2012, on the next defence budget, that if between 2001 and 2010 defence spending increased by 80 per cent in the United States and 70 per cent in East Asia, they increased only by 4 per cent in Europe, whose share in world spending in defence has fallen down from 29 to 20 per cent. Politically this evolution justifies for the French the transfer to the MIC of the experimenting and planning of future complex military operation. NATO keeps, however, its role as provider of proven command structures and of processes to enhance interoperability among allies. For the French, the EU defence perspective is far from being ignored in that scheme; once the dynamic of closer financial, banking and fiscal harmonization will start again, defence will follow. Then the benefit of NATO's heritage as well as the know-how developed at MIC will be by and large transferred to the EU as a military actor when and if the EU under a form or another develops its own defence policy.

In the meantime the French have to maintain coherent, well-trained conventional forces. These forces have been in 2011 engaged, for actual military operations, in Kosovo, Ivory Coast, the Sahel region, Lebanon, Libya, the Indian Ocean and Afghanistan. As a whole, these operations amounted to around €1.3 bn for 2011.

The Libya operation started for the French under Operation *Harmattan*, which later was included in the Coalition Operation *Unified Protector*. The French entered first on that theatre when *Rafale* fighter bombers took off from Saint-Dizier air base, in North East France, on 19 March 2011 to attack targets around the city of Benghazi. From that moment France became a key political actor in the operation against Gaddafi and the decisive engine of the military intervention. French air force and navy planes carried out 30 per cent of the overall air sorties of the coalition and 25 per cent of the offensive mission. Combat helicopters made 90 per cent of the offensive sorties destroying 550 targets. The *Marine Nationale*, dubbed *La Royale*, has mobilized, during 7 months, 25 ships and submarines to be able to maintain an operational presence nearby Libyan coasts; the aircraft carrier *Charles-de-Gaulle* has seen its planes realizing 1,573 combat missions (*E2C AEW, Super Etendard* and *Rafale*).[4]

Operation *Harmattan* was the most important naval engagement since the Suez operation in 1956. It has, indeed, mobilized a significant part of the French navy already engaged in the *Atalanta* EU operation alongside Somalia and compelled the French to momentarily postpone Operation *Corymbe* which, since 1970, consists of naval presence on the gulf of Guinea.

The US-led military intervention in Afghanistan was originally intended to get rid of Al-Qaeda and eradicate its accomplice, the Taliban regime. Soon after, it was understood that political and societal stability could not prevail in Afghanistan without a comprehensive programme of reconstruction and nation-building. The international community, notably NATO countries and the EU, were thus called to back that process by providing security guarantee to what would become the PRTs (Provincial Reconstruction Teams), as well as economic, financial and technical support. At first, the whole operation took place under a UN mandate, which was relatively easy to obtain since most nations recognized in the Taliban regime a threat to global security.

UNSCR 1386 (December 2001) allowed the creation of the International Security Assistance Force (ISAF) with military assets and manpower borrowed from 18 countries. UNSCR 1510 (13 October 2003) gave mandate to ISAF to operate everywhere in Afghanistan under the command of NATO. Initially ISAF comprised 9,000 personnel in a country the size of France plus the Benelux; in 2011 they were about 135,000 if one includes US forces directly led by the US chain of command. In its early days, ISAF was responsible for providing a secure umbrella upon reconstruction activities; it has been growingly caught into combating the Taliban, which cannot be seen merely as 'terrorists' since they are an integral part of the Afghan society. After a period, where NATO officials were talking about maintaining a presence in Afghanistan for an indeterminate period of time, 2012 became the time for undertaking an organized withdrawal.

Under a period of 'cohabitation', when President Chirac (right) was at the Élysée palace and Lionel Jospin was Prime Minister (left), France decided to side with the Americans in sending the aircraft carrier *Charles-de-Gaulle* (Task Force 473) to the Indian Ocean; the first bombardment in Afghanistan from French naval aircraft happened on 19 December

2001. Later, the duration of the intervention in Afghanistan was justified by a series of arguments to begin with the instauration of 'democracy', human rights and the fight against Al Qaeda/terrorism. Indeed, Western involvement in Afghan affairs put into motion complex internal and external dynamics that significantly impacted the duration, the nature and the scope of Western objectives.

The rationale of the Western intervention could no longer be assessed merely in relation with the sole eradication of the Taliban and the gradual instauration of democracy in a country which never experienced it. The absence of a right understanding of the nature of the opponents that met in Afghan provinces was symptomatic of a lack of a clear vision of what should be achieved in Afghanistan. Such imprecision led to growing difficulties in establishing the basis of action. Actually, Western engagement encompassed different types of concerns mixing up together. Gradually, the gap between official rhetoric and reality have been wide years after years. Public opinion poll throughout Europe expressed growing doubts about the success of military commitments in Afghanistan: 63 per cent of the French and the British, 66 per cent of the Italians and 69 per cent of the Germans thought it has been a failure at the end of the 2000 decade. In 2008, 68 per cent of the French population opposed president Sarkozy's plan to send additional French troops to the East of Afghanistan when only 15 per cent were in favour.

In France, most of the analysts having a particular knowledge of that country expressed doubts about the chance of the international community to work out a durable and peaceful transition in Afghanistan. On the military side, Afghanistan was seen as challenging tasks that gradually led to modify and adapt the training of the units to be sent to that country. Most of the French army regiments sent some of their element, giving junior officers and NCOs an experience of combat. The higher echelon of the French military hierarchy took very seriously its new tasks and accomplished its duty in a very professional way; some of the officers, although, expressed confidentially that they were not fully convinced that there will be any chance to alter significantly the political situation prevailing in Afghanistan. General Vincent Desportes, when commanding the *Collège Interarmées de Défense* (*Ecole de Guerre*) in Paris, expressed open criticism about the war in Afghanistan, arguing that if the fight against Al Qaeda brought success, the Taliban will come back to power once the coalition leaves the country. He was then forced to resign. Public opinion was supporting the soldiers but, also, expressed growing doubts about the rationale of the intervention.

In total there was no frontal opposition to the commitment of forces in Afghanistan but the sense that, after ten years, the war did not bring the expected results and that it became in a way absurd to see unarmed French soldiers being shot at by Afghan trainees they were in charge of. Once elected, President Hollande decided to speed up the repatriation of French forces. He announced his decision at the NATO's Chicago summit of May 2012. His decision should be largely implemented by the end of that year. As a whole, between 2001 and 2011 the French had 83 soldiers killed and paid about €2.36 bn for their presence in Afghanistan. The mood in Paris as probably in other Western capitals is now about preparing the political transition in Kabul in 2014, hoping that the Taliban will not be successful.

### The structuring effect of nuclear deterrence on French defence policy

The current reduced level of immediate threat in Europe does not mean the absence of any threat, hence the strong reaffirmation in the NATO's Strategic Concept adopted in Lisbon of the role of nuclear deterrence in the defence of the allies. France is particularly sensitive on this issue. Besides historical reasons, nuclear deterrence has become the central and structuring element of French defence policy. Having reduced the size of its nuclear forces in the last two decades, Paris is determined to maintain a robust nuclear posture, still benefiting, internally, of a large political consensus. President François Hollande, during his electoral campaign, conspicuously indicated to its allies from the green party (EEVL, *Europe Écologie Les Verts*) that nuclear deterrence will continue to be the backbone of France's military posture.

Indeed nuclear deterrence has kept for the French its relevance. Former French President Nicolas Sarkozy enunciated in 2008 the role of deterrence for France in full continuity with his predecessors, a declaration that without doubt François Hollande will confirm: to defend France from aggression against its vital interest; to preserve France's independence and strategic autonomy; to guarantee the ability of a limited nuclear warning shot against any adversary who may misread the delineation of French vital interest; to conceive and build in total national autonomy the necessary tools for possessing and maintaining a credible nuclear deterrence; to plan and execute strategic strike. The place and role of nuclear deterrence explains that a significant part of the defence budget (26 per cent of the equipment budget, i.e., €3.7 bn) is allotted to deterrence.

150 *Application: Case Studies*

With approximately 300 operational warheads, France has reached what is considered as the proper level of sufficiency. These capabilities are split into two components: four SSBN of a new generation are carrying each 16 M51 missiles with an approximate range of 9,000 km carrying 6 MIRVs of about 100 kt each and penetration aids; 2 squadrons of *Rafale* mod.3 fighter-bombers are carrying a supersonic cruise missile (ASMP-A) with a 100/300 kt warhead. The technological and industrial capacities that led to develop and build these nuclear components have, in fact, given France a special position within NATO. A fact barely understood for its consequences by most of NATO's allies with the exception of the United Kingdom and the United States.

Indeed the possession and the control of nuclear weapons are not in themselves enough to explain that situation. The issue there is about retaining and maintaining a specific technological and industrial base in the domain of nuclear weapons as well as in some related domains, such as key intelligence assets notably space-based. Both provide strategic benefits and open the way to bilateral cooperation which go far beyond their initial purpose in bringing strategic and political values. Numerous examples can support this assertion.

### Technology and strategy

The military nuclear R&D complex is central to explore new domains related notably to nuclear simulation. Simulation has become a priority after France renounced, with the other nuclear powers part of the TNP, to nuclear testing. Billions of euros have been spent on these programmes in the last decade; they brought results and many strategic side effects with political consequences. Among the many simulation processes built one can mention the cooperation on an equal footing between the French Atomic Establishment (CEA-DAM) and its US equivalent to design and build, in each country, a highly sophisticated Laser. The *Laser Méga Joule* has been built near Bordeaux, in southern France, and its US equivalent is the National Ignition Facility at Lawrence Livermore National Laboratory. Not only the cooperation carried the expected scientific and technological advantages but it led to the agreement between France and Great Britain on nuclear issues signed in December 2010 in Lancaster House (FCO, 2010).

The British efforts in the field of nuclear deterrence are assigned to the Atomic Weapons Establishment (AWE), where in Aldermaston (Berkshire) components for British nuclear warheads are designed, produced and maintained, in Burghfield final warhead assembly is realized and in Cardiff non-fissile nuclear warhead components are produced.

In the mid-1990s AWE was in great part privatized, being jointly owned by the British government, through its stake in British Nuclear Fuels, and two companies – Serco and Lockheed Martin – which have bought British Nuclear Fuels' one-third share in AWE Management, which makes and maintains the warheads for Britain's nuclear missiles, giving Americans a controlling influence of the facility. In fact, such move and the previous absence of significant programmes have led the AWE towards declining capabilities and difficulties to maintain quality in terms of the researcher team. This situation, in conjunction with enduring doubts about the future of Britain's nuclear deterrent due to a political climate with strong opposition to nuclear weapons, led the French to fear that Britain could sooner or later abandon nuclear deterrence.

Thus the combination of the very good climate between the United States and France on nuclear weapons cooperation on one hand and the quality of French nuclear research capacities and the need to back Britain on maintaining the state of its deterrent forces on the other hand led to the agreement between London and Paris in December 2010. The treaty sates that both countries agreed

> ... to collaborate in the technology associated with nuclear stockpile stewardship in support of our respective independent nuclear deterrent capabilities, in full compliance with our international obligations, through unprecedented co-operation at a new joint facility at Valduc in France that will model performance of our nuclear warheads and materials to ensure long-term viability, security and safety – this will be supported by a joint Technology Development Centre at Aldermaston in the UK.
>
> (FCO, 2010)

Indeed, the constant effort made by France since decades in creating, maintaining and developing a comprehensive programme on nuclear weapons brought added political and strategic benefit, including for the EU and NATO. For the next 50 years both the United Kingdom and France will share the same installation to look at the safety and reliability of their respective nuclear weapons at the CEA-DAM facilities in Valduc. The shift for Britain is significant and has potentially very important political implications. For the first time since the Anglo-American agreements of the 1950s on nuclear cooperation in the field of defence, London is no longer turning its back to the French.

Technology also plays a role in bringing together other NATO European countries on very sensitive technological cooperation that binds countries closer together. This is the case between Germany and France in different sectors. As example, two programmes are worth mentioning. At the CEA-DAM centre at Bruyères-le-Châtel, near Paris, a 'super computer' has been built in cooperation with Germany. Operational since 2009, it is the most powerful in Europe and allows various forms of activities that benefit both countries besides the French use for nuclear simulation. In the domain of space surveillance, Berlin and Paris have also developed very fruitful cooperation. The French radar-based space surveillance system GRAVES (*Grand Réseau Adapté à la VEille Spatiale*) allows surveillance of activities in space near the earth. When mixing the information collected by GRAVES with those of the German TIRA (Tracking & Imaging Radar located in Wachtberg near Bonn) very valuable intelligence is gathered on space activities. Such capabilities offer new perspective on dialogue, such as with the United States in having a better knowledge about their various and sometimes undeclared activities. They may also provide useful capabilities in the framework of developing NATO's BMD (Ballistic Missile Defence).

Space is indeed becoming an important field of activity for the French. The architect of the French space programme is the national agency CNES (*Centre National d'Etudes Spatiales*), the equivalent of DGA and CEA-DAM for leading both civilian and military space activities. In the field of optical satellites the two Helios II satellites are helping significantly in the collection of intelligence materials from areas where international crisis or conflict do exist, to planning nuclear or conventional long-range precision strikes. HELIOS II opens a partnership between France's EU and NATO partners such as Germany (Sar-Lupe radar satellite) and Italy (dual-use Cosmo-SkyMed X-band radar observation satellites).

A successor to Helios II is anticipated in 2016 with two MUSIS satellites with a higher optical resolution as well enhanced infrared detectors. In other fields of intelligence gathering, various demonstrators have been built and launched. ESSAIM is a constellation of four small satellites tasked to collect and map signals intelligence (COMINT) across the world. Launched in 2004, the constellation provided, up to 2010, invaluable data. ELISA (ELectronic Intelligence SAtellites) is another demonstrator of four small satellites designed, under control by DGA and CNES to pave the way for an operational programme to map and characterize radar emissions around the world. Last but not least the demonstrator SPIRALE, a space-based early warning system for missile detection, tracking and identification, has surpassed the objectives of the demonstration phase, both in terms of the volume and the level of detail of the acquired data.

The achievement of SPIRALE, which is unique in Europe, opens the way for a future space-based early warning system, particularly at a time when NATO is embarked in a comprehensive BMD policy. Again, one realizes that technological capabilities requires a significant effort for France, who spent €4.7 bn in 2009 in RT&D (€3.3 bn in the United Kingdom and €1.5 bn in Germany), and serves many purposes, including those of framing the condition of a political and strategic dialogue among Western partners at a time when different objectives are pursued at once by a country like France: to preserve its autonomy of decision which implies having independent strategic awareness capabilities, the necessity to pursue the long-term goal of building a European defence policy and maintaining close link with the United States through bilateral cooperation as well as through NATO.

## The geopolitical and geostrategic context of French defence policy

The NATO Strategic Concept (NSC) adopted in Lisbon in 2010 reaffirmed the military nature of the Atlantic alliance and its primary responsibility to protect the population and the territory of its members (NATO, 2010). This has been a long-lasting objective of the Alliance as stated in the Washington treaty's Article 5. Such positive reaffirmation of the indivisibility of allies' security confirmed the enduring strength of the link binding them together; it did not, however, add new supplementary tasks for the Western alliance. In addition, the disappearance of direct military threat in the European area lessened the practical implication of this traditional goal of the alliance. At the same time, the complexity and the great fluidity of the international scene have significantly reduced the ability of the Atlantic alliance to provide solutions to the many external challenges confronting the Western allies.

On the European continent perspective of conflicts has almost vanished. Although a difficult partner still haunted by a Cold War mindset, Russia, with the exception of its significant nuclear forces, can no longer be considered as a direct threat. From a military standpoint the bulk of Russian military forces have been significantly reduced in quantity and in quality. They are generally lacking hi-tech equipment in number and conventional forces, with the exception of selected units for rapid intervention, are, in term of training, lagging far behind the professionalism of most Western forces. Lastly, deployment of Russian military units, particularly ground forces, is no longer oriented towards Eastern and Central Europe. If one looks, as example, at the disposition of the 11 existing Russian army corps, 9 are located far away from the western borders of Russia on a line spreading from the Caucasus to the Far East. The NSC confirmed the strategic character of the partnership the Alliance is seeking to develop with Moscow. If the Kremlin may pose difficulties with its rather controversial internal governance, France tends to consider Russia as an essential component of any future security architecture of Europe. If scepticism remains strong about democratic life in Russia, the French have not, with few exceptions, significant grievances concerning Russia that still haunt the Baltic states or Eastern and Central Europe countries where criticism have been extremely strong when Paris sold two *Mistral* class helicopter carrier to Russia.

### The NATO dimension: Malaise and necessity

The Chicago summit of May 2012 had, in many ways, confirmed the slow decline of NATO's military organization and the diminished place it has for the United States who, nevertheless, continue to consider the organization as the main channel of its political influence throughout Europe. Seen from Washington the symptoms of the relative decline of NATO are numerous, however largely camouflaged by an active policy of lobbying and communication. One can only be bemused by the use of the term 'historic' to describe NATO's Lisbon summit of November 2010 that was said to be 'the most important in NATO's history'. NATO's Chicago Summit – the city of President Obama – was the first to be held in the United States in 13 years, having been initially billed as an 'implementation summit' at which the alliance's political leaders assessed the evolution of the ambitious plan agreed on in Lisbon to speed up NATO's efforts to adapt to the twenty-first century. Its purpose was, also, to back President Obama stature in the current presidential election year.

However, behind nice depictions, the withdrawal of American forces from Europe is continuing with the repatriation of two US Army brigades (both stationed in Germany: the 170th in Baumholder and 171st in Grafenwöhr). The strength of US Army in Europe will amount to 30,000 men against 270,000 men 25 years ago. In total, the United States will maintain around 70,000 personnel in Europe. The reasons of such withdrawal are various; to begin with US internal policy as well as the shift of US national interest towards new horizon.

First, budgetary pressures are becoming strong in America with a Federal budget deficit almost out of control. The debt interest is now the third budgetary item after the Department of Health and Human Security and the Department of Defence outlays. In such circumstances, the planned $487 bn reduction in the US military budget in the next decade reinforces the determination of US authorities to question the growing imbalance between the effort made by the United States and the stagnation, if not the constant diminishing, of defence spending, throughout Europe. Already the United States represents 3/4 of NATO spending as a whole and, even France or Great Britain, represents a relatively modest portion of the US defence budget (around 6 per cent each).

For the US administration it is becoming easier in a period of reduction of spending to ask for closing bases outside of the United States in the framework of the BRAC – Base Realignment and Closure – process than closing bases in the United States where unemployment at home is already high. Warnings are coming at in an increased rate from the United States about that imbalance. As recalled by US secretary of Defence, Leon Panetta, in a speech made in Brussels in October 2011 such imbalance is harming NATO. His predecessor, Robert Gates, earlier in June of the same year, declared that such situation may lead to 'a "dim, if not dismal, future" for the alliance' (Gates, 2011).

If Europeans' low defence budget amplified exasperation in Washington about NATO's allies, the apparition of a new generation of American leaders, far less inclined to look towards Europe as their predecessors, may accentuate the relative distance that the Americans are taking with NATO. Already, it is striking to see how few hearings at the US Congress are devoted to NATO and to security issues in Europe. The same applies to big US foundations that practically no longer finance research on those topics, a dramatic departure in their policies not so long ago.

The reassessment of US national interests is principally linked to the growing importance of the Middle East, Central Asia and the Far East in the world game. It is striking to see that, in the strategic guidance, released by President Barack Obama, early January 2012, on US defence priorities for the years ahead, the word Asia appeared nine times, while NATO makes just two appearances (DoD, 2012). These shifts, also, correspond to a transformation in the way the Americans intend to use force. The lessons of the last 15 years led them to limit military engagements in circumstances which are not linked to the preservation of major US interests. Consequently, if they are willing to continue supporting their allies in the framework of ad hoc coalition they will do it as 'off-shore balancer' as they did during the operations against Gaddafi's Libya. They will offer logistical support and intelligence but will refrain to commit active forces participating to the kinetic part of the operations.

The US military organization has taken into account the current decline of NATO from the Washington strategic perspective. When Secretary Gates disbanded the US Joint Forces Command (JFCOM) in 2010 he, indirectly, upset NATO since the collocation of NATO's Allied Command Transformation (ACT) with JFCOM manifested the closeness existing between the US high-command structures and the European allies. Today the cooperation between ACT and the US Command structure has become loose. It goes through the Joint Staff, a bureaucratic structure supporting the work of the JCS (Joint Chiefs of Staff) that has a far less important status and weight than a Combatant Command in the US system.

In that context of decline, Washington is offering diverse form of cooperation to the NATO's partners. These offers also relate to US national interests in perpetuating US leadership on European security affairs. Among those new commitments offered by Washington one finds cyber warfare, anti-terrorist activities, rotation of US military units that will come back regularly for training and, for the East and Central European countries, the maintenance of the SPP (National Guard's State Partnership Program) which linked very tightly armed forces of those countries with the National Guard of various states of the United States, 'one of EUCOM's most effective security cooperation programs' (USEC, 2012).

ABM is a new domain for cooperation. The United States has decided to permanently base four *Aegis* cruisers in Rota (Spain); planned a radar system in Turkey and announced the possible deployment of ABM missiles in Poland and Rumania. Washington is thus *killing two birds with one stone*. It reaffirms its leadership through complex system that no European countries master and control; it allows defending one of the key components of its positioning in Europe: Ramstein (air transport hub) and Landsthul (medical centre). Indeed, Ramstein is becoming a critical spot for the transit of all US troops moving towards the Middle East or Central Asia (about 80 per cent of the soldiers participating to OIF and OEF operations have transited through Ramstein).

In a short and snappy manner one can argue that, now, the relative interest of the United States into NATO stays on three elements: the sharing of common values with the European which is not in itself sufficient to justify NATO; the preservation of their national interest in having a critical hub for their movement towards the Middle East and Central Asia and; lastly, the preservation of their political leadership through new form of protection with the setting up of a comprehensive BMD system in Europe.

Indeed, this gloomy appraisal is linked, for Washington, to the successive failure of European members of NATO in making enduring effort to maintain and modernize potent forces. There is an acknowledgement that past efforts have not brought the awaited result: the 1999's Defence Capabilities Initiative; the NRF; the 2002's Prague Capabilities Commitment; the NRF proved to be largely unsuccessful. As evoked by the US analyst Robert Kaplan (2012):

> 'Europe is dead militarily,' a US general told me. In 1980, European countries accounted for 40 percent of NATO's total defense spending; now they account for 20 percent. One numbered air force within the US Air Force is larger than the British Ministry of Defense. Western Europe's military budgets are plummeting, even as their armed forces are not allowed by local politicians to do much besides participate in humanitarian relief exercises.

During the Lisbon NATO's summit the 'Critical Capabilities Package' concept was launched which led the NATO's General Secretary to evoke the concept of 'smart defence'. As Fogh Rasmussen mentioned at the 2012 Munich Security Conference, this initiative would amount to 'a new way for NATO and Allies to do business... this is about doing more by doing it together' (Rasmussen, 2012).

Smart defence embodies three components: prioritization (aligning national capability priorities more closely with NATO's capability goals), cooperation (pooling of military capability among allies to generate economies of scale and improve inter-operability) and specialization. French fears are that there are risks that this proposal will be translated by a new drain of European financial resources to the benefit of US defence industries as already seen with the growing costs of the F-35 fighter that will impinge on the capacity of various European air forces to operate enough fighters to sustain military operation of a certain duration. Accordingly, as example, the Dutch air force will, in the present circumstances, see its fleet of fighters reduced from about 140 F-16 to probably less than 60 F-35 with enormous operating costs.

Another sign of that evolution has been manifested in the aftermath of the Chicago summit with the signature of a contract worth of $1.7 bn with Northrop Grumman to equip NATO with 5 *Global Hawk* block 40 drones that will be based in Sigonella in Italy. In that perspective, BMD is a potential bone of contention within the alliance. Its costs are far from being realistically assessed and new investments required may be done at the detriment of conventional forces already in a very bad shape in most European countries. This type of complex programme raises again the question of the European industrial and technological base: will European participation to an American-led effort have the same effect than the JSF programme sucking meagre European R&D funds? Will the Europeans be totally absent from the design, the production and the real control of complex system, a situation that will be a retreat to an old age as when in the mid-1950s most if not all military equipment used in Europe were provided by the Americans? Is this situation compatible with the status, the wealth, the technological capabilities and the collective organization so far reached by the Europeans?

## Conclusion

Today NATO is under the pressure of different forces and constraints which are politically disruptive. The United States is now looking towards new horizon than Europe, still maintaining its commitments to NATO. The Baltic States are obsessed by a resurgence of a possible Russian military threat and are accepting to fully defer their security to the United States in exchange of the protection offered by Washington. The Scandinavian countries have still the Russian factor in mind due to their geostrategic proximity to Russia but are in a position where it is probably easier to compromise with the Americans than to choose the difficult path towards European defence policy still in limbo. That will compel them to work and cooperate with a country like France they do not understand and towards which they express certain form of mistrust and suspicion.

The Eastern and Central European countries of NATO are for most of them in the same position than the Baltic States with the exception of Poland whose commitments to defence have to be taken seriously although having little to offer in terms of budgetary and military capabilities. However, Poland, without harming NATO, has shown a real commitment to enhancing European defence perspective and it is worth mentioning that in the framework of the Weimar Triangle, Warsaw associated with Berlin and Paris to plea for the creation of a European strategic headquarters (OHQ). Berlin itself is modernizing its forces in a very interesting manner although the internal political condition existing in Germany makes Berlin largely absent when committing forces out of area as witnessed during the Libyan campaign of spring/summer 2011.

The United Kingdom is in a state of disarray regarding its defence policy. Having one of the best military in Europe, the British defence posture has been dramatically impacted by the deflationary effect of the 2010's SDR which has been translated by internal incoherence. The United Kingdom shares with France the will to remain a key player in defence but is at present haunted by a kind of existential crisis which resurrects new appeals towards a rapprochement with former associates within the Commonwealth as if it represented a genuine opportunity. This crisis may endure as long as they will have not cut the Gordian knot about their relations with Europe leaving, in the meantime, their partners with uncertainties about the degree to which further cooperation with London is achievable.

France is, as many other European countries, suffering from the financial and economic crisis. Temptation to retreat on oneself exists. However, as for the British, this does not represent a promising opportunity. What remains is the option of continuing a traditional ambiguous politic: working for preserving a certain degree of autonomy, acting as a fair player in NATO to wait for the favourable moment to speed up a genuine European defence policy while developing ad hoc bilateral cooperation with the American ally.

## Notes

1. Article 14 of the constitution of the 5th Republic, 4 October 1958.
2. In the framework of the defence agreement of 1995 and the strategic partnership signed in 1997, President Nicolas Sarkozy opened, in May 2009, the first permanent French military base in Abu Dhabi, giving Paris a presence in a geopolitically strategic location on a key global oil supply route. France deploys in Abu Dhabi 6 *Rafale* fighter-bomber; elements of the 13th half-brigade of the Foreign Legion; maritime elements as well as the Headquarters of French naval forces operating in the Indian Ocean. In addition, Fudjeirah, on the Eastern coast of Abu Dhabi, provide facilities to French SSN.
3. The defence budget for 2012 is €40.2 bn.
4. Contrary to other country there has been no shortage of munitions: the French has used 950 guided bombs; 225 guided bomb AASM (SBU-18 'Hammer'); 15 SCALP cruise missiles; 431 HOT helicopter launched missiles and fired 3,000 rounds of 100 and 76 artillery shells.

## Bibliography

Boyer, Y. (2005) 'Les opérations en coalition', in Bruylant (ed.) *Annuaire Français de Relations Internationales 2005* (Brussels: Bruylant).

DoD (2012) *Sustaining US Global Leadership: Priorities for 21st Century Defence* (Washington: DoD).

FCO (2010) 'EM on the UK-France Defence and Security Co-operation Treaty', 8 December 2010, www.fco.gov.uk (homepage), date accessed 20 June 2012.

Gates, R. (2011) 'The Security and Defense Agenda (Future of NATO)', http://www.defense.gov (homepage), date accessed 26 May 2012.

Kaplan, R. D. (2012) 'NATO's Ordinary Future', 9 May 2012, www.stratfor.com (homepage), date accessed 20 June 2012.

MIC (2012) 'Multilateral Interoperability Council', January 2012, https://community.apan.org (homepage), date accessed 27 June 2012.

NATO (2010) *Active Engagement, Modern Defence* (Brussels: NATO).

Rasmussen, A. F. (2012) 'Speech at the 48th Munich Security Conference', http://www.securityconference.de (homepage), date accessed 20 June 2012.

USEC (2012) 'National Guard State Partnership Program', http://www.eucom.mil (homepage), date accessed 20 June 2012.

Verhofstadt, G. (2010) *How Can We Save the Euro?* (Gütersloh: Bertelsmann Stiftung).

# 9
# The Reluctant Ally? Germany, NATO and the Use of Force

*B. Schreer*

Germany's behaviour in the run-up of NATO's 2011 *Operation Unified Protector* (OUP) in Libya came as a surprise to many allies since Germany did not participate in a military operation which fulfilled the criteria of a right cause (a 'responsibility to protect') and proper authority (a UN Security Council mandate), and which was supported by its most important European allies, France and Germany. Consequently, Germany was accused by the international media of moving away from 'European unity' while German commentators explained this decision with the country's pacifist preference, immaturity in foreign and security policy and a preoccupation with domestic politics (Erlanger and Dempsey, 2011). German Foreign Minister Guido Westerwelle also pointed to his country's 'tradition of [military] restraint' as an explanation for Germany's abstention (Der Spiegel, 2011).

Some saw Germany, therefore, on another *Sonderweg* of becoming an even more 'unwilling' or 'unreliable' NATO ally (Joffe, 2011). This view also seemed warranted since the German government had not even consulted with its French counterpart in the run-up of the UN Security Council vote (von Thadden, 2011). Worse, Germany's behaviour contributed to yet another split of NATO into a 'coalition of the willing' and those opting out of an operation to stop another 'Srebrenica' on Europe's doorstep. Had Germany, as one of the major European NATO allies, chosen to participate, it is doubtful that other smaller allies would have found it easy to opt out, too. In the end, only 8 out of 28 NATO members contributed troops to the operation. Arguably, Germany's 'no' in the Libya campaign demonstrated its potential to organize 'coalitions of the unwilling' within the alliance.

Is Germany unwilling and unable to play a major military role within a changing NATO? This is a key question for the future of the alliance. Alongside France and the United Kingdom, Germany is one of the top three military powers in Europe. Particularly in the current climate of financial austerity and NATO discussions about 'smart defence', greater German military contribution will be critical to common European defence efforts within the alliance. Yet, German defence spending in recent years has all but stagnated. While at the end of the Cold War in 1990 the country spent 2.8 per cent of its gross domestic product (GDP) on defence, in 2010 the figure was a mere 1.4 per cent. Indeed, German defence expenditure as a percentage of GDP has been rather stagnating for over two decades (SIPRI, 2012). This fact has been recognized by Germany's allies. For example, the UK House of Lords EU Committee in May 2012 asked Berlin to pull its weight militarily to enable the Europeans to shoulder more of the burden in NATO as the US ally shifts its strategic priorities towards the Asia-Pacific (Stacey, 2012).

Against this background, this chapter looks at the evolution of German military power with an emphasis on the twin pillars of political will to use force and the actual ability of the German armed forces (the *Bundeswehr*) to conduct military operations at the high-end of the spectrum, that is, combat operations. Obviously, these two key elements of German military power are influenced by a range of factors. Germany's political will to use force is not only influenced by its strategic culture and domestic opinion but also Berlin's interests in a new European geostrategic setting which define its current approach to NATO operations. Germany's ability to conduct operations depends not only on its willingness to spend enough on defence but also on implementing much-needed defence reform, particularly with regard to the structure of *Bundeswehr*.

To provide context, the chapter will first introduce a brief historical discussion of Germany's defence policy. The main focus will then be on Germany's evolution as a military power in the modern era by analysing both the question of political will and military capability. It finds that Germany has turned into a much more selective ally when it comes to supporting NATO operations. While it is not reluctant *per se* to use military force, including at the sharp end of the spectrum, it has grown more sceptical about the utility of 'wars of choice'. As a result, the German armed forces will only develop a relatively limited capability for high-end expeditionary operations.

## German defence policy in the early post-Cold War period

Any serious discussion of German defence policy has to take into consideration this country's unique historical evolution. It is beyond the scope of this chapter to engage in a detailed elaboration of Germany's NATO policy during the Cold War. Suffice to say that West Germany, stripped of its full sovereignty in security and defence policy, became tightly integrated into NATO's deterrent posture *vis-à-vis* the Warsaw Pact. Moreover, unlike other Western European powers such as France or the United Kingdom, Germany's military power exclusively focussed on territorial defence. In fact, by law the *Bundeswehr* could not be deployed in 'out-of-area' operations. In addition, Germany developed a strategic culture of military restraint supported by European allies' expectations and reservations, and the *Bundeswehr*'s force structure reflected a defence and security policy that was decisively 'non-strategic'. In fact, the 'tight integration of Germany in the alliance was designed to prevent independent German strategic thinking from emerging' (Asmus, 1994, p. 11). As a result, due to this semi-sovereignty in strategic affairs, German policy-makers did not develop strategic ambitions for their country (Paterson, 1996). Instead, the 'Bonn Republic' strongly focused on the economic dimension of its foreign policy.

With the demise of the Soviet Union, the strategic situation for Germany also changed dramatically. Not only had unified Germany regained its full sovereignty in security and defence policy. Given its geostrategic location in the heart of Europe, its demographic and economic weight and the partial disengagement of the United States from the continent, many observers argued that Germany would now reassert its position as the 'natural hegemon' in Europe (Wallace, 1995), which also implied a leadership role in security and defence affairs. This included its contribution to a renewed NATO which had moved to extend its mission spectrum from collective defence to collective security. At the same time, the collapse of the existential Soviet threat enabled the 'Berlin Republic' to play a more independent policy within the Atlantic alliance. During the Cold War, the common threat had disciplined divergent views among the allies. This also concerned undisputed US leadership within the alliance. Freed from such necessities, particularly larger European allies such as Germany also enjoyed a reduced dependence on the most powerful player within the alliance. As will be argued later on, over time this led to a greater willingness of Germany to challenge US alliance policies.

However, in the immediate post-Cold War period the German government of Chancellor Helmut Kohl was very cautious to avoid any impression among the European allies that his country would quickly come to regard the use of military force as a normal instrument of statecraft again. Instead, not only did the German government conduct classical 'check book diplomacy' during the First Gulf War in 1990–1991. In line with most other NATO allies, including the United States, it also planned to reduce the armed forces which at the end of the Cold War comprised roughly 470,000 troops (IISS, 1992, p. 44). These efforts will be discussed in greater detail below.

That said, incrementally the Kohl government moved towards greater 'normalization' in security and defence policy. In 1994, the Constitutional Court ruled in a landmark decision that German forces were allowed to be deployed in 'out-of-area' operations. This paved the way for Germany's offer to contribute up to 1,800 troops to a possible NATO force to secure the retreat of the unsuccessful UNPROFOR mission in Croatia and Bosnia and Herzegowina in February 1995. Moreover, the *Bundeswehr* participated in the NATO-led Implementation Force (IFOR) in Bosnia-Herzegowina in 1995 with about 3,000 troops, mostly medical and combat support elements. When the NATO-led Stabilisation Force (SFOR) took over from IFOR in 1996 the German troop contribution included combat elements stationed in the theatre of operations. Arguably, German defence policy had transformed significantly since the end of the Cold War:

> Germany's full participation in SFOR demonstrated that the country had gone a long way since its military absence from the Gulf War coalition six years earlier. This was not only indicated by the mere fact of the contribution to SFOR, but also by the fact that there was no controversial discussion about this contribution, with a large majority of the Bundestag faction of the SPD [Social Democrats] and even a majority of the Green faction supporting it.
> 
> (Baumann and Hellmann, 2001, p. 75)

That Germany was on a trajectory of becoming a more 'normal' power when it came to the use of military force clearly showed itself only three years later when a Red–Green coalition government decided to contribute combat forces to NATO's air campaign against Serbia in 1999. The participation in Operation Allied Force was all the more remarkable since the mission was not mandated by the UN Security Council. Chancellor Gerhard Schröder argued that Germany had a 'historical responsibility' to 'prevent mass murder by any means' and that his country stood ready 'without any reservations, to assume responsibility as a "normal ally" ' (Schröder, 1999). German public opinion supported the decision to use force in Kosovo with a majority agreeing that the *Bundeswehr*'s participation not only adequately reflected Germany's new role in world politics but that it should continue even in the case of German casualties in the war (Baumann and Hellmann, 2001, p. 77). After the operation, Chancellor Schröder linked the use of military force to Germany's growing power position in Europe. In September 1999, for example, he argued that Germany had 'every interest in considering itself as a great power in Europe' and that German policy had to consequently be based on 'fully acknowledged self-interest' (New York Times News Service, 1999). Long-time observers of German foreign and security policy saw the country having evolved as a 'self-assured middle power' with an ambition to play a more active role in international security (Haftendorn, 2008). This was also reflected in Germany's decision in June 1999 to deploy 8,000 troops as part of NATO's Kosovo peace-keeping Force (KFOR).

## A new approach to the use of force?

Germany's participation in the Kosovo campaign raised deeper conceptual questions about Germany's role as a military power. The core issue was how to explain Germany's new security and defence policy behaviour since the 1990s and its greater willingness to use military force as a tool of statecraft.

As already mentioned above, during the Cold War it was widely accepted that Germany pursued a 'Sonderweg' (special path) in military affairs, including limited sovereignty, when it came to force structure and defence policy decision-making. When the Cold War ended, a new debate started about whether a unified, fully sovereign Germany would move beyond the culture of military restraint. Not surprisingly, competing visions emerged. On the far end of the realist spectrum, scholars like John Mearsheimer argued that Germany would eventually use military force as an instrument of great power politics in Europe (Mearsheimer, 1990). On the other hand of the spectrum, and much more influential, were cultural explanations that saw a continuation of Germany's military 'culture of restraint', based on the lessons learned from the Second World War (Berger, 1998; Duffield, 1999). Most prominent, was the concept of Germany as a *Zivilmacht* (civilian power) developed in the early 1990s by Hans Maull. His basic argument was that due to Germany's self-identification as a 'civilian power' during the Cold War, its political elites and public opinion would remain reserved towards the use of force for the foreseeable future (Maull, 1990, 1992). Yet, particularly with Germany's participation in the Kosovo operation this approach seemed no longer adequate to fully explain the country's military behaviour. While Maull argued that the Kosovo campaign still fitted the 'civilian power' paradigm (Maull, 2000), others maintained that Germany's approach to the use of force during the 1990s combined both structural (distribution of the international system, etc.) and actor-related factors (intentionality, decision-making, etc.), moving beyond the civilian power model (Baumann and Hellmann, 2001, pp. 64–65). Others agreed that the 'civilian power' concept needed 'refinement' (Hyde-Price, 2001), without necessarily providing greater insight into how exactly such a refinement would look like.

What was obvious, however, was that Germany was more willing to use military force in order to contribute to NATO operations at the end of the millennium. Germany also initiated first steps to reform the *Bundeswehr* from a Cold War legacy force into a more expeditionary one; even so during the 1990s such reforms were rather half-hearted and hampered by declining defence budgets. This problem was also due to a focus on the costs of unification and a lacking sense of urgency on part of German policy-makers (Sarotte, 2001). Still, as indicated above, Germany contributed quite sizeable force components to NATO's operations in the Western Balkans. Moreover, it was by no means the only European NATO member state struggling with its adapted armed forces. Indeed, most European allies during the 1990s experienced a defence 'procurement holiday'.

## German defence policy post-2001: The Schröder years

When the US ally was attacked on 11 September 2001 the German government, just like the other allies, threw its full political support behind Washington and NATO's subsequent decision to evoke Article 5 of the North Atlantic Treaty for the first time in history. As the United States government prepared to use force to topple the Taliban from power in Afghanistan, Chancellor Schröder pledged 3,900 troops to support American war efforts in the context of Operation Enduring Freedom (OEF), including a special forces (Dalgaard-Nielsen, 2003, p. 107).

The government also seemed to support the widespread notion of a 'new geography of national security' (Zelikow, 2003), namely that globalized security threats had removed geographic boundaries also when it came to military responses. Then German Defence Minister Peter Struck famously remarked that Germany was now 'also defended at the Hindu Kush'. Finally, post-September 11 the German government deployed forces to a number of operations in the context of the European Security and Defence Policy (ESDP), including in Macedonia (Operation Concordia) and the Democratic Republic of Congo (Operation Artemis).

Yet, two events were much more defining for Germany's behaviour as a NATO ally during this period: the US-led war in Iraq in 2003 and the emerging NATO-led ISAF mission in Afghanistan. The Schröder government's 'No' to the Iraq War came to many as a surprise, particularly since Berlin openly confronted the US ally. This style signalled the end of traditional German alliance politics when opposition to American positions was usually only voiced behind closed doors. While the Chancellor surely had the backing of a majority of a sceptical population, his anti-Iraq stance reflected more than just a cultural reflex against the use of military force. It was also due to the 'emergence of greater self-confidence, the introduction of a more "national" vocabulary into foreign policy statements and a less reflective attitude to transatlantic security' (Buras and Longhurst, 2004, p. 215).

In other words, Germany displayed the characteristics of a European great power, including a greater degree of (just like France and Great Britain) unpredictability and unreliability as a NATO ally. While it is probably a bridge too far to regard the German 'No' in Iraq as the expression of a foreign and security policy based on 'defensive realism' (Dettke, 2009), it was evident that structural factors, for example, Germany's greater degree of manoeuvrability in foreign and security affairs, played as much an impact on the Schröder government's decision in the Iraq case, as did cultural predispositions against the use of military force. As a result, post-2003 the German government was also more willing to challenge NATO allies on a whole range of other strategic issues. It developed a much more pragmatic approach to the alliance which ever since has been governed by a selective mix of discord and collaboration (Schreer, 2009).

That Germany's opposition to the Iraq War did not represent a return to the traditional 'culture of military restraint' was also plain in greater efforts post-September to transform the *Bundeswehr*. As mentioned above, a number of initiatives during the 1990s already aimed to reform a largely territorial defence force; yet, they remained piecemeal due to limited funding and lack of political will. With the new Defence Policy Guidelines (DPG) of 2003, the Schröder government made a fresh attempt to transform the *Bundeswehr* into a modern, expeditionary force to deploy on operations beyond the European territory (Federal Ministry of Defence, 2003). The DPG paved the way for the *Konzeption der Bundeswehr* of 2004, a framework document to establish reduce the total force from 280,000 to 250,000 troops and to establish a three-layered force structure by 2010. This force structure was to consist of

- 35,000 for combat operations. These forces would provide the German contingents to the NATO Response Force (NRF) as well as to other NATO/EU war-fighting operations;
- 70,000 troops for stability and reconstruction operations. These forces would be deployed in low-intensity conflicts for longer periods of time; and
- 147,500 support troops to provide joint logistics for operations and the *Bundeswehr* at home (Federal Ministry of Defence, 2004).

This ambitious plan demonstrated that the German government was willing to develop significant forces for NATO operations also at the sharp end of the mission spectrum. It was also a recognition that the modern operations had laid bare the still existing deficiencies of the *Bundeswehr* as an expeditionary force and the ability of the Ministry of Defence to lead effectively in such missions (Noetzel and Schreer, 2008).

German participation in the NATO-led ISAF operation in Afghanistan had displayed exactly some of those limitations. Berlin was quick to pledge 1,200 troops when the international ISAF deployed to Kabul upon the fall of the Taliban in 2001. Yet, the Schröder government emphasized that they were deployed on a stabilization and reconstruction mission (Daalgard-Nielsen, 2003, p. 109). This did not change when NATO took over the lead of ISAF and expanded its reach to the Northern part of Afghanistan in the Autumn of 2003. That said, the *Bundeswehr* took command of the Provincial Reconstruction Team (PRT) in the province of Kunduz. In 2004, it also led a second PRT in Faizabad. Finally, one year later Germany agreed to lead the Regional Command North (RCN).

When Chancellor Schröder left office in 2005, Germany's defence and NATO policy had been evolved quite dramatically from when he first got elected in 1998. Not only had he demonstrated a greater willingness to use military force in the context of NATO operations in order to facilitate German national interests in a changing international setting. Moreover, traditional patterns of German scepticism towards the use of military power, that is, the self-perception as a civilian power, changed somewhat even if the Afghanistan operation showed that elements still persisted. The Schröder government, however, also was willing to oppose military action in the case of Iraq even at the cost of splitting the alliance. Importantly, this opposition was not due to a general, cultural adversity towards the use of force but was also the result of a changing power dynamic influencing Germany's foreign and security policy. As a major power in Europe, Germany had become more independent to assess if the use of force was in its national interests.

In terms of capability, the *Bundeswehr* proved able to take on leadership roles in NATO's expeditionary operation in Afghanistan. This included combat operations; even so these were largely conducted by special forces and therefore out of the public domain. Still, in combination with a quite sizeable force contingent deployed to the Balkans, the *Bundeswehr* incrementally learned how to conduct and sustain such demanding out-of-area missions. Shortfalls persisted including an almost chronic underfunding of the transformation efforts (Szabo and Hampton, 2003). Overall, however the *Bundeswehr*'s performance in a NATO context during that period was acceptable even though key operational and political challenges in Afghanistan were yet to come.

## German defence policy under Chancellor Angela Merkel

Upon taking office at the end of 2005, the government of Chancellor Angela Merkel did pursue more continuity than change in Germany's security and defence policy. For example, the 2006 Defence White Paper, the first since 1994, also recognized that the country's security and defence policy had to readjust to the international security setting, including a willingness to contribute to multinational coalition operations (Federal Ministry of Defence, 2006, pp. 5–6).

However, the government also faced a slowly deteriorating security situation in Afghanistan where insurgent forces increasingly confronted ISAF forces, including in the country's relatively stable northern part where Germany as the third largest troop contributor was still in command of the RCN. As fighting intensified in Southern Afghanistan, more and more allies demanded help also by redeploying German combat elements from the Northern part in a common spirit of burden-sharing and alliance solidarity. Yet, Chancellor Merkel made it clear that she did not support such a shift, with leading German security experts argued that Afghanistan did not constitute a case of alliance solidarity. Instead, in their view each ally could choose his individual force contribution according to his own interests and risk assessment (Bertram, 2008).

German reluctance to get involved into a sustained counterinsurgency operation also revealed that political elites in Berlin were still reluctant to send the *Bundeswehr* into regular ground combat missions. They contested the very notion that the nature of the conflict in Afghanistan had shifted and avoided using the term 'war'. In a sense, elements of German strategic culture still promoted scepticism towards high-intensity conflict (Noetzel and Schreer, 2009a).

However, over time the *Bundeswehr*'s strategic and operational approach in Afghanistan adjusted to the new reality. Not only did then Defence Minister Karl Theodor zu Guttenberg took the lead to reframe the political debate by calling the ISAF mission a 'war', the Army also moved to adjust its doctrine towards counterinsurgency (COIN) operations and the German ISAF contingent conducted more regular offensive COIN operations. This included the German lead in a major offensive against Taliban forces in October 2007, *Operation Harekate Yolo II*. In July 2008, the German contingent also deployed a Quick Reaction Force (QRF) in RCN, taking over from the Norwegian forces, responsible for kinetic operations against insurgent forces. In subsequent years, German forces became frequently engaged in high-end operations against insurgents which also led to the loss of German soldiers. Until May 2012, the *Bundeswehr* had lost 52 soldiers in Afghanistan of which 34 were combat related (Federal Ministry of Defence 2012). Compared with other ISAF contributors, only the United States (1973), the United Kingdom (414), Canada (158) and France (83) had suffered more casualties (icasualties.org, 2012). Finally, in February 2010 the German Parliament mandated to increase the *Bundeswehr*'s ISAF contingent from 4,500 to 5,350 troops, a mandate that was renewed in 2011 and 2012. Therefore, Germany has persistently been the third largest troop contributor to ISAF.

Consequently, Germany has proven a reliable and also relatively capable ally in the ISAF operation. To be sure, the *Bundeswehr* (just like most of the other European allies) suffered from shortages of critical military equipment such as tactical airlift and specialized infantry units. Yet, over time it adapted to the operational challenge and also overcame its resistance to the use of force, including high-intensity combat operations. Despite the fact that the Merkel government was also willing to challenge US leadership in NATO on a whole number of strategic issues, ranging from enlargement, global partnership to strategic missile defence (Schreer, 2009), it remained steadfast in its support for the ISAF mission. Moreover, apart from the left party (*Die Linke*) there was also by and large broad support for the operation on part of the opposition.

Regarding Germany's abstention in the Libya campaign much has been made of its alleged return to pacifist traditions, supported by the aforementioned statement by Foreign Minister Westerwelle that he favoured a military culture of restraint. Moreover, it should be noted that this decision also met with bipartisan support (Brössler, 2011). While Germany during the operation did not completely abstain, keeping for example some military staff in operational headquarters, it did remove two frigates and, more importantly, also AWACS surveillance plane crews from the Mediterranean theatre of operations. Berlin's behaviour was greeted by its major NATO allies with disbelief and anger; its decision was seen as yet another proof that Berlin has become a much more unreliable ally, unwilling to take a leading role when it comes to military affairs (Demmer and Schult, 2012).

Some analysts concluded that Germany had become a 'geo-economic power', focused primarily on economic interests and increasingly disinterested in the use of military force for political purposes. For them Germany has turned into a 'Great Switzerland' (Kundnani, 2011). Undoubtedly, Germany places greater emphasis on economic than on military power. Moreover, political elites and the broader public are still sceptical about the use of military force. Still, there are also a number of structural factors that can explain why the German government did not support the campaign.

First, there is now a firm understanding among the German political elite that Germany's security does no longer fundamentally depend on the Atlantic alliance (absent a dramatic shift in the external strategic environment), which allows for much greater room for manoeuvre inside NATO, including opting out of operations. NATO in general has become much more institutionally flexible and in which 'coalitions of the willing' have become the norm rather than the exception. Libya was a case in point (Hallams and Schreer, 2012). Berlin no longer automatically supports NATO's 'wars of choice' simply because of alliance solidarity.

Libya did also not directly threaten core German interests. Indeed, the Gaddafi regime had in recent years become a more reliable and interesting business partner. Furthermore, Berlin has developed a considerable scepticism towards 'humanitarian interventions'; it not only wonders about the chances for long-term success of these missions but, more importantly, questions the domestic and international gains to be made from using military power. In fact, one can even argue that the German government exerted some sort of leadership during the crisis for those countries that were also not willing to participate. In the end, only 8 out of 28 NATO members contributed to Operation Unified Protector.

Consequently, Germany's behaviour in the Libya crisis could also be explained in terms of great power politics:

> The alleged damage caused by Berlin's abstention to Germany's reputation of reliability, can be rectified when seen through the lens of traditional great power politics. Following this line, Germany may have only gained in reputation by becoming equally 'unpredictable' in its foreign policy approach as the French, the Britons or the Americans by choosing to follow up on 'national interest'. Reliability and followership may be a formula of success for small states, but not for great powers. This is one of the foreign policy lessons learned in Berlin if one compares Afghanistan 2001, Iraq 2003 and Libya 2011.
> (Hellmann, 2011)

The combination of structural and cultural factors informing contemporary German defence policy and the use of force, including its approach to the Atlantic alliance, leads to a much selective approach when it comes to the use of force. As demonstrated in Afghanistan and elsewhere, German decision-makers are not per se reluctant to use military power to support national interests. However, in an era of 'humanitarian interventions', diffuse global security threats and risks, and rather limited success of military interventions in places such as Afghanistan or Africa, Germany has recently become more sceptical about more NATO (and EU) operations outside the European theatre. On an alliance spectrum from countries favouring the evolution of a truly 'global NATO' on one end and those arguing for a focus on traditional tasks of collective defence, Germany prefers a middle position – or 'Status quo' – which sees the necessity of selectively employing force 'out-of-area' but does not support what it sees as global military adventurism (Noetzel and Schreer, 2009b; Keller, 2012).

This cautious and selective approach has also been reflected on the capability side of German military power. In fact, current trends in German force modernization seem to indicate that the *Bundeswehr* will only develop a limited expeditionary capability. For one, the armed forces were also affected by budget cuts. In June 2010, the German government decided on defence cuts of €8.3 bn between 2011 and

2014. The total defence budget for 2012 was €32.68 bn and forecasted to decline to €30.43 bn by 2015. These targets placed a huge pressure on the *Bundeswehr* leadership to cut manpower which also led to downsizing the level of ambition in terms of deployable forces for expeditionary operations. In 2010, new reform plans were revealed to sustain an actual maximum deployment of 7,000 troops abroad (10,000 for a short period without rotations), bringing the level of ambition down from the previous target of 14,000 to now only 10,000 troops (IISS, 2012, p. 79). Germany also moved to switch to an all-volunteer force, basically ending the old conscription model.

Yet, in May 2011, new Minister for Defence Thomas de Maizière announced a new DPG which renewed the ambition to retain a 'full spectrum force' to participate in international coalition operations. It contained another significant reduction of the *Bundeswehr*. Over the course of the next six to eight years, the force will be cut from roughly 220,000 to 170,000 professional and contracted soldiers plus 5,000–15,000 voluntary conscripts. The three-layered force structure (combat, stabilization and support forces) will be abandoned. Overall, the ambition is still to deploy up to 10,000 troops abroad. However, the German land force for example, will only be able to provide 5,000 troops to such operations (Federal Ministry of Defence, 2011, p. 35). This fairly limited number has led to consternation on part of the NATO allies who wondered why out of a future force of 185,000 troops the *Bundeswehr* will only be able or willing to deploy a relatively small portion. Moreover, Germany recently announced to reduce the number of new fighter aircraft, strategic airlift, as well as attack and transport helicopters. Even its contribution to much-needed NATO high-altitude unmanned surveillance platforms (Global Hawk) hung in the balance (Demmer and Schult, 2012).

## Conclusion

This chapter has shown that Germany has come quite a long way since the end of the Cold War when it comes to the political will to use military force as an NATO ally. The changing geostrategic landscape in Europe and changing perceptions among the political elites led to a greater willingness during the 1990s and the early 2000s to use military power as an instrument of statecraft. Steps were also taken to transform the *Bundeswehr* into a more expeditionary force. It should be noted that particularly in the context of NATO's ISAF operation in Afghanistan and Berlin has proven to be a reliable and significant troop contributor.

At the same time, however, the Berlin Republic grew more self-confident in terms of taking decisions about the use of force from a purely national interest perspective. This led to its opposition to the Iraq War and NATO's Libya campaign. While elements of a strategic culture of military restraint partly informed these decisions, they were also based on the conclusion that these conflicts were not in the country's interests. In other words, Germany has become more sceptical about the wisdom to engage in 'wars of choice' outside NATO territory. As a result, its defence transformation process is currently geared towards obtaining only a limited expeditionary capability, particularly with regard to land operations.

Germany will thus most likely remain a selective NATO ally. It will choose its participation to NATO operations on a case-by-case basis. Berlin is not generally allergic to the use of force, including at the high end of the military spectrum. It will also retain some military capability to contribute to multinational operations. Yet, it will not thrive to play a leadership role inside the alliance. In times of financial austerity and a partial reorientation of the United States towards the Asia-Pacific this lack of leadership creates a problem for the alliance. Berlin's lukewarm approach to improving its capability to act jeopardizes attempts in NATO to increase overall European allied capability through investments in 'smart defence'. Allies increasingly view Germany's lack of European leadership within the alliance as a serious problem. As a 2012 report by the renowned Atlantic Council argued:

> A weak Germany that lacks a capacity to act globally will inevitably weaken NATO. Europe cannot remain a major force within the NATO Alliance if a country of Germany's size, geography, and prosperity makes the kind of deep reductions in defense spending.
>
> (2012, p. 5)

Unfortunately, a major shift in German defence policy is unlikely to occur in the foreseeable future.

## Bibliography

Asmus, R. (1994) *German Strategy and Public Opinion after the Wall, 1990–1993* (Santa Monica, CA: RAND).
Atlantic Council (2012) *Anchoring the Alliance* (Washington, DC: Atlantic Council).

Baumann, R. and Hellmann, G. (2001) 'Germany and the Use of Military Force: "Total War", the "Culture of Restraint" and the Quest for Normality', *German Politics*, vol. 10, no. 1, pp. 61–82.
Berger, T. U. (1998) *Cultures of Antimilitarism*. National Security in Germany and Japan (Baltimore, MD: Johns Hopkins University Press).
Bertram, C. (2008) 'Afghanistan ist kein Bündnisfall', *Die Zeit*, 16 February, http://www.zeit.de/online/2008/08/nato-kolumne-bertram, accessed 26 September 2012.
Brössler, D. (2011) 'Wir woollen nicht Kriegspartei warden', *Süddeutsche Zeitung*, 17 March.
Buras, P. and Longhurst, K. (2004) 'The Berlin Republic, Iraq, and the Use of Force', *European Security*, vol. 13, no. 3, pp. 215–245.
Dalgaard-Nielsen, A. (2003) 'Gulf War: The German Resistance', *Survival*, vol. 45, no. 1, pp. 99–116.
Demmer, U. and Schult, C. (2012) 'Unreliable Partners? Germany's Reputation in NATO Has Hit Rock Bottom', *Der Spiegel*, 17 May, http://www.spiegel.de (homepage), date accessed 2 July 2012.
Der Spiegel (2011) 'Spiegel Interview with German Foreign Minister', 21 March, http://www.spiegel.de/international/germany/0,1518,752164,00.html, date accessed 26 September 2012.
Dettke, D. (2009) *Germany Says 'No': The Iraq War and the Future of German Foreign and Security Policy* (Washington, DC: Woodrow Wilson Center Press).
Duffield, J. S. (1999) 'Political Culture and State Behavior: Why Germany Confounds Neorealism', *International Organization*, vol. 53, no. 4, pp. 765–803.
Erlanger, S. and Dempsey, J. (2011) 'Germany Steps away From European Unity', *New York Times*, 23 March.
Federal Ministry of Defence (2003) *VerteidigungspolitischeRichtlinien* (Berlin: Federal Ministry of Defence).
Federal Ministry of Defence (2004) *Konzeption der Bundeswehr* (Berlin: Federal Ministry of Defence).
Federal Ministry of Defence (2006) *German Security Policy and the Future of the Bundeswehr* (Berlin: Federal Ministry of Defence).
Federal Ministry of Defence (2011) *Defence Policy Guidelines 2011* (Berlin: Federal Ministry of Defence).
Federal Ministry of Defence (2012a) *Neuausrichtung der Bundeswehr* (Berlin: Federal Ministry of Defence).
Federal Ministry of Defence (2012b), *TodesfälleimAuslandseinsatz*, www.bundeswehr.de (homepage), date accessed 15 May 2012.
Haftendorn, H. (2008) 'The View from Berlin: Germany as a Self-assured European Middle Power', in Peter Schmidt (ed.) *A Hybrid Relationship: Transatlantic Security Cooperation Beyond NATO* (Frankfurt: Peter Lang), pp. 213–220.
Hallams, E. and Schreer, B. (2012) 'Towards a Post-American Alliance? NATO Burden-sharing after Libya', *International Affairs*, vol. 88, no. 2, pp. 313–327.
Hellmann, G. (2011) 'Berlin, Great Power Politics, and Libya', *Commentaries*, American Institute for Contemporary German Studies, 22 September, http://www.aicgs.org/issue/berlin-great-power-politics-and-libya/, accessed 26 September 2012.

Hyde-Price, A. (2001) 'Germany and the Kosovo War: Still a Civilian Power?', *German Politics*, vol. 10, no. 1, pp. 19–34.
icasualties.org (2012) http://icasualties.org (homepage), date accessed 15 May 2012.
International Institute for Strategic Studies (IISS) (1992) *The Military Balance, 1992–1993* (London: International Institute for Strategic Studies).
International Institute for Strategic Studies (2012) *The Military Balance 2012* (London: International Institute for Strategic Studies).
Joffe, J. (2011) 'Der neue deutsche Sonderweg', *Handelsblatt*, 30 March.
Keller, P. (2012) 'Germany and NATO: The Status Quo Ally', *Survival*, vol. 54, no. 3, pp. 95–110.
Kundnani, H. (2011) 'Germany as a "Geo-economic" Power', *Washington Quarterly*, vol. 34, no. 3, pp. 31–45.
Maull, H. W. (1990) 'Germany and Japan: The New Civilian Powers', *Foreign Affairs*, vol. 69, no. 5, pp. 91–106.
Maull, H. W. (1992) 'ZivilmachtBundesrepublik Deutschland: VierzehnThesenfüreineneue deutsche Außenpolitik', *Europa Archiv*, vol. 43, no. 10, pp. 269–278.
Maull, H. W. (2000) 'Germany and the Use of Force: Still a Civilian Power?', *Survival*, vol. 42, no. 2, pp. 56–80.
Mearsheimer, J. (1990) 'Back to the Future: Instability in Europe after the Cold War', *International Security*, vol. 15, no. 1, pp. 5–56.
New York Times News Service (1999) 'Schroeder Signals Shift, Calls Germany a "Great Power"', 12 September, http://articles.baltimoresun.com/1999-09-12/news/9909120181_1_germany-german-foreign-policy-chancellor
Noetzel, T. and Schreer, B. (2008) 'All the Way? The Evolution of German Military Power', *International Affairs*, vol. 84, no. 2, pp. 211–221.
Noetzel, T. and Schreer, B. (2009a) 'NATO's Vietnam? Afghanistan and the Future of the Atlantic Alliance', *Contemporary Security Policy*, vol. 30, no. 3, pp. 529–547.
Noetzel, T. and Schreer, B. (2009b) 'Does a "Multi-tier" NATO Matter? The Atlantic Alliance and the Process of Strategic Change', *International Affairs*, vol. 85, no. 2, pp. 211–226.
Paterson, W. E. (1996) 'Beyond Semi-sovereignty: The New Germany in a New Europe', *German Politics*, vol. 5, no. 2, pp. 167–184.
Sarotte, M. E. (2001) *German Military Reform and European Security*, Adelphi Paper no. 340 (London: International Institute for Strategic Studies).
Schreer, B. (2009) 'A New "Pragmatism": Germany's NATO Policy', *International Journal*, vol. 64, no. 2, pp. 383–398.
Schröder, G. (1999) 'Deutsche Sicherheitspolitik an der Schwelle des 21. Jahrhunderts', *Rede auf der 35.MünchenerSicherheitskonferenz*, 6 February.
Stacey, K. (2012) 'Germany Urged to Pay More on Defence', *Financial Times*, 4 May 2012.
Stockholm Peace Research Institute (SIPRI) (2012) *Military Expenditure Database*, http://milexdata.sipri.org (homepage), date accessed 9 May 2012.
Szabo, S. F. and Hampton, M. N. (2003) 'Reinventing the German Military', *AICGS Policy Report* 11.

von Thadden, R. (2011) 'Woist das deutsch-französischePaar?', *Frankfurter Allgemeine Zeitung*, 29 March 2011.

Wallace, W. (1995) 'Germany as the Leading Power in Europe', *The World Today*, vol. 51, no. 8/9, pp. 162–164.

Zelikow, P. (2003) 'The Transformation of National Security', *The National Interest*, 1 March, pp. 17–28.

# 10
# Willing and Able? Spanish Statecraft as Brokerage

D. Coletta and D. García

## Introduction

As the premier power of early modern Europe, Spain did much to perfect the art of statecraft. The lead state of the Hapsburg Empire lost in the end, but for 30 years during the great war of the seventeenth century, Spain managed to fend off all comers bent on displacing her from the apex of military capability in Europe.[1] Observers living in the Anglo-American epoch after the Second World War often look back to nineteenth-century England, at the height of her influence, for models of naval dominance and hegemonic control. Yet, as twenty-first-century Spanish Prime Minister José Aznar reminded an American audience on his valedictory tour, before England there was Spain, controlling a vast empire of millions in the New World stretching from southern Argentina to northern California. After the *Unión Ibérica* between Spain and Portugal from 1580 to 1640, the Empire on which the sun never set (*El Imperio en el que nunca se ponía el sol*) included the Philippines and Guam in the Asia Pacific, Morocco, and trading outposts in greater Africa and India (Boustay, 2004; Sciolino, 2004).[2]

Though the reputation of Spanish statecraft and the use of force suffers from the Black Legend promulgated by her imperial era rivals and the American propagandists who cheered the last gasp of her empire at the end of the nineteenth century, it would be a mistake to overlook the potential for innovative diplomacy, including the full range of foreign policy instruments, from today's Spain or her capacity to benefit from a wealth of experience. In asking the larger question of whether NATO, the most important alliance in the twenty-first century, can muster the capability and the will to fulfil the ambition of its new Strategic Concept, the answer may well depend, among other, more obvious factors, on how a mid-size ally like Spain manages its strategic assets.[3]

The reason statecraft matters so much in this mid-size case is that Spain sits between important blocs of the transatlantic relationship at the same time that it bears the brunt as a vital frontline state for major international crises, including sovereign debt in Europe, political instability in North Africa, vulnerability to international terrorism, and the rattling of state institutions before the forces of globalization. Due to historical, cultural and financial ties, Spain has a special voice in Western Hemispheric affairs even while its size, location and successful transition to democracy make it a central player in the European project. By institutional measures, Spain has been a reliable partner for NATO efforts in the Balkans and Afghanistan and, under the pro-American government of the *Partido Popular* (*PP*), an early contributor to the US-led Operation Iraqi Freedom. Spain's Atlanticism at the turn of the twenty-first century was uniquely complemented by its extraordinary role in the European Union as the largest beneficiary over several years and a model steward of EU cohesion funds (Katsarova, 2007).[4]

In short, Spain with its fiscal house in order would be well-positioned to exercise an influence in global affairs disproportionate to its medium size. It can do so by swinging its diplomatic and material support between blocs within NATO, still the most successful alliance in the world. Because cooperation within NATO is crucial for advancing security and justice in several key regions, including Europe, North Africa and the Middle East, and because NATO military operations in some sense free the United States, with its remaining economic and military strength, to engage East Asia, the strategic role of broker among contending factions within the Transatlantic Alliance offers ripe opportunities for mid-size members to make a global difference.

For Spain, the most productive crease in NATO runs down the Atlantic, separating the United States from long-time allies on the European continent. Especially when the United Kingdom and newer members in Central and Eastern Europe are in the balance, Spanish statecraft, albeit bounded by modest military deployments that only generate on the order of a few thousand troops, can yet build bridges to ameliorate the transatlantic divide – raising the Alliance, and the West's, chance for success in world affairs.

In spite of its central importance, statecraft as the context for use of force has a rather unusual status in contemporary social science and international relations theory: factors that might constrain state

180  *Application: Case Studies*

behaviour also create opportunities. The high-level stakes and potential violence notwithstanding, statecraft is as much art as science. Basic awareness and empirical assessment protect decision-makers from likely threats. At the same time, a kind of sixth sense, or acute perception, can discern combinations of events that would advance national goals. Statecraft takes place under circumstances of constant crisis – in double-edged situations that bring danger but also prospects of significant rewards. Which side the outcomes fall depends on how statesmen interpret and portray, to both domestic and foreign audiences, factors highlighted in this volume: history, culture, economy and policy risk.

In terms of a metaphor closely linked to opportunity and risk, Spanish statecraft in particular may be usefully framed as brokerage. Just as it always has, NATO's decision-making strains under tensions from intense conflicts of interest among internal factions whose cooperation nevertheless fuels Alliance achievements. Relative to Spain, the most important constituents are the United States, Continental Western Europe led by France and Germany, the United Kingdom, Eastern Europe, and depending on the location and nature of the crisis, Turkey. As in brokerage, each manoeuvre, each decision to align for or against certain blocs, involves potential losses. Yet, the various actors, and especially the big investors, must be in play in order for the broker to win.

For Spain, the North Atlantic Treaty creates brokerage opportunities along the transatlantic fault line. In terms of geography, national interests, and world view, it is that line which separates the United States – the most powerful member – from all other Alliance factions. Whether the crisis involves burden-sharing for NATO crisis management, territorial access for force projection or missile defence, or industrial contracts and command headquarters for modernizing NATO's defence posture, there is no shortage of difficult demands crisscrossing the transatlantic gap.

When Spain's economy, democracy and military are strong relative to its size and its own contemporary standard – not the impossible one relative to the global hegemon – Spain is in fine form to modulate the steady stream of weighty transatlantic petitions. The diplomatic record after 9/11 also indicates that however strong the United States becomes in economic and military terms, it will not have sufficient strength to compel other NATO constituencies on decisions to employ their militaries. Real negotiations will be necessary, and while it might make intuitive sense that a weaker United States would need its Spanish ally more, American institutions and strategic traditions turn this logic on its head. The hard task befalling the Spanish broker ends up being 'to keep the United States in'. The European factions are generally in need of convincing that diplomatic concessions and military sacrifices on their part are worthwhile for fixing US attention and resources. This sort of persuasion actually presents greater challenges for Spanish statecraft as the United States gets *weaker*.

Spain may be a mid-size country on the periphery of Europe, but given the world situation today, it can play an important role in helping NATO meet two of its most recently announced core missions: out-of-area crisis management and cooperative security. The need for perspicacious Spanish statecraft, particularly during crises involving the threat of force, is as great as ever. Unfortunately, mounting evidence of US decline indicates that windows of opportunity for Spanish statesmen may be closing: This makes good defence policy harder to come by but no less beneficial for the Alliance and ultimately Spain.

## Spain's assets and liabilities in the NATO context

In order to evaluate consequences of American withdrawal, or at least retraction of US force projection capabilities and financial influence from the extended area of NATO operations, for defence policy of a mid-size ally like Spain, we can first tally Spain's assets and liabilities. With respect to this volume's framework, the usual background factors from classical realism in International Relations theory, including history, culture and economy of a state actor, supplement what may be gleaned from a state's power position in the system.[5] Normally, the highly institutionalized protocols of the Transatlantic Alliance push analysts away from realism, that is, the standard list of geopolitical incentives for state actors (Haftendorn, Keohane, and Wallander, 1999; Duffield, 1994–1995). At the same time, most realists view reasons of state as reasons to undermine NATO's military potential; in fact without the common state-level threat of the Soviet Union, the organization's years as a close alliance, capable of its original mission in common defence, by realist lights ought to be numbered (Mearsheimer, 1990; Waltz, 2000; Rupp, 2006; Layne, 2008).[6]

On the other hand, realist, state-level factors also constitute much of the hand of cards states are dealt when negotiating tradeoffs between their conventional geopolitical interests and obligations to international institutions. Leading intellectuals of the realist camp on statecraft often oppose institutional demands against the national interest: For example, the US administration of George W. Bush withdrew from the Anti-Ballistic Missile Treaty and opposed the Comprehensive Test Ban Treaty, the Kyoto Protocol on greenhouse gas emissions, and the International Criminal Court purportedly because they committed the United States to act against its security and economic interests. All of these arrangements except the first, however, had been signed or negotiated by the previous president. The disagreement was not just a political fight between the American parties or an ideological dispute about the proper role of institutions in international life. Those rejected institutions also reflected a portrait of the national interest, albeit of a longer term and less specific geographic character. The old line factors in our framework – history, culture and economy – actually play into states' institutional commitments like NATO as well as their geopolitical imperatives.

NATO has always evinced traits of international bargaining (Olson and Zeckhauser, 1966; Beer, 1972; Lepgold, 1998; Kaplan, 2004). The dominant threat of the Soviet Union and the proliferation of intergovernmental organizations within the Alliance tended to overshadow the negotiations, but statesmen and NATO's secretary generals have been acutely aware of nearly continuous, vigorous horse trading among the members (Hendrickson, 2006; Deni, 2007;Thies, 2009). In truth, NATO fits rather uneasily within either the realist or institutionalist models for cooperation. In both of these mainstream perspectives the Alliance appears to be in constant crisis: every proposal to respond to changed circumstances – the European Defence Community, the incorporation of West Germany, the Multilateral Nuclear Force, Flexible Response, insertion or withdrawal of American nuclear weapons, out-of-area crisis management – has elicited wildly inconsistent interpretations. The Alliance is either in its death throes or Germany and new members from the East no longer hold legitimate interests apart from servicing a web of institutions to integrate Europe, a task notably requiring few major defence expenditures.

In one sense, these polar interpretations need to continue. After all, it is always possible that NATO could break apart or that it could successfully take on global security missions not in the immediate interests of European member states and executed on the back of unique US military capabilities.[7] However, the heterodox bargaining approach is also useful because, if history is any guide, the most likely pattern for NATO runs consistent with New Institutionalism at the international level. NATO membership provides long-term benefits that mix in without displacing conventional economic and security concerns. Alliance institutions reduce the transaction costs of cooperation as liberal institutionalists expect, but the specifics of protocols, especially those like force generation for coalition missions, which involve redistributive consequences, are fair game in continuous inter-state negotiations. NATO arrangements – from command headquarters and burden-sharing to language in the Strategic Concept – thus reflect both realist and liberal institutionalist impulses: they may reinforce as much as reform member states' perception of their own national interest.[8]

One can acknowledge that NATO has survived the loss of its enemy, its original *raison d'être*, and still see a role for statecraft in shaping individual members' use of force. Spain's diplomatic options are in fact limited by its geography, its culture and its economic circumstances. Yet, much of the movement, the proposals for furthering or withholding defence cooperation, must take place in a fog of uncertainty. If Spain refuses to supply strike aircraft or bases as Libya implodes, no one can be precisely sure what level of difficulty this will create for NATO or the United States.[9] Without specific foreknowledge of costs and benefits – pleasure and pain as a result of certain actions – the art of statecraft could fairly be described as knowing when to invest in improbable outcomes.

Much has been written about the decline of old state preferences, with respect to both traditional ends and conventional military means, after the shift from a bipolar world order and the rise of globalization (Van Evera, 1990–1991; Haftendorn, Keohane, and Wallander, 1999; McCormick, 2006; Baylis, Wirtz, and Gray, 2010, esp. pp. 247–265). At the same time, NATO's member states have not unravelled. The practice of statecraft that remains is richer in the sense that porous sovereign boundaries intensify the pressure on statesmen – from expanding international organizations above and newly mobilized domestic constituencies below. Rather than eliminating statecraft, globalization and democratization may have added a new factor in its formulation. Ulrich Beck (1999, 2006), Michael Williams (2008) and Christopher Coker (2009) have argued that democratic leaders, in order to stay in power, have had to adjust their policies according to prevailing attitudes in their societies towards risk.

Surveying the security policy of the United States once it was cast adrift from its Cold War moorings, some see a pattern in the string of military interventions across the Horn of Africa, the Balkans, Afghanistan and Iraq. The United States, lacking a great power adversary, lashed out to quell brewing threats in the hinterlands, practically ungoverned spaces from which disorder could spill over and perturb the vast zone of peace connecting East Asia and Western Europe with the Americas (Huntington, 1996; Barnett, 2004; Cohen, 2009).

A key difficulty highlighted by the Risk Society theorists is that inordinate fear on the part of citizens combined with electoral pressures in a democracy could trap statesmen in the United States, and possibly Europe, into a briar patch of endless shadow wars, to the detriment of basic defence preparations, which despite the stabilization and nation building missions remain both necessary and expensive (Kagan, 2011). The Risk Society thesis, however, would not be very useful if the warning already came too late. Indeed, defence establishments have begun to shrink, but proposals to go much further are still being debated. Now is the time to recall the science and art of statecraft, recognizing that in addition to the standard considerations of history, culture and economy, democratic statesmen will also be expected to address fears for personal security, which animate calls for crisis management and other complex military missions abroad.

## Spain's rich history

After 200 years of Anglo-American primacy in the international system, it is easy for scholars to discount Spain's rich historical experience with statecraft. If statecraft is the science and art of conjuring diplomatic alignments and rivalries to maximize the benefits from a state's power position for national security, then Spain has practised statecraft under a variety of challenging circumstances (Parker, 1994; Lobell, 2003; Nexon, 2009).[10] Certain facts, that Spain, today, is merely the fifth-largest economy in Europe, that its defence spending is just one thirty-fifth that of the United States, should not – however – be taken as insurmountable obstacles against the country's capacity for effective global policy.[11] During its long diplomatic history, Spain has been the strong man, the sick man, and at still other times, the recovering man of Europe. In all those years, rare indeed have been moments when Spain could do nothing to affect positively the global balance of power.

From the long sixteenth century, 1492–1648, when Spain attained and then fell from the summit of world power, the lessons are mostly negative but nonetheless relevant for today's challenges.[12] On the positive side of the ledger, Castile and Aragon dominated and coordinated administrations across a territory on the vast scale of a modern nation-state, this despite pressures from below and above, including the threat from a competing and in several ways more advanced Islamic civilization with revanchist ambitions.[13] Rather than merely hold its own, Spain created an administration and mobilized the resources to construct the first transoceanic, in a sense the first global, empire (Parker, 1998, 2010; Rodríguez Marcos, 2010).

Now, as the Anglo-authored Black Legend trumpeted, methods in Europe as well as the New World for accomplishing these feats were militaristic, and consequences for 'developing peoples', especially indigenous societies across the Americas, were dire. Yet, the incalculable misery occasioned by this first world order was not in vain. The extreme inequality, the entrenched injustice, left the Iberian system vulnerable to attack without from peer competitors and within through revolutionary and independence movements.[14]

Great Britain and the United States, as instigators and beneficiaries of the Spanish Empire's decline, might be expected to have learned all there is to know from Spain's failures; their subsequent empires have after all been more democratic, more market-based, and less coercive. Crucial questions remain, however. For several populations across the contemporary developing world – in South Asia, the Middle East, East Africa, Vietnam and Central America – the Anglo-American order despite its superior liberal values has been the handmaiden for tragic, Iberian levels of destruction.[15]

This does not mean the United States somehow bears responsibility for redressing every grievance and fixing all the world's problems, but it does indicate that free speech and competitive political parties notwithstanding, the Americans are likely biased in judging their own case, and further this prejudice needs correcting as it contributes to the vulnerability of American leadership. NATO Allies such as Spain, which do not share the same bias even if they have held in the past a similar position in the international system, will soberly perceive the damage done by rapier attacks on US legitimacy. Spain, once the scourge of the Americans, is now a democratic ally of the twenty-first-century hegemon: it finds itself in position to become a trusted, constructive critic, especially where contemporary US influence overlaps with imperial Spain's old radius of action – in the Western Hemisphere, the Maghreb, formerly Catholic Europe, and former Ottoman areas stretching south from modern Turkey into the Middle East.

To be sure, Spain does not wield much coercive power in this vast geopolitical zone, save perhaps for leverage purchased from investment in Latin America worth $125 bn between 1995 and 2007 and ranking second behind that of the United States over the past 20 years (Aragüetes, 2011). Yet, by dint of its history – the triumphs and the disasters – Spain does have credibility as a broker between Washington and governments across this rich expanse, governments which may not yet be behaving as adversaries but are nevertheless buffeted by the sweep of US power.

If seventeenth-century Spain learned what it was like to be feared as US economic size, military might and cultural influence are feared, then during the twentieth century Spain understood what it was to be torn by foreign military and ideological forces colliding on its homeland. To leaders in today's developing regions who dread the prospect of a hyper-power intervention, Spain's voice resonates with comparatively recent experience. Actions undertaken on behalf of national unity under the rule of Generalissimo Francisco Franco still reside in that society's political consciousness (Preston, 1996; Payne, 2000).[16] Even under the repression of a conservative, authoritarian state, though, it should be remembered that Spanish statecraft persevered.

When Spanish diplomats come to call in our time, they may frame history to their advantage. Indeed, no other state after 1945 had occasion to navigate the treacherous waters from neutrality in the global fight against fascism to NATO membership, all the while maintaining its sovereign independence.[17] Of course, this impressive feat of statecraft, a salient example of maximizing influence and increasing security with limited material resources, does not excuse the violence, repression or intimidation of the Franco regime. In answer to that concern, Spain also boasts a dramatically successful transition story, which ought to engage today's fledgling democracies. Many of their leaders, concerned about their electability and the crowding effect of US military power or economic influence, yet ride the so-called Third Wave of democratization inspired by developments in Portugal and Spain some 35 years ago (Huntington, 1991).[18]

### Spain's reticent culture

If history clearly aids Spain in becoming an empathetic interlocutor among small and mid-size powers, i.e., the states Kenneth Waltz once labelled as price-takers in the international system, Spain's culture pushes in multiple directions with regard to statecraft. Here, culture relates to habits of mind emerging from history and moulding Spanish decision-makers' approach to the world. Culture is strategic in the sense that it imports valuations for both geopolitical ends and the effectiveness of military means.[19]

When analysing history, students of statecraft develop objective links between previous experience and future policies. The cultural framework, by contrast, helps explain Spanish subjectivity. Culture may still work within the constraints of instrumental rationality, so patterns of military employment remain predictable. Yet, due to differences in strategic culture, Spain's reliance on force, for example, might diverge from US behaviour in a similar situation. Considering culture in this way, Spain is reticent, creating both advantages and complications for Spanish statecraft. Most importantly, greater awareness of Spain's strategic culture, on the part of allies, officials, and the people, can improve the chances for successful international cooperation and more productive coalition missions when the use of force is in play.

With respect to strategic ends, the long dismantlement of Spain's Catholic Monarchy and the gaping wounds inflicted on society by the Spanish Civil War taught Spaniards to eschew utopian visions of global order and the ideological triumph that would mark the end of history. Soon after the Cold War, with both superpowers straining under heavy defence burdens and bristling with nuclear weapons, political scientist Robert Jervis asked, 'Is the Game Worth the Candle?' If the game was the classical one of great power domination, Spain long ago decided it was not. Rather than forge a single world civilization out of overwhelming destructive power, Spanish culture – the mindset – is more likely to imagine an Alliance of Civilizations (BBC News, 2004; Turkish Daily News, 2006).[20]

Like the historical idiosyncrasies, Spain's distinctive strategic culture is not so detrimental to NATO or to a relatively decentralized, democratic international order under benign US hegemony. In fact when it comes to ambitious geopolitical ends, pluralism among Western allies could be instrumental while military coercion becomes less cost effective. Once again, as brokerage, Spanish statecraft could take the edge off less astute US belligerence.

Because of America's own strategic culture – rejecting the norms of great power balancing developed in Europe after the Thirty Years War and enlisting free citizens under the banner of universal ideals, especially democracy and human rights, in order to mobilize for national defence – the United States as current system leader is prone to ill-advised international crusades. Spanish pragmatism can help modulate strident US policy. Utilitarian peace, prosperity and justice – the greatest good for the greatest number – in a world of coexisting sovereigns adhering to diverse ideologies can help balance American triumphalism. Moreover, when Spain endorses a US mission as it did before the Iraq War, its strategic culture, a credential difficult to hide or counterfeit, lends weight to its brokerage so that adversaries and neutrals may not easily indict US or Anglo-American motives before the international community (Economist, 2004).

By contrast, culture as it connects to means, or, the instruments of power, places certain obstacles on the path for twenty-first-century Spanish statecraft. While the United States with its $600 bn defence budget may overestimate the effectiveness of military force, Spanish habits of mind point in the opposite direction. Underestimating the importance or utility of force can create at least two types of problems for Spain as a NATO ally. First, if Spain decides to employ brokerage and lend its political support to a US-led operation, its military commitment will be open to question. In fact, after the Socialist election victory in 2004, Spain struggled with this issue in both Iraq and Afghanistan, where the Spanish military worked under a cloud: the widely held perception on the American side, and perhaps unfair, that well-placed attacks in the field or on the homeland would be sufficient to knock Spain out of the war.[21] Again, culture is difficult to hide, and in the extreme, Spain's intuitive scepticism about the use of force could increase the danger for her troops and those of her allies.

The second problem occurs when Spain's devaluation of force as a means keeps it on the sidelines instead of shoulder-to-shoulder with NATO partners. Spanish pragmatism naturally encourages optimism towards the democratic and human rights potential of the Arab Spring that energized youth across North Africa in 2011, but early that same year it appeared that Spain underestimated the value of Western military intervention for checking Libya's Colonel Gaddafi at the gates of Benghazi, and in relatively short order building conditions for accountable government on Spain's southern periphery (Cloud, 2011).[22]

In terms of both ends and means, Spain's strategic culture nudges its statesmen towards prudence and reticence. For refining US-style, muscular internationalism, prudence and ideological pragmatism serve as bulwarks in defence of Spanish and NATO interests. Yet, if the Transatlantic Alliance is to guide global developments, if Spain is to realize its potential for positive influence on political and economic changes, military force will be among the policy instruments – not just as a last resort or when vital interests are already jeopardized. Facing an adversary bent on violence, Spain by its culture will be slow to see how such a foe could be disarmed at practical cost. That habitual reticence merits careful attention, for neglected it threatens to unravel statecraft, separating Spain's methods from its objectives.

## The once and future economy

Given recent headlines, spotlighting Spain's sovereign debt crisis and speculating on the future of the European currency should the government in Madrid imperil a €1 tn economy by defaulting on foreign creditors, it is difficult to envision right now how Spain could mobilize sufficient resources to sustain statecraft worthy of its history or its strategic culture. Economic problems may yet force a debilitating separation between Spain's methods and its objectives. On the other hand, even though Republican candidate John McCain elicited howls of criticism when he asserted that US economic fundamentals remained sound as housing, financial and employment indicators crumbled during late-summer of the 2008 election campaign, in the sense of underwriting American statecraft, McCain had a point (Gross, 2008). Three years later, the United States spends less on its wars, but its engagement, backed by military force close to Iraq, inside Afghanistan, and across critical theatres all over the globe continues.[23] Mainstream observers are not prepared to demote the United States from its hegemonic perch just yet (Nye, 2010).[24]

In similar fashion, Spain in 2010 spent some €17 bn on defence, below the 2 per cent NATO guideline but still around 1.6 per cent of GDP.[25] Spain faces defence cuts as part of the plan for attracting outside aid and putting its fiscal house in order. Yet, there is enough to continue Spanish participation in coalition missions through either NATO or the European Union in the Balkans and Afghanistan, which is to say sufficient defence resources to fulfil a broker role: within Europe along the East–West or North–South axes; between the United States and Europe; or between the United States and Europe on one hand and democratizing nations (in Latin America or south and east along the Mediterranean coast) on the other.

Following the trend of the United States and other NATO Allies, Spain's budgets for defence-related research and development are shrinking.[26] For the medium-run, though, quality modernization programmes continue and may yet survive. Despite the economic troubles, aircraft plants in Spain have reached the next milestone in certifying the crucial A400M airlifter for Europe. On the ground, Spain continues to invest in armoured vehicles such as the Leopard and Pizarro systems, and at sea, modernization efforts include the F-100 frigate and the S-80 submarine (Ortega and Bohigas, 2009, pp. 7–8; Ing, 2011).[27]

In space, perhaps the fastest evolving environment for navigation and communication, Spain maintains its position as a mid-size investor in satellite technology (O'Dwyer, 2010). Madrid does not yet control its own imaging satellites, but the Spanish air base at Torrejón hosts the European Union Satellite Centre, with an international staff for producing joint data analysis from shared space assets. In summary, the concerns over low growth and potential default, while dire, do not erase certain fundamentals. Technological knowhow and international business experience keep Spain's defence skills and equipment in being until the next economic upturn. To be sure, present conditions in Spain are not good for production, investment or innovation. Yet, regarding muscle for statecraft, less bulk than sophistication is required for a twenty-first-century broker as opposed to a super-powered hegemon in the US mode. Spain's housing bubble, though it created trouble for financial and other business sectors, did not imply a defence bubble: the Spanish state may yet intervene to preserve key programmes for the military.[28]

As long as Spain can execute sophisticated contracts, particularly in cooperation with sought after industrial partners in Western Europe and the United States, Madrid will have opportunities to engage the global economy (DefenceWeb, 2012). Engagement may not have worked in the case of Spain's 2005 agreement to sell €500 million in transport and maritime patrol aircraft for Hugo Chavez's Venezuela (Defense Industry Daily, 2006).[29] The United States ended up advertising Spain's material weakness in Western Hemispheric affairs, forcing it to cancel the transaction, which also involved American technology. Yet, what Spain lacked in this negotiation was not economic size or sophistication but imaginative statecraft. At the time, there were reasons, including Venezuela's continuing dependence on US demand for oil and deteriorating professional relations between the Venezuelan and US militaries, to believe that rapprochement through a broker in the field of external defence might be fruitful for both sides. Instead, the olive branch inside the aircraft sale was snared by Chavez's anti-American bluster and Spain's objections to the Iraq War, Socialist Prime Minister José Luis Rodríguez Zapatero having pulled Spanish troops from Iraq soon after his election in 2004.

During the boom years of the 1990s, Spain became a leading recipient of economic aid from the European Union – earning plaudits for protecting the cohesion funds from political squabbling in its young democracy and instead investing them in infrastructure such as modern transportation and communication systems. Spain attracted foreign exchange through tourism and an influx of foreign direct investment at the same time that it rose to second place behind the United States as a source of private investment in Latin America. Spain accomplished these feats with an economy less than one-tenth the size of the United States. Though Spain needs to restore economic growth and lower unemployment before it can reach its potential in global diplomacy as a broker state, its small size, especially given the adaptability of NATO and the diffusion of power across the United States, Asia and Europe, is no barrier to effective statecraft or the strategic use of force. As long as Spain fulfils the promise of a once and *future* economy, it should be able to convert interdependence into advantageous cooperation for its own national interests as well as those of important allies.

## Spain's risk society

If and when the Spanish economy does turn around, effective defence, as it does for democracies in general, will depend on how Spain's policy-makers reconcile the demands and risks of foreign policy initiative with societal attitudes. Without societal support for adequate military spending, without, at minimum, acquiescence in the deployment of young men and women to seemingly remote contingencies, and without steady support for whichever party holds power in the face of setbacks abroad, Spanish statecraft, however brilliantly conceived, will not inspire the necessary confidence or international cooperation to reach strategic objectives, outside or in conjunction with NATO. Of the four criteria discussed in this chapter, societal attitude towards risk poses the greatest obstacle for Spanish willingness and ability to undertake military combat operations.

Compared to its more powerful US partner, Spain's risk society has an opposite but nonetheless deleterious effect. Williams (2008) noted how the American Government, and the Bush administration in particular, after the 9/11 attacks faced an increasingly acute risk trap. The US public demanded protection from shadowy terrorist networks who posed no threat to national survival or the United States' rank among the great powers. Because these networks grafted themselves onto state structures, often in places suffering profound governance problems, the situation was more dangerous than it might first appear: in order to respond to the clamour for protection, the President would project force to hit the targets he could, that is, the states harbouring or abetting terrorist organizations. As the Iraq invasion demonstrated, the United States' favoured military instrument bludgeoned its victims, creating more governance failures, opening political vacuums for proliferating networks, and increasing on net the risk of further 9/11-style attacks against the US public (Williams, 2008, Chapters 5 and 6).

Spain's risk society also catalyses a destructive spiral – not towards hopeless overextension but a paralysing tortoise syndrome. On 11 March 2004, a few days before the Spanish general elections, young backpack bombers affiliated with Al Qaeda destroyed several cars on the Madrid metro, a symbol of Spain's post-EU modernization, killing nearly 200 commuters. The outgoing Prime Minister, José Aznar of the conservative *PP*, appeared to protect Spain's policy of active aid to US stabilization operations in Iraq by casting suspicion for the devastating attacks on domestic terrorists of ETA.[30]

If this was the intention, the gambit proved disastrous. Within days evidence mounted against Al Qaeda, and Spaniards saw the government of the *PP* as incompetent or perhaps corrupted by political ambition. The *PP*'s efforts to hold onto power became enmeshed with an ideological tilt towards the United States at the expense of EU leaders France and Germany, to the extreme it appeared of mistaking the security threat against Spain.[31] Socialist candidate José Luis Rodríguez Zapatero surged from behind to win the election and, with a new parliamentary majority, his mandate to remove Spanish troops from Iraq (Simons, 2004).

Though the Socialists insisted that withdrawal was a course correction owing to a more clear-eyed view of Spain's national interest and had been discussed by the then-opposition party well before the election, the United States expressed open displeasure at what it viewed as Spain's abandonment of a multidimensional geopolitical initiative – a crucial mission in the Middle East – out of fear of terrorist reprisals against the public. American suspicions would revive after subsequent decisions by Spain to impose strict caveats on its troops in Afghanistan and to refuse participation in strike missions for the NATO operation against Colonel Gaddafi's murderous army in Libya. If the Risk Society thesis holds in Spain, it operates to cow democratic statesmen, to sap their energy and preclude entrepreneurship in international affairs as popular notions of danger crowd out less politically viable *raison d'etat*.[32]

Although the risk trap poses a grave challenge to robust Spanish statecraft, this pathology is not irreversible. Unlike a real tortoise, Spain will not naturally or easily retreat completely within its shell. Even in 2011, Spain is only one of 12 countries worldwide to host a contingent of more than one thousand US service members. When the US Department of Defense maps its global presence, Spain occupies an important tier in Europe, behind Germany, of course, but on par with Turkey, Italy and the United Kingdom (Oliveri, 2011, p. 2438).[33] Caveats notwithstanding, Spain still suffered casualties with the Taliban resurgence in Afghanistan towards the end of the Bush administration and again during the Allied troop surge there promoted by President Obama. Neither did withdrawal from Iraq obviate Spain's commitments in the Balkans, Lebanon, the Mediterranean, or off the Horn of Africa, nor ironically did it spare the Socialist government from championing the Spanish state against ETA on home soil (Burke, 2010; Sebastián, 2010; NATO, 2011; VOA News, 2012; BBC News, 2011b).

Just nine months before leaving office under an economic cloud, Socialist Prime Minister Zapatero concluded a missile defence agreement, lending Spanish basing support to a revised European architecture, authored by the Obama administration and employing Aegis platforms of the US Navy (Hale, 2011; Fellman, 2011).[34] Despite difficulties with low growth, unemployment and sovereign debt, the very harbingers often linked to US retrenchment from global obligations, Spain remains exposed; the tortoise, risk society or not, remains half-in-half-out from the nominal safety of its shell. Spanish officials, like democratic politicians everywhere, must acknowledge public opinion and popular desire to bring the troops home. At the same time, as demonstrated even during the Iraq withdrawal, Spanish statesmen continue to resist Risk Society logic, lest with every tactical adjustment – every consolidation of state commitments – they invite further assaults upon the Spanish people.[35]

## Conclusion: Rediscovering statecraft

On first pass of news headlines or commentary from the chattering classes, Spain can do little militarily to help itself or the NATO alliance. In none of the elements from our basic framework – history, culture, economy and risk perception – does Spain at first blush appear prepared for innovative or incisive statecraft, the kind required for a mid-size NATO ally to broker significant changes in world politics.

Even so, much of the disrespect against Spain rings hollow inasmuch as it stems from longstanding Anglo-American prejudices, formed over a remote period when British or American interests benefitted by accentuating Spanish sins and burying any of Spain's geopolitical achievements.[36] In present circumstances, however, with US economic power and capacity to project military force called into question, US, European and Spanish interests overlap substantially. A few observers on both sides of the Atlantic might argue otherwise, but Western solidarity, anchored by a militarily formidable NATO alliance, would aid former antagonists – Spain, the United States, the United Kingdom and several other partners – as they confront today's global security threats. Appreciating Spain's potential for effective statecraft and accepting Spain for twenty-first-century diplomacy in a broker's role requires a shift in perspective from the typical Anglo-American lens. Indeed, Spanish, NATO and Western interests might best be served only after certain education took place both outside and inside Spanish territory. To recall the four pillars of this volume's framework, the *history* of Spanish imperialism and Spain's neutrality during the Second World War ought to be faced squarely, accounting for the illiberal character of Spanish policies but acknowledging also the skill with which Spain across multiple centuries negotiated the twisting and at times violent course of great power competition. While pragmatism often provokes mistrust from hegemonic states, who like the United States draw strength from faith in their ideological creed, Spain's strategic *culture* emerged from a school of wide-ranging experience, including reconciliation and democratic transformation as well as imperial decline and civil war. Spanish prudence in the broker's role, a role of no direct threat to the United States, can serve as a useful corrective – leavening stridently ideological, crusading impulses in both the United States and NATO.

The Spanish *economy* and *risk society* pose serious obstacles to Spain's success as a twenty-first-century geopolitical broker, a type of state that must wield military credibility with great powers and developing countries alike. Nevertheless, a broad view undertaken by outside observers and by the Spanish public could prepare the way for reinvigoration of Spanish statecraft. Not so long ago the Spanish economy set the standard for a New Europe, whole and free. While difficult days and additional austerity packages lie ahead, it is unlikely that the pain of unemployment or debt restructuring will make Spanish producers, particularly those leading the defence industry, forget how to succeed. Even now, the most probable scenario in the medium term is that Spain's resources for statecraft, including military readiness for use of force within a NATO context, will grow once again.[37]

The opportunities for Spain to grow in diplomatic terms, to become in its own right a leading voice from the West in global affairs, expand dramatically if the Spanish Government can restore popular trust. Brilliant statecraft goes for naught if citizens can neither see a state worth defending nor feel the emotional tug of republican virtue. In order for Spain to succeed as a twenty-first-century broker – to benefit itself and larger coalitions, especially NATO – *España tiene que involucrarse*.[38] It needs to take stands on inter-state disputes, accepting military risk from calculated exposure and investment of precious Spanish resources in order to increase the likelihood of achieving geopolitical objectives.

Rather than the false security of the inert tortoise, Spain might rediscover the restless and tenacious spirit of the venture capitalist. Is Spain willing and able? A timely metamorphosis towards firmer will and improved ability in its broker role will demand public outreach from Spain's statesmen, an inside as well as an outside game for Spanish democracy. Only extraordinary democratic communication, sorely lacking from the late Aznar and Zapatero governments, can refocus Spain's priorities.

From the sharp rhetoric at election time, a common temptation is to overstate the debilitating effects of current ideological and partisan divisions within Spain. Under Socialist Prime Minister Zapatero (2004–2011), Spain remained exposed and could not abandon relationships with the United States and NATO in order to court France, Germany or the European Union. Now, Mariano Rajoy of the *PP* is unlikely to defy public opinion by placing Spanish forces at the beck and call of any US secretary of defence, regardless of the party's Atlanticist preferences or diplomatic reputations in Brussels. A party change to the conservative *PP* in the prime minister's residence at Moncloa matters, of course, but not as much as a change in personalities. Back on 11 March 2004, Mariano Rajoy was next in line when the Al Qaeda train bombings and Aznar's War, as Rajoy reportedly called it, derailed the *PP's* planned succession. In Spain's democracy, institutional norms supply the person of the Spanish prime minister, also known as the Spanish president, of either party ample room to conduct foreign policy. At this juncture, after waiting eight years in opposition, Rajoy may be less likely than his predecessors to overexploit parliamentary deference from the *Congreso de los Diputados*.[39] If so, Spanish statecraft will soon have the opportunity to overcome its highest hurdle.

Democracy's solution to the Risk Society syndrome bedevilling the effective use of force involves heavy doses of executive transparency and parliamentary debate. Almost regardless of the role in twenty-first-century NATO – hegemon, regional leader, broker or specialist – generating will and ability to practice statecraft requires, in addition to negotiating skills abroad, statesmanship at home. Otherwise, no Western Ally, not even one with Spain's historical and strategic assets, can escape the narrow, predominantly private, fear for public safety in order to better engage civic-minded concerns. For Spain, these include material contributions to NATO missions and transatlantic brokerage towards wise action in defence of a just and peaceful international order.

## Notes

1. Since the battle of Garellano in 1503, in the Second Campaign of Italy by Gonzalo Fernández de Cordoba the so-called 'Gran Capitán' fairly until the battle of Rocroi in 1643, Spanish military dominance was almost absolute on Europe's battlefields thanks to the 'Tercios' (Parker, 1998, 1991, 1996).
2. Two recent exceptions to the US academic preference for examining the British Empire are Nexon (2009) and Lobell (2003). Lobell's is a partial exception since he included two chapters on Britain, one on imperial Spain.
3. The introduction to this volume terms Spain a large state in NATO-Europe along with the United Kingdom, Germany and France. By population, Spain at 46 million is as far from the United Kingdom and France (62 and 65 million) as those two are from Germany at 85 million. Perhaps more tellingly with respect to the ability to use force, Spain's military expenditure ($16 bn) is closer to that of Norway ($6 bn) than the other large powers (Germany at $47 bn; the United Kingdom at $57 bn; France at $61 bn). For purposes of this country study, we refer to Spain as a mid-size power to express that the difference in resource level factors into Spain's distinct role, apart from how other allies such as the United Kingdom, France or Germany on the one hand, Norway or Denmark on the other, would incorporate force into their statecraft. (Population figures are from an on-line compilation of official estimates. Defence budget figures are quoted from the Stockholm International Peace Research Institute [SIPRI] Database for 2010 in constant 2009 US dollars.)
4. See also EUROPA (2009) and a report from the European Commission (2009).
5. Core neoclassical texts bring these factors back into analysis of international conflict and cooperation (Schweller, 1998; Dueck, 2006; Lobell, Ripsman, and Taliaferro, 2009). From this point of view, regarding the Spanish case, see García Cantalapiedra (forthcoming).
6. See also the comments by Norwegian Defense Minister Espen Barth Eide in Washington, DC (Majumdar, 2012).
7. It is hard to imagine, for example, how the NATO mission in Libya, Operation Unified Protector, could have resulted merely from the mutual pursuit by members of their traditional security interests.
8. On new institutionalism applied to European organization, see Olsen (2010).
9. In 1986, the Spanish government (and France and Italy's) denied overflight rights to US planes for carrying out the El Dorado Canyon Operation against Libya, adding almost 3,000 km to the mission.
10. For Spanish statecraft during the Second World War era, see Balfour and Preston (1999); Crawford (2008); and Payne (2008).
11. Experts debate what to include as part of defence spending. A Catalan think tank that advocates defence budget reductions tallied official numbers and placed Spanish defence-related spending closer to €17 bn, approximately $23 bn for 2010 (Ortega and Bohigas, 2009, esp. p. 4).

12. In his widely read volume on modern strategy, the Clausewitz scholar, Paret (1986), neglected to include a case on Habsburg Spain, an oversight that Parker (1994), Lobell (2003) and Nexon (2009) have led the way in correcting.
13. There were independently administered kingdoms under the Catholic Monarchy until Philip V unified Spain as a single state under the *Nueva Planta* decrees of 1707.
14. These independence movements to open the nineteenth century were more complex than Right versus Spanish Might. The movements split *criollos*, American-born elites, among themselves. Iberian models also had positive aspects: representatives of Spain's Latin American territories came to Iberia in order to create a liberal constitution for all Spain in 1812. This was only the second such constitution authored in Europe after a short-lived predecessor from the French Revolution.
15. For a critique of the Anglo-American record, see Bowden (2009), especially Chapter 5 – 'The Expansion of Europe and the Classical Standard of Civilization' and Chapter 8 – 'The "New Realities" of Imperialism'.
16. See conflicting sentiments with respect to the Franco years stirred by the legal proceedings against Judge Garzon (BBC News, 2012).
17. See the final three chapters (pp. 210–267) in Balfour and Preston (1999). In fact, before 1943 Spain aligned with the Axis Powers. The Cold War shift towards eventual alliance with the United States, the United Kingdom, and France required substantial negotiation and political manoeuvring. See Marquina Barrio (1986, 2003).
18. On the Spanish transition as a model, see, for example, Karl and Schmitter (1991) and De Villiers (ca. 1994).
19. Here, we emphasize the character of Spain in its approach to geopolitical competition as opposed to the military's tendencies within the 'Spanish Way of War'. The state rather than the armed forces is the key protagonist of strategic culture in this case, given we are assessing a broker rather than a hegemon or a normal great power (Johnston, 1995; Echevarria, 2004; Sondhaus, 2006; Lock, 2010).
20. See the current United Nations website for the forum at www.unaoc.org. Regarding the Spanish plan, see Ministerio de AsuntosExteriores de España (2005). For a critique that Socialist party ideology burdened the diplomatic initiative in practice, see Powell (2009) and García Cantalapiedra (2011).
21. Here is representative analysis from Peter Smith's highly regarded, centre-left textbook on US–Latin American relations: 'Above all, they [other nations] did not want to become targets themselves... [The war had long been highly unpopular in Spain, where the electorate promptly dismissed the pro-Bush ruling party from power after a terrorist attack on Madrid; Britain would remain a target of continuing terrorist plots.]' (Smith, 2008, p. 317). With the perception of increasing possibility for a higher number of casualties, Spanish public opinion reduced support for Spanish Armed Forces operations overseas (Noya, 2007).
22. US Defense Secretary Gates singled out Spain, but the facts imply a more complex situation: Spanish air and naval forces participated discreetly from the very beginning under AFRICOM in Operation Odyssey Dawn, and on 22 March, the Spanish Parliament under the Socialist Government approved

198  *Application: Case Studies*

contributions to NATO Operation Unified Protector under UNSCR 1973, including four F-18 fighters, one P-3C Orion surveillance aircraft, one tanker, one Aegis-class frigate, one submarine, one patrol boat and some 500 personnel.

23. As of this writing, US House and Senate negotiators agreed on a $662 bn budget for the Department of Defense in FY2012, staving off real cuts at least one more year.
24. This opinion, nevertheless, is a matter of debate; see, for example, Rachman (2011).
25. This figure includes expenditures under SIPRI criteria that are in addition to the budget for the Spanish government department of defence. Extras include programmes for retired soldiers, the *Guardia Civil*, and military-related research and development loans from the Ministry of Industry. The exclusive department of defence figure for 2010 is just €7.69 (Ortega and Bohigas, 2009, p. 4).
26. The Spanish departmental defence budget for 2012 will amount to almost €7 bn, with a €340 million cut that represents a return to 2003 levels. In addition, the department has spent more than originally authorized, amassing a huge debt of €27 bn. See Cortes Españolas (2012).
27. The Spanish company Navantia has been building for Norway the F-310 frigates series. Two more Aegis Frigates F-100 with missile defence capability are expected for the Spanish Navy in two to four years; the future S-80 attack submarines are armed with conventional Tomahawk cruise missiles that have land attack capabilities. There is a future carrier project, the *Carlos III* R-21, similar in design to the new French carriers. The Spanish Armed Forces are waiting for Tiger attack helicopters, the Strategic Airlift Airbus A-400, and a Strategic Projection Ship, the *Juan Carlos I* (L-61), a strategic lift ship, similar to the US LHD Wasp-class, which could be also used as a carrier (30 planes and helicopters) thanks to a ski-jump.
28. For instance, at the height of the housing bubble in 2004, authorized defence exports reached €439,632,519; in 2005, €1,230,272,576; in 2006, the value reached €1,295,656,156. Moreover, according to SIPRI (2010), Spain is the sixth largest arms exporter in the world. 'España, con 925 millones de dólares en armas vendidas, se encuentra en la posición de número seis en el "ranking" de los países exportadores. Un puesto por delante de todo un gigante como China, con...870 millones' (ElMundo.es, 2010).
29. This aircraft deal was originally part of an even larger contract worth €1.7 bn that included Corvette-class ships and maritime patrol boats.
30. *Euskadi Ta Askatasuna* (Basque Homeland and Freedom). Debate surrounding the 3/11 attacks in Madrid is still hot in Spain. Court cases related to who organized the bombing and how preliminary evidence was handled by Spanish authorities are still active: these may ultimately point more towards incompetence than unbridled political ambition.
31. This does not imply that a shift away from the United States was without real complications. For a critical review of the strategic rationale behind Spain's shift towards the EU, see García Cantalapiedra (2012).
32. For a parallel application of the Risk Society thesis to British statecraft and the use of force in an age of defence austerity, see the following panel at the Inter-University Seminar on Armed Forces and Society Biennial Conference,

Chicago, IL, 21–23 October 2011. *The Next Generation of Civil-Military Relations: A View from the UK* (Saturday, 22 October, 8:00–9:30 am), especially Edmunds (2011) and Dorman (2011).
33. The US Department of Defense category encompassing these strategic countries spans from 1,000 to 25,000 US service members. GlobalSecurity.org (2012) reports 1,942 US service members in Spain, just under one fifth the levels in Italy and the United Kingdom. Moreover, 'the Spanish government mainly offered during the review of the 1988 US–Spain Defense and Cooperation Agreement in 2002 the enlargement of the Rota Naval Station and the use of Moron Air base and to allow US Navy and Air Force information services to operate in Spain under the supervision of national authorities.' The Socialist government 'approved a protocol allowing these services to really operate in Spanish territory in April 2007' (García Cantalapiedra, 2009).
34. Under Zapatero, for the first time a Socialist government designated transatlantic relations second only behind Europe among Spain's foreign policy priorities (Zapatero, 2008).
35. See analysis of Prime Minister Zapatero's decision to withdraw Spanish troops from Iraq in Woodworth (2004).
36. An example of criticism that resonated with English-speaking sceptics was 'P.I.G.S'. Portugal, Ireland and Greece were lumped together with Spain as profligate, barely competent democracies, struggling to manage sovereign debt without dragging down more productive economies, particularly Germany or, just outside the Eurozone, the United Kingdom (BBC News, 2011a; Mansori, 2011).
37. In any case, official documents codify this ambition. Ministerio de Defensa (2009), which addresses constraints brought on by the financial crisis on pp. 2–3. See also Ley Orgánica 5/2005, de 17 de noviembre, de la DefensaNacional (2005); Ministerio de Defensa (2002), 'Requerimientos Básicos y Capácidades Críticas' [Basic Requirements and Critical Capacities], which begins on p. 63, and 'Criterio Básico 3, Fuerzas preparadas para las acciones más exigentes del combate y sostenimiento del esfuerzo' [force readiness and sustainability], pp. 91–93. At present, the new PP government has embarked on a Defense Strategic Review, a new National Defense Directive, and probably a review of the Spanish Security Strategy approved by the Spanish Government on 24 June 2011 (Gobierno de España, 2011).
38. 'Spain needs to involve itself' in major issues and international crises of the day.
39. The 'Congress of Deputies' is the more powerful house of the *Cortes Generales*, the Spanish Legislature, on matters related to foreign and defence budgets.

# Bibliography

Aragüetes, A. (2011) 'Las Inversiones Directas Españolas en America Latina en el Periodo 2001–2010', *Anuario Iberoamericano*, http://www.anuarioiberoamericano.es/pdf/analisis/6_alfredo_arahuetes.pdf, date accessed 26 September 2012.

Balfour, S. and Preston, P. (eds) (1999) *Spain and the Great Powers in the Twentieth Century* (London: Routledge).
Barnett, T. (2004) *The Pentagon's New Map: War and Peace in the Twenty-First Century* (New York: G.P. Putnam's Sons).
Baylis, J., J. Wirtz and C. Gray (2010) *Strategy in the Contemporary World*, 3rd ed. (Oxford: Oxford University Press).
BBC News (2004) 'Spain Proposes Cultural Alliance', *BBC News*, 22 September 2004, http://www.bbc.co.uk (homepage), date accessed 5 June 2012.
BBC News (2011a) 'Europe's PIGS: Country by Country', *BBC News*, 11 October 2011, http://www.bbc.co.uk (homepage), date accessed 5 June 2012.
BBC News (2011b) 'Spanish PM Zapatero Hails End to Basque Eta Violence', *BBC News*, 21 October 2011, http://www.bbc.co.uk (homepage), date accessed 5 June 2012.
BBC News (2012) 'Spain's Franco-era Probe Judge BaltasarGarzon on Trial', *BBC News*, 24 January 2012, http://www.bbc.co.uk (homepage), date accessed 5 June 2012.
Beck, U. (1999) *World Risk Society* (Cambridge: Polity Press).
Beck, U. (2006) 'Living in the World Risk Society' (published lecture), *Economy & Society*, Vol. 35, No. 3, pp. 329–345.
Beer, F. (1972) *The Political Economy of Alliances: Benefits, Costs, and Institutions in NATO* (Beverly Hills, CA: Sage Publications).
Boustay, N. (2004) 'The View from Spain', *Washington Post*, 14 January 2004.
Bowden, B. (2009) *The Empire of Civilization: The Evolution of an Imperial Idea* (Chicago, IL: University of Chicago Press).
Burke, E. (2010) *Spain's War in Afghanistan*, FRIDE Policy Brief No. 23 (Madrid, Spain: Fundación para las Relaciones Internacionales y el Diálogo Exterior).
Cloud, D. (2011) 'Gates Calls for more NATO Allies to Join Libya Air Campaign', *Los Angeles Times*, 9 June 2011, http://articles.latimes.com (homepage), date accessed 5 June 2012.
Cohen, S. (2009) *Geopolitics: The Geography of International Relations*, 2nd ed. (Lanham, MD: Rowman & Littlefield Publishers).
Coker, C. (2009) *War in an Age of Risk* (Cambridge: Polity Press).
Cortes Españolas (2012) 'Comparecencia del Señor Ministro de Defensa Morenés Eulatepara Informar de Las Lineas Generales de la Política de su Departamento Comisión de Defensa del Congreso de los Diputados, Sesión n° 2 (extraordinaria), 26 de enero, X Legislatura. N° 28, http://www.congreso.es/public_oficiales/L10/CONG/DS/CO/CO_028.PDF
Crawford, T. (2008) 'Wedge Strategy, Balancing, and the Deviant Case of Spain, 1940–41', *Security Studies*, Vol. 17, No. 1, pp. 1–38.
De Villiers, D. (ca. 1994) 'Spain: A Model Transition to Democracy – Lessons for South Africa', UNISA Press Online (South Africa), https://my.unisa.ac.za/portal/tool/f3abf0c2-de8b-48c4-8080-a493efce0099/Default.asp?Cmd=View Content&ContentID= 11576&P_XSLFile= unisa/lms.xsl, date accessed 26 January 2012.
DefenceWeb (2012) 'Spain's Indra Develops Light Maritime Surveillance Aircraft', *DefenceWeb*, 24 January 2012, http://www.defenceweb.co.za (homepage), date accessed 27 January 2012.
Defense Industry Daily (2006) 'Love on the Rocks: CASA's $600 Million Venezuelan Plane Sale Hits Heavy Turbulence, Crashes', *DID*, 14 February 2006, http://www.defenseindustrydaily.com (homepage), date accessed 27 January 2012.

Deni, J. (2007) *Alliance Management and Maintenance: Restructuring NATO for the 21st Century* (Hampshire: Ashgate Publishing).

Dorman, A. (2011) 'Managing Risk in an "Age of Austerity": Revolutionary Change or the Continuation of Incrementalism?', Paper presented on 'The Next Generation of Civil-Military Relations: A View from the UK' at the Inter-University Seminar on Armed Forces & Society Biennial Conference, Chicago, IL, 21–23 October.

Dueck, C. (2006) *Reluctant Crusaders: Power, Culture, and Change in American Grand Strategy* (Princeton, NJ: Princeton University Press).

Duffield, J. (1994–1995) 'NATO's Functions after the Cold War', *Political Science Quarterly*, Vol. 109, No. 5, pp. 763–787.

Echevarria II, A. (2004) *Toward an American Way of War* (Carlisle, PA: US Army War College, Strategic Studies Institute).

Economist (2004) 'Charlemagne: Europe without Aznar', *Economist* (online), 18 March 2004, http://www.economist.com (homepage), date accessed 5 June 2012.

Edmunds, T. (2011) 'New Civil-Military Relations', Paper presented on 'The Next Generation of Civil-Military Relations: A View from the UK' at the Inter-University Seminar on Armed Forces & Society Biennial Conference, Chicago, IL, 21–23 October.

ElMundo.es (2010) 'Españapordelante de China en el "Ranking" de los MayoresExportadores deArmas', *ElMundo.es*, 15 March 2010, http://www.elmundo.es (homepage), date accessed 5 June 2012.

EUROPA (2009) 'Commissioner Hüber in La Rioja (Spain): Maximising Cohesion Policy Investment to Tackle the Crisis', *EUROPA*, 27 March 2009. http://europa.eu (homepage), date accessed 24 January 2012.

European Commission (2009), 'European Cohesion Policy in Spain'. http://ec.europa.eu/regional_policy/sources/docgener/informat/country2009/es_en.pdf, date accessed 24 January 2012.

Fellman, S. (2011) 'US to Base Anti-Missile Ships in Spain', *Defense News*, 10 October 2011.

García Cantalapiedra, D. (2009) 'Spain, Burden-Sharing, and NATO Deterrence Policy', *Strategic Insights*, Vol. VIII, No. 4, pp. 1–9.

García Cantalapiedra, D. (2011) 'Entre *Bandwagoning, y Appeasement*. La Política Exterior de España hacia EEUU 2001–2011', UNISCI Discussion Papers (Madrid) No. 27 (October), pp. 63–72.

GlobalSecurity (2011) 'World Wide Military Deployments', http://www.globalsecurity.org (homepage), date accessed 28 January 2012.

Gobierno de España (2011) *Estrategia Española de Seguridad: Una Responsabilidad de Todos* (Madrid, España: Imprenta Nacional del Boletín Oficial del Estado): http://www.lamoncloa.gob.es/NR/rdonlyres/D0D9A8EB-17D0-45A5-ADFF-46A8AF4C2931/0/EstrategiaEspanolaDeSeguridad.pdf

Gross, D. (2008) ' "The Fundamentals of our Economy Are Strong". Is There any Excuse for McCain's Gaffe?' *Slate.com*, 17 September 2008, http://www.slate.com (homepage), date accessed 27 January 2012.

Haftendorn, H., Keohane, R. and Wallander, C. (eds) (1999) *Imperfect Unions; Security Institutions Over Time and Space* (Oxford: Oxford University Press).

Hale, J. (2011) 'Spain to Host US Ships for NATO Missile Defense', *Defense News*, 5 October 2011, http://www.defensenews.com (homepage), date accessed 5 June 2012.

Hendrickson, R. (2006) *Diplomacy and War at NATO: The Secretary General and Military Action after the Cold War* (Columbia, MO: University of Missouri Press).
Huntington, S. (1991) *The Third Wave: Democratization in the Late Twentieth century* (Norman, OK: University of Oklahoma Press).
Huntington, S. (1996) *The Clash of Civilizations and the Remaking of World Order* (New York: Simon & Schuster).
Ing, D. (2011) 'Spain's S-80 Submarines Delayed by Funding Cuts', *HIS Jane's: Defense & Security Intelligence and Analysis*, 7 November 2011, http://www.janes.com (homepage), date accessed 5 June 2012.
Johnston, A.I. (1995) 'Thinking about Strategic Culture', *International Security*, Vol. 19, No. 4, pp. 32–64.
Kagan, R. (2011) 'The Price of Power: The Benefits of US Defense Spending Far Outweigh the Costs', *Weekly Standard*, 24 January 2011, www.weeklystandard.com (homepage), date accessed 5 June 2012.
Kaplan, L. (2004) *NATO Divided, NATO United: The Evolution of an Alliance* (Westport, CT: Praeger Publishers).
Karl, T. and Schmitter, P. (1991) 'Modes of Transition in Latin America, Southern and Eastern Europe', *International Social Science Journal*, Vol. 128, pp. 269–284.
Katsarova, I. (2007) 'The Cohesion Fund' (memo), European Parliament (January). http://www.europarl.europa.eu/ftu/pdf/en/FTU_4.5.3.pdf, date accessed 23 January 2012.
Layne, C. (2008) 'It's Over Over There: The Coming Crack-Up in Transatlantic Relations', *International Politics*, Vol. 45, No. 3, pp. 325–347.
Lepgold, J. (1998) 'NATO's Post-Cold War Collective Action Problem', *International Security*, Vol. 23, No. 1, pp. 78–106.
Ley Orgánica 5/2005, de 17 de noviembre, de la Defensa Nacional (2005) http://noticias.juridicas.com/base_datos/Admin/lo5-2005.html
Lobell, S. (2003) *The Challenge of Hegemony: Grand Strategy, Trade, and Domestic Politics* (Ann Arbor: University of Michigan Press).
Lobell, S., Ripsman, N. and Taliaferro, J. (eds) (2009) *Neoclassical Realism, the State, and Foreign Policy* (Cambridge: Cambridge University Press).
Lock, E. (2010) 'Refining Strategic Culture: Return of the Second Generation', *Review of International Studies*, Vol. 36, No. 3, pp. 685–708.
Majumdar, D. (2012) 'Norway: NATO Losing Self-Defense Ability', *Defense News*, 12 January 2012, http://www.defensenews.com (homepage), date accessed 24 January 2012.
Mansori, K. (2011) 'Why Greece, Spain, and Ireland Aren't to Blame for Europe's Woes', *The New Republic* (October 11), http://www.tnr.com (homepage), date accessed 5 June 2012.
Marquina Barrio, A. (1986) *España en la Política de Seguridad Occidental 1939–1986* (Madrid, España: EdicionesEjército).
Marquina Barrio, A. (2003) *Las Negociaciones entre España y los Estados Unidos (1953–1982): Algunas Cuestiones Centrales en Retrospectiva*, UNISCI Discusión Papers No. 3 (October): http://www.ucm.es/info/unisci/revistas/Marquina5.pdf
McCormick, J. (2006) *The European Superpower* (New York: Palgrave Macmillan).
Mearsheimer, J. (1990) 'Back to the Future: Instability in Europe after the Cold War', *International Security*, Vol. 15, No. 1, pp. 5–56.

Ministerio de Asuntos Exteriores de España (2005) *Alianza de Civilizaciones*, Dirección General de Comunicación Exterior MAE (November): http://www.spainun.org/binarydata/files/alianzacivilizaciones.pdf
Ministerio de Defensa (2002) *Revisión Estratégica de la Defensa* [Defense Strategic Review] (Madrid, Spain: Government of Spain), http://www.defensa.gob.es/Galerias/politica/seguridad-defensa/ficheros/DGL_RevisionEstrategica.pdf
Ministerio de Defensa (2009) 'Resumen Ejecutivo de la Directiva de Defensa' (January), http://www.defensa.gob.es/Galerias/politica/seguridad-defensa/ficheros/DGL_ResumenEjecutivDPD_1-2009.pdf
NATO (2011) 'Operation Active Endeavor', 22 February 2011, http://www.nato.int (homepage), date accessed 28 January 2012.
Nexon, D. (2009) *The Struggle for Power in Early Modern Europe: Religious Conflict, Dynastic Empires and International Change* (Princeton, NJ: Princeton University Press).
Noya, J. (2007) 'La Opinión Pública Española y las Misiones de las Fuerzas Armadas en el Exterior', *Real Instituto Elcano* ARI No. 121 (November).
Nye, J. (2010) 'American and Chinese Power after the Financial Crisis', *Washington Quarterly*, Vol. 33, No. 4, pp. 143–153.
O'Dwyer, G. (2010) 'Norway, Spain Sign Satellite MoU', *Defense News*, 15 September 2010, http://www.defensenews.com (homepage), date accessed 4 June 2012.
Oliveri, F. (2011) 'The Power of Inertia', *CQ Weekly*, 21 November 2011.
Olsen, J. (2010) *Governing Through Institution Building: Institutional Theory and Recent European Experiments in Democratic Organization* (Oxford: Oxford University Press).
Olson, M. and Zeckhauser, R. (1966) 'An Economic Theory of Alliances', *The Review of Economics and Statistics*, Vol. 48, No. 3, pp. 266–279.
Ortega, P. and X. Bohigas (2009) *Spanish Military Expenditure and R&D 2010*, Report No. 5 (Barcelona, Spain: Centre d'Estudis per a la Pau J.M. Delàs – Justícia i Pau).
Paret, P. (ed.) (1986) *Makers of Modern Strategy: From Machiavelli to the Nuclear Age* (Princeton, NJ: Princeton University Press).
Parker, G. (1991) *El Ejército de Flandes y el Camino Español* (Madrid, España: Alianza Editorial).
Parker, G. (1994) 'The Making of Strategy in Habsburg Spain: Philip II's "Bid for Mastery", 1556–1598', in W. Murray, M. Knox and A. Bernstein (eds) *The Making of Strategy: Rulers, States, and War* (Cambridge: Cambridge University Press), pp. 115–150.
Parker, G. (1996) *The Military Revolution: Military Innovation and the Rise of the West, 1500–1800*, 2nd ed. (Cambridge: Press Syndicate of the University of Cambridge).
Parker, G. (1998) *La Gran Estrategia de Felipe II* (Madrid, España: Alianza Editorial, S.A.).
Parker, G. (2010) *Felipe II* (Madrid, España: Planeta).
Payne, S. (2000) *Fascism in Spain, 1923–1977* (Madison, WI: University of Wisconsin Press).
Payne, S. (2008) *Franco and Hitler: Spain, Germany, and World War II* (New Haven, CT: Yale University Press).

Powell, C. (2009) 'A Second Transition or More of the Same?' Spanish Foreign Policy under Zapatero', *South European Society and Politics*, Vol. 14, No. 4, pp. 519–536.
Preston, P. (1996) *Franco: A Biography* (New York: Basic Books).
Rachman, G. (2011) 'Think Again: American Decline: This Time It's for Real', *Foreign Policy* (January/February), http://www.foreignpolicy.com (homepage), date accessed 4 June 2012.
Rodríguez Marcos, J. (2010) 'Geoffrey Parker: 'Felipe II gobernó el primer imperio global en la historia', *El Pais* (España), 21 September 2010, http://www.elpais.com (homepage), date accessed 4 May 2012.
Rupp, R. (2006) *NATO after 9/11: An Alliance in Continuing Decline* (New York: Palgrave Macmillan).
Schweller, R. (1998) *Deadly Imbalances: Tripolarity and Hitler's Strategy of World Conquest* (New York: Columbia University Press).
Sciolino, E. (2004) 'A Departing Bush Ally Hails an Ascendant Spain', *New York Times*, 11 March 2004.
Sebastián, S. (2010) *Spanish Foreign Policy in the Balkans: Wasted Potential*, FRIDE Policy Brief No. 28 (Madrid, Spain: Fundación para las Relaciones Internacionales y el Diálogo Exterior).
Simons, M. (2004) 'Spain's New Leader Promises Sweeping Changes', *New York Times*, 18 April 2004, http://www.nytimes.com (homepage), date accessed 27 January 2012.
SIPRI (2010) *SIPRI Yearbook 2010* (Oxford: Oxford University Press for Stockholm International Peace Research Institute).
Smith, P. (2008) *Talons of the Eagle: Latin America, The United States, and the World*, 3rd ed. (Oxford: Oxford University Press).
Sondhaus, L. (2006) *Strategic Culture and Ways of War* (Oxon: Routledge).
Thies, W. (2009) *Why NATO Endures* (Cambridge: Cambridge University Press).
Turkish Daily News (2006) 'Gül, Zapatero Agree to Extend Alliance of Civilizations', *Turkish Daily News*, 4 March 2006, http://www.hurriyetdailynews.com (Homepage), date accessed 27 January 2012.
Van Evera, S. (1990–1991) 'Primed for Peace: Europe after the Cold War', *International Security*, Vol. 15, No. 3, pp. 7–57.
VOA News (2012) 'Spanish Navy Thwarts Pirate Attack in Indian Ocean', *Voice of America*, 12 January 2012, http://www.voanews.com (Hoempage), date accessed 28 January 2012.
Waltz, K. (2000) 'Structural Realism after the Cold War', *International Security*, Vol. 25, No. 1, pp. 5–41.
Williams, M. (2008) *NATO, Security and Risk Management* (Oxon: Routledge).
Woodworth, P. (2004) 'Spain Changes Course: Aznar's Legacy, Zapatero's Prospects', *World Policy Journal*, Vol. 21, No. 2, pp. 7–26.
Zapatero, J. (Spanish Prime Minister) (2008) 'En Interés de España: UnaPoliticaExterior Comprometida', address at the Museo del Prado, 16 June 2008, printed in *ARI* No. 9, Real Instituto Elcano, 17 June 2008.

# 11
# Poland's Participation in NATO Operations

*M. Pietras*

Poland has taken part in NATO operations since 1996 – even before its membership in NATO. From the very beginning this involvement was connected with the implementation of the changing objectives of Poland's foreign policy. Hence, the distinguished feature of these activities was high level of political will to use force for clearly defined political purposes. Before Poland became a NATO member in 1999, the goal of Poland's participation in NATO operations was to demonstrate that it was a valuable candidate for Alliance membership. After its entry into NATO in the early years of the twenty-first century, Poland, by taking part in Alliance operations, sought to prove that the decision of membership was justified. In the late first decade of the twenty-first century the aim of Poland's participation in NATO operations was to strengthen its political position in the Alliance.

This evolution and changing goals clearly confirms that Poland tries to find its position and role in the structure and functioning of the international order emerging after the end of the Cold War. Consequently, this reflects the rationality of the state adjusting to the changing reality and seeking there its place corresponding with the changing position and changing aspirations. Poland aims at being not only 'a consumer' but also a 'producer' of security. Its membership of the Atlantic Alliance and striving for privileged relations with the United States play a special role in this process. These activities were accompanied by shortcomings of both the quality of military equipment and limited financial possibilities of the Polish state. Moreover, at the beginning of the second decade of the twenty-first century, and particularly from the side of the President's office were raised arguments that high costs of Poland's involvement in Afghanistan are becoming barrier to modernization of Poland's military forces.

The implementation of the foregoing goals was also accompanied by Poland's preferences concerning the vision of the NATO Alliance in the conditions of its transformation and adaptation to the post-Cold War international arena. One of the tendencies of this process is the practice of undertaking missions not mandated by Article 5 of the Washington Treaty, that is, not confined to collective defence, but the missions which involve operations outside the Euro-Atlantic area, or even on a global scale. Poland's acceptance of this tendency towards evolution in NATO's functioning, especially preferred by the United States, was accompanied by fears that the capability for collective defence might be weakened.

The collective defence issue is particularly significant for Poland, given its geopolitical situation. Paradoxically, the formula (emphasized by Poland) of selective involvement in out-of-area operations was intended to strengthen rather than weaken the Alliance's collective defence capability since Poland assumed that it was possible to maintain the meaning of Article 5 of the Washington Treaty through actions in the spirit of Allied solidarity by supporting NATO's political and military activities. Poland concluded that participation in NATO missions created conditions for the country's rising position in the Alliance and provided grounds for expecting reciprocity and solidarity on the part of the other member states also under Article 5. It was explicitly emphasized that NATO's existence and its efficacy also in solving global security problems was of vital interest for Poland, hence its approval for selective globalization of operations (Pawłowski, 2010, pp. 98–99).

Poland's participation in NATO operations is a complex and dynamic process. It is assumed that its analysis requires taking into account the factors that determine it, with special consideration for Poland's changed geopolitical situation after the Cold War, historical experiences of Poland's involvement in UN peacekeeping operations, and for the role of public opinion. It is also necessary to analyse the political strategy which is served by Poland's participation in NATO operations and to examine the implementation of this process. Of significance for the reconstruction of the political strategy will be the analysis of NATO's significance for Poland's security policy, evolution in understanding threats to international security, and preferences for the mechanism of collective defence. The key elements in the analysis of the process of implementing Poland's participation in NATO operations include normative grounds, decision-making process and operational activities.

# Determinants of Poland's participation in NATO military operations

The analysis of Poland's involvement in NATO operations after the end of the Cold War requires taking into account the wider context determining and dynamically influencing this process. The main factors should include the change in Poland's geopolitical situation after the end of the Cold War and the choice of the Euro-Atlantic option in its foreign policy. However, the experience and many-year tradition (since 1953) of Poland's participation in UN peacekeeping operations must not be overlooked. Nor can the public opinion be disregarded. These factors first of all conditioned the level of political will. Since the mid-1990s the two first factors were strengthening both the political will and Poland's involvement in NATO-led military operations. On the other hand, since the second half of the first decade of the twenty-first century the factor of public opinion is limiting the level of Poland's political will to be involved in NATO out-of-area operations. The intensity of the two first factors is weakening, and the third is strengthening.

The change in Poland's geopolitical situation under the conditions of the end of Cold War confrontation and the collapse of the bipolar order created grounds for reorienting the security policy and overcoming the specific geopolitical curse of Poland's location between Russia and Germany. The Polish writer, Stefan Żeromski, defined this situation as that of Poland being squeezed between two millstones. A chance to change these circumstances was provided by the Euro-Atlantic option in Poland's foreign policy after 1989. The option makes one aware of how important for Poland's security policy is its NATO membership, and it is in this context that its involvement in Alliance operations should be analysed.

It should be remembered, nevertheless, that Poland's acquisition of NATO membership was a process which required political will and readiness of both Parties. In his exposé delivered after the formation of the government in September 1989, Tadeusz Mazowiecki, prime minister of the first non-communist government, while declaring the Western option in Polish foreign policy, at the same time emphasized the need for the retention of the existing alliances: Warsaw Pact and NATO (Kupiecki, 2000, p. 275). However, the Warsaw Pact, with the significant involvement of Polish, Hungarian and (the then) Czechoslovak diplomacies, was dissolved and ceased to exist as of 1 July 1991 (Nowak, 2011), which meant that several Central European countries found themselves in a peculiar 'grey zone of security'.

Under the conditions of geopolitical change consequent upon the dissolution of the Warsaw Pact and then the collapse of the former Soviet Union, the ways of thinking of European security began to be redefined not only in Poland but also in NATO. Poland established official relations with the Atlantic Alliance already on 21 March 1990, when the NATO Headquarters was visited by the then Foreign Minister Krzysztof Skubiszewski. On 3 July 1991, two days after the dissolution of the Warsaw Pact, the then President of Poland Lech Wałęsa visited the NATO Headquarters. During that visit Poland expressed a view (still relevant today) that NATO is a permanent element of the architecture of security in Europe (Polska Zbrojna, 1991). In this context, the transatlantic orientation began to be explicitly perceived as the solution to Poland's security problems. These activities – as Stanisław Koziej put it – were an element 'of Poland achieving strategic independence' after the period of functioning in the conditions of the Soviet Union's hegemony (Koziej, 2010, p. 2).

One clearly emphasize that almost from the beginning of its ties with NATO, Poland treated its experiences resulting from participation in UN peacekeeping operations as an instrument of achieving objectives in security policy. After the establishment in December 1991 of the North Atlantic Cooperation Council (NACC), Poland became actively involved in the functioning of the Ad Hoc Group on Co-operation in Peacekeeping. Poland presented here its experiences gained during UN peacekeeping operations and declared its readiness to assign a military contingent for NATO operations conducted under the UN mandate or the then Conference for Security and Cooperation and Europe (Kupiecki, 2000, p. 289).

After the conclusion of the first NACC ministerial session on 21 December 1991, in his exposé delivered in the Parliament, the then Prime Minister Jan Olszewski included in the priorities of Poland's foreign policy the cooperation with the Atlantic Alliance, which he recognized as a pillar of security in Europe. At the same time he opted for the development of extensive ties with NATO (Expose, 1991). This direction of thinking became a stable tendency in Poland's security policy. After the change of government, in her exposé delivered on 10 July 1992 Prime Minister Hanna Suchocka explicitly stated that Poland sought to ensure its security through NATO membership (Expose, 1992). Similarly, the strategy for Poland's security adopted on 2 November 1992, reflecting geopolitical change in Europe and the process of systemic transformation in the country, recognized that Poland's strategic goal was NATO membership (Założenia, 1992, p. 5).

This means that the idea of ad hoc cooperation with NATO was abandoned while a broad, cross-party consensus for the prospect of NATO membership was reached, which continues to the present day. This was accompanied by growing public support, which reached even 73 per cent in 1996 (Sakson, 1996, pp. 25–26). Under such circumstances on 1 September 1993, that is, the 54th anniversary of the outbreak of the Second World War, the then Polish President Lech Wałęsa submitted a letter to the NATO Secretary General, in which he confirmed Poland's will to gain membership of the Alliance. A test of interoperability between Poland's armed forces and NATO forces was the participation of Polish units (begun in 1996) in Implementation Force (IFOR) and then Stabilisation Force (SFOR) operations in Bosnia and Herzegovina. For Poland, however, these operations did not merely confirm its ability to interoperate with NATO forces but they also proved the earlier proposition that Poland did not want to be merely a consumer of NATO-produced security but also wished to significantly contribute to enhancing the Alliance's strength by being involved in fulfilling Allied obligations (Kupiecki, 2000, p. 321).

To sum up, it should be explicitly emphasized that the collapse of the international bipolar order created a geopolitical chance for Poland to implement the Euro-Atlantic option in security policy. NATO was recognized as the security pillar in Europe while NATO membership became a priority in Poland's foreign policy. From the very beginning, declarations to take part but also actual involvement in NATO peacekeeping operations became one of Poland's instruments for the accomplishment of this objective.

## The tradition of Poland's participation in UN peacekeeping operations

A vitally significant factor for Poland's participation in NATO peacekeeping operations was the prior experience of participation in UN peacekeeping missions. It should be remembered that when initiating its contacts with NATO in 1991, Poland treated the experience gained through participation in UN peacekeeping operations as some kind of added value for the cooperation begun at that time. This experience also means that involvement in multinational peacekeeping operations is permanently present in Polish defence doctrine and foreign policy. The 1992 strategy for Poland's security assumed continuation of the armed forces' participation in peacekeeping operations and involvement in solving conflicts outside the State frontiers (Założenia, 1992).

Until 1995 Poland participated exclusively in UN-mandated peacekeeping operations. Polish soldiers were first involved in a peacekeeping mission in 1953. They began service lasting until 1989 under the Neutral Nations Supervisory Commission in Korea. From 1954 to 1975 they served on the International Commission for Supervision and Control – Indo-China (ICSC), and in 1968–1970 on the International Observer Team in Nigeria. In the 1970s Poland was involved in the next UN-led peacekeeping operations. From 1974 it took part in the UNDOF operation in the Golan Heights and from 1978 in the UNIFIL operation in Lebanon. Altogether, in 1953–1988 the civil and military personnel from Poland took part in the functioning of four conciliation commissions and three peacekeeping operations. These actions involved approximately 17,000 personnel (Gagor, 1999). For Polish soldiers those operations became a source of experience of living in difficult geographical, climatic conditions and in complex, different cultural environments. One must, however, remember their limitations especially in the context of future functioning in NATO operations. The UN operations were peacekeeping ones, while the Polish contingents mainly performed logistical tasks, which were a kind of specialty of Polish soldiers participating in UN peacekeeping operations.

Poland's involvement in peacekeeping operations significantly rose after 1989. From 1989 to 2009 – the UN operations, from 1996 NATO operations, from 2003 EU operations, and OSCE observer missions as well as in the 'coalition of the willing' operations involved 67,000 soldiers and civilian personnel. The character of participation by Polish soldiers in peacekeeping operations also changed. Apart from earlier, traditional, as it were, operations to keep peace and observer missions, Polish soldiers began to take part in peace enforcement operations. This first took place in 1992 in the UNPROFOR operation in Bosnia and Herzegovina (Balcerowicz, 2009, p. 24). Regardless of their limitations, these experiences became a kind of 'value added' contributed by Poland to NATO operations conducted from 1996.

The example of Polish military presence in the Afghanistan mission conducted under NATO auspices clearly shows that a significant problem in making political decisions on involvement in similar operations is the public opinion factor. The November 2010 survey of Poles' views on the presence of Polish troops in Afghanistan explicitly shows the persistently low public support (approximately 20 per cent) and the high (approximately 80 per cent) level of opposition (see Table 11.1).

The results of the opinion poll explicitly show that as the duration of operation in Afghanistan and the presence of Polish troops grow longer,

*Table 11.1* Attitude of the Poles towards the presence of Polish troops in Afghanistan (%)

|  | January 2007 | September 2007 | September 2008 | September 2009 | November 2010 |
|---|---|---|---|---|---|
| For | 20 | 22 | 21 | 20 | 17 |
| Against | 78 | 72 | 74 | 76 | 79 |
| Don't know | 2 | 6 | 5 | 4 | 4 |

Source: *Udział Polski* (2010, p. 1).

the public support for this operation and military presence declines. Prevalent disapproval is recorded in all demographic and social groups regardless of declared political views and sympathies for political parties. This is a distinct change when compared with Poland's initial military involvement in Afghanistan in 2002. At that time, fresh memories of terrorist attacks on 11 September 2001 and the conviction that the war on terrorism would yield fast and positive results caused even more than half of Polish society to support Poland's involvement in Afghanistan (*Udział Polski*, 2010, p. 1).

There are many reasons for growing disapproval of the presence of Polish troops in Afghanistan. One of them is the low level of belief that the operations of NATO forces will contribute to stability in this country and establish peace. Only 16 per cent of the respondents were optimistic about the final outcome of NATO (including Polish) troops' presence in Afghanistan, while 71 per cent were pessimistic. Moreover, a significant number of Polish citizens (56 per cent) were afraid that one of the negative effects of participation of Polish troops in the stability mission in that country might be a growing danger of terrorist attacks against Poland (*Udział Polski*, 2010, p. 1).

This situation is a serious challenge to Poland's political decisions about involvement in NATO operations, especially in those conducted outside of the Treaty Area, far away from Poland's borders. The problem is even more complicated as Poland's military presence in NATO operations (carried out with the growing number of fatalities, accompanied by the reform of Polish armed forces and growing expenditure) requires acceptance of the public, which is more and more difficult to gain. Clearly noticeable is the growing 'fatigue of public opinion', who often find it increasingly difficult to understand these operations and express less and less willingness to bear the rising costs in terms of funds and personnel (Prymat NATO, 2006, p. 23).

Such conditions make it difficult to continue military involvement and in the case of the NATO operation in Libya in March 2011 this may well have been one of the reasons – before the parliamentary elections planned for October – why Poland refused to take part in the military venture. However, in the context of Polish military presence in Afghanistan, a view emerged in the public debate in Poland that one of the ways of gaining an increase in public support was to influence the public opinion in order to define realistic objectives of operations, thereby enabling the public to better understand the undertaken actions and continue their belief in the final success. Therefore, the problem arose regarding the concept of dialogue with society and the arguments used. It was concluded that the appeal to the argument of fulfilling allied obligations was entirely unsatisfactory (Prymat NATO, 2006, p. 23).

## The political strategy of Poland's participation in NATO military operations

Poland's involvement in NATO military operations conducted beyond obligations as set forth in Article 5 of the Washington Treaty served to achieve exactly defined although evolving political objectives expressing the priorities of Polish foreign policy. Underlying them was the invariable assumption of the fundamental significance of NATO membership for Poland's security and for strengthening its international position. These became the main political will motive for Poland's participation in NATO military operations (Ciechanowski, 2010, p. 72), and the primary element of the implemented political strategy. The analysis of the strategy requires, however, that two more components be taken into account. One is the evolution in defining threats to national security, and transition from focusing on traditional threats in Poland's immediate neighbourhood, to perceiving non-traditional threats occurring even on a global scale The other component is that, in the conditions of globalization of the Atlantic Alliance's operations, Poland attaches particular importance to the principle of collective defence laid down in Article 5 of the Washington Treaty.

Involvement in NATO peacekeeping operations should be examined in the context of the importance of the Atlantic Alliance for Poland as a country striving to secure its security and seeking its position in the post-Cold War international arena. Already in the early 1990s Poland recognized NATO as the main peace and stability factor in Europe (Założenia, 1992, p. 5). One consequence of the recognition of NATO's place and importance for European security was Poland's endeavours to become a member of the Alliance. A form of actions towards this goal was to declare Poland's readiness and then, from 1996, participation in peacekeeping operations under NATO auspices. These actions were intended to demonstrate that Poland's armed forces were able to interoperate with the armed forces of other NATO members, and that Poland was ready to contribute to enhancing security in Europe and outside it (Strategia, 2000, p. 3). This was also a clear signal that Poland was not only 'a consumer' but also 'a producer' of security. Hence the primary goal of these actions taken before gaining NATO membership was to prove that Poland was a valuable candidate able to contribute to the security of the Euro-Atlantic area and the surrounding international environment.

In 1996, as has been stressed before, Poland became involved in the NATO peacemaking mission in Bosnia and Herzegovina. The main motive was the need and necessity to jointly participate in operations carried out primarily by the Atlantic Alliance members in order to solve ethnic conflicts in the Balkans. These actions were in entire conformity with the November 1992 strategy for Poland's national security and with the adopted goal of integration with the Western European structures, chiefly with NATO and the present EU. Participation in multinational military units organized under NATO auspices was to establish closer relations with the Alliance in political and military terms. Poland's military forces treated these actions as a training in military culture, standards and procedures specific to the Atlantic Alliance. They were also an element of building a positive image of the Polish armed forces, an opportunity to show their capability and reliability to the future allies (Balcerowicz, 2009, pp. 25–26).

It is obvious that the political objectives carried out by Poland as a result of involvement in the Alliance's peacekeeping operations after entry in the NATO in 1999 changed when compared with those during the candidacy period. Initially, Poland sought to confirm that the decision of gaining NATO membership was very well founded. With time, the focus of attention shifted more and more towards strengthening Poland's position in the Atlantic Alliance, which also meant striving to enhance Poland's international position, to which participation in peacekeeping operations also contributed.

After 1999 a firm conviction developed that NATO membership (the Alliance being the central institution through which Poland realizes its security interests) significantly changed Poland's geopolitical and geostrategic position (Strategia, 2000, p. 2). It was believed that Poland as an Atlantic Alliance member and then an EU member was becoming, on the one hand, an increasingly important actor in international relations, especially in the Euro-Atlantic area. On the other hand, a conviction was expressed that membership of the two institutions ensured Poland's high level of security (Strategia, 2007, p. 4). Under such conditions, Poland's main strategic goals were defined, inter alia, as the active development of relations in the international arena and promotion of its image as a reliable ally, 'a producer of security' (Strategia, 2007, p. 5). A belief developed that by enhancing Poland's security and position the Alliance increases the freedom of action in the international environment (Kupiecki, 2003, p. 49).

The emphasis on the priority importance of NATO membership for security policy became a constant element of Polish policy, underlying which was a specific kind of cross-party consensus of the major political forces. Continuation of this line of thinking was therefore not surprising after the formation in November 2007 of the coalition government between the liberal party (Civic Platform) and the peasant party (Polish Peasants' Party), while at the same time the ties with the EU were strengthened in Polish security policy. In Prime Minister Donald Tusk's exposé delivered in the Sejm (Parliament) on 23 November, both NATO and the EU were recognized as the pillars of Poland's security. The information of the new government on Poland's foreign policy, presented by Foreign Minister Radosław Sikorski on 7 May 2008, gave distinct priority in security policy to the Atlantic Alliance as performing the political function of the link between the two branches of Western European civilization: North American and European, and the military function in the form of guarantees of collective defence. Minister Sikorski confirmed that Poland's participation in NATO military operations was a way of emphasizing its reliability as an ally (*Informacja rządu*, 2009, p. 18) and realizing the principle of allied solidarity, which Poland regarded as invariable.

With time, an important element of Poland's political strategy after entry in the NATO was to strive to strengthen its position inside the Alliance. One of the activities serving this purpose was its participation in peacemaking operations. A manifestation of Poland's growing international position and its sense were endeavours, as it was put in official statements, to seek a more equitable distribution of costs of and benefits from participation in peacekeeping operations. A conviction arose in Poland that greater involvement in the Atlantic Alliance's expeditionary missions would prompt its member states, especially those playing major roles, to be more interested, from the point of view of Poland's interests, in the Central and Eastern European region and in problems especially significant for Poland, such as energy security. These views were explicitly expressed in the above-mentioned exposé delivered on 23 November 2007 (Expose, 2007) by Prime Minister Donald Tusk, who headed the coalition government formed by the liberal party and peasant party. This government took clear actions to strengthen Poland's position in the NATO, according, at the same time, more importance to the EU in Poland's security policy. Foreign Minister Radosław Sikorski confirmed this direction in the aforementioned government information on Poland's foreign policy presented in the Sejm on 7 May 2008. When emphasizing allied credibility manifested in participation in NATO military operations, he stressed not only Poland's priority in seeking to strengthen collective defence but also expectations concerning the location of military infrastructure in Poland and greater participation of Poland's representatives in NATO structures (*Informacja rządu*, 2009).

Giving priority significance to NATO in ensuring Poland's security, endeavours to enhance the Polish position in the Alliance and balance the costs and benefits of involvement in its military operations was accompanied by activities aimed at building especially privileged relations with the United States. These were expressed in the strategic partnership formula (Madej and Terlikowski, 2009, p. 49). In Poland, the allied relations with the United States, including US military presence in Europe, were believed to be a vital component of national and European security. It was assumed that NATO expressed the institutional substance of special ties between Poland and the United States (Kupiecki, 2003, p. 51).

The treatment of the ties with the United States as a priority in the field of security was significantly prompted by the assessment of the geopolitical and geostrategic situation in post-Cold War Europe. A view was advanced that the process of building the international order was not completed in the eastern part of the European continent, with the existing instabilities and competition for areas of influence. Threats to energy security created by the Russian Federation were perceived as especially significant for Poland (Madej, 2008, p. 58). Under such circumstances the United States was regarded as the only partner which could offer Poland genuine political and military aid, and support in solving security problems (Kaczyński, 2008, p. 58). That is why cooperation with the United States within NATO came to be regarded as the most important element of European security and an element of Poland's *raison d'être*. Consequently, Poland explicitly stressed that it was against any attempts to build European security in opposition to the United States or against those aimed at undermining the US position (Cimoszewicz, 2003, p. 25).

As it perceived the United States as a guarantor of its security, Poland also formulated its expectations towards that country. It first of all expected US commitment to the deployment of anti-missile defence systems in Poland's territory, presence of US troops and more involvement in the modernization of Poland's armed forces. In exchange, Poland offered its fidelity as an ally, one of such manifestations being involvements in military operations with the United States, even in those that were not organized under NATO auspices and were not legitimated by the UN Security Council. A confirmation of this was Poland's symbolic participation in 'the coalition of the willing', which, in March 2003, started military actions against Iraq governed by Saddam Hussein. However, one cannot fail to notice Poland's later disappointment with the US attitude towards Polish expectations from that country. This disillusionment, in the late 2000s, might have caused Poland, while acknowledging NATO's paramount importance, to increase cooperation with the EU in security policy; consequently, in March 2011, although Poland offered political support, it did not take part in the NATO operation against Muammar Gaddafi's Libya, and even came under US criticism.

The analysis of the strategic thought accompanying the involvement in NATO military operations requires taking into account how Poland perceives threats to security. The threats after 1989 are clearly treated as a dynamic process characterized by two tendencies. One is the transition from threats traditionally identified with armed conflicts to non-traditional, asymmetrical threats associated with the activity of non-State actors and globalization processes. The other is the broadening of the geographical range of the identified threats and the transition from those in Poland's immediate neighbourhood to those functioning even on a global scale, which, consequently, has created grounds for broadening the geographical range of security-oriented actions (Pietraś, 2010, pp. 174–193).

Poland's strategy for national security adopted in 1992 primarily focused on fairly traditional threats existing in the immediate vicinity of Poland, first of all in the post-Soviet area. It was emphasized that geopolitical changes produced by the collapse of the former Soviet Union could cause the proliferation of weapons of mass destruction and conventional weaponry. There were also fears of ethnic and border conflicts as well as immigration waves and disruption of delivery of energy raw materials (Założenia, 1992, p. 9).

Distinctly different threats were expressed in Poland's security strategy adopted in 2000, a year after Poland acquired NATO membership. The document emphasized the absence of danger of direct military aggression and the low probability of the outbreak of a global or continental war. However, certain threats to security were highlighted, such as ethnic conflicts, economic crises and upset political stability in some countries, as well as proliferation of weapons of mass destruction; moreover, the emergence of new threats such as terrorism and transnational organized crime was emphasized. Changes in the natural environment were also included in the category of security threats (Strategia, 2000, pp. 2–4).

The security strategy adopted in 2003, that is, after the terrorist attacks on 11 September 2001 and right before Poland's entry in the EU, positively assessed the security environment but pointed out the emergence of threats with qualitatively new characteristics found on a global scale. The document distinctly stressed that Poland's security increasingly depended on the outcomes of globalization and fragmentation processes. In their context, it was explicitly emphasized that the change in Poland's security environment consisted in the shift of the centre of gravity from 'classical', 'traditional' threats to untypical ones: their sources are difficult-to-identify non-State actors (Strategia, 2003, p. 2).

The direction of thinking of security threats outlined in the 2003 security strategy was continued, albeit with certain modifications and change in priorities, in the 2007 strategy, which emphasized threats connected with the interruption of deliveries of energy raw materials, the collapse of European integration processes, and crisis in financial markets. A comparatively lesser importance was attached to threats like international terrorism, transnational organized crime and ecological problems (Strategia, 2007).

A conviction arose in Poland that the change of the character of security threats from traditional ones to those non-traditional with qualitatively new characteristics poses a challenge to the Atlantic Alliance: there is limited capacity to respond to those threats by resorting to a strategy of deterrence through the use of the Alliance's military potential. Support was therefore expressed for NATO's adaptive measures to new threats; it was recognized that an important element of these actions was international military cooperation and involvement in low intensity conflicts and humanitarian crises outside the Alliance's borders. Poland accepted involvement in these kinds of operation, acknowledging that they confirmed its credibility as an ally and were a factor of enhancing the Atlantic Alliance's vitality (*Informacja rządu*, 2009, p. 18). An essential constraint, however, was postulated. These actions should in no way reduce NATO's capacity to perform its function of collective defence pursuant to Article 5 of the Washington Treaty (Ziółkowski, 2007, p. 73).

An especially significant element of Poland's political strategy in the conditions of globalization of security threats was the acceptance of selective involvement in NATO's operational activities, with an absolute preference for the Alliance fulfilling its obligations concerning collective defence. Preference for NATO's performance of obligations under Article 5 of the Washington Treaty in the conditions of the Alliance's transformation and adaptation to the new type of threats became, essentially, an element of Poland's *raison d'être*, a kind of mantra repeated by Polish politicians and the academic circles from the moment Poland gained NATO membership. A specific cross-party political consensus was reached on this matter, which is confirmed, for example, by Poland's security strategies adopted in 2000, 2003 and 2007, and by the speeches of Poland's foreign ministers representing different political orientations. The year 2000 strategy explicitly stated that Poland's priority was that NATO should retain its capacity to fulfil the function of effectively organizing collective defence (Strategia, 2000, p. 10). The strategy of 2003 supported NATO's selective involvement in stability missions in the non-European area, recognizing them as important for the Alliance's vitality, but on condition that it maintained its credible potential and capacity to perform the classical functions of collective defence (Strategia, 2003, p. 5). Almost the same wording was used in the 2007 strategy.

Having given priority to the function of collective defence whilst NATO conducted operations not arising from obligations under Article 5 of the Washington Treaty and even on a global scale, Poland began to observe that with the absence of intense threat, common to all member states, the integrating role of the collective defence clause was weak. It was remarked that the clause comparatively lost in importance as the organizing principle of NATO's functioning and a determinant of the development prospect. This situation was not essentially changed with the invocation of Article 5 after the terrorist attacks of 11 September 2001. For Poland but also for other member states, an important question arose about the understanding of the principle of mutual defence when many threats to security existed far away from the borders of NATO member states (Prymat NATO, 2006, pp. 9–10).

The weakening of NATO's dominant role in transatlantic relations and the diminished importance of the function of collective defence was and is seen by Poland as adverse phenomena. The main reason was its geopolitical situation as one of the NATO easternmost NATO members. Poland found that with its political position it had limited possibilities of influencing the Alliance's evolution, but it was not entirely deprived of them. The focus was on two directions of actions aimed at enhancing the importance of Article 5. First, by influencing the content of documents adopted by the Alliance. Second, by acting on behalf of allied solidarity and by supporting political and military actions also taken in non-European regions. Poland recognized that involvement in military operations created grounds for strengthening its political position in NATO and for the expectance of reciprocity and solidarity, that is, actions in accordance with the logic of the collective defence principle, on the part of the other member states (Prymat NATO, 2006, p. 12).

On the other hand, Poland realized that with the ongoing economic reforms and with the costly reform of the military forces there were financial barriers to Poland's involvement in NATO operations carried out even on a global scale. This means that by globalizing its actions the Atlantic Alliance proves too costly for Poland and also difficult to accept by the public opinion. What became essential, therefore, was to strive to optimally use the resources available. In the context of Polish presence in Afghanistan, the public opinion began to emphasize that apart from fulfilling its obligations as an ally, Poland had no interest in involving its military forces and financial resources (Pacuła, 2009, p. 37).

Under such circumstances, a discussion began on the model of Poland's involvement in international peacekeeping operations conducted not only by NATO. The existing model was deemed ineffective in both political and military terms. There was criticism of the fragmentation of activities into the operations organized by the UN, NATO, EU, and 'the coalitions of the willing', where Poland did not achieve proportional political gains while it incurred considerable costs. Polish decision-makers, therefore, concluded that it was necessary to set forth a 'catalogue of involvement' in international military operations, including those under NATO auspices, which would enable the maximization of political gains and training advantages. Consequently, it was essential that the following questions should be answered: (1) In what situations was Poland ready to participate in military operations? (2) In what role? (3) With what partners? (4) In what political conditions? (5) In what institutional form? It was concluded that Poland should take part in NATO- and EU-led operations

(Prymat NATO, 2006, p. 15). One of the results of this change of priorities in participation in peacekeeping operations was the takeover of responsibility for Afghanistan's Ghazni province in 2008, and the termination in 2009 of participation in operations organized under NATO auspices.

Involvement in military operations outside the Euro-Atlantic area became the subject of discussions and disputes within NATO. In Poland, questions were also asked about what threats and what interests justified involvement in global-scale operations. For such questions asked in Poland, of significant importance were also the rising costs of military ventures. Under such circumstances, two visions of NATO appeared. One, a NATO of proponents of globalized operations, perceived as a structure serving to promote stability, democracy and freedom outside the Euro-Atlantic area. This direction of action is supported first of all by the United States and Great Britain. The other, a NATO of supporters of the 'traditional' vision, consisting in focusing interest on the Euro-Atlantic area and on chiefly military tasks, leaving the 'soft' elements of security to the EU (Kupiecki, 2006, p. 71).

The vision of NATO, which Poland espoused, was closer to the one represented by the United States although with emphasis placed on selective involvement in military operations limited by the capabilities available and preferences for enhancing collective defence. As a point of principle, Poland did not find it necessary to limit the geographical range of Alliance operations, deriving their legitimacy from UN Security Council's resolutions and the North Atlantic Council's decisions in the cases justified by the requirements of collective defence. It was assumed that consensus as a procedure for making decisions on NATO-led missions would reduce the possibility of some member states treating the Alliance as a 'toolbox', from which a member state could choose at will in order to implement its particular interests. Poland opted for joint collective actions, admitting of the possibility of cooperation with other institutions that worked for security, mainly with the EU. This solution should serve to better divide tasks and harmonize modernization efforts enabling effective counteraction to security threats. Poland also believed that NATO would not need to monopolize operations conducted outside the Euro-Atlantic area, while the choice of the place of involvement and the kind of actions to be launched should be subject to discussion by the interested states and should serve to optimize the undertaken actions from the standpoint of their effects on international security (Kupiecki, 2006, p. 71).

## The execution of Poland's participation in NATO military operations

The analysis of the process of Poland's participation in NATO operations will be carried out taking into account three problems. First, this will be the analysis of normative grounds for the undertaken actions. Second, the decision-making process will be taken into consideration. Third, an especially thorough examination will cover operations that confirm Poland's involvement in NATO military operations in different parts of the world.

The *normative grounds* for Poland's participation in NATO military operations are diverse. On the one hand, these are statutory regulations, on the other, political norms. The former include the Statue of 17 December 1998 on the Rules of Use and Stationing of the Republic of Poland's Armed Forces Abroad (Ustawa, 1998). This law regulates all kinds of involvement of Poland's armed forces outside its borders, including NATO operations. It specifies (Article 2) the forms of such involvement and distinguishes between the employment of Poland's armed forces and their stationing outside the State's borders. The term 'employment' means the presence of military units outside Poland's borders in order to participate in an armed conflict, a peace operation or in missions against terrorist attacks and their effects. 'Stationing' covers participation in military training and manoeuvres, rescue, search and humanitarian missions, and in representative events. The Statute also specifies the elements of the decision-making process to use the Polish armed forces abroad, and the soldiers' rights and duties.

Special normative grounds for the decision on Polish participation in international military operations, including NATO missions, are laid down in the 'Strategy for Deployment of The Armed Forces of the Republic of Poland in International Operations' adopted by the Council of Ministers on 13 January 2009. The document is an attempt to specify objectified criteria, in accordance with national interests and free from current short-term political conditions, for making decisions to deploy Polish military units in international peacekeeping operations. The Strategy also reflects Poland's experiences gained during previous participation in these types of operations and conclusions from mistakes. It is an attempt to place the participation in military operations in the broader context of Poland's foreign policy. It contains a thinking instruction and identification of problems which need to be taken into account when deciding on sending Polish military units to take part in a foreign mission (Osica, 2009, p. 41).

This document also tries to detail Poland's political strategy for participation in international military operations. It explicitly states that participation in these types of operations is an instrument of Poland's foreign and security policy, which makes it possible to influence the development of national security. One of the factors justifying these types of activities was, in Polish opinion, a change in the character of threats to security determined by globalization processes which 'require deployment of armed forces in distant theaters'. While indicating Poland's political will to be involved in missions under the auspices of NATO, EU, UN, OSCE or as part of ad hoc coalitions, distinct priority was given to NATO and EU operations. It was explicitly emphasized that participation in these operations would have to reflect Polish national interest, be in accordance with Poland's *raison d'être* and serve to accomplish clearly defined political goals, serve to enhance Poland's international position, contribute to the fulfilment of allied obligations and build Poland's image as a reliable and responsible member of the international community. The document also specified the rules of participation in international missions. These are: (1) advisability or conformity with State interests; (2) freedom of action or ensuring that Polish units have the greatest influence possible on the course of operations; and (3) economy of forces or the optimum use of means towards the intended objectives (Strategia, 2009).

The structure and principles of the *decision-making process* to send Polish military units to be engaged in foreign missions are specified in the above-mentioned Statute on the Rules of Use and Stationing of the Republic of Poland's Armed Forces Abroad of 18 December 1998. Pursuant to its Article 3, the decision to employ Polish military units for a foreign mission is taken by the President of Poland on the motion of the Prime Minister. The decision-making process actually excludes the Parliament. After the President has made a decision, he or she only informs the Marshals [Speakers] of the Sejm and Senate about it. There is no requirement, therefore, to obtain the Parliament's consent (Ustawa, 1998). An indisputable advantage of this solution is the possibility of quickly making decisions and responding to the development of the international situation. A drawback is the absence of special legitimation of such decisions by the Parliament (Pietrzak, 2012, pp. 2–5).

Poland became engaged in NATO's *operational military missions* in 1996, already prior to its Alliance membership. Initially, the operations were concentrated in the Balkans, and then in Afghanistan, Iraq, Pakistan and sporadically in other places.

In the Balkans, Poland participated and still does in several NATO-led military missions: IFOR, SFOR, Allied Force (AFOR) and Kosovo Force (KFOR). The participation in the IFOR mission, which began to operate in Bosnia and Herzegovina after the conclusion of the Dayton Peace Accords ending the war in the Balkans, was the turning point of Poland's participation in NATO-led peacemaking operations. The implementation forces created at the time involved 32 countries and numbered approximately 60 thousand troops. The battalion sent by Poland began its service in the IFOR in February 1996 and was part of the multinational Polish-Nordic Brigade. The sending of this battalion confirmed Poland's aspirations for NATO membership. It was also a test of preparedness of Polish troops for cooperation with NATO military units in the conditions of peace enforcement (Kochanowski, 2000, pp. 303–305; Balcerowicz, 2009, p. 25).

After the ending of the IFOR mission Poland was invited to take part in the SFOR operation. Until the end of 1999, the Polish battalion of 500 soldiers still functioned as part of the Nordic-Polish Brigade belonging to the Multinational Division 'North'. Because of the reorganization of the SFOR mission, the Nordic-Polish Brigade was transformed into the Nordic-Polish Combat Group subordinated to the Multinational Division 'North', which consisted, apart from Polish troops, of soldiers from Denmark, Finland, Norway, Sweden, Latvia, Lithuania and Estonia. The tasks of the Polish unit included supervision over the military activities of the parties to the conflict (Towpik, 2000, p. 26). The SFOR operation ceased to function in 2004, its tasks having been taken over by the military forces of EU member states under the EUFOR-ALTHEA mission.

Poland became a NATO member, together with the Czech Republic and Hungary, on 12 March 1999, and already on 24 March the Atlantic Alliance began the operation against Serbia governed by Slobodan Milosevic because of ethnic cleansing in Kosovo. Poland offered its political support to the operation, without, however, taking part in its military stage. Already during the 'Allied Force' operation and after its cessation, the Atlantic Alliance launched stability operations as part of the AFOR and KFOR missions. The Polish contingent on the NATO mission of Albania numbered 140 soldiers and operated from 1 May to 15 October 1999. Its main responsibilities were to support the activities of the Albanian government and those of the UN High Commissioner for Refugees in connection with the initiated process of the return of refugees from Albania to Kosovo (Kochanowski, 2000, p. 306).

After ending the stage of military operations as part of the 'Allied Force' mission under the UN Security Council Resolution 1244, the

Atlantic Alliance began stability operations in Kosovo as part of the KFOR mission. The 800-strong Polish troop contingent became part of the Multinational Brigade 'East' and was deployed in the so-called American sector along the Macedonian border. In the autumn of 1999, 108 Ukrainian and 30 Lithuanian troops began to serve in the Polish battalion, hence in July 2000 the Polish battalion was renamed as the Polish-Ukrainian battalion (POLUKRBAT). Its principal tasks were to ensure security along the main transport routes, monitor the observance of resolutions on cessation of armed operations, escort humanitarian aid convoys, and check some border crossings. On account of the unstable situation in Kosovo and continuing ethnic riots between the Albanian and Serbian populations, in April 2000, at the request of the NATO Command in Europe, the Polish battalion of the SACEUR Strategic Reserve was sent to Kosovo, to be stationed in Kosovska Mitrovica (Towpik, 2000, p. 26). In this context, it should be emphasized that the KFOR forces and the Polish contingent as their component were modified many times; one of the tendencies was to reduce the number of Polish soldiers. At the end of 2011 their number was 212. They executed their tasks in the central and eastern part of Kosovo.

However, of special importance for Poland and the Alliance is the mission in Afghanistan. For Poland it is a dynamic process of the changing scale and forms of engagement. After the terrorist attacks on the United States on 11 September 2001, already in November that year Poland decided to send a modest contingent to participate in the US-led operation 'Enduring Freedom'. This contingent achieved operational readiness in early January 2002 (Kobieracki, 2002, p. 68). At the same time Poland was invited to participate in the ISAF. In compliance with the request, on 16 March 2002 the first group of Polish soldiers, totalling 300, were sent to the mission area. This was the beginning of involvement alongside the United States in the antiterrorist campaign. In 2003 NATO took over command of the ISAF mission.

It should be stressed that despite Poland's declared priority accorded to engagement in NATO peacemaking operations, in comparison with other organizations, in particular the UN, Polish participation in the Atlantic Alliance missions was negligible in 2004. It happened despite the special importance of the ISAF mission for the antiterrorist campaign and for NATO. This was the first Alliance mission conducted outside Europe and it was part of the broader strategy for cooperation between Central Asian states. At the military level the mission integrated the efforts of the NATO member states; it had a high priority status, and did not arouse significant controversy. Apart from sending a symbolic number of soldiers, Poland also failed to answer the call to manage or only take part in one of the emerging regional reconstruction teams which coordinated international operations in separate Afghan provinces. The Command of the Polish armed forces opted for the use of troops involved in Iraq at that time as a possibility of changing the situation. Therefore, it should come as no surprise that Poland's conduct was criticized by many NATO members, the object of criticism being the way Poland discharged its obligations as an ally (Kupiecki, 2005, p. 66).

In September 2006, with the situation in Afghanistan growing increasingly complicated and with the criticism by many NATO member states, Poland decided to significantly increase its military presence in that country by sending over 1,000 troops. Poland was one of the nine countries which each sent a contingent of over 1,000 troops to Afghanistan, thus being ranked eighth among the 31 states participating in the coalition. What is essential is that Poland placed its contingent at the ISAF Command's disposal without any caveats (operation restrictions) as to its use. This was an unusual solution because many countries imposed such caveats on their contingents (Balcerowicz, 2009, p. 35). Pursuant to the President of Poland's decision of 22 November 2006, the enlarged contingent would be deployed in Afghanistan by April 2007, and would start its operations in May. However, problems with equipping the contingent and logistical difficulties arose, which stemmed from lack of the contingent's transport capability and dependence on the United States in this respect. This delayed the deployment of Polish units in Afghanistan (Gazeta Wyborcza, 2007; Madej, 2008, pp. 63–64).

The military units composing the Polish Battle Group, operating in the structure of the multinational military forces, were deployed in the Ghazni and Paktita provinces in the eastern region of Afghanistan and were responsible for protection of the strategic Kabul–Kandahar highway: they began to conduct patrolling actions in June 2007. They were subordinated to the US troops which had already been deployed there – to the 'East' Command, which conducted counter-terrorist actions as part of the operation 'Enduring Freedom', separate from the ISAF mission. This solution was criticized in Poland. The public opinion stressed that the Polish units were excessively subordinated to the US armed forces, being even reduced to the role of 'a subcontractor' executing the decisions and operations of American units (Balcerowicz, 2009, p. 35). Critics added that the structure and deployment of the Polish units did not ensure adequate influence, commensurate with their size, on the course of ISAF operations. The then Polish government countered the criticism, pointing out the absence of alternative solutions resulting from limited financial and logistical capacities. It was also recognized that such a solution had positive elements, including training gains from close cooperation with the US military forces.

At the end of 2007, two factors triggered a critical discussion on the functioning of Polish military units in Afghanistan, especially their close subordination to US troops. The first factor was the parliamentary election held in October 2007 and the resulting formation of the Civic Platform and Polish People's Party government. The other factor was the arrest in November 2007 by the military prosecutors, of seven Polish soldiers on charges of violations of the Hague Convention of 1907 and the Geneva Conventions of 1949 while shelling the village of Nangar Kehl on 16 August 2007: six civilians were killed.

The discussion held in the contexts of the two conditions resulted in the announcement already in December 2007 that the Polish military contingent operating in Afghanistan under the ISAF mission would be reorganized and consolidated. These measures were expected to culminate in Poland taking over responsibility for security in one of the Afghan provinces in 2008 (Gazeta Wyborcza, 2008). It was believed that this solution would, on the one hand, enhance the effectiveness of operations of the Polish contingent, which operated in dispersed areas and under the US command. On the other hand, the adopted solution would make Polish troop operations more noticeable to their NATO allies and would strengthen Poland's position in the Alliance, thereby enabling Poland to have more influence on the planning and decision-making process during the ISAF mission. The explicit aim was that the Polish military units should undertake actions 'on their own' (Madej, 2008, p. 65).

However, the takeover of responsibility for security in one of the provinces involved rising costs of Polish military presence in Afghanistan because this required self-sufficiency in air shipping, reconnaissance/intelligence and logistics. It was also necessary to undertake new tasks aimed at stabilization of societal life in Afghanistan and its reconstruction. In March 2008 it was decided that the Polish troops deployed mainly in the Ghazni and Paktita provinces would be concentrated in the former. The Ghazni province was distinguished by the lower level of rebel activities when compared with many others and the lower level of drug production, while it was strategically highly significant because of the Kabul–Kandahar highway. Poland took over responsibility for that province on 31 October 2008 (Madej and Terlikowski, 2009, pp. 51–53).

In 2009 Poland twice made a decision to increase its military contingent as part of ISAF. In July that year the contingent was increased to a total of 2000, and in April 2010 to 2,600 troops and civilian personnel. These decisions were followed by reductions in the size of the Polish KFOR contingent in Kosovo (Madej, 2010, pp. 60–61). From 2010 on an 800-strong US battalion is also stationed in the Ghazni province. The Americans are operationally subordinated to the Commander of the Polish garrison and took over control of selected districts along the borders with the Logar, Paktia and Paktika provinces. Apart from patrolling actions the Polish troops are involved in training the Afghan army and police, having formed separate Operational Mentoring and Liaison Team and Police Operational Mentoring and Liaison Team. Poland is also engaged in development aid for Afghanistan. A Polish experts' team is also operating with the Ghazni Provincial Reconstruction Team established by the United States. The subject of special interest and support is to strengthen the structures of the state and civil society, education, health care and development of the city and province of Ghazni. Military actions are thus supplemented with the civilian component. It should be emphasized that Poland plans to withdraw its presence in Afghanistan by 2014; that is why the strength of the Polish contingent will be gradually reduced, which already began at the end of 2011.

Its presence in the Balkans and in Afghanistan does not exhaust Poland's involvement in NATO military operations. Poland participated or participates in several other missions. These are the training mission in Iraq (NTM-I), humanitarian aid operation in Pakistan, as well as the operations *Active Endeavor and Air Policing*. The NATO Training Mission – Iraq (NTM-I) was launched after the NATO summit in Istanbul held in June 2004. Its objective was to support the process of building Iraqi security forces by training high- and mid-level officers. Poland took part in this mission from 2005. The size of the Polish contingent never exceeded 20 persons. It was involved inter alia in training Iraqi sentries and in the implementation of staff functions. In October 2008, after the withdrawal from Iraq of the Polish contingent involved in the operation *Iraqi Freedom*, the NTM-I mission became an independent Polish contingent in Iraq under the NATO operation. Its size varied from 1 to 20 people at that time. The Polish contingent's mission in Iraq under the NTM-1 ended as of 31 December 2011.

In the autumn of 2005 Poland participated in a NATO humanitarian operation in Pakistan after the earthquake in that country. The NATO Response Force was sent in. The NATO contingent contained a

139 soldier-strong engineering company from Poland, which took part in rebuilding road infrastructure in Pakistan and provided assistance to the civilian population. It was an innovative operation showing a new kind of competence exhibited by the military units involved in stability missions, and demonstrating new possibilities of the use of NATO Response Force. However, in Poland this operation provoked a discussion on the costs of participation in NATO military operations and on the ideas of using NATO Response Force. Poland shared the opinion of those countries which believed that these troops should be treated as an elite force and employed in large-scale complicated anti-crisis operations, while ad hoc actions like the humanitarian mission in Pakistan should be conducted by other units. Poland expressed a view that the military units composing the NATO Response Force, trained with great expenditure of means and resources, should not be divided and used in ad hoc operations only because they are available. However, the problem was also that these are the only NATO units capable of being redeployed fast and commencing military operations. In this context Poland feared that the ad hoc use of NATO Response Force may weaken the political will of NATO member states to participate in their successive rotations (Kupiecki, 2006, pp. 73–75).

Poland was also involved in NATO operations *Active Endeavor* and *Air Policing*. The former operation conducted under Article 5 of the Washington Treaty is a response to the terrorist attacks against the United States on 11 September 2001. It is conducted in the Mediterranean Sea, its objective being to ensure navigation security and to prevent terrorist attacks in this major sea basin. Several Polish warships participated in this operation: ORP 'Bielik', ORP 'Kondor', ORP 'Xawery Czernicki' and the rocket frigate ORP 'Gen. K. Pułaski'. The operation *Air Policing* is carried out as part of the joint defence of NATO member states. Its objective is to control the airspace of those members which do not have the capacity to control it by themselves. Poland took part in these missions in 2006, 2008, 2010 and will do so in 2012.

## Conclusion

To sum up, it should be emphasized that Poland's participation in NATO military operations was a dynamic, evolving process, which served to achieve the interests of Polish foreign policy. During the period prior to NATO membership their goal was to prove that Poland was a valuable candidate, which was not merely a consumer but also a producer of international security. After gaining membership, apart from confirming its justifiability, the goal of Poland's participation in NATO military operations was to enhance its international position and attain the status of a US strategic partner. Accomplishment of these goals was determined by high level of political will to use force for clearly defined political purposes. On the other hand, it was limited by financial shortcomings, particularly reflected in the logistic capabilities.

Poland's involvement in NATO operations after the end of the Cold War analysed as a dynamic process was determined by three factors. They are (1) the change in Poland's geopolitical situation after the end of the Cold War and the choice of the Euro-Atlantic option in its foreign policy; (2) the experience and many-year tradition (since 1953) of Poland's participation in UN peacekeeping operations; (3) the public opinion. These factors first of all conditioned the level of political will. The two first were strengthening both the political will and Poland's involvement in NATO-led military operations. However, since the second half of the first decade of the twenty-first century the factor of public opinion limits the level of Poland's political will to be involved in NATO out-of-area operations. The intensity of two first factors is weakening, and the third is strengthening.

Poland took part and is still involved in NATO missions in the Balkans and in Afghanistan. These operations have undoubtedly contributed to the enhancement of Poland's international position but Poland has been disillusioned with its efforts to attain the status of a privileged partner of the United States. Under the influence of that state Poland accepted the globalization of operations of the Atlantic Alliance outside the Euro-Atlantic area; however, fearing that such operations might adversely affect the fulfilment of obligations specified in Article 5 of the Washington Treaty, that is, those concerning collective defence. Poland has, therefore, opted for selective involvement in the so-called 'out of area' operations – those not covered by Article 5 and outside the Euro-Atlantic area, but on condition that they will not impede the discharge of Alliance obligations regarding collective defence. These obligations are of crucial importance for Poland in view of its geopolitical situation. We must not fail to see that for the Polish armed forces the participation in NATO military operations became a factor in their transformation, modernization and acceleration of the process of their professionalization.

# Bibliography

Balcerowicz, B. (2009) 'Polskie wojny', in *Rocznik Strategiczny 2008/09*, Warszawa.
Ciechanowski, G. (2010) *Polskie Kontyngenty Wojskowe w operacjach pokojowych 1990–1999*, Toruń.
Cimoszewicz, W. (2003) 'Polska racja stanu a nowe środowisko międzynarodowe', in *Rocznik polskiej polityki zagranicznej 2003*, Warszawa.
Expose (1991) Prezesa Rady Ministrów Jana Olszewskiego w dniu 21 grudnia 1991 roku, http://orka2.sejm.gov.pl/Debata1.nsf
Expose (1992) Prezes Rady Ministrów Hanny Suchockiej w dniu 10 lipca 1992 roku, http://orka2.sejm.gov.pl/Debata1.nsf
Expose (2007) Delivered by Prime Minister Donald Tusk in the Sejm on 23 November 2007, http://orka2.sejm.gov.pl/Debata6.nsf
Gazeta Wyborcza (2007) of 22 May.
Gazeta Wyborcza (2008) of 22–24 March.
Gagor, F. K. P. (1999) *Międzynarodowe operacje w doktrynie obronnej RP*, Toruń.
*Informacja rządu* (2009) *na temat polskiej polityki zagranicznej w 2008 roku* (presented by Foreign Minsiter Radosław Sikorski in the Sejm on 7 May 2008), in *Rocznik polskiej polityki zagranicznej 2009*, Warszawa.
Kaczyński, P. M. (2008) *Polska polityka zagraniczna w latach 2005–2007: co po konsensusie?* Warszawa.
Kobieracki, A. (2002) *Bezpieczeństwo Polski w roku zagrożeń niekonwencjonalnych*, in: *Rocznik polskiej polityki zagranicznej 2002*, Warszawa.
Kochanowski, F. (2000) *Udział Wojska Polskiego w misjach pokojowych w latach 90-tych*, in: *Rocznik polskiej polityki zagranicznej 2000*, Warszawa.
Koziej, S. (2010) *Obronność Rzeczypospolitej Polskiej w latach 1989–2009*, Warszawa.
Kupiecki, R. (2000) 'Kierunek atlantycki w polskiej polityce zagranicznej po 1989 r.', in R. Kuźniar (ed.) *Polska polityka bezpieczeństwa 1989–2000*, Warszawa.
Kupiecki, R. (2003) 'Polskie interesy w NATO', in *Rocznik polskiej polityki zagranicznej 2003*, Warszawa.
Kupiecki, R. (2005) 'Polityka bezpieczeństwa Polski', in *Rocznik polskiej polityki zagranicznej 2005*, Warszawa.
Kupiecki, R. (2006) 'Główne aspekty polityki bezpieczeństwa Polski', in *Rocznik polskiej polityki zagranicznej 2006*, Warszawa.
Madej, M. (2008) 'Polityka bezpieczeństwa Polski (wymiar polityczno-wojskowy)', in *Rocznik polskiej polityki zagranicznej 2008*, Warszawa.
Madej, M. (2010) 'Polityka bezpieczeństwa Polski – wymiar polityczno-wojskowy', in *Rocznik polskiej polityki zagranicznej 2010*, Warszawa.
Madej, M. and Terlikowski, M. (2009) 'Polityka bezpieczeństwa Polski – wymiar polityczno-wojskowy', in *Rocznik polskiej polityki zagranicznej 2009*, Warszawa.
Markowski, J. (1994) *Polska w operacjach pokojowych. Operacje pokojowe ONZ*, Warszawa.
Nowak, J. M. (2011) *Od hegemonii do agonii. Upadek Układu Warszawskiego. Polska perspektywa*, Warszawa.
Osica, O. (2009) *Fałszywy motyw i słabe państwo. Polityczne aspekty udziału Polski w operacjach międzynarodowych*, in: *Rocznik strategiczny 2008/09*, Warszawa.
Pacuła, P. (2009) '10 lat Polski w NATO – co dalej?', *Bezpieczeństwo Narodowe*, Vol. 11, No. 3, pp. 29–40.

Pawłowski, K. (2010) 'Misje pokojowe i operacje stabilizacyjne sił zbrojnych Rzeczypospolitej Polskiej na początku XXI wieku. Przesłanki i głosy krytyczne', in Jan Gliński (ed) *Teka Komisji Politologii i Stosunków Międzynarodowych* (Lublin: Polska Akademia Nauk. Oddział).

Pietraś, M. (2010) 'Ewolucja strategii bezpieczeństwa Polski po 1989 roku, w', in K. Leszczyńska (ed.) *Rzeczpospolita Polska 1989-2009*, Toruń.

Pietrzak, P. (2012) *Siły Zbrojne RP w operacjach międzynarodowych – podstawy prawne, założenia strategiczne, praktyczna realizacja* (typescript).

Polska Zbrojna (1991) of 4 July.

*Prymat NATO* (2006) *i stosunki transatlantyckie – polski punkt widzenia*. Raport Forum Bezpieczeństwa Centrum Europejskiego Natolin, Warszawa.

Sakson, A. (1996) 'Stosunek społeczeństwa polskiego do bezpieczeństwa kraju i przystąpienia do NATO', in J. Kiwerska (ed.) *Interesy bezpieczeństwa w Europie*, Poznań.

*Strategia* (2000) *bezpieczeństwa Rzeczypospolitej Polskiej*, Warszawa.

*Strategia* (2003) *bezpieczeństwa narodowego Rzeczypospolitej Polskiej*, Warszawa.

*Strategia* (2007) *bezpieczeństwa narodowego Rzeczypospolitej Polskiej*, Warszawa.

*Strategia* (2009) *udziału Sił Zbrojnych Rzeczypospolitej Polskiej w operacjach międzynarodowych*, Warszawa.

Towpik, A. (2000) *Polska w NATO – rok pierwszy*, in: *Rocznik polskiej polityki zagranicznej 2000*, Warszawa.

*Udział Polski* (2010) *w operacji NATO w Afghanistan i jego konsekwencje*, CBOS, Polling announcement BS/159/2010, Warszawa.

*Ustawa* (1998) *z dnia 17 grudnia 1998 r. o zasadach użycia lub pobytu Sił Zbrojnych Rzeczypospolitej Polskiej poza granicami państwa*, Dz. U. of 1998 o. 162, item 1117.

*Założenia* (1992) *polskiej polityki bezpieczeństwa oraz Polityka bezpieczeństwa i strategia obronna Rzeczypospolitej Polskiej*, Warszawa.

Ziółkowski, M. (2007) 'Polityka bezpieczeństwa Polski', in *Rocznik polskiej polityki zagranicznej 2007*, Warszawa.

# 12
# Hungary in NATO: The Case of a Half Empty Glass

*T. Magyarics*

## Introduction

The subtitle might be mutual great expectations and, to a certain extent, mutual disappointment. NATO made a bold decision in the late 1990s to start expanding towards Eastern Europe. It was obvious that none of the candidate countries was militarily prepared to be a full-fledged member of the Alliance; the decision to take some of them into NATO was first and foremost a political one. The expansion wished to prevent the emergence of a potential security grey zone in the middle of Europe, as well as to create a zone of political, economic and social stability as the Atlantic Alliance is not only about a collective security organization in the traditional sense, but it is also a community of states which share the same values. It was also expected in the capitals of the member countries that the new allies would do their best to catch up with the old members in, among others, military matters too. However, by the time the first three Central European countries joined the Alliance, NATO's mission had already substantially changed. 'Out-of-area' missions had replaced the predominantly territorial defence posture and these new missions, as a response to some new types of challenges, had become more complex in nature too. The new members, in general, had been looking for NATO membership mainly because of the Cold War-era security guarantees and were, on the whole, unprepared to contribute meaningfully to the capabilities of the organization. These countries, Hungary one among them, were beset with a long list of military, political, economic and social problems. They were incapable to address all of them simultaneously; the security questions were usually pushed into the background by the more pressing other issues.

This chapter intends to discuss the case of a country which had arguably the highest expectations about NATO membership both within and without. Hungary was a 'poster boy' for setting the pace of transformation from a closed society to an open one. Hungary was also the country, which had become a *de facto* member of the Alliance before formal accession to it on account of its geopolitical position and the role it was playing during the Balkan wars in the 1990s. Nevertheless, Hungary also became the 'whipping boy' in the early 2000s for – often only the perceived – lack of adequate capabilities and political will to be a provider of security instead of a consumer of security. This transition is the subject proper of this chapter. It wishes to assess the actual performance of Hungary as a NATO member as well as the perceived and real weaknesses of its membership. Special attention is paid to the military capabilities, where Budapest has been clearly underperforming, and the political will, in which the country's record is much better.

## Hungary's security environment

Amidst the sweeping changes in East and Central Europe starting in 1989, perhaps the most serious direct challenge to the national security of Hungary was posed by the violent disintegration of Yugoslavia. Contemporary Hungarian Government, and almost each one to follow, was keen on reconciling *Realpolitik* with democratic values in the broadest sense. Thus, despite the potential danger that the Serbs would take steps against the hundreds of thousands of ethnic Hungarians in Voivodina, Budapest sided with the victims of Serbian aggression, foremost among them was Croatia. The rapid downsizing of the military left Hungary extremely vulnerable in face of potential aggression along the southern border; in fact, in some cases Hungarian airspace was violated and even a few bombs were dropped on Hungarian territory during the initial stages of the Balkan wars.[1]

A resurgent Soviet Union (or Russia) or a war in the vicinity meant classic conventional threats to Hungary. It became obvious practically to everyone in Central Europe that the countries in the region would acquire hard security only through membership in the Euro-Atlantic community. Although the countries in the wider Central Europe, that is, from the Baltic to the Adriatic and the Black Sea, naturally do not share 100 per cent the outlook on their own security and threat perceptions, a common characteristic feature of theirs is that the region suffers from 'strategic dependency'. One may add that, by definition, small countries are much more interested in strong and stable alliances and multinational institutions than the bigger ones as they are able to sit at the table where decisions are made and with the help of *ad hoc* coalitions within the appropriate organization they can represent their interests more efficiently than otherwise.

There emerged a rare consensus among the major political forces in Hungary in the early 1990s with regard to the priorities of Hungarian foreign and security policy. It was agreed that the strategic goals should be the integration of the country into the Euro-Atlantic community, a 'good neighbor' policy, and the appropriate protection of the Magyar ethnic minorities in the neighbouring countries. As Budapest had a more than mixed experience with the bilateral talks over the treatment of the Magyar minorities in some neighbouring states, the unifying idea behind these priorities was that the Euro-Atlantic integration of the East and Central European countries would bring about the adoption of the values upon which the Atlantic community were based. Namely, parliamentary democracy, a market economy, the rule of law and the observation of human and civil rights. Thus, the borders could be 'spiritualized' and the long-standing discrepancy of Hungarian politics between the 'state' and the 'nation' could be solved.

Thus NATO was seen as an almost perfect organization to kill, in this case, three birds with one stone from the Hungarians' point of view. As a military organization, it would provide hard security guarantees, and as a community of countries sharing the same democratic principles, it would help address the regional hard and soft security concerns alike. Moreover, it would have a stabilizing influence all over the region in the security, political and economic fields alike. It is worth emphasizing at this point that the NATO Hungary wished to join in the 1990s was a NATO whose missions were more relevant during the Cold War than in the post-Cold War period.

Despite all the just criticisms later on, it is only fair to state that Hungary can be said to have been the only Central European country that joined NATO even before former membership was accorded to Budapest. In fact, it may be more appropriate to say that NATO had already entered Hungary before Hungary acceded to NATO in 1999. Since the mid-1990s Hungary was offering host nation support to NATO (American) troops, Hungarian airspace was put at the disposal of AWACS aircraft (the first time in October 1992), and the former Soviet air-base at Taszár in the southwest of Hungary was one of the staging areas of the US military to be deployed in the Balkans. One can even say that the only period when Hungary was enjoying real geostrategic importance to the Alliance was at a time when the country was not a formal member. The indirect Hungarian participation in the peace enforcement efforts in the Balkans was a 'value-added' to the regular Partnership for Peace (PfP) programmes which had been implemented since 1994 (Végh, 1999, pp. 41–49).

The other Euro-Atlantic organization, the European Union was (and is) seen primarily as a guarantor of the soft security elements in this context. The Hungarians were extremely sensitive about the various wars in the Balkans, and saw how hapless the EU was in trying to put an end to or to prevent bloodshed and ethnic cleansing over there. The disappointing experience may have been one of the reasons why the East and Central European countries supported American policies sometimes against their better conviction and even by defying some major European powers.[2]

The dilemma which briefly emerged on a political level around the time of Hungary's accession to the EU in May 2004, namely, that 'more Europe' should or should not mean 'less America' was never a real one in hard security matters.[3] The recent Hungarian national security strategies declare without exception that the ultimate guarantor of the country's *hard* security is NATO. 'Hard' should be emphasized here because there has been a marked shift towards giving priority to *economic* security and in this area, obviously, the EU comes first. One may argue that it is a sign of the *softening* of Hungarian security concepts across the board in the past few years. This tendency is not unique at all: the stereotypical 'peace dividend', that is, discounting the traditional hard security threats and, consequently, cutting defence budgets characterized almost all the members of the Atlantic community without exception after the collapse of the Soviet Union and the dissolution of the Warsaw Pact.

Downsizing and modernizing the armed forces as well as rebuilding the civil–military relations had to be done simultaneously after 1990. The first element of these often meant across-the-board cuts and thus preserving a top-heavy army in which there were, literally, too many 'desk officers' and relatively few troops on the ground. (This anomaly has been greatly remedied recently.) Modernization was taking place on two levels: on the one hand, the force structure had to be changed and, on the other hand, the equipment had to be converted into a NATO compatible one. Finally, the question of prestige and the social acceptance of the military forces had to be addressed; the results can be said favourable and, perhaps, this was the most successful endeavour from among the three issues indentified above.

The 'softening' of the Hungarian security and defence policies can also be attributed to the successful gradual 'embedding' into the Euro-Atlantic community. While Hungary was an 'island-member' in NATO in the years after 1999, with the accession of especially Slovakia and Romania this geostrategically and geopolitically exposed position came to an end to a large extent – although Hungary is still 'open' towards Ukraine and Serbia. This development can even be termed as a mixed blessing of sorts for the image of Hungary as a NATO member. While the country's territory and airspace themselves were important assets for the Alliance, the lack of appropriate capabilities and the unfounded promises were mostly ignored or, at least, they did not get as much attention publicly as they did subsequently.[4]

The 'softening' of the Hungarian defence and security posture is, naturally, one of the results of the disappearance of the hard security challenges in the extended Central Europe. Parallel with the fading away of hard security challenges, the soft ones, such as illegal migration, drugs trade, arms trade, human trafficking, organized crime, environmental degradation, as well as economic and social problems, have gained ground spectacularly in recent times. Moreover, even within NATO-missions there has been a general tendency towards integrated civil-military (CIMIC) missions (Rácz, 2005). As for the expectations of the United States, they are mostly about a proper support of the 'democracy project' both in the neighbourhood (the Balkans, Moldova and so on) and in countries such as Iraq or Afghanistan.

The security situation in Central Europe cannot be detached from the larger context of the transatlantic relations. The conventional challenges to the United States shifted to the Middle East, Central Asia and the Pacific region to a large extent and though the United States has remained a 'European power', its military 'footprint' in Europe has definitely become much lighter than it used to be in the Cold War years. Washington also capitalized on the post-Cold War 'peace dividend' but not to such a great extent as some (major) European countries did. The end result was (is) that the already existing capabilities gap has widened since 1990 and created considerable tensions within the alliance.[5]

In fact, with regard to defence philosophy and strategic outlook, the East and Central European countries, including Hungary, tend to be more Atlanticist than the majority of the old NATO members and some of them would like to see a heavier (military, economic and even political) US 'footprint' in the region than the existing one. One of the major reasons is a less benign view of potential challenges from a resurgent Russia (see, for instance, Bugajski, 2004). The view that the major continental powers, such as Germany and France, are sometimes too 'soft' and indifferent in these issues is shared by quite a number of people in the region, and they see Washington as a place which is sometimes more willing to share some of their concerns. The fear from finding themselves in a 'lite' strategic vacuum motivated a number of East and Central European politicians and security experts to plead with the Obama Administration of not neglecting or ignoring the region in 2009.[6]

Despite initial American denial of the concerns articulated in the Letter of 22 in 2009, Vice President Joseph Biden was almost immediately despatched to Bucharest where he emphasized that Europe remained the cornerstone of American foreign policy and NATO the bedrock of Washington's commitment to Europe. However, he also indicated that, in return, the United States was expecting Europe to take on *global* responsibility and 'growing *capacity and willingness* to meet [challenges] with us' (Biden, 2009, italics mine). Herein lies the source of some of the mutual frustrations: while the East and Central European countries perceived NATO as primarily an organization to protect them against conventional threats, Washington started to operate on the basis of a new approach to security in the world which was more inclusive geographically and functionally than that of the former states'. There emerged a clear-cut asynchronism in the perception of common threats spatially as well as temporally between the Americans and the Europeans at large (with the possible exception of the British and, at times, the French). The East and Central Europeans were not able to bridge this gap militarily, but they tried hard to do it politically – witness the Letter of Eight and the declaration of the Vilnius Ten on the eve of the Iraq War.

## The half empty glass: capabilities

### Defence-related expenditures

Field-Marshal Raimondo Montecuccoli, a military commander on the payroll of the Habsburgs in the seventeenth century, is attributed to have declared that there are three things needed for a war: 'Money, money, and money.' His maxim can be applied to peacetime military forces as well: a well-functioning and properly equipped army cannot be brought into being and sustained on the cheap. The gaps in training, equipment and so on can be covered over for some time but bluffing in the long term is hopeless and counterproductive.

Though the cornerstone of NATO-membership is Article 5 of the Washington Treaty, it does not mean that the individual members should not do their very best to provide for their own defence and be ready to give assistance in case another member becomes a victim of an unprovoked armed attack. As it has already been mentioned above, the majority of the European countries reassessed the threat perceptions after the conclusion of Cold War and, among others, started to cut their defence budgets. So again, when we talk about Hungary's unfulfilled promises concerning the required level of defence spending, we can talk as well about a general European trend – although this phenomenon in itself does not justify Hungarian underperformance in this respect.

When Hungary joined the Alliance on 12 March 1999, the defence-related expenditure amounted to about 1.6 per cent of the GDP and the government promised to increase it to 1.8 per cent by 2002. That year there was a change of government in Hungary and the incoming Socialist-Free Democrat government committed itself at the Prague Summit of NATO to bring the defence budget up to 2.01 per cent by 2006. Nevertheless, the actual figures showed a diametrically opposed trend, that is, a sharp decrease of the defence budget. It amounted to 1.69 per cent of the GDP in 2004, 1.27 per cent in 2005, 1.15 per cent in 2006 and as low as 1.1 per cent in 2007. There was a slight increase in the next two years (1.14 and 1.16 per cent, respectively) and Defense Minister Imre Szekeres repeatedly announced in 2008 that the government intended to raise defence spending between 2009 and 2013 by 0.2 per cent annually. These figures were incorporated into the National Military Strategy accepted in January 2009 too (Kern, 2009, p. 77).

The promises repeated at regular intervals by a number of member countries started to frustrate Washington and some other states which kept their defence spending around the ideal 2.0 per cent of the GDP. Sensing the unfeasibility of the promises it was informally agreed at the Bucharest Summit of NATO in 2008 that the member states whose defence-related expenditures did not reach 1.3 per cent of their GDPs should raise them at least to this level within five years. Prior to the NATO summit, the Hungarian National Assembly stipulated in 2007 that Hungary's defence spending should be lifted close to the Alliance average (1.9 per cent of the national GDPs) with the proviso that it was to be realized in conjunction with the economic conditions in the country. Clearly, the government provided itself an escape route with this precondition. And it resorted to it in due course. With the economic downturn in the late 2008 and early 2009 the Hungarian government took austerity measures and decided upon across the board budget cuts.

Furthermore it provided that the defence sector would get 1.1 per cent of the GDP if revenues topped 102.9 per cent of the originally planned ones. The end result was that the Ministry of Defense received less than 1 per cent of the GDP and the Hungarian defence budget has not been able to exceed the 1 per cent threshold ever since (Kern, 2009, p. 80).[7]

The defence budget was standing at 0.97 per cent in 2011 (with 275 billion HUF); actually, it meant an increase in real value as the economy was also expanding (Kern, 2011, p. 72). The latest announcement by Defense Minister Csaba Hende in April 2012 on the projected defence budgets promises that the defence-related expenditures will not and cannot be lower in 2013–2015 than the current level, while they will be growing by 0.1 per cent of the GDP annually after 2016. At the same time, the government guarantees that the defence budget will have been fixed at 1.39 per cent of the GDP by 2022 (hirado.hu, 2012).

It goes without saying that the figures themselves tell only one part of the story. Much depends on the structure of the budget, how efficiently the relatively scarce resources are allocated, and what output can be produced with this input. Another issue is how the Hungarian defence budgets fit into the overall goals of NATO, that is, how they provide for an appropriate level of home defence and to what extent they contribute to the Article 5 obligations, that is, what capabilities they support which can be used in international missions. The picture emerging after analysing these factors is not so bleak as the sheer budget numbers would suggest; in other words, the output is sometimes much better than one would expect from the input.

The ideal structure of a defence budget would be 40:30:30, that is, 40 per cent of the budget should go to cover the salaries and wages in the military forces, and 30 per cent each for material expenditures and procurement and modernization. However, personal expenses have been consistently over 40 per cent since Hungary's accession to NATO: they were close to 50 per cent in the first half of the past decade and even the 2012 defence budget plans to spend around 44 per cent of the total on them (Kern, 2011, p. 72; Szenes, 2011, p. 2). The material expenses have always been higher in the past decade than they should have been in an ideal case: they hovered above 40 per cent. Therefore, the real loser of the defence budgets has been modernization: the amount spent on this purpose has never been above 5 per cent of the total layout[8] – one may even go as far as to say that the successive governments in Hungary wished to implement the modernization of the Hungarian Defense Forces (HDF) on the cheap. Some experts call this process as 'second-hand' modernization (Szenes, 2009, p. 38) as the HDF often has to make shift with used equipment which is supplied to the Hungarian troops free of charge or for a nominal amount of money. In some other cases equipment, especially military armoured or transport vehicles are leased or lent to the HDF (primarily by the United States), as it happened in Iraq and Afghanistan.[9]

One exception is the lease of the Gripen JAS-39 fighter aircraft – however, the deal is widely thought to be the albatross and the white elephant of the HDF, the defence budgets and also a reflection on the confusion and discontinuity of defence planning and philosophy in Hungary. Hungary received altogether 28 MiG-29s in the early 1990s in compensation for the debt accumulated by the former Soviet Union. The Horn-cabinet (1994–1998) decided to have them modernized and to procure new Western-made fighter planes – at that time the F-16, the F-18, the Mirage and the Gripen aircraft were taken into consideration. Later on only the F-16 and the Gripen were considered as real options; in point of fact the National Security Cabinet decided in favour of obtaining used F-16s in early 2001. The issue was not only a technical one despite the fact that the MiG-29s were not compatible with the NATO standards; the political and security considerations enjoyed a priority.[10]

Nevertheless, in a sudden turnabout the government finally decided in favour of the leasing of Gripen Jas 39 A/B aircraft for 130 billion HUF for ten years. (The deal was 'sweetened' by SAAB with a promise of 118 billion HUF offset.) Though the then opposition parties (especially the Socialists) criticized the decision vehemently, when they came into power in 2002 they started negotiations for equipping the aircraft with aerial refuelling capabilities – making the deal even more expensive than it was originally. The original contract was first modified in 2003[11]; it provided that Hungary would pay 210 billion HUF over 2016 when the aircraft would get into Hungarian ownership and the Swedes would make investment in Hungary in the amount of 191 billion HUF. The deal meant that a huge portion of the defence budgets has been being eaten up by the lease and the HDF has not been able to implement the much needed modernization in other areas. The latest chapter of the Gripen-agreement was concluded in early 2012 when Defense Minister Csaba Hende signed a new contract with the Swedish partners. It stipulates that the term of the lease is extended for another ten years and thus lifting some burden from the strained defence budget between 2012 and 2016. It is true that the original total cost increases by 45 per cent, but it is going hand in hand with a 95 per cent increase in services provided. The amount of money thus saved will be spent on lubricants for the vehicles, the purchase of the Norwegian Kongsberg URH-radios, armoured vehicles and the operation of the HDF's signal and information systems (népszabadság.online, 2012). (Another source for modernization might be the money deriving from the potential sale of the MiG-29s.)

The other area in which the Hungarian governments have been relatively generous financially is international missions. If we take only the latest defence budget, some 42 billion HUF were spent on them (out of a total of some 270 billion HUF); the bulk of the money went to sustain the Hungarian missions in Afghanistan (19 billion HUF, a 7 billion HUF increase compared with 2010) and Kosovo (3.7 billion HUF) (Kern, 2010b, p. 58). Hungarian laws allow the stationing of about 1,000 troops abroad and the overall number of Hungarian soldiers in international missions[12] has been very close to or even above this figure in the past decade. Currently, about half of these troops serve in Afghanistan, predominantly in the Provincial Reconstruction Team (PRT), and the rest as members of KFOR and various other missions, which are not necessarily NATO operations but are administered by the UN. As the overall number of troops is around 20,000, and given the needs for rotations, about a sixth of the HDF is being deployed abroad, or is training to be deployed or has just returned from deployment at any given time. This proportion is quite high and their deployment eats up some 8–9 per cent of the overall defence budget every year.

Besides the ongoing financing of the Hungarian troops in Afghanistan in various capacities from the PRT to running Kabul Airport, among other things, Hungary committed itself at the Chicago Summit of NATO in May 2012 to contribute 0.5 million USD a year between 2015–2107 (that is, altogether 1.5 million USD) for the maintenance of the Afghan security forces after the conclusion of the ISAF mission in 2014.

## What capabilities Hungary brings to the table

*The Balkans*

By way of introduction we should repeat that Hungary has been punching above its weight in some areas which are important for NATO and/or the United States.[13] Even before formal accession to NATO on 12 March 1999, Hungary had been playing a crucial role as a host nation during the Balkan wars. First, it was in October 1992 that the National Assembly made it possible for AWACS planes to use the Hungarian airspace to monitor the no-fly zones over Bosnia-Herzegovina. After the 5 February 1994 massacre at the Sarajevo market place, NATO threatened the

Serb forces with airstrikes if they did not withdraw their heavy artillery from the mountains surrounding the city. The Hungarian Government was put on the spot to a certain extent and, finally, announced that the AWACS could continue monitoring the airspace over Bosnia-Herzegovina but the aircraft cannot be used as command platforms for combat missions with a view to the precarious situation of the 400,000 or so ethnic Hungarians in Voivodina.

The participation in the IFOR/SFOR missions was the first international operation Hungary was joining after the Cold War. Richard Holbrooke indicated in September 1995 that Hungary was expected to provide logistical support and participation in the multinational forces after the conclusion of peace. The National Assembly responded by allowing transit for IFOR troops and the establishment of logistics bases at Kaposvár and Taszár.[14] At the end of the year, legislative green light was given to send an engineering corps to Bosnia-Herzegovina as part of the IFOR, but NATO was dissatisfied with this meagre commitment. Finally, the number was increased to some 400 and the last soldiers of this mission were pulled out of the area in late April 2002. These commitments helped a lot in Hungary's case when the NATO-members were considering the list of the first group of invitees from Central Europe during the latter half of the 1990s (Ilisics, 2004, p. 105; Szenes, 2000, pp. 67–78). Moreover, the manoeuvres carried out within the framework of the PfP, especially the Cooperative Light and the Cooperative Nugget (Deák, 2000), proved to be useful for Hungary's adapting to NATO's 'ways and means' and a different way of thinking about security, cooperation and solidarity.

Basically, Hungary's contribution did not change in the KFOR operations, which succeeded the IFOR mission. Budapest continued its dual role: on the one hand, a third logistics base was added to the existing two ones (Kaposújlak). On the other hand, around 300 soldiers were integrated into the Multinational Task Force (Italian–Slovene–Hungarian) under Italian command and served in Pristina, while the novelty was meant by about 110 military police who performed second-generation peacekeeping tasks; in this case it meant, among others, the resettlement of the refugees.

The Defense Review in July 2002 then doctrinally shifted the tasks towards peacekeeping, peace-enforcement, conflict prevention, humanitarian missions and peace building as well. As a follow-up, the National Assembly passed a resolution along similar lines as far as it concentrated on new expeditionary capabilities (by implicitly prioritizing NATO commitments to purely national ones), including, among other things, a special operations battalion, psychological operations units (PSYOPS), human intelligence (HUMINT), water cleansing and medical capabilities and so on (Szenes, 2000, p. 71).

At the end of the first decade in the twenty-first century, troops from the HDF were serving on four continents, 14 countries, 28 missions. The bulk of the peacekeeping forces, 70 per cent, were deployed in NATO missions (Szenes, 2000, p. 68). Some of the international missions were carried out in close cooperation with other countries; for example, with reference to ISAF, air bridge agreements were concluded with Germany, the Netherlands, Norway, Denmark and Canada. This practice also applied to ground operations: a Hungarian–Italian–Slovene Multinational Land Force (MLF) was operating in Kosovo, or the forces offered to the NATO Response Force (HRF) and the EU Battle Groups (EUBG) are usually immediately or in a short time used in peacekeeping missions. In general, the missions in the Balkans, though they were not intended to be so, proved to be extremely useful 'laboratories' for subsequent deployments farther away from the homeland; in fact, we may even create a sequence of foreign missions as the HDF units were predominantly serving in the Balkans before 2004, while after that date there was a definite shift to Iraq and Afghanistan (Szenes, 2000, p. 77).

At the same time, this shift created some domestic political problems. While the importance of the security in the Balkans did not need very elaborate explanations, the public at large (whose majority supported NATO's membership at the referendum held in 1999)[15] easily understood why Hungary should take an active part in the peacekeeping operations. However, public opinion was more split upon the questions of Afghanistan and Iraq, especially regarding the latter, in which case even an UN resolution was missing.

The air strikes against Serbia commenced a few weeks after Hungary's admission into the Alliance and the use of the airbase at Taszár, as well as the Hungarian airspace were instrumental in suppressing Serbian resistance and rotating troops. It must also be mentioned that the Orbán government took relatively great risk with the military and political support of the NATO operations because there was the danger that Slobodan Milosević might take hostile steps against the Hungarian minority in Voivodina.

The Hungarian commitment to improving security in the Balkans did not cease after the conclusion of the armed conflicts there. One of Hungary's major national security concerns is the Southeastern neighbourhood; it is not only peaceful conditions that are of interest to Budapest but it is also the Euro-Atlantic integration of the region and its concomitant adoption of the values of the Atlantic community. It is especially the centre-right led governments that have been emphasizing the importance of the reconciliation of hard-headed interests and democratic values in foreign policy. They recognize that long-term peace and ethnic reconciliation cannot be imposed on the Balkans, where inter-ethnic strife has been century old, exclusively from outside and above; that is why Hungary has been trying to promote and assist civilian and bottom-up programmes, such as community building, women empowerment and the like in cooperation with some NGOs, among them is the International Center for Democratic Transition (ICDT), established in 2005.[16]

## Afghanistan and Iraq

The deployment of Hungarian troops is mostly about alliance loyalty or alliance dependence (to put it less charitably) and values, national interests as such are downplayed.[17] The three major public concerns in Afghanistan – terrorism, drug production and trafficking – and potential mass migration out of the country are only remotely relevant to Hungary (Marton, 2011, pp. 11–21). The first Hungarian units to arrive in Afghanistan were from a transport battalion in Summer 2003 and though the deployment originally enjoyed a five-party support in the National Assembly, when the Hungarian camp at al-Hillal was attacked in early February 2004, the universal support started to evaporate and some parties openly demanded the withdrawal of the soldiers. The next two years saw a gradual expansion of the Hungarian presence in Afghanistan; the breakthrough came in 2006 when Hungary took over the leadership of a PRT from the Dutch in Baghlan Province, in the north of the country, that is, in a territory that can be characterized as a relatively low-intensity conflict area. However, troops died in road accidents and because of IED attacks; after such an incident in 2010 the majority of the public (52 per cent of the people) turned against Hungarian presence in Afghanistan (Marton, 2011, p. 19).

A number of politicians, therefore, think the whole issue too sensitive to touch and conceive the deployment of Hungarian troops in Afghanistan as a 'compulsory exercise': since 2006 no Hungarian Foreign Minister or Prime Minister has visited the country and Camp Pannonia (Marton and Wagner, 2011, p. 12).

The PRTs are engaged in primarily a relatively new type of civil–military cooperation ('Marshall Plan Hindu Kush'), though traditional military tasks are also part of their responsibilities. The basically 'nation-building' (in fact, 'state-building' would be a more correct term) endeavour theoretically can be traced back to the Cold War struggle for the 'hearts and minds' of the people, in which the West (the United States) won hands down against Communism. However, the ideological adversary in Afghanistan is not one which is imposed on the local people from outside and which is not organically rooted in the traditions and history of the people affected, but an ideology which has extremely deep roots in the local society and in the broader region as well. The other ideological source of the civil–military cooperation comes from the American belief in the 'democracy project', which has encountered some setbacks recently and the impression is that its successful penetration into tribal, religiously and ethnically divided societies is fairly uncertain. The Hungarian PRT has been engaged in creating self-sustaining economic conditions, jobs, the rule of law and in developing institutions for education.

Similarly to the operations in the Balkans, Hungarian NGOs and charities have also been trying to assist the military in community-building, training of future politicians, monitoring local and national elections and so on. Hungary also contributed quite substantially, in comparison to its economic possibilities, to the civil-military (CIMIC) stabilization and development projects in Afghanistan. Budapest was spending in the excess of one billion HUF on these programmes mainly through such NGOs as the ICDT, the Magyar Ökumenikus Segélyszervezet [*Hungarian Ecumenical Aid Organization*] or the Baptista Szeretetszolgálat [*Baptist Love Service*]. In a number of cases, the Hungarian resources were complemented with ones coming from other countries, for instance, Japan and Greece. The development programmes fit into the needs of Baghlan province and the Afghan National Development Strategy (ANDS) (Kulugyminiszterium, 2012). Another project in which Hungarians are taking part is EUPOL Afghanistan, which is training the policemen.

Although most of the Hungarian troops are deployed within the framework of the PRT, Hungarians were training Afghan pilots on Mi-17 transport helicopters, some 60 were taking part in the activities of an US–Hungarian Operational Mentoring and Liaison Team (OMLT) under Hungarian leadership, which in turn, operates within the ISAF. At the same time, a Special Operations Task Unit (SOTU) was deployed in eastern Afghanistan in January 2009 under US command. Altogether 24 Hungarian pilots were deployed in the Air Mentor Team until 1 May 2012. In addition, Hungarian special forces were teamed up with the Ohio National Guard (OHG) (Kulugyminiszterium, 2012).

The Hungarian contribution was complemented with an additional number of troops when then Prime Minister Gordon Bajnai offered 200 soldiers to assist President Obama's 'surge strategy' in December 2009. When evaluating the Hungarian contribution to the efforts to create a safe and secure environment in Afghanistan, first we should emphasize the human dimension. The Hungarian troops have been acting professionally, responsibly and with distinction in a hostile environment. However, they have had to put up with a number of difficulties arising from the financial straitjacket in which the Ministry of Defense has had to operate. Thus, one is not too far off the mark to claim that the Hungarian troops despite their dedication and expertise would not have been (and would not be currently) able to fulfil their tasks without substantial material assistance from especially the Americans. The US forces (and others as well to a lesser degree) have provided logistical support, training, equipment, technical assistance (such as, for instance, armoured vehicles), even combat troops when needed as well as civilian help through the USAID (Kulugyminiszterium, 2012).

One of the lessons of the deployment in Afghanistan is that the HDF in its present state is hard put to carry out sustained operations in a great distance away from the mother country. Each of the member states in NATO is required to provide for home defence and expeditionary capability simultaneously in an ideal case; Hungary seems to have fallen between two stools. The gap between them is attempted to be bridged and hidden by extra efforts to increase the visibility of Hungarian troops in international missions. On the one hand, the soldiers who take part in them and, by extension, the HDF profit a lot from these experiences and their level of professionalism gets boosted. However, on the other hand, the relatively high costs of these deployments siphon resources away from other fields and, in the medium and long term, postpone the necessary modernization of the HDF and put off long overdue procurements. It is true, though, that considerable pressure has been put on Hungary (and other European members of NATO) by the United States to share burden with the US military services which, in turn, have become overstretched in recent years. The expected and – after all – justifiable shift of American attention towards the Pacific region (as demonstrated most recently by the military strategy made public in January 2012) is likely to maintain if not increase this (immediate) burden-sharing demand on the Europeans allies and thus it may contribute to the perpetuation of relatively short-term planning in those countries.

The Hungarian contribution to the military efforts in Iraq, which was primarily important for the US–Hungarian relations and only indirectly for the Alliance, was mostly symbolic; in fact, it can be labelled as simply an expression of alliance solidarity. Both in the Gulf War in 1990–1991 and the Iraq War a decade later the 'passive military contribution' was more substantial than the active one insofar as in both cases Hungary provided free overflight for the US aircraft heading for the conflict area. In the former case, this decision was all the more significant as Hungary was still formally a member of the Warsaw Pact at that time. The actual assistance was meant the stationing of a small number of voluntary medical personnel at Dahran, Saudi Arabia. In the latter case, the political support in the form of the Letter of Eight was perhaps the most important factor for Washington. After the initial phase of the war, a battalion of 300 Hungarian troops engaged mostly in transport and humanitarian tasks as part of the Polish-led multinational division, which itself was preoccupied with so-called second-generation peacekeeping operations such as restoring administration and preventing the outbreak of armed clashes between rival ethnic and religious groups. The Iraq War was not enjoying widespread popularity in Hungary and the deployment of Hungarian troops in 'Mr Bush's War' was rather controversial. The Hungarian Government took almost the first opportunity to withdraw them in late 2004. There was another hotly debated issue related to the Iraq War: Washington requested Hungarian cooperation in training hundreds of Iraqi 'opposition people' at Taszár. Ultimately, only some 100–120 Iraqis arrived at the base and the programme was folded in two months on 31 March 2003.[18]

Hungary also volunteered to assume some minor responsibilities in the post-war stabilization: 19 officers were working within the framework of the NATO Training Mission (NTM-I) until 30 September 2006 and another 15 officers took over the leadership of the Military Advice and Liaison Team (MALT) in the latter half of 2007; the organization was supposed to control the military readiness of the trained Iraqi forces (Kulugyminiszterium, 2012).

*Airspace control, early warning system, airlift capability, missile defence*
Hungary became an important partner of the NATO-forces before accession in 1999 – primarily by offering its airspace for the AWACS. The Taszár Airbase served as an important staging area for the rotation of US troops into and out of the Balkans. At the same time, as part of the 'trade-off' the USAF protected the Hungarian airspace against any enemy overflights or even attacks. The controversial Gripen-deal in 2001 at least solved the question of patrolling the Hungarian airspace and

Budapest does not have to rely on fellow NATO-members' aid in this respect in a way the Baltic states do. In fact, Hungary volunteered at the Chicago Summit in May 2012 that sometime between 2015 and 2018 four Hungarian Gripen JAS-39s will be deployed at the Šiaulia airbase (Lithuania) for four months within a rotation system under the Baltic Air Policing (BAP). The mission will require the deployment of some 100 personnel and the bulk of the costs will also burden the Hungarian defence budget despite the fact that the host nation contribution to the costs will be raised as well.

Hungary inherited a more or less outdated radar system from the Warsaw Pact times and it was obvious that the country had to modernize and develop it in order to be able to be part of one of the most significant elements of common defence: the early warning system. In fact, the Alliance approved the project to modernize the whole early warning system and committed itself to bear the brunt of the costs – to the tune of some 90 per cent of the money needed for the individual stations. Thus, the resources did not seem to be an obstacle for the development and modernization of the Hungarian elements of the system. Three 3D-radars were planned and the set-up of two, one at Bánkút in the northeast, the other at Békés in the southeast (produced by the Italian Alenia Marconi systems), went without any problem. However, the third one ran into fierce civilian opposition: environmental protectionists, conservationists and pacifists repeatedly demonstrated against and even blocked access to the planned site of the third radar station in the Mecsek-mountains in the south of Hungary.[19] The planned construction was finally dropped by the Government and, as a compromise, a new site was found at Medina not too far from the originally planned one; the only problem is that this new site is not on such a high elevation as the original one is and, therefore, the airspace it can 'see' is more limited.[20] (The operation of the three radars will cost around 1.5 billion HUF/year for the Hungarian state.)

The Washington Summit in 1999 accepted the Defense Capabilities Initiative (DCI), which aimed at creating mobile military capabilities, especially for the out-of-area operations. The DCI established the so-called Deployability and Mobility (DM) requirements for the individual members. From among the various DMs, DM3 covers sea and air transport and applies to Hungary as well among other countries. Moreover, the EU Headline Goal 2010 also provided for eight 'milestones' and four of them were about DMs. The technical requirements were coupled with the NATO Response Force (NRF) concept which mandated that the units involved in the operations were to be deployed within six days and that their missions were to be sustained up to 30 days even without supplies.

The HDF has got two major tasks regarding airlift. One of them requires capabilities to transport smaller amounts of material, VIPs and so on over shorter distances. Hungary can meet these obligations with its own air force (primarily using five recently modernized AN-26 aircraft). The other one is more demanding: the capabilities should incorporate the transport of large amounts of material and a substantial number of people for over large distances; in other words, it requires strategic airlift capability (SAC). Hungary joined the Strategic Airlift Interim Solution (SALIS) in June 2004; the grouping had as many as 18 members from NATO and the EU in 2008. This multinational cooperation is complemented with bilateral agreements with the German, the Canadian and the Rumanian militaries. SALIS intends to use Airbus-400M aircraft but their introduction into service has suffered delays. At the same time, the North Atlantic Council (NAC) accepted the Charter of the NATO Airlift Management Organization (NAMO) in June 2007 and was ready to deploy the Boing C-17 'Globemasters' without any delay. Hungary joined NAMO in 2006 and took on the smallest possible number of flying time, altogether 40 hours. Meanwhile, the Germans did not want to create a competitor to Ramstein and the A-400Ms and the United States asked for alternative offers for the stationing and registration of the C-17 Heavy Airlift Wing. Then Hungarian Defense Minister Imre Szekeres put forward Hungary's application in March 2007 and after a few on-site inspections, the United States decided upon a former Soviet airbase at Pápa in the west of the country. Altogether 12 countries are taking part in the SAC programme; the first C-17 took off from the Pápa airfield in July 2008 and since then the aircraft using the Hungarian facility have logged in more than 7,000 flight hours.[21] Most recently, Hungary joined the European Air Transport Fleet (EATF) programme in March 2012.

Missile Defense (MD) as a national security concern first appeared in Hungarian security thinking as early as 1993. Prime Minister Antall suggested to NATO Secretary General Manfred Wörner that Patriot antimissile batteries be deployed in Hungary in the face of a perceived threat by the Serbs. Manfred Wörner and, among others, Volker Rühe, then German Defense Minister concluded that the threat was not 'clear and present' and imminent and, therefore, there was no need to take the precautionary measure asked for by the Hungarian Government.

Hungary was not seriously considered to host elements of the MD system as planned by the George W. Bush Administration. In fact, one may even say that it was for all purposes a non-issue for both the national security establishment and the public at large. The political leaders lent their support to the planned deployment in principle in a rather subdued way because they did not want to pick a public fight with the Russians either. The cancellation of the original plans by the Obama Administration and the announcement of a somewhat scaled-down phased adaptive missile defence system did create some stir among the political elite. The issue was not really the merits of the new planned system, but the rather heavy-handed and insensitive manner in which it was made public, as well as the general framework of the new strategy.[22]

The impression was that the Democratic Administration was willing to make a deal with Moscow over the heads of the Central and East European Allies in the (somewhat illusionary) hope of Russian cooperation in questions such as Iran, Afghanistan, the Middle East and the Far East, and in fighting such transnational challenges such as international terrorism, drug trafficking and the like. A number of people also thought that the Obama Administration deliberately snubbed the Central and East Europeans and the circumstances of the announcement simply meant as a message to the region. The reaction was the widely discussed 'Letter of 22'; though the idea of an open letter to the President of the United States may be questioned (partly because acting in accordance with its content might have been a sign of weakness), the contents reflected real concerns. Hungary, together with the other Central and East European members of the Atlantic Alliance, considers Article 5 as the cornerstone of NATO, and they still perceive the nuclear weapons and, in conjunction with them, missile defence as the ultimate guarantee of their national security.[23]

## The glass is half full: willingness

Hungary was indisputably in the vanguard of dismantling the Warsaw Pact and seeking ways to establish links with NATO. The National Assembly passed a resolution as early as July 1990 to leave the Warsaw Pact and it also declared that the country suspended its participation in the military operations within the Soviet-led military organization and it would not allow Warsaw Pact troops to enter Hungary either. It was the then Foreign Minister Géza Jeszenszky who had first paid a visit to NATO HQ in Brussels from among the Central European leaders in June 1990 and there he announced that the security of the region could only be guaranteed by the Atlantic Alliance. The strategic goal was unequivocally set by PM József Antall at the annual Ambassadors' Conference in July 1993 where he stated that 'Our paramount goal in this decade is to join the European Communities and accession to NATO.' PM Antall, Czech President Václav Hável és Polish President Lech Wałesa went a step further in Prague in May 1992 with a joint declaration that their common goal was a full-fledged NATO-membership. The dice was cast; now it was up to the members of the Alliance to decide whether they were ready and willing or not to admit the applicants from Central Europe. The initial push was made by the Clinton Administration's 'engagement and enlargement' strategy and its vision of a 'Europe whole and free (and prosperous)'.[24]

Another crucial principle was also set early by PM Antall: he firmly believed that European integration without strong transatlantic ties would be doomed. The idea has basically been shared by each of the mainstream political forces in Hungary ever since the very beginning of the 1990s; arguments questioning one or other of these parties' commitment to the Atlantic Alliance are purely politically motivated for short-term tactical gains in domestic politics. The only anti-NATO political forces, which are anti-globalization, anti-EU and anti-American at the same time, can only be found on the far right and the far left. This idea of organic relationship between the two sides of the Atlantic explains in the first place the determined efforts by the Hungarian governments to avoid having to choose between America and Europe. One of the worst possible scenarios for Hungarian national security would be an American disengagement from Europe in general or East and Central Europe in particular at a time when the EU is not in a position, and will not be in one for some time to come, to offer similar security guarantees to the region than the United States is able to at the moment. Hungary's political willingness to support Alliance (and within it, United States) policies should, therefore, be interpreted within this general framework.

The priority given to the transatlantic relationship and NATO has become almost a pattern in Hungary's security policies even in cases when other serious national security issues, such as the security of Hungarian minorities in the neighbouring states or the unity of Europe, were at stake. In fact, the first open alignment with the United States came as early as 1991 when Hungary, still a member of the Warsaw Pact, gave overflight rights to the USAF during the Gulf War. Then throughout the Balkan wars there was the possibility that the Serbian leadership would take punitive steps against the Hungarian population in Voivodina. The sanctions introduced against 'Little Yugoslavia' in the early 1990s unquestionably hurt the Hungarian economy but the Antall and later Boross Governments joined the sanctions regimes despite the fact that some even within the ruling MDF [*Hungarian Democratic Forum*] openly opposed the step. (Their somewhat oblique argument was that economic sanctions never work against autocratic regimes.)

Hungary's commitment and alliance loyalty was seriously tested in March 1999 when only a few weeks after Hungary's accession to NATO, the Alliance commenced airstrikes against Serbia. The first dilemma for the Orbán Government was the legality of the operations. As the Alliance did not have the UNSC authorization, the military actions – strictly speaking – violated international law. The introduction of the notion of humanitarian intervention was a rather feeble surrogate. Second, the airstrikes targeted objects in Voivodina as well, foremost among them were bridges and factories; collateral damage, including human casualties, could not be excluded at all, especially given the relatively high-altitude bombing which was intended to evade anti-aircraft fire. Third, as the airstrikes did not bring about quick success (partly because of the preferred strategy of gradual escalation of the war), consideration was given to the deployment of ground forces as well – and one potential and logical point of departure would have been Hungary. In such a case Voivodina would have become a battleground. Ultimately, Slobodan Milosević yielded before ground forces would have been deployed but even the distant possibility of such a step created much headache for the Hungarian government.

Besides alliance loyalty, long-term *Realpolitik* considerations also dictated that Hungary should actively support the Allied forces in their campaign against Serbia. Hungary's national security, just like any other nations, requires peaceful neighbourhood. The successive wars in the Balkans did not only threaten with a potential spillover of the armed conflict onto Hungarian territory but they also substantially hurt the Hungarian economy because of the sanctions and the blocking of important trade routes for Hungarian exports. In addition, the challenge posed by drug trafficking grew; Hungary became a safer transit route for drug shipments sent from Central Asia to Western Europe than the war-torn Balkans. This also meant that organized crime activities picked up in Hungary, and in some extreme cases firefights broke out in the middle of Budapest in broad daylight between rival gangs of Ukrainian, Chechen and Russian origins. Money-laundering, prostitution rings and human trafficking were some of the other by-products of the continued instability in Hungary's southern neighbourhood providing a textbook case of how external and internal security is interconnected and interdependent. The realization of this rule is one of the chief reasons why Hungary decided to stay engaged in the Balkans even after the conclusion of the NATO operations and to continue its efforts to help build elements of civil society and facilitate ethnic reconciliation. One of the lessons drawn from the Balkan wars is the importance of keeping up NATO's 'Open Door' policy. NATO expansion is not an issue that has been enjoying universal support ever since the first serious suggestions were made in the early 1990s. The counterarguments run from *Realpolitik* considerations (for instance, isolating a defeated great power, that is Russia, is not a good idea; the United States would stretch itself thin by assuming new defence commitments and so on) through financial considerations (military assistance to the new members would require an enormous sum of money) to fearing from watering down the Alliance. On the other hand, Hungary's exposed geopolitical and geostrategic position dictates a pro-expansion policy. Therefore, Budapest has consistently promoted the eventual membership of all the East and Central European countries with a special reference to its immediate neighbours. The Hungarian government did not miss the opportunity at the Chicago Summit to keep the question on the agenda in general and, in particular, to support the future membership of Montenegro and Macedonia. The Alliance did not take a decision in May 2012 about new members to the Alliance but it was agreed that the next summit will be an 'expansion' summit again, that is, one or two countries may expect to be invited to join. In addition, Hungary also welcomes the cooperation of like-minded democracies in a new form of 'partnership' with NATO.

The question of having to choose between America and Europe, which each of the East and Central European countries so eagerly wish to avoid, cropped up on the eve of the Iraq War in early 2003. Although very few people were convinced in Hungary by the Bush Administration's justification for the war, the Medgyessy Government sided with Washington in opposition to Paris and Berlin in the form of the Letter of Eight. It does not seem to be only by accident that all the East and Central European nations lent political support to the United States despite their misgivings. If we want to put the question into perspective, we can go back to 1989–1990 when, as latest research on the topic proves, none of the so-called great European powers, especially the United Kingdom and France, was very keen on supporting the withdrawal of the Soviet forces from Central Europe and, consequently, the political changes in the area. With regard to the first issue they feared that a re-united Germany would be the winner by extending its influence over Central Europe and it would thus alter power relations in Europe at the expense of London and Paris.

Concerning the latter question, they feared that too fast and radical political transformation in the former satellites would undermine the power of Mikhail Gorbachev and trigger a conservative backlash in the Soviet Union. It was the George H. W. Bush Administration that had made the greatest efforts to support the political transition in East and Central Europe, though it also wished to hold the radicals back. Then, the initiative to expand NATO to the East was also an American idea – this time it was Paris, which had been traditionally sceptical about the United States as a 'European power', that primarily feared that the new members would be staunch US-allies and, therefore, would strengthen American positions on the Continent. Third, the emerging Paris–Berlin–Moscow 'axis' in opposition to the United States in this question evoked rather tragic memories in East and Central Europe. Finally, the countries in the region shared, and still share, the view that it is only the United States that possesses credible deterrent power and can offer real security guarantees.[25]

NATO responded to terrorist attacks on 11 September 2001 by evoking Article 5 – this was ironic to some extent because the famous 'three musketeers' clause was originally envisaged primarily as an American commitment to come to the assistance of the weaker European allies in case. The Hungarian military contribution is remarkable itself given the financial and the technological conditions under which the Hungarian troops have to work in Afghanistan. However, equally important is Budapest's commitment to the 'in together, out together' principle, which is a significant contribution to the solidarity, unity and – by extension – the future of the Alliance as well. There is no *Realpolitik* justification for the presence of Hungarian military units in this faraway country (though such indirect security threats as mass migration, drug trafficking and so on may be mentioned), but it is the values NATO stands for that explain why the various governments in Hungary, whether they are centre-right or centre-left, are equally supportive of the efforts made in Afghanistan not only by NATO but also by like-minded nations like Australia, Japan and so on. Hungary adheres to the policies accepted at the Lisbon Summit of NATO and reinforced in Chicago. The Hungarian troops will be withdrawn from Baghlan province in Tranche 4 by 31 October 2013. However, the military withdrawal will not affect Hungary's political commitment towards Afghanistan after 2014; meanwhile, the military role will also be undergoing some changes and emphasis will be laid on training and advising the Afghan military, security and law enforcement forces.

The wisdom of the acquisition of the 14 fighter planes in 2001 in the first place, then the addition of the refuelling capability were repeatedly called into question as NATO has an excess number of fighter aircraft and the Hungarian ones do not mean a meaningful contribution to either to common defence or out-of-area operations.[26] A number of experts argued that Hungary should have developed niche-capabilities instead, such as, for instance, strategic airlift. In fact, there is an underlying defence and security philosophy debate in the whole issue. One camp argues that priority should be given to developing and modernizing national defence capabilities as NATO requires that each member provide for its own defence first and foremost and be capable to defend itself – at least for some time – in case of an attack until NATO forces come to its defence under Article 5 obligations. The other one claims that the possibility of a conventional armed attack against Hungary can be practically discounted and NATO's modern missions are 'out-of-area' operations which are not necessarily of pure military nature. In reality, the Defense Capabilities Initiative at the Washington Summit of 1999 and the Prague Capabilities Package (2002) set the general framework for the member states insofar as it refocused NATO's force posture. There is 'less and less emphasis on home defense, and more and more forces offered for use outside' of the Euro-Atlantic area (Gyarmati, 2005, p. 32).

Hungary promised one battalion and special operations forces besides such niche capabilities as water-cleansing, pontoon-construction and military police. However, Hungary has rarely delivered on these and other promises and there arose a suspicion that Budapest wanted a 'free ride' primarily because of the lack of adequate funding but sometimes the political will was also missing (Gyarmati, 2005, p. 32).

The issue of the existence or the lack of political will is a complex one with internal and external implications too. The single major domestic factor is that defence has not been a priority any time in the past 20 years. The questions of political, economic and social transition – rightfully – pushed defence into the background. None of the prime ministers has really been seriously interested in matters related to this sector; the political leadership of the Ministry of Defense became too often a hostage of inter- and/or intraparty machinations and the top post was frequently used to satisfy the personal ambitions of politicians with little or absolutely no experience in defence and security issues.

Military leadership also often lacked continuity and integrity as the successive governments (the centre-right and centre-left ones alternated quite regularly) tended to play politics with it. There was no 'constituency' for defence; public opinion was, at best, indifferent to defence-related questions; the best example is the referendum on NATO-membership in 1999 when hardly half of the population bothered to show up at the polling booths. The country was undergoing a number of economic hardships: the Western-type welfare state has never taken roots in Hungary and the various imbalances in the economy have been reinforced by globalization in the recent years. None of the political forces risked to lose hard-fought political support by initiating a comprehensive and, by definition, costly reorganization and modernization of the military forces. In addition, the scarce resources have not always been spent the most efficient way; sometimes so-called prestige-procurements diverted badly needed sums from other more worthy projects and corruption was also a serious problem.

## Conclusion

Without exonerating the Hungarian political and military leaderships, it is just fair to state that they have often had to shoot at a moving target. To put it bluntly, NATO has been in search of a mission since the disappearance of the Soviet Union and the Warsaw Pact. Alliances are glued together by the commonly perceived enemy or outside threat; to be honest, both have been missing recently. In general, while the United States is busy converting NATO into a sort of 'global sheriff', by asking its allies to think more globally than they are sometimes willing, the European allies (except for the United Kingdom and France) are less and less capable of thinking globally as far as military matters concerned.

First, they reject the notion theoretically that power politics should play a prominent role in international affairs. Second, because of their own seriously underfunded militaries they lack the necessary expeditionary capabilities as well. Alliance solidarity and unity are not what they used to be during the Cold War years: US policies and leadership are publicly criticized and opposed by key allies in issues which are deemed vital by Washington. The smaller countries at times find themselves between the American hammer and the European anvil; it is hard or next to impossible for them to please Washington, Brussels, London, Paris and Berlin at the same time. NATO is about alliance unity, but it seems that there are cracks in it as national security interests are gaining grounds at the expense of some of the commonly shared mostly tactical, but to a lesser degree strategic positions too. The burden-sharing debate, which has been following the history of NATO since at least 1951, is likely to become more and more embittered: while the European allies covered close to 50 per cent of the costs during the Cold War, nowadays this ratio dropped to some 25 per cent in a situation in which the US (strategic) interests seem to be shifting primarily towards the Pacific region and the Pentagon is facing relatively deep budget cuts in the next few years.

This is not all welcome news to Hungary. A benevolent neglect of the East and Central European region by the United States may be a proper approach if an extremely stable political, economic, social and ethnic environment were coupled here with a strong, capable and united European leadership. In the absence of these conditions, Hungary should do its best to strengthen the Atlantic Community because it may have its own faults but any other alternative looks much less attractive both in the short and the long term.

Regarding the political will, the track record of the Hungarian governments in the past 20 years or so is definitely positive. It was Prime Minister Antall, who was among the first politicians in Central Europe, who initiated the dissolution of the Warsaw Pact, and who suggested that Hungary join NATO. The Hungarian political and military leaders, as well as the fledgling security establishment, have been aware of the fact that the ultimate guarantor of Hungary's is the United States within NATO. Thus a healthy and robust transatlantic cooperation is also a *sine qua non* for Hungarian security; it explains why the Hungarian governments have invariably been trying to maintain close relations with Washington even if they sometimes found themselves in opposition to some major states in Europe.

Concerning military capabilities, however, the record is rather mixed. The Hungarian armed forces started with such huge handicaps as oversized and top-heavy personnel, outdated hardware and software, which were not naturally not compatible with NATO standards. The military had to be downsized, modernized, restructured, re-trained – and all at the same time. The command structure had to be revamped as well. A new legislative and executive framework for the civil control of the military had to put in place. The human dimension should not be forgotten either: the prestige of the military service had to be restored after decades in which the armed forces had been seen not more by most in the public at large than an organization in the service of the Communist Party in Hungary and the Soviet interests internationally.

All of these sweeping changes had to be carried out in very difficult economic circumstances in which the governments were rather reluctant to spend resources badly needed elsewhere on the armed forces. This situation was exacerbated by the fact that NATO was 'sold' to some extent to the public as a cure-all for all Hungarian security concerns, while the message to NATO erred on the other side: Budapest repeatedly promised more than it has been able to deliver. The process to come clean about the real capabilities with both the Hungarian public and the Atlantic community has already started and it is only hoped that Hungary will not be punching below its weight in NATO in the future.

## Notes

1. 27 October 1991 on Barcs in Southern Hungary. It is still unknown whether they were dropped as conscious provocation or by accident.
2. The classic case is, of course, the Iraq War, the so-called Letter of Eight and the angry and patronizing French reaction to the latter in 2003.
3. Charles Gati claims that 'To a large extent, membership in the European Union in 2004 [except for Romania and Bulgaria, which joined in 2007] made Washington's loss of influence all but inevitable.' He adds that 'surprisingly large majority has now joined other Europeans in questioning America's aptitude for leadership in a post-Cold War environment'. Gati labels the US policy towards East and Central Europe as 'Checkmark Diplomacy'. See Gati (2008).
4. The most widely discussed such statement at the time when it was published was Celeste A. Wallender's (2002). Some of her comments, such as Hungary's territorial claims against its neighbours or missing an opportunity to play a constructive role in the Balkans were clearly off the mark.
5. The most recent and public American frustration with this situation was the outgoing Secretary of Defense, Robert Gates's speech in Brussels on 10 June 2011. He painted an extremely dark picture of the future of NATO if current trends are continuing. See Barnes and Fidler (2011). A strongly-worded unofficial criticism appeared in the *Foreign Affairs* was Cimbalo's (2004).
6. The Letter of Twenty-Two may be criticized as ill-timed or an unhelpful public statement but the perception is real and shared by quite a number of people in the national security establishments in East and Central Europe.
7. The National Assembly passed a Resolution (57/2007) which obliged the governments to increase the defence budget but it was ignored by both the Gyurcsány and Bajnai governments between 2007 and 2010 (Kern, 2010a, p. 81).
8. Hungary promised at the Prague Summit of NATO in 2002 that it would spend 30 billion HUF in four years on procurement and modernization; this target amount was never achieved. See Szenes (2009, p. 38).
9. The latest 'second-hand' acquisitions are two Mi8 transport helicopters from Finland.
10. Then Prime Minister Viktor Orbán stated on 1 March 2001 that 'Hungary wishes to have good economic relations with Russia but there is a clear-cut dividing line between us concerning defense policies and security matters.' Quoted by Kern (2008), p. 100.
11. 2021/2003 Government Resolution.
12. The Basic Law of Hungary discusses the terms of foreign deployment under the general heading of the 'Hungarian Defense Forces' and the subheading

of 'Decision on Participation in Military Operations': 'Art. 47 (1) The Government shall decide on troop movements of the Hungarian Defense Forces and of foreign armed forces that involve border crossing. (2) The Parliament with a two-thirds majority of the votes of the Members...at present shall decide...on the use of the HDF abroad or within the territory of Hungary...(3) The Government shall decide on the troop movements of the HDF and of foreign armed forces...on the basis of the decisions of the European Union or the NATO ...'.

13. As for Hungary's operational contributions, it ranked about sixth to seventh place in proportion of the size of its ground forces in the mid-2000s, and it was the fourth on this imaginary ladder in 2009 (Németh, 2009, p. 8).
14. National Assembly Resolution 112/1995. Hungary was the first non-NATO country to grant Alliance-troops transit rights in December 1995.
15. Participation at the referendum was remarkable low, around 50 per cent of the eligible voters; 85 per cent of those voting supported membership in NATO.
16. For a comprehensive review of Hungarian participation in international peace-supporting missions in a historical context, see Isaszegi (2008).
17. Former Minister of Defence Ferenc Juhász openly declared that 'This is about NATO, not Afghanistan.' Cited in Marton and Wagner (2011, p. 7).
18. On the technical details see Dr Isaszegi János, 'Magyar katonák a nemzetközi béketámogató műveletekben' (Budapest, 2008), Manuscript.
19. The best-known proponent of those opposing the planned radar station was former President László Sólyom.
20. The constructor will be Marconi's successor the Selex Sistemi Integrati.
21. This section is predominantly based on Szarvas (2008, pp. 60–76).
22. The Czechs and the Poles were the last minute before the public announcement which was made on 17 September 2009, on the 60th anniversary of the Soviet invasion of Poland in 1939.
23. 'Missile defense...is a capability that will definitely strengthen transatlantic ties. Hungary recognizes the threat posed by advances in ballistic missile technology and by the proliferation of ballistic missiles themselves .... Missile defense will complement but certainly not substitute NATO's nuclear capabilities. The preservation of NATO's credible nuclear capabilities remains a key pillar of collective defense and solidarity between Allies' (Siklósi, 2012, pp. 8–9). The official Hungarian national security documents gradually realized the importance of the defence against Weapons of Mass Destruction (WMD): while in 1994 there was no mention whatsoever of them, the 1998 NSS made a brief reference to them, while the one issued in 2004 listed them as the second most significant threat to the national security of Hungary (after terrorism).
24. Arguably the best single account of the NATO-enlargement process from the Americans' point of view is Asmus, 2002. The story of the Hungarian side is summarized, among others, in a bilingual volume (Joó, 1999). As NATO is a community based on commonly shared values, a part of political commitment includes the adoption of the democratic values, the rule of law and so on. Here, suffice it to refer to the importance of the introduction of civil control over the military.

25. The current issue of missile defence in East and Central Europe is also about 'keeping the Americans in'. It is true that the countries involved urge that the system be operated nominally by NATO, but in reality it is obvious that missile defence will be US technology and will be controlled by the United States as well.
26. István Gyarmati és György Szentesi are cited by Kern (2008, p. 108).

## Bibliography

Asmus, R. D. (2002) *Opening NATO's Door. How the Alliance Remade Itself for a New Era* (New York: Columbia University Press).
Barnes, J. E. and Fidler, S. (2011) 'Gates Questions NATO's Future', *Wall Street Journal*, 11 June 2011, http://online.wsj.com (home page), date accessed 18 March 2012.
Biden, J. (2009) 'Remarks By Vice President Biden on America, Central Europe and a Partnership for the 21st Century', Central University Library, Bucharest, 22 October 2009, http://www.whitehouse.gov (homepage), date accessed 9 November 2009.
Bugajski, J. (2004) *Cold Peace: Russia's New Imperialism* (Westport, CT: Praeger/CSIS).
Cimbalo, J. L. (2004) 'Saving NATO from Europe', *Foreign Affairs*, Vol. 83, No. 6, pp. 111–120.
Deák, J. (2000) 'A nemzeti katonai stratégia néhány aktuális kérdéséről', *Hadtudomány*, Vol. 10, No. 3, www.zmne.hu (homepage), date accessed 26 May 2012.
Gati, C. (2008) 'Faded Romance. How Mitteleuropa Fell Out of Love with America', *The American Interest*, Vol. 4, No. 2, pp. 35–43.
Gyarmati, I. (2005) 'Hungary and NATO', *The Analyst*, Vol. 1, No. 2, pp. 27–38.
hirado.hu (2012) 'Hende: Tíz évig folyamatosan nő a honvédség költségvetése', *hirado.hu*, 5 April 2012, http://www.hirado.hu (homepage), date accessed 4 May 2012.
Ilisics, Z. (2004) *Válságkezelés az ezredfordulón. Magyarország részvétele katonai béketámogató műveletekben*, Ph. D. Dissertation (Budapest: Corvinus University).
Isaszegi, J. (2008) *Magyar katonák a nemzetközi béketámogató műveletekben (1895–2000)* (Budapest), in manuscript.
Joó, R. (1999) *Hungary, a Member of NATO* (Budapest: Ministry of Foreign Affairs).
Kern, T. (2008) 'A Gripen-projekt. Egy elhibázott katonai beszerzés margójára', *Kommentár*, No. 2, pp. 95–109.
Kern, T. (2009) 'A magyar honvédelem központi finanszírozása a 2010. évi költségvetésben', *Nemzet és Biztonság*, December, pp. 76–84.
Kern, T. (2010a) 'Katonapolitika: prioritás vagy nem? Egy kormányprogram margójára', *Nemzet és Biztonság*, June, pp. 74–83.
Kern, T. (2010b) 'A 2011-es védelmi költségvetés a gazdasági stabilizáció fogságában', *Nemzet és Biztonság*, December, pp. 52–59.
Kern, T. (2011) 'Több mint fél siker – a második Orbán-kormány védelempolitikájának első évéről', *Nemzet és Biztonság*, June, pp. 70–80.
Kulugyminiszterium (2012) 'Biztonságpolitika – Magyarország a NATO-ban – Magyar szerepvállalás Afganisztánban', http://www.kulugyminiszterium.hu (homepage), date accessed 6 June 2012.

Marton, P. (2011) '9/11 hatása kül- és biztonságpolitikai helyzetünkre', *Nemzet és Biztonság*, October, pp. 11–21.
Marton, P. and Wagner, P. (2011) 'Hungary's Involvement in Afghanistan. Proudly Going through the Motions?' in Hynek, N. and Márton, P. (eds) *Statebuilding in Afghanistan. Multinational Contributions to Reconstruction* (London: Routledge), pp. 192–211.
Németh, A. (2009) *Magyarország Euro-Atlanti kapcsolatrendszere: Az ország szerepe és helye az EU-ban, a NATO-ban és az EBESZ-ben* (Budapest: Pécsi Tudományegyetem BTK Politológia Szak, IV. évf.).
népszabadság.online (2012) 'Költségvetési lyukakat is betömnek a Gripenpénzből', *népszabadság.online*, 1 May 2012, http://nol.hu (homepage) date accessed 1 May 2012.
Rácz, A. (2005) 'Hungary: A Most Reluctant Ally', *Contemporary Security Policy*, Vol. 26, No. 3, pp. 544–557.
Siklósi, P. (2012) 'NATO Summit in Chicago – Hungarian Perspective', *Transatlantické Listy*, No. 1, pp. 8–10.
Szarvas, L. (2008), 'Stratégiai Légi Szállítási Képesség – egy új többnemzeti megoldás', *Nemzet és Biztonság*, July, pp. 60–76.
Szenes, Z. (2000) 'Koncepcióváltás a magyar békefenntartásban?', *Nemzet és Biztonság*, April, pp. 67–80.
Szenes, Z. (2009) 'Magyar haderő-átalakítás a NATO-tagság idején', *Nemzet és Biztonság*, April, pp. 33–43.
Szenes, Z. (2011) 'Védelmi költségvetés 2012', *Nemzet és Biztonság*, November, p. 2.
Tálas, P. (2009) 'A NATO új stratégiai koncepciója – adalékok a magyar szemponthoz', *Nemzet és Biztonság*, October, 61–73.
Végh, F. (1999) 'The Hungarian Defense Forces: From Preparation to Full Interoperability', in Rudolf, J. (ed.) *Hungary: A Member of NATO; A NATO-tag Magyarország* (Budapest: Ministry of Foreign Affairs).
Wallender, C. A. (2002) 'NATO's Price: Shape Up or Ship Out', *Foreign Affairs*, Vol. 81, No. 6, pp. 2–8.

# 13
# Punching above Its Weight: Denmark's Legitimate Peripheral Participation in NATO's Wars

*M. V. Rasmussen*

## Introduction

'In the Libya operation, Norway and Denmark, have provided 12 per cent of allied strike aircraft yet have struck about one third of the targets', US Defence Secretary Robert Gates noted in June 2011, 'These countries have, with their constrained resources, found ways to do the training, buy the equipment, and field the platforms necessary to make a credible military contribution' (Gates, 2011). Along with Belgium, Canada and Norway the outgoing US Secretary of Defence mentioned Denmark as an example for the rest of the Alliance to follow. For 10–20 years Denmark has increasingly become a more willing and able NATO-partner committing troops to NATO operations in Afghanistan and fighter planes to Unified Protector over Libya. The Danish government and its armed forces have prided themselves in being able to commit troops that were able to get the job done without caveats and, in Afghanistan at least, able to tolerate considerable casualties while doing so. When Secretary Gates described Denmark as a country that punched above its weight, it confirmed the new-found Danish self-image of being among the most willing and able NATO-partners.

This chapter will investigate how this strategic commitment has been translated into operational experiences and how these operational experiences in turn have come to define Denmark's military capabilities, strategic outlook and role in the Alliance. Taking its point of departure in Jean Lave and Etienne Wenger's notion of 'situated learning', this chapter will describe the way in which the Danish armed forces have used military operations, particularly in Afghanistan's Helmand province, to define a new role for Denmark as country in the Alliance's core. That core is disappearing, however, producing new challenges for Danish NATO-policy.

This chapter will proceed by, first, an introduction to the ideological positions that defines Danish foreign policy discourse and thus the Danish 'willingness' to participate in NATO operations. It is argued that these ideological positions can only be understood in the context of a Danish security policy practice. In other words, willingness and ability are two sides of the same coin in the Danish case. Second, this practice is described in terms of Jean Lave and Etienne Wenger's notion of 'situated learning'. The Danish armed forces deployed troops to Afghanistan in order to learn from the British and thus transform the Danish army to an expeditionary force. This deployment is described in section "Activism as practice". Fourthly, the Danish deployment to Libya is described as an example on how the Danish ability to deploy troops has transformed. Finally, the chapter discusses how Denmark can use its new-found status in the Alliance to find a position at a time when NATO is being increasingly fragmented.

## Cosmopolitanism, defencism and activism

I have previously argued (Rasmussen, 2005) that Danish strategic culture is constituted by a debate between 'cosmopolitanism' and 'defencism'. Cosmopolitanism holds that there is a certain virtue in being a small country. Denmark should, therefore, stay out of great power politics in favour of an engagement with civil societies in order to create a better world. In opposition to the cosmopolitan view, defencists argue that Denmark has no such special mission, but should instead pursue its interest like any other state, including by the use of military force. Accordingly to cosmopolitans, Denmark should thus be a 'humanitarian actor' (Villaume, 2009), while defencists want Denmark to be a 'strategic actor' (Rynning, 2003).

It is important to note that cosmopolitanism and defencism are competing discourses on Danish foreign policy. Danish security and defence policy have seldom corresponded to either of the discourses, and that is to a certain extent the very point of these discourses. They constitute critiques of the prevalent policy and thus make sense only in dialogue with each other. The policy itself is most often a compromise between cosmopolitanism and defencism, as the discourses manifest themselves in political programmes of a particular government or opposition party, and the foreign policy environment in which Denmark has to operate at a particular point in time. Together the discourses and the policy constitute the practice of Danish security policy.

Since 1945 Danish security and defence policy have been constituted by a number of practices that provided a compromise between cosmopolitan and defencist view on Danish foreign policy. Since the end of the Cold War one such practice has been named 'activism'. The outcome of activism has been what Bertel Heurlin has termed the 'militarisation' of Danish foreign policy (Heurlin, 1993, pp. 45–46). This militarization has mostly taken place within a NATO-context where Denmark has been amongst the most willing and able members of the Alliance. Activism is a practice rather than a policy. This is demonstrated by the fact that cosmopolitans and defencists have passionately disagreed on what kind of activism Denmark should pursue – should Denmark be a humanitarian or strategic actor? In 2003, Prime Minister Anders Fogh Rasmussen asked, 'who can best guarantee Denmark's security? My answer is very clear. Denmark's security is better guaranteed by a super power in North America than by the fragile and ever shifting balance of power between Germany, France and Britain' (Rasmussen, 2003).

Rasmussen's argument was defencism classic. The utility of security policy was defined in terms of national survival and interest, rather than in terms of an active engagement with world civil society. Denmark was thus regarded as a strategic actor that could ally itself with an 'off-shore balancer' (Mearsheimer, 2001) in order to gain more freedom of manoeuvre in relation to the European great powers. The then leader of the opposition, Mogens Lykketoft from the Social Democratic Party, accused the Prime Minister of a 'false activism': 'Nobody rejects the need for Danish engagement in global issues,' the labour politician asserted, 'but underneath the consensus on the doctrine of an activist foreign policy there are huge differences in opinion about the concrete political content of activism.' Lykketoft finds that Fogh's commitment to the United States as an 'off-shore balancer' focuses on 'hard security issues' as opposed to 'the broader aspects of human security' (Lykketoft, 2003).

The US ambassador to Denmark, James Cain, summed this debate up nicely in a cable to Washington on the 2008 parliamentary election. According to *Wikileaks*, the ambassador assessed US–Danish relations thus:

> A change to a social democratic-led government would present significant challenges for the United States – the current government has been among our closest allies – but not insurmountable ones. Pressed to bet, our money is on Rasmussen to win, but we can take

satisfaction in the conviction that Denmark will remain a valued partner even if we lose that wager.

(Cain, 2008)

The ambassador realized, perhaps more clearly than the protagonists themselves, that Denmark was set on an 'activist' course. The question was 'how' Denmark would be activist rather than 'whether' Denmark would pursue activist policies. When the social democrats came to power in 2011, Prime Minister Helle Thorning-Schmidt stated in Parliament that her government would be 'active – from Africa to Afghanistan' (Prime Minister's Office, 2011). This leads us to take a closer look at how the Danish government implemented the activist agenda in a NATO context and how the practice of activism shaped the conduct of Danish security policy.

## Activism as practice

Danish security policy has become 'activist', regardless of whether the government is inclined to pursue a cosmopolitan or defencist agenda. Denmark developed its willingness to engage in the sharpest of missions at the same time as the Danish armed forces was transformed to be able to deploy to this type of mission. In 2003, the then Prime Minister Anders Fogh Rasmussen stated that the armed forces should be able to deploy twice as many (that is 2,000) troops in international operations (Prime Minister's Office, 2003). In the period from 1985 to 2004 Denmark had cut its defence expenditure back by 28.6 per cent (Ringsmose, 2008, p. 356).

This dramatic attempt to cash 'the peace dividend' after the Cold War had been conducted in a piecemeal way, however, which had essentially left the Danish armed forces with the same organization as during the Cold War – just with far fewer resources. The main concession to the new European security environment had been the formation of an International Brigade, which had been used for deployment in the Balkans. The fact that only one of the army's brigades was designated to be the 'international' clearly demonstrated that the armed forces in general was still organized with territorial defence in mind. The international brigade was the exception that proved the point. Anders Fogh Rasmussen wanted to change that making international deployments the raison d'être of the armed forces as such. Such reforms were necessary because having cut costs without focusing the mission there was a mismatch between ends, ways and means. The defence budget was thus in the red, with the Defence Minister needing to ask Parliament for 1 million DKK in further funds. The Defence budget did not get any bigger following Primer Rasmussen's speech, but the budget got focused on a certain type of mission with a clear end state (deploying 2,000 soldiers) to plan after. In the coming years, the Danish armed forces developed the capability to deploy one battle-group of one army brigade with heavy support (including tanks), 1–2 frigates and up to 16 F-16s. In 2010, McKinsey concluded that 23 per cent of the Danish armed forces were in combat functions, placing Denmark comfortably in the middle of the consultancy's bench marking exercise. The study even indirectly mentions Demark as an example of how a country can transform its tooth-to-tail ratio by centralizing support functions (Gebicke and Magid, 2010, pp. 5–6).

The answer to why Denmark is a willing and able NATO-ally is neither to be found on the ideational, ideological level nor in terms of military capability. The reality of the operations and the ideological commitment to doing them has fed one another. In the course of this transformation, the Danish armed forces have become fond of referring to the armed forces' capabilities as a 'tool kit', which Parliament can use for various tasks. This reflects the extent to which the armed forces have embraced a transformation from a force dedicated to fighting a war of necessity in the defence of the national territory to a force that fights wars of choice. This 'capability-based approach' closely follows NATO's adaptation of 'capability based defence planning'.

This serves to show how Danish military capabilities and the way in which they are organized have been shaped not only by changes in Danish policy, but also changes in the way the Alliance conceived of defence planning. Thus, it is not only the military hardware that constitutes a tool kit. The concepts offered by NATO became 'conceptual tools' by which the armed forces could be transformed, and this in turn offered the government a new way of using the armed forces. At the same time changes in policy necessitated a transformation of the armed forces in ways that made them more useful in a global context. This creation of a new 'security policy tool box' can be explained in theoretical terms as the constitution of a new cultural practice. Ann Swidler defines culture as the 'tool kit' enabling agents to form strategies of actions. Swidler sees 'culture's casual significance in providing cultural components that are used to construct strategies of action' (Swidler, 1986, p. 273). Practice studies describe *how* actors act rather than why and for what purpose. Barry Barnes notes that 'the practice should be treated as involving thought and action together' (Barnes, 2001, p. 33). From a practice perspective 'will' and 'ability' become mutually constitutive factors, as they form part of the tool kit that defines what types of policy are possible for the Danish government to undertake.

The advantage of practice theory is that it allows us to regard cosmopolitanism and defencism as concepts of how to use the same security policy 'tool kit'. Thus by focusing on the way policy is done we can escape a political discussion of the merits of cosmopolitanism compared to defencism and instead explore the activism which both ideological positions inform. This integration of discourse and political action into practice also makes it possible to penetrate the shroud of the spin that often prevents one from describing the operational realities. This is especially important in the Danish case since Denmark's activism has been created in interaction between abstract political ideas and the experience in concrete missions. The Danes have been very good at selling the Danish commitment to NATO operations; perhaps better than the operational realities allowed (Rasmussen, 2011). This process of acquiring a practice is at the centre of Jean Lave and Etienne Wenger's theory of practice (Lave and Wenger, 1991).

Lave and Wenger study apprenticeship in order to demonstrate how 'learning is an integral part of generative social practice in the lived-in world' (Lave and Wenger, 1991, p. 35). Training to become a carpenter is not only about learning a specific skill-set, but learning these skills while working as a part of a carpenter's workshop. The apprentice engages in 'legitimate peripheral participation', in Lave and Wenger's terms. This is not learning by doing, in Lave and Wenger's account, but learning *in* doing. Learning is 'situated' in the specific assignments of the workshop rather than defined by the student acquiring a predefined curriculum. In the carpenter shop 'understanding and experience are in constant interaction – indeed, are mutually constitutive' (Lave and Wenger, 1991, pp. 51–52). In the course of one's apprenticeship one is not only training certain skills, one becomes part of a 'community of practice' which defines not only what one does but also who one is in terms of a professional identity. 'Learning is never simply a process of transfer or assimilation', Lave and Wenger notes (Lave and Wenger, 1991: 57).

The apprentice engages with the master and the journeymen and in that engagement. The apprentice not only learns his trade, but learns it by working side by side with the journeymen. In that process of learning the journeymen renegotiate the nature of the trade itself, confirming its skills and codes, as well as creating new ones, together with the apprentice. For that reason, Lave and Wenger argues, the power relations of an apprenticeship are situational rather than hierarchical. The apprentice does not move in a straight line from the periphery of the workshop to its centre, but rather assumes a number of different positions in relation to the specific tasks the workshop is engaged in, and thus power relations are constantly negotiated with the surrounding environment (Lave and Wenger, 1991: 36).

In its 2006 vision statement the Danish Armed Forces defined its transformation to an expeditionary force as a case of situational learning: 'The Armed Forces must be a sought-after partner for prioritised alliance and coalition partners. In other words, we must measure our own capabilities in relation to our partners. This means at minimum the United States and Great Britain' (Danish Defence, 2006, p. 13). Danish military capabilities were to be measured in relationship to their relevance in operations with the United States and Great Britain. This vision statement is a good example of how discourse and action interact in a practice. Pegging the organization's performance to 'industry leaders' was one element in the new public management approach prevalent in the Danish state administration at the time. The military leadership thus followed a management discourse by benchmarking their organization. In doing so they translated political ambitions for cooperating with the United States and the United Kingdom into an operational and an organizational-development goal at the same time. The armed forces wanted to create situations in which Danish forces could participate in coalition operations and thus learn from the best. In sum, Denmark did not just become activist, it learned to be activist by placing its armed forces in situations from which they could learn. In order to illustrate this, we will focus on how Danish troops were deployed to Afghanistan in 2006.

## The Goldilocks solution

The mission in Afghanistan appealed to the Danish government because it offered an opportunity to engage NATO in an out-of-area mission that would confirm the global scope of the alliance. Apart from this strategic rationale the operation had the political benefit that it brought France and Germany into a mission with Great Britain thus making up for the disagreements surrounding the Iraq War. For a small country it was unpleasant – the Prime Minister's commitment to the off-shore-balancer regardless – to be caught on the side of Britain and the United States against the most important powers in the EU. This political willingness to take part in the ISAF-mission suited the Armed Forces reform agenda. The Chief of Defence, General Jesper Helsø, wanted a mission that 'belonged to the military métier' (Interview Helsø, 2010). To General Helsø, 'the military métier' was combined arms operations along the lines of those the general had trained as a young artillery officer during the Cold War. This was 'real war', as opposed the 'operations other than war' Danish troops had taking part in the Balkans and in the occupation duties in Basra. The transformation process had enabled the army to deploy one battalion of mechanised infantry in a battle group heavy with support troops, and General Helsø and his staff wanted to be able to prove that battle group in the field. This followed logically from the Armed Forces' mission statement. Helmand province was to be the site of situated learning for the Danish army.

The Ministry of Defence's Permanent Secretary Anders Troldborg supported deploying as a part of the British Task Force for slightly different reasons. The Ministry of Defence considered the option of adding more troops to the contingents already part of the Swedish and the German Provisional Reconstruction Teams (PRT) in Northern Afghanistan. It would serve to make up for the diplomatic points lost during in Iraq War and the areas in which the Germans and the Swedes deployed were considered less dangerous than Helmand province. Furthermore, the deployments themselves would be easier since one could use already established logistical arrangements. These pragmatic considerations were challenged from the political level because the government wanted to prove its defencist commitment to fight where challenges were the greatest and challenged from the armed forces that wanted a mission which could improve the army's ability to do the 'military métier'. From a political perspective the Germans and the Swedes were too soft. From a military perspective their contribution was soft too, and that concerned Troldborg. When Danish troops were put in harm's way he wanted to make sure that they could get the back-up they needed. Neither the German nor the Swedish contribution had the powerful reserves of the British and this was an important factor for the Permanent Secretary.

Another factor was the Danish ability to influence operations. No matter who the Danes joined forces with, Denmark would be the junior partner. The Danish experience with the Germans and the Swedes in Afghanistan did not compare well with the experience of working together with the British in Iraq. Even if that mission was far from successful, Secretary Troldborg felt that the British and the Danes had shared experience which would form a foundation for cooperation in

Afghanistan. It is interesting to note how it mattered to the Danish Ministry of Defence that the Danish army was in a situation of 'legitimate peripheral participation' with the British. The cooperation with the British was regarded as an ongoing relationship from which the Danish army could benefit, and this organizational consideration was an important part of the decision. In the end deploying with the British was, in Anders Troldborg's words, the 'Goldilocks solution'. The Germans and the Swedes were too 'cold' in the sense that their military engagement was too small to guarantee Danish troops and their level of ambition to low. The Americans were too 'hot' because their level of ambition was higher than the Danish one and their technological level was something the Danish forces could not match. The British, however, was just right (Interview Troldborg, 2010).

Troldborg still feared that the British might use the Danish troops for the tasks which were either too dangerous or too unglamorous for the British to do themselves (Interview Troldborg, 2010). In order to maintain some control of the troops, the Danish force was increased to 700 as soon as the army was able to withdraw from Iraq, and this battle group was put in charge of its own area in North of Gereshk in the Helmand river valley. In the Balkans the Danes had maintained their own area of operations and they wanted to do the same in Afghanistan. This gave the Danish commander operational command of his own troops most of the time – at the same time as it put Dannebrog on a map highlighting the Danish achievements in that area.

The Danish approach to the British task force is captured by Lave and Wenger's notion of the situational nature of power in a community of practice. The Danish wanted to participate in the British operations in order to improve the operational capabilities of the army. Therefore it would make little sense to have drawn up legal documents that explicitly forbade Danish troops from being used in certain ways. Such 'caveats' would work against the political signal the government wanted to send and prevent Danish soldiers and officers from achieving the organizational goal of learning from the British. Yet, the Danes had their fears and reservations which other nations in ISAF put into print in formal caveats. Danish experience in the Balkans and the organizational culture in the Danish defence establishment in Copenhagen make them choose other means to secure against these fears than formal caveats. Sten Rynning and Jens Ringsmose note that 'significantly, and quite unusually in the ISAF context, Denmark has imposed none of the so-called national caveats on the deployed troops' (Rynning and Ringsmose, 2008: 62); they overlook the most interesting part of the story. The lack of caveats is a fact which Danish politicians and civil servants are proud to proclaim; in more quiet moments, however, they are equally proud to assert that they have been successful to secure informally what other nations use formal caveats to ensure (Interview Troldborg, 2010; Interview Bisserup, 2010).

Acquiring a distinct area of operations was one way to gain control of the way in which Danish troops were used. Another was to place Danish officers in various British headquarters in order to ensure information about British intentions and to have an officer in place to influence planning in ways preferable to the Danes (Interview Helsø, 2010). At the personal level, the commanding Danish officer worked hard to ensure that his British superiors appreciated how the Danish units could be put to best use – one Danish commander termed this his 'psyops' towards the British (Interview Mathiesen, 2010).

Power in the Anglo-Danish relationship was thus situationally defined. The British task-force commander had to negotiate with his Danish subordinate about how to use the Danish troops, and in these discussions in theatre the foreign ministries in London and Copenhagen was always just off-stage. Secondly, the relationship between the Danish army units deployed and their British counterparts depended a lot on the nature of these units. For a while the Danish contingent was the heaviest in theatre and that made the Danish force attractive to the British commanders (Interview Mathiesen, 2010). It seems that Danish mechanised infantry had a better relationship to UK mechanised infantry, than the Danish Dragon reconnaissance unit first deployed to Helmand had it with the British paratroopers then deployed (Johannesen, 2009; Tootal, 2009). As Lave and Wenger would expect, the Danish contingent's influence within the task force depended on the missions the task force undertook and the role the Danes played in these missions.

While the Danes created considerable room for manoeuvre in relation to the British Task Force, the Danish contingent was still an apprentice. As the Danes had wanted, the British treated the Danish battle group as any other unit in the task force, but that also meant that the British commander was not always interested in the effects of Task Force operations within the Danish area. This might be one reason why Danish officers complained that they were treated with 'British arrogance' by the Task Force headquarter. The Danes thus repeatedly complained about adverse effects of British operations on the Danish area, to little effect. On the same note, the Task Force commander often requested Danish troops for operations outside the Danish area that left the Danish positions weakened. When the Danish troops returned to their own bases they thus had to clear the area for the Taliban fighters that had returned while the Danish soldiers were away on British-led missions (Jakobsen and Thruelsen, 2011).

## From Afghanistan to Libya

On the operational and on the organizational level the Danish army openly embraced the role as an apprentice of the British in Afghanistan. On the strategic and political level decision-makers in Copenhagen had a lot to learn as well. However, this learning process was less straightforward, than the one which the Danish contingent went through in Helmand. First of all it was difficult to establish what the Danish government should learn by the engagement in Afghanistan. In many ways the Kingdom's grand strategic goals were achieved when the Danish contingent arrived in Helmand and would remain so as long as the troops remained in Afghanistan (Jakobsen, 2011a, 2011b). By taking part in the operation Denmark was proving itself to be a willing and able member of the Alliance; a point that was emphasized by the high number of casualties the Danish forces sustained from 2007. Since the organizational goal for the army was to learn from the British, the armed forces did not demand a set of operational end-states as a condition for success. Being in Afghanistan was an end in itself for the Foreign Ministry, the Ministry of Defence and Defence Command Denmark. Setting priorities for the troops deployed was to a large extent left for the individual commanders (Interview Mathiesen, 2010; Rasmussen, 2011).

If the Danish preference thus was for muddling through, the Danes had picked just the right senior partner. The House of Commons Public Administration Committee thus concluded that the British had no systematic way of doing strategy (House of Commons, 2010). This was reflected in the British approach to the war in Helmand. As one senior British officer sulkily concluded, 'we went into Helmand with our eyes closed and our fingers crossed' (Haynes, 2010). The chief of the British army at the time of the initial deployment to Helmand told *The Times* that he had no idea why Helmand was chosen as the theatre of operations. According to *The Times* the British were warned by the Americans that the British Task Force was too small for the job, but unable to field more troops at a time when the UK army was still engaged in Iraq, the British went ahead with the piecemeal deployment of only 4,000 troops (*The Times*, 2010). While the Danes had no immediate interest in doing strategy, they ended up with a coalition-partner who was not able to do strategy.

In that situation practice took over. The strength of Lave and Wenger's theory of situated learning is that it is able to account for learning in situations where 'the student' has no formal intention about being taught, but where the situation becomes the teacher. In Afghanistan, the Danes learned to do strategy, not because they wanted to, but because the situation left them with little choice. In 2008 there was widespread disquiet with the mission in Afghanistan in Armed Forces (Interview Helsø, 2010) and for the first time opinion polls showed a negative trend. This challenged the wide majority in Parliament behind the mission at the same time as it questioned the wisdom of the government's belief that showing up was a success in itself. An Afghanistan strategy and a Helmand plan were thus developed (Rasmussen, 2011).

This strategy work made it possible to align cosmopolitan and defencist goals. Aid to building schools and promoting women's rights were part of a plan which also defined military benchmarks in Helmand. Thus cementing the political consensus, the plan set the 'afghanisation' of the conflict as the end goal of the Danish military effort. The Helmand plan was in many ways a flawed document. The need to talk to a cosmopolitan as well as a defencist constituency made it difficult to integrate civilian and military means into a coherent campaign plan. The Danish plan was a de facto subset of the British Helmand Road Map, and thus it was difficult for Copenhagen to be more specific than London was able to. Despite its flaws the fact that a plan was made at all was a revolution in the Danish approach to military affairs. It was the first time that Danish civil servants and generals actually produced a strategy and the first time such a strategy defined benchmarks that placed the military endeavour as a part of a coherent plan with military as well as civilian elements (Rasmussen, 2011). This will have long-term effects on the way in which the Foreign Ministry and the Ministry of Defence does business. In 2009, the Foreign Ministry was reorganized in order to be able to integrate security policy and development issues with the stated aim of thus being better able at operating in Afghanistan. At the same time the ministry set up a Policy Planning section to strengthen its ability to formulate strategy. In 2012, Defence Minister Hækkerup proposed that the Ministry of Defence was to be merged with Defence Command Denmark in order to strengthen the Ministry's ability exercise its strategic responsibilities.

The engagement in Afghanistan thus made Denmark more willing and able to participate in Alliance operations. This was demonstrated in March 2011 when Parliament voted unanimously to contribute F-16s to NATO operations in Libya. Not only did Parliament expedite the matter in a day; the air force had the planes in the air by 6 am the next morning. Six F-16s flew from Skydstrup Airbase to Signonella airbase in Sicily loaded with ordnance ready to be deployed right after arrival (Rex, 2011). This demonstrated a willingness to take part in missions and ability to do so at very short notice that had simply not being a part of neither Danish defence policy nor Danish force planning before Afghanistan. During operation Unified Protector the six Danish F-16s contributed around 10 per cent of the total number of strike sorties. Again, the fact that the Danish contribution arrived with no formal caveats made it possible for the Allied commanders to use the planes in a large number of missions. Once again, Denmark preferred to keep the government's reservations informal – once such means was to place a Danish military lawyer in the coalition's headquarter to approve the targets assigned to the Danish planes. Following a week when the Danish planes had been especially active the US Secretary of Defence and the Chairman of the Joint Chief of Staff testified before Congress. Thus it seems plausible that Admiral Mullen was particularly referring to the Danish contribution when he told Senator John McCain: 'Our allies – Denmark, Belgium, France, the U.K., Canada – along with us, have actually been very, very impressive, over the course of the last week' (US Senate, 2011). *The Times* described the Danish pilots as 'Tøp Guns' (*The Times*, 2011).

What an apprentice wants the most is recognition from the master and the journeymen. During the Libya operation Denmark achieved recognition for its willingness and ability to contribute to the operations. In fact cursory evidence suggests that high-level officials were surprised at just how much praise they got from the allies. For ten years contributing to the Alliance's operation had been a way to transform the Danish military and score foreign policy points especially with the United States. This policy came full circle when in November 2011 the NATO Secretary General congratulated the new Danish Prime Minister Helle Thorning-Schmidt on the Danish engagement in Libya, which the Secretary General described as the culmination of many years of active Danish engagement. That Secretary General was of course Anders Fogh Rasmussen who as Danish Prime Minister from 2001–2010 had made an active engagement a cornerstone of his foreign policy (Hjortdal, 2011).

## Journeyman

An apprentice becomes a journeyman when he or she has acquired the skills of the trade and learned the ways of the workshop. At that point the apprentice is no longer a peripheral participant, but one of those who can legitimately define the trade. Lave and Wenger do not believe that a journeyman necessarily has more power than an apprentice – the power relationships of the workshop are situational and relational. When the social democrats came to power in 2011, the new government did emphasize that Denmark was a 'small country' (Prime Minister's Office, 2011, p. 39).

This was a cosmopolitan statement meant to signal a departure from the previous government's defencist focus on Denmark as global power. Yet, Helle Thorning-Schmidt's government also wanted to 'punch above' Denmark's weight as an 'active and responsible' country. A very important part of the defence reforms the new government undertook was to maintain Danish ability to deploy troops even when the defence budget was cut more than 10 per cent. Denmark was still willing and able. 'We need not ask ourselves whether we will face the world's problems,' Minister of Defence Nick Hækkerup said when he assumed office, 'the question is how we face the world, which we are a part of. Do we make a stand or will we attempt to be a Lilliput nation hiding from the world? We have taken a stand since the fall of the Berlin Wall and we will continue to do so' (Brøndum, 2011).

With the experience from Afghanistan and Libya the Danish armed forces had acquired the skills of expeditionary warfare. The Danish government and Parliament was not as well versed in the strategic side of the expeditionary equation as the troops they committed to combat. Unfortunately, this was a problem they shared with many other NATO-countries and thus a fact which confirmed that they had learned the ways of the workshop – the good as well as the bad.

The Danish status as journeyman was confirmed by the fact that the former Prime Minister Anders Fogh Rasmussen was NATO's Secretary General. Rasmussen's appointment as Secretary General was in many ways a symbol of Denmark's new status. Out of loyalty to 'our man in Bruxelles' the civil servants in Copenhagen went out of their way to support the Secretary General's reform agenda which made sure that Denmark remained committed to 'smart defence'.

When an apprentice becomes a journeyman, he or she realizes that the new status entails new responsibilities and new skills to learn. In spite of the highly capable forces Denmark had developed, the country could only deploy a battalion, a number of frigates and 16 F-16s. These forces were of high quality, but quantity matters as well. Because of its very limited military resources Denmark would never become a NATO great power even if it had graduated to the core of the Alliance. Denmark had begun its process as an apprentice in the expectation that European geopolitics were defined by a number of concentric circles (Wæver, 1992; Defence Commission, 1998) in which each circle defined one of the European organizations (EU, NATO, OSCE, etc.). By putting political commitments and troops on the table a country was able to move from the less integrated outer circles to the fully integrated core. While Denmark might still have its reservations with regard to EU integration, it was able to compensate by committing even more to NATO (Mouritzen, 2007).

Even if one argued like Anders Fogh Rasmussen that a small country needed an off-shore balancer, this was exactly because the integration process brought Denmark closer and closer to the EU, and the power wielded by France and Germany in that organization. In 2011, these concentric circles had morphed into a number of regional and functional zones of integration that supported one another, but also increasingly worked against the notion of overall European integration. The EURO-zone was one such functional zone while the Visegrad group was a regional zone of integration. As 'smart defence' increasingly defined NATO in terms of cooperation between a number of countries on the procurement and deployment of specific capabilities, more specialized partnerships are becoming the norm. The Danish armed forces benchmarking in terms of British capabilities was an early recognition of this. Yet, the Danish NATO policy presupposed that Denmark was one contributor amongst others, instead of regarding Denmark as a part of one or more networks that contributed to the overall effort. If Denmark wants to maintain its status as a 'journeyman' in NATO, the Danish government will have to continue to develop its ability to network the Danish armed forces with partners.

## Bibliography

Barnes, B. (2001) 'Practice as Collective Action', in T. R. Schatzki, K. K. Cetina and E. von Savigny (eds) *The Practice Turn in Contemporary Theory* (London: Routledge), pp. 17–28.

Brøndum, C. (2011) 'Forsvarsminister overrasker med stålsat tale', *Berlingske*, 3 October 2011, http://www.b.dk (homepage), date accessed 6 December 2011.

Cain, J. P. (2008) 'Danish Parliamentary Elections: Rasmussen's to Lose', US Embassy Cables Related to Denmark, Randoom, 2011. Available at: http:

//friism.com/us-embassy-cables-related-to-denmark, date accessed 6 December 2011.

Defence commission (1998) *The Danish Defence Commission of 1997*, *Defence for the Future*, English Summary (Copenhagen: Statens Information).

Gates, R. (2011) 'The Security and Defense Agenda (Future of NATO)', http://www.defense.gov (homepage), date accessed 6 December 2011.

Gebicke, S. and Magid, S. (2010) *Lessons from Around the World: Benchmarking Performance in Defence* (Copenhagen and San Francisco: McKinsey and Company).

Danish Defence (2006) *Forsvarets Mission og Vision* (Copenhagen: Danish Armed Forces).

Haynes, D. (2010) 'They Went to Helmand with Eyes Shut and Fingers Crossed', *The Times*, 9 June 2010.

Heurlin, B. (1993). 'Nye prioriteringer i dansk udenrigspolitik', in N. Pedersen and C. Thune (eds) *Dansk udenrigspolitisk årbog 1993* (Copenhagen: Dansk Udenrigspolitisk Institut/Jurist- og økonomforbundets forlag), pp. 30–50.

Hjortdal, M. (2011) 'Helle Thorning får roser af Fogh', *Politiken*, 4 November 2011, http://i.pol.dk (homepage), date accessed 6 December 2011.

House of Commons (2010) House of Commons Public Administration Select Committee, 2010. *Who Does UK National Strategy?* First Report of Session 2010–11, HC 435, 18 October.

Interview with Lieutenant General Bjørn Bisserup, 7 June 2010.

Interview with General (ret.) Jesper Helsø, 8 April 2010.

Interview with Colonel H. C. Mathiesen, 26 May 2010.

Interview with Permanent Secretary (ret.) Anders Troldborg, 14 April 2010.

Jakobsen, P. V. (2011a) 'Forsvarets deltagelse i farligemissioner giver prestige, indflydelse og sikkerhed', http://www.dkvs.dk/debat.asp (homepage), date accessed 8 December 2011.

Jakobsen, P. V. (2011b) *Fra Ferie til Flagskib. Forsvaret og de internationale operationer* (København: Forsvarsakademiet).

Jakobsen, P. V, and Thruelsen, P. D. (2011) 'Clear, Hold, Train: Denmark's Military Operations in Helmand 2006–2010', in N. Hvidt and H. Mouritzen (eds) *Danish Foreign Policy Yearbook 2011* (Copenhagen: Danish Institute for International Studies), pp. 78–105.

Johannesen, L. U. (2009) *De danske tigre [In Danish: The Danish Tigers]* (Copenhagen: Gyldendal).

Lave, J. and Wenger, E. (1991) *Situated Learning. Legitimate Peripheral Participation* (Cambridge: Cambridge University Press).

Lykketoft, M. (2003) 'Fogh dyrker falsk aktivisme', *Berlingske*, 20 May, http://www.b.dk (homepage), date accessed 5 June 2012.

Mearsheimer, J. J. (2001) *The Tragedy of Great Power Politics* (New York: W. W. Norton).

Mouritzen, H. (2007) 'Denmark's Super Atlanticism', *Journal of Transatlantic Studies*, Vol. 5, No. 2, pp. 155–167.

Prime Minister's Office (2003) *Prime Minister Anders Fogh Rasmussen's Speech at the Royal Danish Defence Academy*, 31 October 2003, http://www.stm.dk (homepage), date accessed 30 January 2012.

Prime Minister's Office (2011) *Et Danmark der står sammen*, http://www.stm.dk (homepage), date accessed 6 December 2011.

Rasmussen, A. F. (2003) 'Hvad skal det nytte?', *Berlingske Tidende*, 25 March 2003.

Rasmussen, M. V. (2005) ' "What's the use of it?": Danish Strategic Culture and the Utility of Armed Force', *Cooperation and Conflict*, Vol. 40, No. 1, pp 67–89.

Rasmussen, M. V. (2011) *Den Gode Krig?* (Copenhagen: Gyldendal).

Rex, A. (2011) 'Dansk deltagelse i Operation Unified Protector', Presentation at the Center for Military Studies, University of Copenhagen, 23 May.

Ringsmose, J. (2008) *Frihedens Assuranceprømie: Danmark, NATO ogforsvarsbudgetterne* (Odense: Syddanskuniversitetsforlag).

Ringsmose, J. and Rynning, S. (2008) 'The Impeccable Ally? Denmark, NATO, and the Uncertain Future of Top Tier Membership', in N. Hvidt and H. Mourtizen (eds) *Danish Foreign Policy Yearbook 2008* (Copenhagen: Danish Institute for International Studies), pp. 55–84.

Rynning, S. (2003) 'Denmark as a StrategicActor? Danish Security Policy after September 11', in P. Carlsen and H. Mouritzen (eds) *Danish Foreign Policy Yearbook 2003* (Copenhagen: Danish Institute for International Studies), pp. 23–47.

Swidler, A. (1986) 'Culture in Action: Symbols and Strategies', *American Sociological Review*, Vol. 51, No. 2, pp. 273–286.

*The Times* (2011) 'Denmark's Tøpguns Trump RAF in Libya', *The Times*, 29 September 2011.

*The Times* (2010) 'US Warned Britain: You Must Send More Troops to Afghanistan', *The Times*, 9 June 2010.

Tootal, S. (2009) *Danger Close. Commanding 3 Para in Afghanistan* (London: John Murray).

US Senate (2011) Committee on the Armed Services, *Hearing To Receive Testimony on Operation Odyssey Dawn and The Situation in Libya*, 31 March 2011, http://armed-services.senate.gov (homepage), date accessed 6 December 2011.

Villaume, P. (2009) *Aktivisme – eller tilpasning?* Rådet for International Konfliktløsning, http://riko.nu (homepage), date accessed 6 December 2011.

Wæver, O. (1992) 'Nordic Nostalgia: Northern Europe after the Cold War', *International Affairs*, Vol. 68, No. 1, pp. 77–102.

# 14
# Norway: Militarily Able but Politically Divided

*J. H. Matlary*

Prior to the NATO summit in Chicago Jon Stewart at 'The Daily Show' hosted the American NATO-ambassador Ivo Daalder. Asking whether any NATO members increased their defence budget in times of austerity, he replied: 'Norway'. 'So this is the new great power?' said Stewart, 'are we going to attack them next?'

In fact Norway, with its oil riches, was the only member state that could report a slight increase in its defence budget for 2012, as was also the case for 2011. This stood out in the company of so many NATO allies that reduced their, this time also including the United States.

In this chapter, we will analyse Norway's political willingness and military ability to contribute to sharp operations.

Norway was one of the founding members of NATO and has maintained close ties to the United States throughout the history of the alliance. In the Cold War one used to speak about an 'alliance in the alliance', akin to the British 'special relationship', and there was a very integrated relationship also on the materiel side. Norway maintained a policy of close integration with the United States while cooperating with the USSR when possible; and had a specific policy of self-restraint in order to defuse potential tensions. Norwegian governments were sometimes in disagreement with the United States – alliance solidarity was not one of automaticity (Eriksen and Pharo, 1997, especially Chapter 3).

After the Cold War the close transatlantic relationship continued, vested in consensus across the political party spectrum. The exception to this broad consensus on the importance of NATO and US leadership of the latter was the left-Socialist Party SV, formerly SF. As we shall see later in this chapter, SV is the main explanation with regard to political unwillingness to contribute in the few cases where this has been the case.

In this chapter, I proceed as follows: First I analyse the variable 'military capability', then I turn to the variable 'political willingness'. I define 'military capability' as the ability to deploy rapidly with state-of-the-art capabilities and to inter-operate with the leading states in NATO, such as the United States, United Kingdom, France, the Netherlands, Canada, Denmark, to mention the key ones. I do not go into details about the defence budget apart from a general overview at the outset.

As for 'political willingness', Norway is one of the countries that still has the FPP – the foreign policy prerogative – whereby the government can deploy troops. However, by custom Parliament is always consulted and informed, although there is no formal need for its approval. But as it holds the purse strings, it needs to be in agreement after a short while anyway.[1] The broad consensus on contributing to NATO operations was broken only by one party, SV, which paradoxically has opposed the government it has been part of since 2005 on various occasions. But also other parties have been wary of types of contributions and types of operations. As we shall see later in this chapter, the conflict lines are over alliance loyalty and UN mandates for operations. The Cold War consensus has become weakened after 1990, with clear and permanent opposition in many cases. I operationalize the concept 'political willingness' to the will to contribute what is requested and needed in sharp-end operations where major allies are involved. These can be 'coalitions of the willing', NATO or UN-operations. If Norway is asked for combat forces and sends medical personnel, this does not count as a contribution by this definition.

## Military capability

Norway was, as mentioned earlier, the only NATO country that increased its defence budget in 2012, at a time of austerity. The total defence budget for 2012 was 40.5 billion NOK (7 billion USD), where about 30 billion NOK is operating cost and about 10 billion is materiel investments (NMOD, 2012, p. 20). The budget is set to grow in the years ahead by an annual 800 million NOK.

The investment is aimed at modernization of old materiel, in the *army* new artillery (Swedish 'Archer') is being procured, as well as new heavily armoured patrol vehicles and remote weapons stations. In the *navy* procurement of new frigates has been accomplished as well as new MTBs ('Skjold class stealth'), making the Norwegian navy one of the best-equipped in NATO. The navy will also get new helicopters that will serve both the coast guard and the frigates, and 'substantial' sums will be invested in new anti-ship weapons systems (NSM – Norwegian cruise missile) (NMOD, 2012). In the *air force*, the major decision on procuring F-35 'Lightning II' was taken in 2011, and this major procurement of 56 planes will be dominant in budget discussion in the years ahead. For the immediate future, however, the upgrade of F-16s and P-3 Orion aircraft will be the main tasks.

The defence structure of Norway is a reflection of the geopolitical situation of being a small state next to Russia and of having sea areas that are six times greater than the land mass, mostly in the North. Security and defence policy therefore requires the ability to offer a *threshold of resistance* to any type of attack, and 'maintaining Norway's sovereignty, territorial integrity and political freedom of action constitutes a fundamental security interest' (NMOD, 2012, p. 8).

The goals of Norwegian defence policy is listed in this order:

> To prevent war and the emergence of various kinds of threats to Norwegian and collective security, to contribute to peace, stability, and the further development of the rule of law under the auspices of the UN, to uphold Norwegian sovereignty, rights, interests and values and to protect Norwegian freedom of action in the face of political, military, or other pressure, together with our Allies, to defend Norway and NATO against assault or attack, to protect the society against assault and attack from state and non-state actors.
> (NMOD, 2012, p. 20)

As we see, this is very traditional security and defence policy where the integrity of the state and its borders is key, and where the idea that the state may be put under pressure from foreign states is spelt out. Norwegian policy is designed with deter against transgressions of sovereignty and against pressure in terms of coercive diplomacy. Norwegian military capability must be able to deal with these traditional tasks in a very large area at sea and on land. NATO membership is therefore extremely important as a basis for deterrence, but Norwegian national capacity must be able to deal with most threats and risks alone, as there is no longer any invasion scenario in Europe. Paradoxically, as the gap between Article 5 situations and likely scenarios is greater, the demands on Norwegian capacity are also greater. In the Cold War, any strategic attack or coercive diplomacy would quickly ascend to Article 5 status, but in the present diffuse risk picture this is not so.

Unlike states on the continent, such as the Benelux and Denmark, Norway has to maintain a robust national defence structure at sea, on land and in the air. Fortunately for the country, oil revenue ensures that this is economically possible. There is an increased emphasis on the High North in government policies, to the point of describing this as 'of the greatest strategic importance to Norway' (NMOD, 2012, p. 9). Here the security aspects of heightened national interests are underlined: 'we are witnessing a gradual transformation of the global security policy landscape, which in turn underlines the need for a sharper focus on our interests in the High North' (NMOD, 2012, p. 9). It is further emphasized that NATO is very important, and that participation in international operations is key.

The armed forces, therefore, cannot abolish important capabilities. They must be able to wage conventional war as well as being able to contribute to expeditionary operations. They cannot, like Denmark, abandon submarines, or for that matter abandon any of the three services. The potential for defence integration is more limited in the Norwegian case than in states situated in the middle of the European continent.

Norway is well-heeled militarily[2] today, but what about the readiness to deploy in operations? It is one thing to have balanced forces with good equipment, but training is essential for rapid and professional deployment.

### Readiness and military contributions

Norway had a mobilization defence structure until about 2000, when major and rapid transformation towards expeditionary forces started. Yet deployment to various operations in the Cold War period went rather well. Norway has been a contributor to more than 100 operations in 40 countries after WWII (Forsvarsmuseet, 2012). Early UN operations recruited 'from the street' and the contingents had little or no training, yet deployments were quite rapid.

These international operations can be grouped in three: traditional peacekeeping until about 1990, peace enforcement and stabilization in the 1990s, and war-fighting after that. When we look at historical operations, we find a great deal of eagerness to contribute and to deploy rapidly. In the Cold War UN peacekeeping was not seen as important security and defence policy, but more as idealism and often also as an 'alternative' to the defence policy of NATO. There was a sharp political separation between UN 'do goodism' and NATO security policy in Norwegian politics and diplomacy in this period. Norway with its strong emphasis on the UN and idealism contributed to many peacekeeping operations. These were politically uncontroversial.

The largest contribution was to the allied occupation of *Germany* after the war. In the 'German Brigade' Norwegians served alongside the British for six years after the Second World War, from 1947 to 1953. More than 50,000 Norwegian conscripts served in six month rotations, making this the largest international operation to date. In this case the importation of British military materiel after the war was a key factor: the British promised Norway aid in developing its own defence structure after the war, but expected Norwegian contributions of manpower in Germany. After the occupation of Norway which lasted for five years, the country had no national army and was wholly dependent on the United Kingdom, where its exile government and King had spent the war years. As the Cold War developed, there was a need to bring the forces home in order to develop national defence (Gjeseth, 2012, pp. 180–185).

The next deployment was to *Korea* in 1951. In this case the United States asked for combat forces but received a military hospital (Leraand, 2012, pp. 352–363). Yet this contribution, like others, are deemed to have been well prepared and rapidly deployed as a main rule. Leraand makes the point that the Norwegian word *dugnad* – meaning effort made by all and mutual help – is relevant here: 'Is everything ready?' one asked. 'No', was the reply. 'Shall we go ahead anyway?' 'Yes' (Leraand, 2012, p. 363). Even if politics and bureaucracy made deployment difficult, the soldiers and officers made all efforts to deploy: 'When there is mismatch between mission and resources, the solution lies in improvisation – *dugnadsånd* – the military basic attitude: the task must be performed' (Leraand, 2012, p. 363).

In the classic UN operations there was no sharp capability beyond self-defence, as most missions were lightly armed and had mandates that stopped at self-defence. Norwegian deployments were swift, although the military structure at the time was not prepared for international operations. Both political decision-making and actual deployment went rapidly: for example, in UNEF in 1956 – the first UN force, deployed to *Gaza and Sinai* to observe the peace agreement between Egypt and Israel – saw deployment from Norway the same day parliament dealt with the issue (Leraand, 2012, p. 353). The same swiftness was evidenced in the ONUC deployment to the *Congo* in 1960, and this time there was no long lead time. Also the UNIFIL deployment in 1978 was swift, but the volunteer force, recruited from untrained reserves and 'from the street', had minimal training, only one week. This basically amounted to nothing, and the battalion that was deployed was unprepared for being attacked. It was not equipped and poorly trained, and this fact has since led to much soul-searching and public debate. The fact that 'peace keeping' could turn into war-fighting, even in self-defence, was only gradually recognized. As stated, UN operations were not thought to be dangerous and did not count as security and defence policy in the Cold War.

When the Cold War is over, NATO enters an era of using force in international operations. A new strategic concept is adopted in 1991, where internal armed conflict is a major feature, and NATO develops a rapid reaction force called the IRF (Immediate Reaction Force). Member states have to adapt to the new reality. In Norway the mobilization army did not really start restructuring towards expeditionary force until 2000 – almost ten years later. Inertia and bureaucratic interests of all sorts explain this. The fear of downsizing had to do with the long shadow of the Soviet Union – could one really believe that the invasion scenario was gone?

Norway's army bore the brunt of changes and was also the focus of expectations. The navy and the air force had operated in multinational mode in NATO throughout the Cold War, but it was the army that had to deploy to most international operations. When the war in *Bosnia* broke out in 1991, NATO eventually used some air force to quell the worst atrocities by Milosevic, but there were no land forces until IFOR in 1995, the peace enforcement operation following the Dayton accords. Norway deployed a battalion, alternating the rotation between the one professional battalion, Telemark Battalion, and conscripts trained for 12 months as general soldiers, with 6 weeks at the end of this period as mission-specific training. There was a steep learning curve, and the whole defence structure adapted to the fact that international, sharp operations were a fact of daily life. From 1998 the government integrated 'intops' into the mainstream of the defence system, and this made the set-up much more professional.[3] Now service in international operations became a gateway to one's career.

But it was *Kosovo* that really made it clear to Europeans that they had to do better than gradual adaptation to a new reality. Again the Telemark battalion was to be deployed to KFOR, but instead of four weeks it took almost four months to deploy. There was simply a need for getting ready that did not allow for rapid deployment, but COMKFOR General Sir Michael Jackson famously inquired: 'What took you so long – did you have to walk?'

Kosovo was a lesson not only for the Norwegians but for Europe. Prime Minister Tony Blair was both shocked and humiliated at the lack of European interoperability in the air, and the French–British defence cooperation in the EU started against this background.[4]

In Kosovo, however, Norway could deploy a very attractive military capacity, special forces (special operations forces – SOFs). Norwegian SOFs were among the first on the ground there, and ever since the SOFs have been very much sought after by allies, especially the United States and the United Kingdom. These SOFs has been developed in the 1990s, and were used in the Balkans prior to Kosovo. When Operation Allied Force was under way, Norwegian SOFs were deployed in two days (Leraand, 2012, p. 303). Later the same forces have been among the most desired by allies in Afghanistan.

### War-fighting in Afghanistan and Libya

Norway was, like most allies, *tous Americans* on 12 September 2001, as *Le Monde* wrote. There was a unison expression of political solidarity, and this was translated into military solidarity when NAC declared that an Article 5 situation obtained. But as we know, the United States did not want a repetition of the Kosovo 'war by committee' and preferred a coalition of the willing. Norway offered several capacities to the ensuing *Operation Enduring Freedom* (OEF): Six F-16s, four Bell helicopters, one DA 20 electronic war-fighting plane, specialists in winter warfare – these were in fact SOFs – staff officers and logistics (Leraand, 2012, p. 305; see also Bøifot, 2007). Initially there was no clear mention of SOFs as these have been surrounded by the utmost secrecy in Norway, but American sources revealed that the contribution was 78, as 78 soldiers and officers were decorated by the United States (Bøifot, 2007, p. 18). They received the Navy Presidential Unit Citation, the second-highest decoration in the United States. It was the first time since the Vietnam War that it had been given to SOFs (Bøifot, 2007, p. 19).

Norway deployed SOFs to OEF three times, and they participated in major fighting under American command. The first contingent went to Kandahar and fought in Task Force K-Bar, earmarked for the hunt for Al-Qaeda. Other contributing states were Denmark, Australia, New Zealand, Turkey and Germany (Leraand, 2012, p. 307; Bøifot, 2007, p. 19). They participated among others in Operation Anaconda in March 2002 which represented intense war-fighting. Between 100 and 1,000 insurgents were killed in this operation.

Norway continued to send SOFs to Afghanistan. The second deployment was in 2003, this time apparently working more on intelligence and reconnaissance than being engaged directly. Also this time the United States was very pleased with Norwegian SOFs (Leraand, 2012, p. 308). The third deployment was in 2005, this time to Helmand where the forces tracked down Taliban and Al-Qaeda and came into much contact with the enemy. The participation in OEF was 'an occasion to show allies that Norway has the ability to deploy professional forces at short notice, of high quality, with competence to work on a high level in a multinational scenario', concludes Torunn Laugen Haaland (Haaland and Guldhav, 2004, p. 13).

Norway continued the deployments to ISAF from early 2002, *inter alia* with a multinational task force in Kabul consisting of elements from Telemark battalion. From 2005 Norway took over responsibility for PRT Maymaneh in the then peaceful Faryab province in the North. From 2006 Norway replaced the British as the quick reaction force (QRF) for all of RC North, and manned this force for two years. During this period IEDs attacks grew and the QRF saw battle on a regular basis. The unruly area of Ghwormach was added to the Norwegian 'turf' in 2009 after Norwegians had been unable to penetrate this area in hunting the Taliban due to bureaucratic difficulties. Norway has continued to deploy OMLT-instructors and operated a forward base in Ghwormach for a period, but due to frequent attacks this base was closed.

The military contributions to OEF and ISAF have included a wide range of force – from F-16s to SOFs and rapid reaction forces – and the fighting encountered has been the toughest so far for Norwegian soldiers since the few battles in the Second World War (Gjerde, 2012, pp. 312–323). Afghanistan has marked the total departure from traditional peacekeeping and represents the most difficult of COIN operations. The major deployments have been from the Norwegian army, which has gone through a major learning exercise on the job, so to speak. Colonel Ingrid Gjerde writes that 'participation in Afghanistan has increased competence in the army and strengthened operative ability' (Gjerde, 2012, p. 320), but it is also true that rotations have been far too frequent for officers in particular and that contingents have had little time to prepare, made up as they have been of elements from battalions and not by battalions *in toto*.

Come 2011 and *Libya*. The Norwegian air force is able to deploy six F-16s to Crete within 100 hours of the go-ahead from the government. The decision is taken on a Friday, the planes are deployed on Monday morning. This rapid deployment is jokingly said to be possible only on weekends where the Ministry of Defence officials are off duty and cannot meddle. In the Libyan case, the deployment was not only rapid but the Norwegians punched above their weight, as the international press reported. A senior American official said that

'Danish and Norwegian rates were significantly higher than normal' whereas Germany and Poland were chided for not contributing, also by the then Secretary of Defence Robert Gates (*Financial Times*, 2011). The burden was borne by eight allies, he reportedly said, and also named other states that did not contribute enough: Spain, Turkey and the Dutch.

Norway flew may combat sorties of great difficulty, and was able to do so because of its intense preparation over the last few years. Norway had enough ammunition for the entire mission while other, bigger states ran out (International Herald Tribune, 2011b). There were severe shortages of equipment: intelligence, logistics, targeters, aerial refuelling and so on. The United States was therefore an essential ally also in this operation where it expressly did not want a leading role. Only 14 out of 28 member states contributed, and of these only 8 carried out the actual campaign with combat assets (Hallams and Schreer, 2012). 'The operation simply exposed how little real combat power the Europeans could put into such operations, how reluctant they were collectively to commit even to something in Europe's back yard, and how great a gulf has now opened up between US and European military capacities and their relative perspectives on global security' (Clark, 2012, p. 11).

What can be concluded about Norway's military capability? The status as of 2012 is good. As we have seen, all three services are in the process of becoming well equipped and the defence budget is rising somewhat, despite international austerity. Surveying contributions to international operations, we have noticed a strong tradition of continuous participation in both UN peacekeeping operations as well as NATO operations. Deployment has been quick in most cases, many times due to '*dugnad*', getting things done despite a lack of resources and readiness in the system. Improvisation and pride in getting ready have been key elements, and also Norwegian interest in going far abroad – perhaps a legacy from both sailors and missionaries. The equipment in early missions was not always very sophisticated and soldiers had far too little preparation, but they deployed nonetheless. Learning on the job, so to speak, the military structure learnt lessons and improved. As operations became sharper, professionalism became a must. From 1998 intops became a key element of Norwegian defence policy and a major career path for officers. By this time NATO had become the main player in intops, and Norway has always contributed to NATO-led operations.

In terms of military capacity, Norway has been able to deliver to sharp-end operations and has done so, with some few exceptions.

## Politically willing?

We now turn to an analysis of Norway's willingness to contribute to sharp operations. As stated, the political consensus on the importance of NATO has been strong in Norway, but after 1990 the need for NATO has been interpreted differently: for some, the need is stronger, for others, there is less ally dependence. Whereas realists will interpret alliance dependence as greater because there is no automaticity in assistance like in the bipolar, existential threat picture of the Cold War, others will maintain that since there is no existential threat, there is no need to cater to the hegemonic ally (Østerud, 1999, p. 180). The interpretation depends on one's basic belief about the state system and how anarchic it is. We don't have to 'solve' this issue here, suffice it to notice that most Norwegian politicians have entertained the realist version of the world: alliance dependence continues to be seen as vital to Norwegian security interest. Labour Party Foreign Minister Gahr Støre underlined this as late as in May 2012: 'Norway's anchor of security, NATO, is an alliance also for the 21$^{st}$ century... art 5 about collective security is and remains our security guarantee, and likewise, the Atlantic dimension is crucial' (Støre, 2012, my translation).

With regard to strategic culture, the Cold War was one of a clear separation of UN idealism and NATO realism. Security and defence policy was in the latter category. UN operations in this period were mostly peacekeeping, not war-fighting. In Norway there was a political consensus among the major parties on the importance of NATO and its Article 5, and only the left Socialists (SV, formerly SF), was in opposition to this and to NATO membership as such. After 1990 Norway was very slow to modernize its armed forces and continued to maintain an invasion scenario. The Bosnian and Kosovo operations brought change, as we have seen, and in 1998 intops became a key feature of security and defence policy, as they were by this time also mainstream NATO activity.

In the period from 2000 to the present we see interesting changes in the patterns of support for such operations. I will argue below that this period evidences both a change of strategic culture and much more diversity than before in the political support for the use of force: ideological stances matter.

First, the *change in strategic culture*: my argument below is that Norway went through a period of denial of the war-fighting reality of intops – especially concerning ISAF – but that facts from the operation itself have finally made an impact on both public opinion and politicians.

There is no longer the general reluctance to talk about and recognize war-fighting for what it is, there is support for soldiers and decorations and ceremonies as one should expect in a country that conducts war-fighting. ISAF represents a steep learning curve for Norwegians, but the lesson seems to finally have been learnt.

In terms of strategic culture, one might place Norway in a position between the Germans and the British. The use of military force in an explicit security and defence policy has a strong standing and a long tradition, but this applies to the North and specific national interests. With regard to 'out-of-area' or global security and defence policy, there has been an emphasis on doing good in terms of humanitarian interventions. These have been optional and have not been regarded as part of security policy proper.

But the ISAF case was different, an 'eye-opener'. It has turned out to be much more war-like than previous operations. This happens while Norway had developed more and more of a 'peace culture' domestically, as a view of itself in the world. In a report from NUPI in 2007, Leira and his colleagues define this self-image as 'Norway as a peace nation, Norway as a humanitarian giant, and Norway as the best friend of the UN' (Leira et al., 2007, p. 9).

Second, the *importance of political ideology*: We can trace ideological differences between left and right, not only from the SV Party, but as a general phenomenon. SV is the most opposed to the use of force, but also the Center Party (agrarian) has reservations about intops that involve war-fighting. Further, in this period Norway had a Conservative government from 2001 to 2005, a Socialist government where SV played a strong role from 2005 to 2009, and yet another Socialist government from 2009 to the present, but one where SV plays a very small role. In the 2005–2009 government we can trace the influence of SV in the refusal of SOFs and certain other contributions to ISAF, whereas this influence is gone in the present period. We can also trace clear changes in general security and defence policy from the Conservative to the Socialist government.

These changes that vary with ideology are not major ones, but are nonetheless significant. They concern in particular the relationship to the United States under President Bush and the relationship to NATO. One may argue, but of course not prove, that the influence of SV weakened Norway's position in NATO. This may be a major reason why Norway contributed so much to the Libya operation. It was important to rectify this situation.

In the following sections, I first analyse the political willingness to contribute to operations and then conclude with an assessment of political willingness.

## Political restraints on deployments

The Norwegian government after 9/11 was non-Socialist, consisting of the Conservative Party (H), Christian-democrats (KrF) and Liberals (V). The PM was the Christian-democrat Kjell Magne Bondevik. But the elections took place on 10 September, so the Socialist government continued until October.

Like in most NATO states, the Norwegian government was in complete solidarity with the United States after 9/11. It offered a united front in NATO to fight international terrorism and supported the NAC declaration of Article 5 on 12 September. On 4 October the government decided to support the US militarily, like other NATO states.

The change of government on 19 October continued this policy line. Norwegian officers were deployed to CENTCOM in Tampa to prepare Norwegian contributions to OEF. The only dissenters politically were SV and the right-wing Progress Party that both wanted an open plenary in parliament to discuss the Norwegian contributions, thus deviating from the standard practice of classified internal committee meetings on military contributions.[5] The reasons for this were different, SV refusing to place Norwegian forces under American command and the Progress Party wanting a bigger role for Parliament in the sending of troops. As mentioned above, Norway enjoys the FPP, but governments consult the party leaders and the foreign relations committee regularly, and it is considered customary law that this be so.[6] The Progress Party fully supported the United States and is the keenest party on alliance loyalty, but from the vantage point of being outside of government, it wanted a role in the process.

The contributions made to OEF are detailed previously. The SOFs were not controversial at all under the new non-Socialist government, they operated in Helmand under American command and were highly decorated. Only SV voted against the contributions (Bøifot, 2007, p. 17).

The issue of supporting the US-led coalition that attacked Iraq in 2003 was, however, controversial both inside the new Norwegian government and in the Norwegian political landscape in general. Prime Minister Bondevik was very sceptical to the Bush policy on Iraq, whereas both the foreign minister and the defence minister, both from the Conservative Party, were much more positive. A debate developed on whether a new UN mandate was necessary, which ended in 'victory' for the Prime

Minister, but prior to this he got entangled in a debate on whether Norway would accept an attack if a UN mandate were given. The Labour Party leader Jagland stated that a mandate must be accepted – legality implies legitimacy – whereas Bondevik disagreed. This debate showed that Labour was ready to support the Iraq War if a mandate was produced and that the Christian-democrats were quite averse to the use of force. The mandate debate became irrelevant when no new mandate was agreed to, but we can see ideological differences between the Christian-democrats and the conservatives within the government. The dilemma between alliance loyalty and public opinion, opposed to the war, persisted. Prime Minister Bondevik finally had to make a personal telephone call to President Bush about the matter, explaining why Norway did not side with him on Iraq (Engelstad, 2011). Norway contributed to the Iraq stabilization mission once there was a UN mandated, primarily with engineers. This contribution was withdrawn when Stoltenberg became Prime Minister again in 2005.

As we have seen, Norway contributed sharp capacities to OEF, most notably SOFs who fought in Helmand with the Americans. These contributions were opposed by SV, and sometimes questioned by politicians from the Centre Party where the Party Leader Åslaug Haga expressed dismay when deployed F-16s actually dropped bombs: 'We have been active bombing Hekmatayar, and I fear that Norway now can be seen as an actor in internal conflicts in Afghanistan, something which can endanger Norwegian humanitarian workers', she said (NTB, 2003). We could deploy planes, but not use them. This attitude – that military capacities are nice and civilian – can also be found in the Christian-Democratic Party where the then Party Leader Valgerd S. Haugland famously said during the Kosovo operation – when the party was in government – 'I do not like bombs' (Skjervøy, 1999). We have also seen Prime Minister Bondevik from the same party being very much opposed to the Iraq War. Thus, there are three parties in the Norwegian political landscape with a reluctant attitude to the actual use of force, but SV has a principled stance against what it calls 'offensive' use of force, NATO-membership, and American command of Norwegian forces.

The new Socialist government in 2005 announced changes to security policy, communicated directly to President Bush by the new Prime Minister Jens Stoltenberg. After this telephone call he was not invited to the customary visit to the White House as long as President Bush was in office. Explicitly writing that Norway is to be a 'distinct peace nation' in the government declaration (Regjeringen, 2005, p. 5), no doubt to please SV; the changes amounted to a criticism of US policy: the contributions to Iraq would be withdrawn, as a UN mandate would be required for all operations, OEF contributions would be discontinued, Norwegian contributions to ISAF would be in the North only. Norway would contribute more F-16s, however. The latter contribution was met with resistance from SV – then in government – which staged a demonstration against its own government – itself (!) – outside Parliament.

SV, true to its ideological basis, continued to protest against ongoing operations and tried to limit them even when in government. The SOFs in Afghanistan were a particular problem for the party, which operates with a notion of offensive versus defensive use of force. The latter is acceptable, it is self-defence and the party entertains an almost comically tough stance on the need for strong defence of Norway and talks about 'national interests' in the North. Socialist and therefore internationalist, one should expect the party to embrace humanitarian intervention as a 'force for good' in the world, but it is instead very wary of international operations, akin to the deeply conservative and nationalist Centre Party, the agrarians. Also they want defence at home but no use of force abroad, and try to distinguish between fighting and non-fighting down to interfering with military capacities on the ground: Norway may deploy F-16s, but they may not drop any bombs, as Haga of the Agrarians said. The same issue made the SOPs a problem for SV: they are close to the Americans and they actually use force.

In the first Stoltenberg government, SV played an important role, and since it was the first time the party was in government ever, it was vital to make this experiment work. Labour therefore ceded to SV in its opposition to much of the security policy in order to avoid the impression that Labour could dictate. After all, anti-NATO stances formed the core of SV Party ideology. The result was that SV resistance to SOFs in particular opened for the Norwegian government's 'no's' to two NATO requests for such troops, and eventually also the caveat that the SOFs that went to Afghanistan were not allowed to operate in the south. There was a curious debate about this where this caveat was a 'red line' for SV, also telling the world that the Norwegians were not ready to assume the risk that other allies assume. The Norwegian caveat of not sending any troops to the dangerous South was negative for Norway's traditional place in NATO's 'inner circle', something which diplomats and opposition commented on in private.

SV imposed a demand on the Labour majority that a NATO request for SOFs be refused in 2006. The Labour Party finally accepted this demand, and the request was denied. When NATO made the same request a month later – to underline the point about alliance solidarity – the government again said no. The SOFs were finally sent to Afghanistan again at a later time, but with the caveat that they could only operate in Kabul. The academic literature on this concludes that keeping the government together trumped the Labour Party's initial priority of accepting NATO's request:

> the focus for the government's Afghanistan policy...developed into keeping the government together. SV was given concessions with regard to Norwegian contributions to Afghanistan. This did not lead to a radical change in Norwegian Afghanistan-policy, but definitively to an adjustment of it.
> (Bøifot, 2007, p. 64, my translation)

This finding is corroborated by Oma. She concludes her study of the impact of SV in this question thus. 'The hypothesis that it has not been possible to contribute entirely as desired by NATO because of the need to keep the government together, is clearly brought out.... The Labour Party has had to accept influence from SV in security policy' (Oma, 2008. p. 99).

The reluctance to award the highest military decoration to war heroes from the Afghanistan mission also seems to be due to SV resistance in the government, which had two petitions for such awards on its table (Bakkeli and Johnsen, 2008). The Defence Spokesman of the party, Bjørn Jacobsen, stated that he is 'against arranging decoration ceremonies for the awarding of honours' (Bakkeli and Johnsen, 2008). This rather revealing statement was never corrected by the defence minister. The SOFs were finally awarded the Military Cross in 2011, several years after having been recommended for such by the then Chief of Defence, General Sverre Diesen. One of the officers, Trond Bolle, had by then been killed by a car bomb and thus did not experience this honour, which his little son and wife received on his behalf. The tardiness on the part of the government in deciding on the decorations was conspicuous.

The first Stoltenberg government also tried to find a suitable UN operation for Norwegian deployment, again to be acceptable on the left. SV could stomach UN operations much better than NATO ones, and it seems that this 'name game' was politically important even though it should not have been. In 2006 preparations were suddenly made for a deployment to Darfur, but because Omar Al-Bashir refused to guarantee the safety of this operation, it came to nothing. There was no real discussion about the reasons for such a deployment, but it fit in nicely with the new government's insistence that Norway put much more priority on the UN than in the previous one. Another deployment that was also decided quickly and without much consultation with parliament was also a UN-operation, in the wake of the war in Lebanon in the summer of 2006. Norway offered a small contribution of MTBs, a deployment not motivated by real military needs, according to the then Chief of Defence General Diesen, but by the need to contribute under the UN flag (Nilsen, 2011, p. 238). He found the MTB contribution militarily useless, according to the same source.

In the first Stoltenberg government there was also a protracted reluctance to call things military by their real name. The Minister of Defence, Anne-Grete Strøm-Erichsen, talked about civilian aspects of the ISAF operation whenever possible and refused to discuss war-fighting, the warriors and military successes. When the author wrote that 'the sharp shooter aims on behalf of the government, kills on behalf of the government, but the government is not pleased', she replied that Norway has no tradition for celebrating military victories and military decorations (Matlary, 2008a, 2008b; Strøm-Erichsen, 2008). At this time a national debate in the media and academia on the lack of a warrior culture developed (Edström, Lunde and Matlary, 2009). The 'cognitive dissonance' of calling war peace, like in Orwell's '1984', was clearly present, and endless discussions about whether Norway is at war in Afghanistan ensued. The problem was not the formal-juridical one of war or not, but the self-image of Norway as a 'peace nation' and the fragility of a government with SV in its midst. Words had to be calibrated, more carefully than ammunition. As the Grenader Emil Johansen said, 'No Norwegian government has managed to convey to the Norwegian people why soldiers are sent into war in Afghanistan' (Norges Forsvar, 2012, p. 52). He even wrote a book, *Blood Brothers*, about this lack of realistic description and recognition of the war effort on the part of politicians.

Bøifot's study found that Norwegian politicians used the security argument about NATO as the main argument for ISAF contributions, but the humanitarian argument as the second. His study covers all formal political statements about ISAF from 2001 until 2008, spanning three governments (Bøifot, 2007). The significance of this is what is missing, namely, a security-related reason connected to the fight against the Taliban. This security-related reason is only stated when there are Norwegian injured and fallen, which luckily has been a very rare occurrence. But when a soldier fell in November 2007, both the prime minister and the foreign minister advanced the security reason for being in Afghanistan: '(Afghanistan) became a free zone for

Al-Qaida, something which threatened security far beyond the borders of Afghanistan, 9/11 being the most dramatic', Foreign Minister Støre said on that occasion. At the same time Prime Minister Stoltenberg wrote an op-ed in Norway's main paper *Aftenposten* where he cited security as reason no. 1 for the ISAF participation: 'Priority number one: We are there to stabilise the country and contribute to security' (Stoltenberg, 2007).

But apart from these rare cases, the security rationale is absent from the political vocabulary when related to fighting terrorism (Nordvik, 2009). It is only logical that it has to be presented when there are fallen, as one cannot justify the sacrifice of dying for anything less than either a security threat of the noblest of causes, the saving of human life. To die for a development project is hardly acceptable.

General Robert Mood of the Norwegian army argues that the Norwegian peace image stands in the way of recognizing the war-fighting that takes place in ISAF. In a large interview he stated that 'the politicians do not dare to define this as being at war. The question is whether this matters to the soldiers on the ground when the bullets fly about their ears' (Winge, 2009). The journalist adds, 'He thinks that the reluctance to talk about Norway at war is not due to the legal implications of using the term "war", but to the view we entertain of ourselves as a peace nation' (Ibid.). General Mood is concerned that there develops a 'newsspeak' about the military tool; that is what the soldiers actually do when their fight goes unrecognized by politicians and public. 'It is a very good thing that they (Norwegian soldiers in Afghanistan) succeed without losses and with minimal use of violence. I know that they can be lethally effective when they have to', he said.

The 'cognitive dissonance' that occurs when Norwegian soldiers are fighting and suffering losses and injuries and the communication about the rationale for ISAF at home, in the peace nation, is detectable, as we have seen. Former Prime Minister Bondevik called the NATO attack on Kosovo a 'campaign', and only much later admitted under pressure from officers that it was a military attack. The Socialist-left government had the added problem that it had to accommodate SV.

In 2009 a new Stoltenberg government came into office, this time without much power on the part of the SV partner. The latter had done poorly in elections and could not wield the same power as before in the coalition. It consequently lost the major post of finance minister, and stopped 'interfering' with security policy altogether. In fact, SV in the present Stoltenberg government has been mute in these questions. This is a major change, explicable by loss of power.

The Labour Party is now in full control of security and defence policy, with a new Minister of Defence, Espen Barth Eide, who is an expert in the field and who has long experience as Deputy Minister in both the MFA and the Ministry of Defence. The Labour Party along with Conservative Høyre are the two largest parties and the only ones where security and foreign affairs are major portfolios. Labour is now back to its traditional role as leader in this field, and conducts a policy that is close to NATO and where there are few if any differences between it and the Conservative Party.

Alliance loyalty is a key factor which explains the important Norwegian war-fighting contributions, and security analysis is now centred on Article 5, deterrence and the core concerns of a military alliance. The 'near abroad' of Norway is the High North, and realist analysis of strategic interests there has replaced the rhetoric of idealism of the former Stoltenberg government. Values of course still matter, but the political analysis offered by ministers Støre and Barth Eide are sophisticated, realistic and do not shrink from discussions of power and interest. The major security policy talk by Støre on 16 May 2012, serves as a case in point: It talks about the new multi-polarity, the importance of geopolitics, territorial interests and of how NATO and the United States are of an almost absolute importance to Norwegian security (Støre, 2012).

There is also a major change in strategic culture under way: the 'cognitive dissonance' discussed above is disappearing quickly. Norway 'has become familiar with using military power': in 2003 politicians were appalled when Norwegian planes dropped bombs, in 2011 the same planes drop 600 bombs on Libya and politicians are applauding (Espenes and Haug, 2012, p. 42). Likewise, in 2011 war-fighting by the SOFs was celebrated and they were decorated with the highest military honour for the first time since the Second World War, while the politicians some few years before refused to recognize their heroism and preferred to talk about humanitarian issues.

In conclusion, Norwegian strategic culture has changed in the last few years, and the catalyst for change has above all been the war in Afghanistan. Also, the rise of non-democratic great powers like China and Russia play a role. The state is back as an actor in traditional security policy. But as we have seen, domestic politics has played a key role in the first Stoltenberg government where SV influenced Norwegian NATO policy.

In the introductory chapter of this book, we discuss the literature on burden-sharing. The research findings agree on the importance of alliance dependence, but also that underlying variables here are both threat/national interest as well as national prestige. Davidson's study concluded that the latter two variables explain far more than usually thought, but he concedes that there is probably a high degree of covariance between all three (Davidson, 2011). In the Norwegian case it is clear that security policy of the geopolitical kind plays the central role in explaining contributions to burden-sharing. This is corroborated by other research and seems to be borne out by most of the examples analysed here.

Norway has, on the whole, been militarily able. It has been swift in deployments historically, although far from state-of-art in terms of military equipment and preparations in early UN operations. Today it is clearly militarily able, in all three services. Norway has also for the most part been politically willing. The exceptions to this are mostly found in the first Stoltenberg government under the influence of SV. The literature on the role of domestic factors in determining and influencing burden-sharing shows that it plays little role. Only if opposition parties use this as a platform for elections do we see a role for public opinion, but as long as the consensus among parties on security policy holds together, there is no real effect of public opinion, be it negative or positive (Krebs, 2010; Davidson, 2011).

In the Norwegian case it was not the opposition that opposed, but a party in the government coalition. We have seen that SV was influential in security policy for as long as it was powerful in the coalition, but that it lost all influence in this policy area when it lost general standing. We can conclude that Labour put government survival as their priority no. 1 in this period, but that it quickly returned to 'normal' Norwegian NATO policy afterwards. SV has not had any lasting impact on Norwegian security and defence policy. On the contrary, the notion of Norway as a particular kind of 'peace nation' has all but disappeared and there is no celebration of war heroes for the first time since 1945.

As we have seen, being in the inner circle of the alliance matters much, and the Libya contribution must be understood in this light. With a UN mandate, a real humanitarian cause, the main variables co-varied, to the delight of the Labour Party, and there was no political resistance at all to the sharp contribution offered.

Norway showed its political willingness and military ability in Libya. This role is also the most common we have played in NATO. There is not one NATO-operation in the history of the alliance without a Norwegian contribution. As Jan Tore Nilsen points out, 'the strategic thinking in Norway has been surprisingly stable and is to a great extent based on the same security policy logic as before...a perusal of government documents in the period from 1998 to 2006 reveal a surprising continuity... Norway has to take the Russian neighbour into account' (Nilsen, 2011, p. 205, my translation).

Geopolitics and NATO's Article 5 guarantee are the perennial elements of Norwegian security and defence policy and explain the political willingness to contribute.

## Notes

1. The FPP is found in the constitution, para 26.
2. The army thus maintains heavy battle tanks (Leopard II) as well as the smaller CV-90 armoured infantry fighting vehicle. The latter were used in Afghanistan. The army as well as the navy has developed SOFs that have played very important roles in international operations. The navy is as said, very well equipped at present. It has five new frigates (Fridtjof Nansen Class, built in Spain at the IZAR works in Ferrol) and six MTBs of the Skjold Class (built in Mandal, Norway), one ice reinforced coast guard ship (Svalbard class) and a number of other that are on constant patrol in the Barents sea. The submarines are old (6 Ula Class) and will have to be replaced in the coming years, this being the next major investment after the F-35s. The frigates will get new NH-90 helicopters, these are currently phased in. In addition to the regular navy, there are as said SOFs and also a rapid deployment naval ranger command. The air force is equipped with 57 F-16s, 12 sea king helicopters for search and rescue, 6 maritime patrol aircraft, 4 Hercules transport aircraft, NASAMS anti-air batteries, helicopters, etc. The major investment is as said the new F-35s.
3. NMOD (1999) was a turning point. Hitherto intops had been a peripheral activity for the officer; now it was the key thing. This naturally had everything to do with the fact that NATO was conducting intops and that they were no longer mere peace keeping, but increasingly war-fighting.
4. See Matlary (2009) for an analysis of the reasons behind the UK-French St Malo cooperation and the development of 'autonomous' European military capacity.
5. The Norwegian parliamentary foreign relations committee, DDUK, has secret meetings as the standard. A minority of a certain size can demand open proceedings in the plenary. The frequency of such is small, but increasing, see Sjåstad (2006).
6. For a discussion of this legal question, see Eriksen (2006).

## Bibliography

Bakkeli, T. and Johnsen, A. B. (2008) 'SV misliker krigsmedaljer. Vil ikke gi utmerkelse til soldater', *VG*, 8 December 2008.
Bøifot, E. (2007) 'Det norske militære engasjementet i Afghanistan: idealisme eller egeninteresse?', Master Thesis (Oslo: The Norwegian Defence University College).

Clark, M. (2012) 'The Making of Britain's Libya Strategy', in A. Johnson and S. Mueen (eds) *Short War, Long Shadow* (London: RUSI, London).
Davidson, J. (2011) *America's Allies and War: Kosovo, Afghanistan, and Iraq* (Basingstoke: Palgrave Macmillan).
Edström, H., Lunde, N. T. and Matlary, J. H. (eds) (2009) *Krigerkultur i en fredsnasjon* (Oslo: Abstrakt Forlag).
Engelstad, A. M. (2011) 'What Determines Norwegian Participation in International Military Operations in the New Millenium?', Master Thesis (Oslo: University of Oslo).
Eriksen, C. (2006) 'Utenrikspolitisk praksis og norsk rett', in B. K. Fonn, I. B. Neumann and Ole Jacob Sending (eds) *Norsk Utenrikspolitisk Praksis: Aktører og prosesser* (Oslo: Cappelen Akademisk Forlag), pp. 97–112.
Eriksen, K. E. and Pharo, H. Ø. (1997) *Kald krig og internasjonalisering, 1949–1965*, Vol. 5, Norsk Utenrikspolitikks Historie (Oslo: Universitetsforlaget).
Espenes, Ø. and Haug, K. E. (2012) 'Norge er blitt vant til å bruke makt', *Norges Forsvar*, May 2012.
*Financial Times* (2011) 'Gates Accuses NATO Members of Failing to Act in Libya Air War', *Financial Times*, 9 June 2011.
Forsvarsmuseet (2012) *Intops: Norske soldater, internasjonale operasjoner 1947–2012*, Forsvarsmuseets skrifter No. 9 (Oslo: Forsvarsmuseet).
Gjerde, I. (2012) 'Ti år i Afghanistan – ti år for Hæren', in *Forsvarsmuseet: Intops: Norske soldater, internasjonale operasjoner 1947–2012*, Forsvarsmuseets skrifter No. 9 (Oslo: Forsvarsmuseet).
Gjeseth, G. (2012) 'Til Tyskland – for freden', in *Forsvarsmuseet: Intops: Norske soldater, internasjonale operasjoner 1947–2012*, Forsvarsmuseets skrifter No. 9 (Oslo: Forsvarsmuseet).
Krebs, S. (2010) 'Elite Consensus as a Determinant of Alliance Cohesion: Why Public Opinion Hardly Matters for NATO-led Operations in Afghanistan', *Foreign Policy Analysis*, Vol. 6, No. 3, pp. 191–215.
Haaland, T. H. and Guldhav, E. (2004) *Bruk av norske styrker i kampen mot internasjonal terrorisme* (Oslo: The Norwegian Institute for Defence Studies).
Hallams, E. and Schreer, B. (2012) 'Towards a "post-American" Alliance? NATO Burden-sharing after Libya', *International Affairs*, Vol. 88, No. 2, pp. 313–327.
*International Herald Tribune* (2011a) 'Norway to Reduce Libya Airstrike Role', *International Herald Tribune*, 10 May 2011.
*International Herald Tribune* (2011b) 'Libya Role Revealed NATO Deficiencies', *International Herald Tribune*, 22 October 2011.
Leira, H. et al. (2007) *Norske selvbilder og norsk utenrikspolitikk* (Oslo: NUPI).
Leraand, D. (2012) 'Militær Evne', in *Forsvarsmuseet: Intops: Norske soldater, internasjonale operasjoner 1947–2012*, Forsvarsmuseets skrifter No. 9 (Oslo: Forsvarsmuseet).
Matlary, J. H. (2008a) 'Jobb på liv og død', *VG*, 6 November 2008.
Matlary, J. H. (2008b) 'Kriger i kamuflasje', *VG*, 23 November 2008.
Matlary, J. H. (2009) *European Union Security Dynamics* (Basingstoke: Palgrave Macmillan).
Nilsen, J. T. (2011) 'Strategi og politiske prosesser', in H. Edstrøm and P. Ydstebø (eds) *Militærstrategi på norsk: En innføring* (Oslo: Abstrakt Forlag).

NMOD (1999) *Tilpasning av Forsvaret til deltakelse i internasjonale operasjoner* (Oslo: Ministry of Defence).

NMOD (2012) *Facts and Figures. Norwegian Defence 2012* (Oslo: Ministry of Defence).

Nordvik, A. M. (2009) 'Så sivilt som mulig – så militært som nødvendig: en analyse av Stoltenberg II regjeringens legitimering avden norske innsatsen i Afghanistan', Master Thesis (Oslo: University of Oslo).

Norges Forsvar (2012) 'Sterke ord fra veteran', *Norges Forsvar*, May 2012.

NTB (2003) 'Frykter at Norge kan dras inn i afghansk maktkamp', NTB, 28 January 2003.

Oma, I. (2008) *Internasjonal militær deltagelse*, Master's Thesis, University of Oslo.

Østerud, Ø. (1999) *Globaliseringen og nasjonalstaten* (Oslo: Ad notam Forlag).

Regjeringen (2005) *Plattform for regjeringssamarbeidet mellom Arbeiderpartiet, Sosialistisk Venstreparti og Senterpartiet 2005–09*, https://regjeringen.no (Homepage), date accessed 2 June 2012.

Sjaastad, A. (2006) 'Stortinget som utenrikspolitisk organ', in B. K. Fonn, I. B. Neumann and Ole Jacob Sending (eds), *Norsk Utenrikspolitisk Praksis: Aktører og prosesser* (Oslo: Cappelen Akademisk Forlag), pp. 19–47.

Skjervøy, A. (1999) 'Leiar: Bomber og hån', *Dag og Tid*, 22 April 1999.

Stoltenberg, J. (2007) 'Derfor er Norge i Afghanistan', *Aftenposten*, 22 November 2007.

Støre, J. G. (2006) 'Norge som fredsnasjon – myte eller virkelighet?', Speech at Norges Fredssenter, 24 April 2006, https://regjeringen.no (Homepage), date accessed 3 June 2012.

Støre, J. G (2012): 'Suverenitet, stabilitet og samarbeid. Norsk sikkerhetspolitikk i en brytningstid', Speech at the University of Oslo, 16 May 2012, https://regjeringen.no (Homepage), date accessed 2 June 2012.

Strøm-Erichsen, A-G. (2008) 'Norsk krigsinnsats', *VG*, 17 November 2008.

Winge, Å. (2009) 'Kan denne mannen sikre fred i Midtøsten?', *Dagens Næringsliv*, 10 January 2009.

# Index

Notes: Locators followed by 'n' refer to note numbers.

Abbott, K. W., 104–5
ABM (Anti-Ballistic Missile) system, 156, 181–2
Acheson, D., 102
ACT. *see* allied command transformation (ACT)
actors, 4, 17, 46, 106, 123, 133, 180–1, 216–17, 266, 281
Afghanistan war
  Denmark's role in, 272–4
  Hungary's role in, 244–6
  ISAF in, 25, 31, 81–2, 88, 167
  NATO strategy, 81–3
  Norway in, 285–7
  transatlantic relationship and, 109–10, 112–17
*AHA* (newsletter), 72
airborne warning and control system (AWACS), 62
airspace control, 247–50
  *see also* Hungary
air war, in Libya, 33
Alliance of Civilizations. *see* Spain
alliance dependence, 3, 4, 5, 7, 13–14, 20, 244, 288, 296–7
alliance dilemma. *see* Denmark
allied command transformation (ACT), 156
Allison, G. T., 4
American power, 54, 97, 100, 118, 128
  *see also* USA, hegemony
Amery, J., 122
Anderson, D., 131
Anderson, S., 29
anti-missile defence sytem, 79, 132, 216
Al Qaeda, 147–8, 192, 195, 285–6
Aragüetes, A., 185
Arbuthnot, J., 134
Ash, T. G., 127

Asmus, R. D., 77, 163
Atlantic Council report, 174
Attlee, C., 132
AWACS. *see* airborne warning and control system (AWACS)
Aylwin-Foster, N. R. F., 130
Aznar, J., 13, 178, 192, 195

Bakkeli, T., 293
balance of power, 46, 71, 73, 124–5, 184, 264
Balcerowicz, B., 210, 213, 223, 225
Balfour, S., 196 n10, 197 n17
Balkan crisis
  America's role in, 115, 117–18
  EU's political unity, absence of, 42
  Germany in, 169
  Hungary in, 233–6, 241–5, 247, 251–3
  NATO's strategic concept, 78, 79–80
  Poland in, 213, 222–3, 227, 229
  Spain in, 179, 183, 189, 193
Ballistic Missile Treaty, 181–2
Barnes, B., 266–7
Barnes, J. E., 258 n5
Barnett, T., 183
Barry, B., 266
Barry, J., 39
Bateman, R. L., 26
Baugh, D. A., 124
Baumann, R., 164-5, 166
Baylis, J., 183
*BBC News*, 123, 135, 187, 193
Beck, U., 46, 183
Bellamy, A. J., 31
Bennett, H., 131
Berger, S., 109
Berger, T. U., 165
Bernard, J-Y., 30
Bertram, C., 170

301

Biddle, S., 136
Biden, J., 87, 237
Bielik. *see* Poland, air policing operations
Black, J., 29
Blagden, D., 90, 123
Blair, T., 18, 133–4, 284
Bland, D., 50
Bobbit, P., 136
Bohigas X., 189
Bohlen, C. E., 100
Bøifot, E., 285, 290, 293–4
Borchert, H., 61
Bosnia
　Anglo-American relationship, 127
　AWACS planes (Hungary), 241–2
　crisis management (NATO), 79–81, 104, 107
　IFOR and SFOR operations, 209, 223, 242, 284
　Norway forces in, 288
　peacemaking mission, 213
　UNPROFOR mission, 164, 210
Boustay, N., 178
Bowden, B., 197 n15
Boyer, Y., 12, 16, 18, 141–59
Bozo, F., 73, 87
BRICs (Brazil, Russia, India and China), 39
Britain
　American relationship, 127–9
　in Cold War, 132–5
　commitments, 124–7
　hegemony, 178
　imperial myths, 130–2
　nuclear policy, 132–5
　overview, 121–4
　political will, 135–7
Brockpähler, J., 76
Brøndum, C., 275
Brössler, D., 171
Brussels Treaty, 72, 100
Brzezinski, Z., 78
Bucharest Summit, 238
Bugajski, J., 237
Bumiller, E., 118 n3
Buras, P., 167

burden sharing, in NATO
　British resources, 114. *see also* Lippmann gap
　European allies and, 4–7
　existing strategic plan, 114
　German defence policy, 169
　ISAF mission, 9
　military spending, 105–6
　research findings, 296–7
　Soviet Union's demise and, 72, 77
　Spain, brokerage opportunities, 180, 183
　structural conditions, 98–104
　sustainability, lacking of, 31
　transatlantic relationship, 98–104
　US criticism, 2
　use of force, implication on, 16, 17
Burgess, L., 108
Burke, E., 193
Burns, J. F., 117
Bush, G.W. administration
　Afghanistan war, 109
　American military under, 53
　Franco-American clashes, 86
　international obligations, withdrawal from, 181–2
　Iraq War, justification, 253, 290
　missile defense (MD), in Hungary, 249–50
　Norway's relationship, 289–91
　political transition, in East, 254
　Taliban resurgence, 193
Byman, D., 9

Cain, J. P., 265
Cameron, D., 17–18, 39, 117
Canada, 45, 50–2, 111, 123, 170, 243, 262, 274, 280
Carr, E. H., 32
case studies
　Britain, 121–38
　Denmark, 262–76
　France, 141–59
　Germany, 161–74
　Hungary, 232–58
　Norway, 279–98
　Poland, 205–29
　Spain, 178–96

Index 303

CDSP. see common security and defence policy (CDSP)
Center for Strategic & International Studies (CSIS), 69
Chalmers, M., 123–4
Chicago Summit, 149, 154, 157, 241, 248, 253
Chin, W., 31
Churchill, W. S., 125
Ciechanowski, G., 212
Cimoszewicz, W., 216
Clark, M., 135, 136, 287
Clark, W., 42
Cloud, D., 188
Cohen, R., 84
Cohen, S., 183
Coker, C., 10, 37–55, 183
Cold War
  American power, 97–9, 102–4
  Britain, during, 132–5
  collective action problem, 104, 106
  creation, 72–6
  defence procurement, end of, 59
  demilitarization, Europe, 50
  Denmark, 265, 269
  European security, after, 114–16
  France, reluctant ally, 85–6, 153
  German defence and, 162–6
  Hungary in, 232, 234, 236, 238, 242, 245
  NATO forces, 62
  NATO member countries, end of, 66
  NATO, implication on, 77–9
  Norway in, 279–84, 288
  Poland, 205–7, 212, 215, 229
  post-modern European use of force, 31–2
  re-arming, Germany, 44
  Spain in, 183, 187
  transatlantic relationship, 112
Coletta, D., 13, 15, 178–96
collective action problem, 82, 99, 104–8, 220
Cologne Declaration, 42
common security and defence policy (CDSP), 39, 66, 80
Comprehensive Test Ban Treaty, 181–2
Condit, D. M., 25–6
Cooper, R., 28, 46, 48

Cortes Españolas, 198 n26
cosmopolitan states, 46
Crawford, T., 196 n10
Croft, S., 134
CSIS. see Center for Strategic & International Studies (CSIS)
Daalder, I. H., 91, 279
Dalgaard-Nielsen, A., 28, 29–30, 166
Danish Defence, 268, 270, 274
Davidson, J. W., 4–5, 297
Deák, J., 242
Defence commission, 276
Defense Industry Daily, 190
DefenceWeb, 190
De Gaulle, C., 75, 85, 147
demilitarization
  cosmopolitans, 45–9
  overview, 38–9
  status, 49–52
  value, 52–4
  war discourses, 39–45
Demmer, U., 171
Dempsey, J., 83, 89, 161
Deni, J., 182
Denmark
  activism, 265–8
  Afghanistan operations, 272–4
  Anglo-Danish relationship, 168–72
  in Cold war, 265, 269
  cosmopolitanism, 263–5
  defencism, 263–5
  Libyan operation, 262–3, 272–4
  new status, 275–6
Deporte, A. W., 74
Der Spiegel, 161
Dettke, D., 167
De Villiers, D., 197 n18
Devore, M. C., 31
De Young, K., 111
Diesen, S., 10, 57–70, 293, 294
Dixon, P., 131
DoD (US Department of Defence), 98, 114–15, 155, 192–3
domestic factors, security policy, 2, 4, 5, 17, 255, 297
Donnelly, T., 130
Dorman, A., 198-9 n32
Doyle, M. W., 31

## 304 Index

Drozdiak, W., 80
Dueck, C., 196 n5
Duffield, J., 165, 181
Duke, S., 81, 102

Echevarria II, A., 197 n19
economic crisis, 12, 38, 68, 107, 114, 142, 159
*The Economist*, 113, 187
Edmunds, T., 198–9 n32
Eggenberger, R., 61
Ellis, J. O., 109
ElMundo.es., 198 n28
Engelstad, A. M., 291
Eriksen, C., 279
Erlanger, S., 109, 112, 161
ESDP. *see* European Security and Defence Policy (ESDP)
Espenes, Ø., 296
European defence
  after Cold War, 114–16
  critcal mass, 58–61
  formal alliances, 65–8
  integration strategies, 61–5
  overview, 57–8
  rational structure, 68–9
  technology-driven cost, 58–61
European Security and Defence Policy (ESDP), 42, 66, 167
European strategic culture, 28, 42, 45
Expose, 208, 215

Farrell, T., 8
FCO. *see* Foreign and Commonwealth Office (FCO)
Feaver, P. D., 136
Federal Ministry of Defence, 168–70, 173
Fellman, S., 193
Fidler, S., 258 n5
*Financial Times*, 90, 287
Fonte, J., 47, 49
Foreign and Commonwealth Office (FCO), 150, 151
Foreign Policy Prerogative (FPP), 16–19, 280, 290
Foreign Relations of the United States (FRUS), 100–1, 103
*Forsvarsmuseet*, 282

Fox, L., 135
FPP. *see* Foreign Policy Prerogative (FPP)
France
  Chicago Summit, 154
  Cold War, 85–6, 153
  conventional forces, 145–9
  defence budget, 141–2
  defence organization, 142–5
  geopolitics and geostrategic policies, 153–4
  nuclear policy, 149–50
  technical strategy, 150–3
  US Army budget deficit, impact on, 154–8
Freedman, L., 127
free riding. *see* transatlantic relationships
*Friedenspolitik*, 37, 48
FRUS. *see* Foreign Relations of the United States (FRUS)
Fursdon, E., 73–4

Gaddis, J. L., 33
Gates, R., 1, 25, 38–9, 84, 90, 97, 114, 155–6, 262, 287
*Gazeta Wyborcza*, 225, 226
Gebicke, S., 266
Gelpi, C., 136
Germany
  Cold War, 162–6
  defence budget, 161–2
  defence policy, 163–5
  hegemonic power, 163
  Merkel's government, 169–73
  national interest, 169, 172, 174
  new strategies, use of force, 165–6
  Schröder's government, 166–9
Giegerich, B., 113
Gillingham, J., 72
global security, 2, 147, 172, 182, 194, 206, 282, 287, 289
Gjerde, I., 286
Gjeseth, G., 283
Gobierno de España, 199 n37
Goddard, T., 51
Golden, J. R., 102
Goldgeier, J., 91
Gray, C., 137, 183

Groove, E., 30
Gross, D., 189
Guldhav, E., 286
Gulf War, 30, 69, 135, 164, 247, 251
Guttenberg, K. T. z., 170
Gyarmati, I., 255

Haaland, T. H., 14, 286
Habermas, J., 40, 48, 52
Haftendorn, H., 165, 181, 183
Hale, J., 193
Hall, P., 46
Hallams, E., 2, 25, 31, 79, 90, 171, 287
Hampton, M. N., 169
Harder, H-J., 73
Harding, T., 111
Haug, K. E., 296
Haynes, D., 272
Heller, F. H., 72
Hellmann, G., 164–6, 172
Hendrickson, R., 182
Herring, E., 8
Heurlin, B., 264
Hjortdal, M., 274
HM Government, 59
Hoffmann, S., 66
Hopkins, N., 132
House of Commons, 134–5, 272
Howard, M., 29, 33–4, 124, 126
humanitarian interventions, 1, 9, 49, 106, 111, 127, 157, 171–2, 217, 221, 224, 227–8, 242, 247, 252, 263–4, 289, 292–2, 294, 296–7
Human Security Centre, 127
Hungary
 Afghanistan operations, 244–6
 Balkan crisis, 233–6, 241–5, 247, 251–3
 Cold war, 232, 234, 236, 238, 242, 245
 defence budget, 237–41
 Iraq war, 246–7
 missile defense (MD), 247–50
 national interest, 244
 NATO membership, 233
 political willingness, 250–6
 security environment, 233–7
Huntington, S., 183, 186
Hyde-Price, A., 28, 166

Iatrides, J. O., 30
IISS. see International Institute for Strategic Studies (IISS)
Ilisics, Z., 242
Ing, D., 189
Innset, B., 60
*International Herald Tribune*, 287
International Institute for Strategic Studies (IISS), 83, 89, 106, 164, 173
International Security Assistance Force (ISAF), 3, 147
 in Afghanistan, 25, 31, 81–2, 88, 167
 American criticism, 110
 British strategy, 122
 creation of, 147. see also United Nations Security Council Resolution (UNSCR 1386)
 Denmark, 269–70
 German participation, 168–71, 173
 Hungary in, 241, 243, 245
 Norway, 286, 288–9, 292, 294–5
 Poland, 224–7
Iraq War, 13, 39, 42, 98, 167, 174, 187, 190, 237, 247, 253, 268–9, 291
ISAF. see International Security Assistance Force (ISAF)
Isaszegi, J., 259 n16, n18

Jackson, A., 131
Jackson, Sir, Michael, 284
Jaffe, G., 111
Jakobsen, P. V., 272
James, B., 104
JFCOM. see Joint Forces Command (JFCOM)
Joffe, J., 161
Johannesen, L. U., 271
Johnsen, A. B., 293, 156
Joint Forces Command (JFCOM), 156
joint force generation, European defence policy, 61, 64–5, 67, 68
Jones, J., 107
Joó, R., 259 n24
Jospin, L., 147
journeyman, Denmark as, 14, 275–6

Kaczyński, P. M., 215
Kagan, R., 2, 26–8, 31, 184
Kaldor, M., 71
Kanarowski, S. M., 74
Kaplan, L., 182
Kaplan, L. S., 103,
Kaplan, R. D., 157
Katsarova, I., 179
Kay, S., 11, 16, 97–118
Keller, P., 172
Kennedy, P., 127
Keohane, R. O., 105, 181, 183
Kern, T., 238–9, 241
KFOR forces. *see* Kosovo peace-keeping Forces
Khan, S., 110
King, A., 42–4
Kirchner, E. J., 5
Kobieracki, A., 224
Kondor. *see*. Poland, air policing operations
Kosovo operation
 alliance history, 83
 American military intervention, 98
 British forces, 49
 collective action problem, 106
 crisis management, 79–81
 European defence, 57
 France in, 146
 German army in, 44, 48, 165–6
 Hungary in, 241, 243
 Norway in, 284–5, 288, 295
 Poland in, 223–4, 227
 pooling and sharing, fleet, 63
 tactics, 108–9, 114
 use of force, post-modern Europe, 31
Kosovo peace-keeping Forces, 44, 79-81, 165, 223–4, 227, 241, 242
Koziej, S., 208
Kreps, S., 3, 5, 297
Kugler, R. L., 73
Kulugyminiszterium, 245–7
Kundnani, H., 171
Kupchan, C., 8–9
Kupiecki, R., 207–9, 214–15, 220, 225, 228
Kyoto Protocol, 182

Lambeth, B. S., 109
Lave, J., 262–3, 267–8, 270, 271, 273, 275
Layne, C., 181
LeCuyer, J. A., 102
Ledwidge, F., 43, 126
Leira, H., 289
Lepgold, J., 106, 182
Lequesne, C., 87
Leraand, D., 283, 285
Ley Orgánica, 199 n37
Libyan operation
 American role in, 38–9, 49
 Britain's role in, 123, 127, 133, 135–6
 Denmark's role in, 262–3, 272, 274–5
 European security policies, 57, 66, 72, 83–6, 88–91
 France's role in, 146–7, 155, 158
 Germany's role in, 161, 171–2, 174
 NATO strategy, 97–8, 106, 108, 110–12, 114–15, 117
 Norway's role in, 285–6, 289, 296–7
 Poland's role in, 212, 216
 Spain's role in, 183, 188, 192
Liddell Hart, B., 125–6
Lippmann gap, 136–7
Lisbon Summit, 154, 157, 254
Lobell, S., 184
Lock, E., 8, 19
Longhurst, K., 167
Lukes, S., 41
Lunde, N. T., 294
Lundestad, G., 73
Lykketoft, M., 264
Lynn, J., 40–1, 46

Macpherson, C. B., 49
Madej, M., 215, 225, 226–7
Magid, S., 266
Majumdar, D., 196 n6
Mansori, K., 199 n36
Marcus, J., 111
Marquina Barrio, A., 197 n17
Marton, P., 244
Matlary J. H., 1–20, 67, 279–98
Maull, H. W., 165–6
McCormick, J., 183

Mearsheimer, J., 165, 181, 264
Menon, A., 87, 90
Merkel, Angela, 17, 169–73
MIC. *see* Multinational
   Interoperability Council (MIC)
military ability
   NATO strategy, 71, 79, 87, 91
   post-modern Europe, 31–4
   *see also specific entries*, use of force
missile defence sytem (MD), 115, 152,
   171, 180, 193, 247, 250
Ministerio de AsuntosExteriores de
   España, 197 n20
Ministerio de Defensa, 199 n37
Moskos, C. C., 49
Mouritzen, H., 276
Multinational Interoperability
   Council (MIC), 145–6
Myers, S. L., 83

Nagl, J., 130–1
National Defence University, 1
national interest, 17, 155–6, 169, 172,
   180, 191, 221, 244, 282, 289, 292
NATO strategy
   Afghanistan operations, 81–3
   crisis management, 79–81. *see also*
      Bosnia; Kosovo
   France, transatlantic bargain, 85–8
   Libyan campaign, 83–5
   nature and function, 72–7
   transatlantic burden sharing, 77–9
NATO treaty, 100–1, 116
Neal, D. J., 31
Németh, A., 259 n13
The Netherlands, 1, 8, 63, 64, 243, 280
Nexon, D., 184
Nilsen, J. T., 294, 297
NMOD, 281–2
Noetzel, T., 4, 6, 32, 168, 170, 172
NORDEFCO. *see* Nordic Defence
   Coooperation (NORDEFCO)
Nordic Defence Coooperation
   (NORDEFCO), 64
Nordvik, A. M., 295
Norges Forsvar, 294
Norton-Taylor, R., 110, 132

Norway
   Afghanistan operation, 285–7
   Cold war, 279–4, 288
   defence budget, 279–80
   defence structure, 282–5
   domestic policies, 290–8
   Libyan operation, 285–7
   military capability, 280–2
   national interest, 282, 289, 292, 297
   naval force, 59
   political willingness, 288–90
Nowak, J. M., 207
Noya, J., 197 n21
Nuland, V., 87
Nurick, R. C., 77
Nye, J., 3, 189

Obama administration
   Afghanistan operations, 82,
      193, 246
   Chicago Summit, 154
   foreign policy, 237
   in *Europapolitik*, 87
   missile defence system, 250
   NATO defence planning and
      budget, 114–15, 155
O'Dwyer, G., 190
Oliveri, F., 193
Olsen, J., 196 n8
Olson, M., 4, 99, 182
Oma, I., 293
Ortega, P., 189
Osica, O., 221
Østerud, Ø., 71–91, 288

Packer, G., 130
Pacuła, P., 219
Panetta, L. E., 25, 31, 82, 112, 115, 155
Paret, P., 197 n12
Park, W. H., 74
Parker, G., 184
Paterson, W. E., 163
Patrick, S., 11, 78
Pawłowski, K., 206
Payne, S., 186
Petersson, M., 1–20, 25–34, 67
Pew Research Center, 98
Pharo, H. Ø., 279
Pietraś, M., 13, 15, 216

Pietrzak, P., 222
Poland
  Active Endeavor, 227–8
  air policing operations, 228
  in Cold war, 205–7, 212, 215, 229
  foreign policy, 205–6
  international strategy, challenges, 221–8
  national interest, 221–2
  NATO operation, 207–9
  political strategy, 212–20
  UN peacekeeping operations, 209–12
  political culture, 4, 10, 15–16, 38–9, 42, 45
  political willingness
    Britain, 135–7
    Cologne Declaration, criticism, 42
    defence strategy, 71, 87
    Denmark, 269
    Germany,, 162, 168, 173
    Hungary, 233, 250–1, 255, 257
    ISAF mission, 25
    Norway, 279–80, 290, 297–8
    Poland, 205, 207, 212, 222, 228–9
    threat perceptions, 79
    use of force, post-modern Europe, 31–4
Polska Zbrojna, 208
pooling and sharing, European defence policy, 61–3, 67, 68
Porter, P., 11–12, 15, 121–38
post-modern age, 26–7, 28, 29–32
Prague Summit, 238
pre-modern age, 28–9
Powell, C., 197 n20
Preston, P., 186
Prime Minister's Office, 265, 275
Prins, G., 124
*Prymat NATO*, 211–12, 218–19, 220

Rachman, G., 198 n24
Rácz, A., 236
Rasmussen, A. F., 14, 16, 157, 262–76
Rees, G. W., 86
Reifler, J., 136
Ringsmose, J., 3, 6–7, 66, 265, 270–1
Ripsman, N., 196 n5
Rizopoulos, N. X., 30

Roberts, H., 85
Rodríguez, Marcos, J., 184, 190, 192
role specialization, European defence policy, 61–2, 64, 67, 68
Rupp, R., 181
Russia
  defence budget, 142
  geostrategic concept of NSC, 153–4
  in Kosovo war, 109
  on NATO's enlargement policy, 78–9
  Norway and, 281, 296
  Poland *vs*, 207, 215
  threat to Hungary, 233, 237, 249, 252
  transatlantic bargain, 85, 88, 90
  *see also* Soviet Union
Rynning, S., 66, 263, 270

SAC. *see* strategic airlift capability (SAC)
SACEUR. *see* Supreme Allied Commander Europe (SACEUR)
Sakson, A., 209
Sarkozy, N., 17, 18, 85–8, 148, 149
Sarotte, M. E., 166
Saxi, H. L., 8, 61, 64
Scales, R., 130
Schmitt, C., 42
Schmitt, E., 2
Schmitter, P., 197 n18
Schreer, B., 2, 4, 6, 12–13, 15, 19, 25, 31–2, 79, 90, 161–74, 287
Schröder, G., 164–9
Schult, C., 171, 173
Schwartz, D. N., 71, 74
Schweller, R., 196 n5
Sciolino, E., 178
Second World War
  America's role in NATO, 98–9
  Britain in, 129
  Germany in, 165
  Hitler's regime, 116
  Norway, 283, 286, 296
  Poland in, 209
  Spain in, 178, 194
  use of force, 27–8, 30–2, 34
Security and Defence Policy (ESDP), 42, 66, 167

security policy
 affordability, European defence, 57–69
 Denmark, 263–7, 273
 France, 144
 Germany, 161, 163, 165, 167, 169
 Hungary, 234
 NATO strategy, 72
 Norway, 282, 289, 291–3, 295–8
 Poland, 206–9, 214–16, 222
 Spain, 183
Sedivy, J., 25
Senghaas, D., 71
Shanker, T., 2
Sheehan, J. J., 2, 27–8, 30–1, 42, 45
Siklósi, P., 259 n23
Simons, M., 192
Sion, L., 45
Skjervøy, A., 291
Sloan, S. R., 74
Smith, P., 197 n21
Snidal, D., 104–5
Snow, C. P., 37–8
Snyder, G., 3, 4, 6
Sondhaus, L., 197 n19
Sontag, S., 52
Soviet Union
 Cold War tensions, 102–3
 collective action problems, 100
 conventional forces of, 25, 233
 demise of, 66, 72, 77, 89, 133, 163, 216, 235, 256
 global commitments, 125, 208
 nuclear weapons, 74, 132
 political transformation, 254
 threat to NATO, 181–2
Spain
 assets, 181–4
 Cold war, 183, 187
 cultural values, 186–8
 defence budget, 189–91
 hegemonic power, 180, 185
 historical importance, 184–6
 liabilities, 181–4
 national interest, 180–3, 191–2
 risk society, 191–3
 statecraft, 178–81
 twenty-first-century statecraft, 178, 185, 188, 190, 194–5

Sperling, J., 5
Spiegel, P., 1, 161
Stacey, K., 162
Stevens, P., 1
Stewart, R., 122
Stoler, M. A., 128
Stoltenberg, J., 291–7
Støre, J. G., 288, 295, 296
Strachan, H., 3, 123, 126, 131
strategic airlift capability (SAC), 249
Strøm-Erichsen, A-G., 294
Stromseth, J. E., 76
Suhrke, A., 81–2
Sullivan Jr, L., 102
Supreme Allied Commander Europe (SACEUR), 42, 63, 224
Swidler, A., 266
Synovitz, R., 110
Szabo, S. F., 169
Szarvas, L., 259 n21
Szenes, Z., 239, 242–3

Taliaferro, J., 196 n5
Taliban, 81, 110, 122, 147–9, 166, 168, 170, 193, 272, 286, 294
Taylor, R., 46
Terlikowski, M., 215, 226
Terriff, T., 8
*The Times*, 272, 274
Thies, W. J., 2, 26, 182
Thruelsen, P. D., 272
Till, G., 123
Toje, A., 11, 71–91
Tootal, S., 271
Towpik, A., 223–4
transatlantic relationships
 Afghanistan war, 109–10
 burden sharing, 98–104
 collective action problem, 104–8
 economic crises, impact on, 112–17
 Kosovo, tactical operation, 108–9
 Libya, 110–11
Turkey, 1, 81, 83, 84, 156, 180, 185, 193, 285, 287
*Turkish Daily News*, 187

UAVs. *see* Unmanned Aerial Vehicles (UAVs)
*Udział Polski*, 211

UK (United Kingdom). *see* Britain
United Nations Security Council Resolution (UNSCR 1386), 147
Unmanned Aerial Vehicles (UAVs), 39
UNSCR 1386. see United Nations Security Council Resolution (UNSCR 1386)
USA
 criticism, on NATO, 1, 26, 216
 defence budget, 102, 155, 157
 Department of Defense, 98, 114–15, 192–3
 hegemony, 3, 11, 85, 187, 189, 190, 194
 military, 42, 53, 73, 84, 91, 131, 155–6, 182, 185–6, 215, 226, 234, 246
 national interest, 154–6
 Secretary of Defense, 90, 104, 112, 114–15
 security policy, 3, 5, 7, 78–9, 183
US Department of Defense, 98, 114–15, 192–3
use of force
 cabinets, 28–9
 commons, 28–9
 courts, 28–9
 historical perspectives, 27
 military ability, 32–3
 overview, 25–7
 political will, 32–3. *see also Specific countries*
 post-modern age, 29–32
 *see also specific Countries*
US Senate, 274
USEC, 156
*Ustawa*, 221, 222

values
 alliance, 4–5
 American norms, 53
 in foreign policy, 244
 political, 2, 150
Van Evera, S., 183
Vasquez, J. A., 41
Végh, F., 235
Vennesson, P., 33

Verhofstadt, G., 141
Villaume, P., 263
vision
 cosmopolitan, 45
 Danish Armed Forces, 268
 NATO's, 206, 220
VOA News, 193
von Thadden, R., 161

Wagner, P., 244
Wallace, W., 26, 113, 163
Wallander, C., 105, 181
Walt, S. M., 111
Waltz, K., 181, 186
War on Terror, 38, 48, 53, 81–2, 86, 132, 211
Warsaw Treaty Organization, 76
Washington Summit, 248, 255
Washington Treaty, 153, 206, 212, 218, 228, 229, 238
Waxman, M., 9
Webb, J., 53
Wenger, A., 72
Wenger, E., 262–3, 267–8, 270–1, 273, 275
*Wikileaks*, 87, 264
Williams, M. J., 3, 183, 191–2
Williams, P. D., 31
Winand, P., 74
Winkler, P., 82
Wirtz, J., 183
Witney, N., 40
Woodworth, P., 199 n35

Xawery Czernicki. *see*, Poland, air policing operations

Yitzhak, R., 30
Yost, D. S., 107

Zaborowski, M., 25
Założenia, 208, 209, 212, 216
Zapatero, J., 13, 190, 192–3, 195
Zeckhauser, R., 4, 99, 182
Zelikow, P., 167
Ziółkowski, M., 218

CPSIA information can be obtained at www.ICGtesting.com
Printed in the USA
LVOW10*1522210214

374698LV00009B/427/P